Fodor's InFocus

LISBON

Welcome to Lisbon

An alluring combination of glorious architecture, deep-rooted musical traditions, and thoroughly modern flair have made Lisbon a top destination for travelers. Famously built on seven hills, Lisbon's terra-cotta–roofed homes, turreted castles, and gleaming white basilicas appear to tumble down the cobblestone slopes towards the glimmering River Tagus as visitors traverse the city on rattling streetcars or head uphill with the help of antique funiculars.

One of Europe's hottest destinations (Lisbon is justifiably proud of its status as Europe's "sunniest capital city"), Lisbon has enthusiastically embraced change without casting aside its much-loved heritage. Colorful murals by internationally renowned street artists make it one of the best cities in Europe to see street art. The city has gained a reputation as one of the best spots on the continent for live music—from rock to jazz and classical—with many outdoor festivals held in the city's numerous leafy green spaces.

Counting some of Europe's finest galleries, museums and cultural centers, and a vast aquarium among its indoor attractions, Lisbon's charms do not abate under rainy skies. You could easily spend days at the UNESCO World Heritage sites and other treasures in the postcard-perfect neighborhood of Belém. An increasingly sophisticated dining scene is building on a growing international appreciation for Portuguese food, with its abundant fresh seafood, fruit, and vegetables, and astonishingly affordable wines. Lisbon is not only a treasure chest of historical monuments, but also a place where you won't use up all your own hard-earned treasure.

As you plan your upcoming travels to Lisbon, please confirm that places are still open and let us know when we need to make updates by emailing us at corrections@fodors.com.

Contents

MAPS

Chapter 1

EXPERIENCE LISBON

12 ULTIMATE EXPERIENCES

Lisbon offers terrific experiences that should be on every traveler's list. Here are Fodor's top picks for a memorable trip.

1 Get lost in Alfama

Despite its steep hills and streets that are actually flights of stairs, the city's most historic neighborhood is best explored on foot. *(Ch. 6)*

2 Admire the street art

A public-private partnership has led to the creation of large murals painted by internationally known artists like Shepard Fairey and PichiAvo.

3 Eat a pastel de nata

Lisbon's famously sweet, eggy custard tarts are the city's favorite breakfast treat. Look for bakeries that make them from scratch.

4 Cross the river for the views

Book a sightseeing cruise or simply take a ferry from Cais do Sodré or Belém to take in a vista of Lisbon from afar. *(Ch. 12)*

5 Get your hands on seafood

From garlicky clams slurped straight from the shell to scarlet shrimp whose brains you suck from the head, Portuguese seafood is delightfully interactive.

6 Shop local in Príncipe Real

The posh hilltop neighborhood of Príncipe Real is home to small boutiques from established and up-and-coming Portuguese designers, particularly in a converted embassy. *(Ch. 5)*

7 Take in some fado

Portugal's famously melancholy vocal music was born in Lisbon, but there's no need to understand Portuguese to feel the emotion that's conveyed.

8 Watch the sunset from a miradouro

Lisbon's "golden viewpoints" are gathering spots for visitors and locals all day, but they especially come alive as the sun bathes everything in gold.

9 See the fantastical palaces of Sintra

From the candy-colored hilltop Pena Palace to the surreal well of Quinta da Regaleira, the royal residences in this village are worth an overnight. *(Ch. 14)*

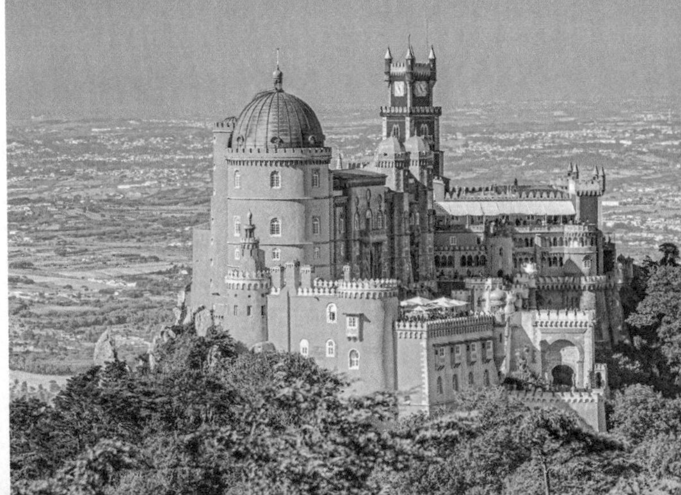

10 Walk along the Tagus River

The stretch that heads west from Docas in Alcântara to the Torre de Belém (Tower of Belém) is excellent for people-watching and river views. *(Ch. 8, 11)*

11 Visit Lisbon's enthusiast museums

Whether it's aristocratic carriages, painted ceramic tiles, old public transportation, or royal treasures, Lisbon has a manageably sized, hyper-specific museum for it.

12 Ride a yellow tram

While long lines and packed cars can make the famous 28 an unpleasant experience, plenty of other vintage trams crisscross the city.

WHAT'S WHERE

1 Baixa. Home to historic architecture and tourist restaurants.

2 Chiado and Bairro Alto. Chiado has upscale shopping, restaurants, and hotels; in Bairro Alto the party goes all night.

3 Avenida da Liberdade, Príncipe Real, and Restauradores. Tree-lined streets with luxury and local shopping.

4 Alfama, Graça, and São Vicente. The oldest neighborhoods in Lisbon feature narrow winding streets.

5 Beato and Marvila. The city's new capitals of cool.

6 Alcântara, Cais do Sodré, and Santos. Hip riverside neighborhoods.

7 Estrela, Campo de Ourique, and Lapa. Residential hilltop neighborhoods where Lisbon's moneyed live.

8 Intendente, Martim Moniz, and Mouraria. Working-class neighborhoods with craft beer, trendy restaurants, and the best Asian food in town.

9 Belém. Hot spot for museums and historic sites.

10 South of the River. Beaches, destination restaurants, and other day trips.

11 Avenidas Novas. Pastel-colored art deco architecture and authentic restaurants off the tourist path.

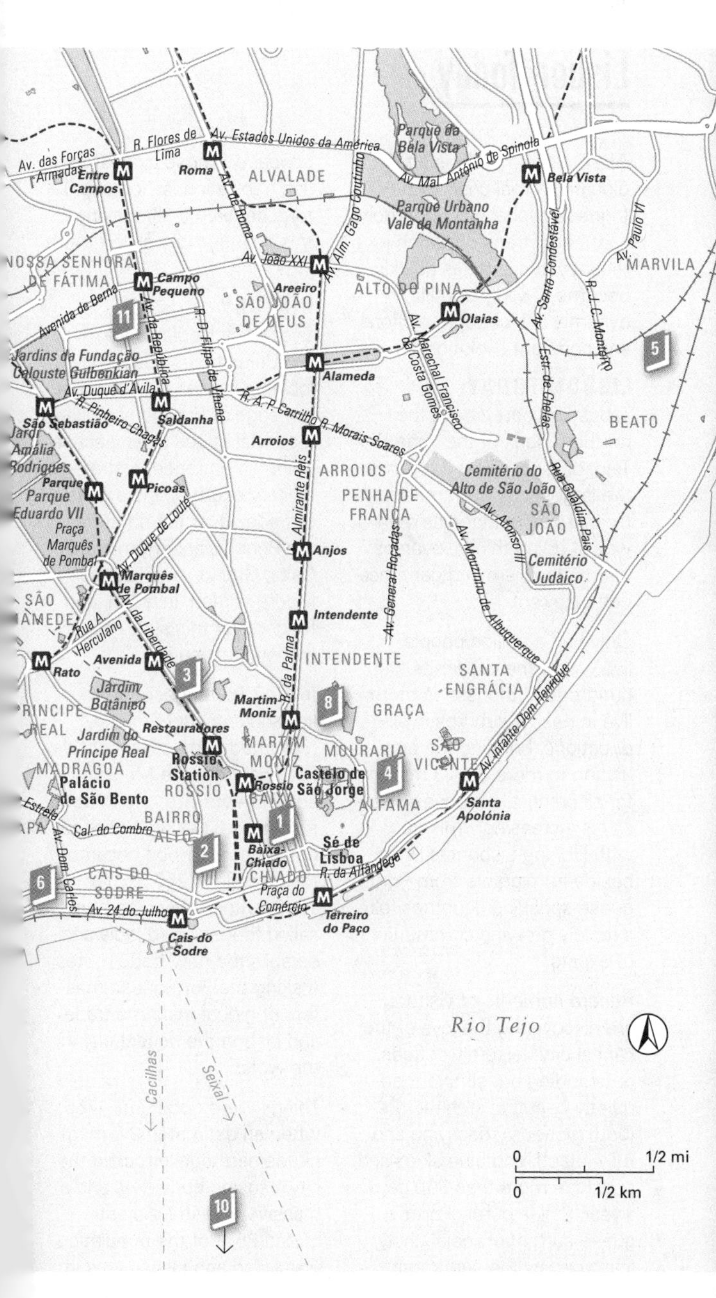

Av. das Forças Armadas
R. Flores de Lima
Av. Estados Unidos da América
Parque da Bela Vista
Av. Mal. António de Spínola
Entre Campos
Roma
ALVALADE
Bela Vista
Parque Urbano Vale da Montanha
NOSSA SENHORA DE FÁTIMA
Campo Pequeno
Av. João XXI
Areeiro
SÃO JOÃO DE DEUS
ALTO DO PINA
MARVILA
Olaias
Avenida de Berna
Jardins da Fundação Calouste Gulbenkian
Alameda
Av. Duque d'Ávila
São Sebastião
Saldanha
Arroios
R. Morais Soares
BEATO
ARROIOS
PENHA DE FRANÇA
Cemitério do Alto de São João
SÃO JOÃO
Parque Eduardo VII
Picoas
Praça Marquês de Pombal
Anjos
Cemitério Judaico
Marquês de Pombal
SÃO MAMEDE
Intendente
Rato
Avenida
INTENDENTE
SANTA ENGRÁCIA
Jardim Botânico
Martim Moniz
GRAÇA
PRINCIPE REAL
Jardim do Príncipe Real
Restauradores
MARTIM MONIZ
MOURARIA
SÃO VICENTE
MADRAGOA
Palácio de São Bento
Rossio Station
Rossio
Castelo de São Jorge
ROSSIO
BAIXA
ALFAMA
Santa Apolónia
BAIRRO ALTO
Baixa-Chiado
Sé de Lisboa
R. da Alfândega
CHIADO
CAIS DO SODRE
Praça do Comércio
Terreiro do Paço
Av. 24 de Julho
Cais do Sodre
Rio Tejo
Cacilhas
Seixal
0
1/2 mi
0
1/2 km

Lisbon Today

After taking a serious hit in the global financial crisis, the Portuguese capital has undergone a stunning transformation in recent years and has quickly become a wildly popular, dynamic city of contradictions and constant evolution.

LISBON TODAY

A bustling port city on the northern bank of the wide Rio Tejo, or Tagus River, Lisbon is the largest city in a small country that has retained its own way of doing things, even as internationalism and gentrification take root.

Only half a million people live within the city limits, but hundreds of thousands more live in nearby suburbs in all directions, bringing the population to more than 3 million for all practical purposes. The city is increasingly mixed, with lifelong Lisboetas living beside immigrants from Portuguese-speaking countries, plus a rapidly growing community of expats.

Record numbers of visitors are discovering the joys of the capital city: leisurely coffees, outstanding but simple food, quietly beautiful architecture (both gloriously decaying and fully intact), and blue skies and sunshine more than 300 days a year. Still, a purely Portuguese current of melancholy (captured by the sentiment *saudade,* whose closest English translation is "longing") runs beneath it all, making this beautiful city all the more intriguing.

HISTORY

Ever since Neolithic and pre-Celtic times, Lisbon's location at the far southwestern edge of Europe has given it special status as an escape point, an entrance, a strategic military enclave, and a center of trade. Over the centuries, the Phoenicians, Romans, Celts, Greeks, and Islamic Moors settled, invaded, and fought over this slice of the Iberian Peninsula.

In 1147, Portuguese Catholics and crusaders forcibly reclaimed parts of present-day Portugal from the Moors, and 32 years later the Pope recognized it as an independent country. Lisbon became the capital in 1255. By the 16th century, Vasco da Gama sailed four ships to India and established new trade routes, making the Portuguese masters of global maritime trade and Lisbon the richest city in the world.

Things were good until 1755, when an estimated 9.0-magnitude earthquake rocked the city, causing huge fires and a massive tsunami. An estimated 25% of the population was killed and Lisbon was in ruins. As the city got back on its feet, the 19th century was defined by class struggle and the decline of the monarchy. The Portuguese Republic was established after a coup d'état in 1910, which was followed by years of political instability and financial chaos: there were 45 government changes over 16 years.

António de Oliveira Salazar, a right-wing dictator, established the Estado Novo (New State), the corporatist authoritarian government that ruled Portugal from 1932 to 1974. Salazar maintained viselike control of the population through censorship, torture, and imprisonment. Democracy was restored on April 25, 1974, through the Carnation Revolution, a largely bloodless military coup coupled with a popular campaign of civil resistance.

THE PORTUGUESE DISCOVERIES

Portugal's sailors and mapmakers were among the best of the 16th century, and they had a knack for colonization, though they refer to places like Mozambique and Brazil as discoveries. Citizens of the onetime colonies see things a bit differently, and some reckonings are underway, but the Portuguese are largely proud of their seafaring heritage and their onetime management of resources from around the world. Lisbon is rife with monuments to those explorers, particularly in Belém, where many expedition ships set sail.

GENTRIFICATION

Lisbon is at something of an inflection point right now. After the 2008 financial crisis, the government courted an influx of tourist dollars, encouraged foreign start-ups to take root, and wooed wealthy foreigners to buy property.

While salaries have remained low, housing prices and rents have been rising quickly. Many of the apartments in the city center are inhabited (or Airbnb-ed) by foreigners, and protests about the lack of affordable housing and high cost of living are increasingly common. Visitors should be respectful of the situation and avoid exclaiming how "cheap" things are.

Regardless of the pros and cons of the current boom, it's an excellent reason to venture beyond the city center and into the suburbs, along the beach toward Cascais, or across the river to the south, to experience how the Portuguese really live—and to sample the most authentic food and wine.

What to Eat and Drink in Lisbon

POLVO À LAGAREIRO

As in neighboring countries, olive oil is an essential part of the Portuguese diet. *Polvo à lagareiro* is the epitome of that: roasted octopus served with greens and baked potatoes and doused with olive oil and garlic.

BACALHAU À BRÁS

Portugal's national dish is salted codfish, better known as *bacalhau*, and one of the most crowd-pleasing cod-based recipes is *bacalhau à Brás*, scrambled eggs with shredded salt cod, onion, and thin potato sticks topped with black olives.

PREGO

Ask for a *prego* in Lisbon and you'll get either a nail or a sandwich. Of course, if you're at a restaurant, odds are you'll get the latter: a garlicky steak sandwich, with a slice of beef that's often bigger than the bread roll.

GRILLED SARDINES

You know summer's arrived in Lisbon when the streets are filled with the aroma of grilled sardines, especially during the street parties that take over the city every June. Locals eat them with potatoes and roasted pepper salad or on bread.

CALDO VERDE

Traditional Portuguese meals often begin with vegetable soup. One of the most famous is *caldo verde*, which combines finely shredded cabbage, potatoes, and a slice or two of chorizo.

PASTÉIS DE BACALHAU

Along with sweets, Lisbon has its share of savory snacks for quick bites. One of the most popular is *pastéis de bacalhau*, salted cod cakes that are held together with potatoes and eggs and then deep-fried.

Caldo verde

VINHO VERDE
There's nothing like a chilled glass of wine on a sunny day, and though produced exclusively in the far northwest of the country, this light (sometimes slightly effervescent) wine is always available at Lisbon tables.

MOSCATEL
This fortified wine, with a sweet fruity flavor, is enjoyed either as an aperitif or a dessert wine. There are several varieties from different regions, but Moscatel de Setúbal comes from a fishing town a few miles south of Lisbon.

GINJA
From morning to night, you can drink *ginja* without anyone raising an eyebrow. This crimson-red sweet liqueur made with sour cherries is ubiquitous in Lisbon.

PASTÉIS DE NATA
Lisbon has plenty of tasty pastries, but if you have to pick only one, make it Portugal's legendary custard tart. A creamy filling is held together by a flaky pastry shell and sometimes sprinkled with cinnamon.

PICA-PAU
The concept is simple: little chunks of meat (usually pork but sometimes beef or tuna) marinated with garlic, served in a small bowl to share.

AMÊIJOAS À BULHÃO PATO
This delicious clam dish is named after writer António de Bulhão Pato. The sauce of garlic, olive oil, white wine, lemon, and cilantro makes it a must-try. (Ask for extra bread.)

What to Buy in Lisbon

CERAMIC TABLEWARE
Handcrafters all over the country produce beautiful and functional items from cabbage-shaped soup tureens inspired by 19th-century artist Bordallo Pinheiro to rough-hewn espresso cups by next-gen artisans.

PORT WINE
Although Porto is the center of production for port wine, the sweet drink is available in bottle shops all over the country. It comes in white, red, and tawny, and with various levels of age and complexity.

ANYTHING CORK
Portugal is the largest cork producer in the world, and quite a lot ends up in Lisbon's boutiques where you can find obvious items like coasters and trivets alongside more surprising ones like handbags and yoga mats.

FILIGREE JEWELRY
The fine, delicate gold- and silver-smithing that goes into producing Portugal's famously ethereal jewelry is impressive. Historic shops in some of Lisbon's oldest districts specialize in this sort of classic jewelry, particularly the stylized Viana hearts that are fabricated in the north of the country, in the city of Viana do Castelo.

OLIVE OIL
Portugal's gourmet olive oil rarely gets the recognition it deserves, but some of the country's small producers are out to change that. Specialty grocery stores carry a variety of high-quality flavorful olive oils that make excellent souvenirs.

Azulejos

TINNED FISH

While North Americans may turn up their noses at canned fish, in Portugal, it's a delicacy. Fresh Algarve tuna, mackerel, sardines, and even octopus and squid are packed at peak freshness into cans with plain or flavored olive oil and beautiful packaging.

DECORATIVE TILES

The painted ceramic tiles (known as *azulejos*) that adorn many of Lisbon's buildings also work as stylish keepsakes. Just shop with caution: some of the sellers at flea markets offer tiles that have been stolen from the sides of buildings, so it's best to go to shops that specialize in new tiles.

HERITAGE COSMETIC BRANDS

From the art deco packaging of Claus Porto soaps to the elegant logo of Couto toothpaste, everyday Portuguese products are often wrapped in iconic papers and labels that make them appealing as souvenirs to take home, beyond their usefulness.

GINJA

Portugal's popular sour-cherry liquor also makes for a long-lasting reminder of a trip to Lisbon—a little of the sweet strong stuff goes a long way. It's easy to find at liquor or souvenir shops.

Lisbon with Kids

Interactive museums, playgrounds in well-kept parks, and even a swath of protected forest within the city limits make entertaining kids easy in Lisbon. Just note that the city's hilly topography and cobblestone streets make it stroller-unfriendly.

WILDLIFE ENCOUNTERS

The Oceanário de Lisboa, in Parque das Nações, is the largest oceanarium in Europe and home to penguins, sea otters, sharks, rays, anemones, seahorses, starfish, octopuses, jellyfish, and all sorts of fish and marine plants. *(Ch. 7)*The Jardim Zoológico is home to more than 2,000 animals from more than 300 species. *(Ch. 13)*

MUSEUMS

The Museu da Marioneta has an extensive collection of puppets from around the world. For kids who like boats and buses, the Museu do Marinha is dedicated to all things related to Portugal's history of navigation, and the Museu da Carris shows historic trolleys and trams. In Sintra, in addition to the palaces, the Museu do Ar is an aviation museum.

PLAY TIME

Many of the city's parks have compact but innovative playgrounds. The ones in Estrela, Príncipe Real, and Campo de Ourique are especially good. Monsanto Forest Park is a protected forest within the city limits that is a good place for hiking or playing in the woods. At the edge of Monsanto there's Hello Park, a supervised space where kids can climb on a simple ropes course, bounce on inflatables, or experiment in a painting studio. At the esplanade outside, parents can have a coffee or a drink as they watch.

What to Watch and Read

LISBON STORY, DIRECTED BY WIM WENDERS

Wim Wenders's *Lisbon Story* (1994) is the saga of a film director who has trouble finishing a movie about Lisbon. He calls his friend for help, who in turn arrives in Lisbon, falls in love with the city and a Portuguese singer, and takes his camcorder all over to capture hidden Lisbon.

NIGHT TRAIN TO LISBON, DIRECTED BY BILLE AUGUST

The 2013 film *Night Train to Lisbon* is based on the 2004 novel of the same name. Told in flashbacks, the story follows a Swiss professor's journey through Lisbon in search of a mysterious woman and an obscure author who, it turns out, was part of the resistance during the Salazar dictatorship.

ON HER MAJESTY'S SECRET SERVICE, DIRECTED BY PETER R: HUNT

Parts of the 1969 James Bond film *On Her Majesty's Secret Service* were filmed in and around Lisbon, although it depicts a city of luxury and Salazarist cosmopolitanism rather than reality.

IN THE WHITE CITY, DIRECTED BY ALAIN TANNER

In the White City (1983) depicts the poor side of the city as a love story between a sailor and a maid is revealed.

THE RUSSIA HOUSE, DIRECTED BY FRED SCHEPISI

Lisbon and its many monuments figure prominently in the 1990 film *The Russia House,* when the protagonist takes refuge in the city amid the espionage of the Cold War.

THE BOOK OF DISQUIET BY FERNANDO PESSOA

Lisbon's most famous writer is Fernando Pessoa, who attributed his prolific writings to a range of alter egos. His *Book of Disquiet,* which was found in a trunk after his death in 1935, is considered his posthumous masterpiece. The collection of short aphoristic paragraphs forms an autobiography of one of his personas and blends diary, prose poetry, and descriptive narrative. Critics have called it one of the greatest works of the 20th century and argued that it "gives to Lisbon the haunting spell of Joyce's Dublin or Kafka's Prague."

What to Watch and Read

THE LUSIADS BY LUÍS DE CAMÕES

Sixteenth-century poet Luís de Camões was the first great European artist to cross into the southern hemisphere, and his works reflect his years in far-off destinations. He is most famous as the author of the great Renaissance epic *The Lusiads,* which tells the story of Vasco da Gama's voyage via southern Africa to India. Another fine introduction is *The Collected Lyric Poems of Luís de Camões,* which includes nearly 300 poems.

THE YEAR OF THE DEATH OF RICARDO REIS BY JOSÉ SARAMAGO

In 1998 José Saramago became the only Portuguese-speaking author to be awarded the Nobel Prize in Literature. His novel, *The Year of the Death of Ricardo Reis*, is set in 1936, in the early days of the dictatorship, and is marked by visits from the spirit of Fernando Pessoa.

THE FIRST GLOBAL VILLAGE: HOW PORTUGAL CHANGED THE WORLD BY MARTIN PAGE

For a good nonfiction overview of the history of Lisbon and Portugal, Martin Page's *The First Global Village: How Portugal Changed the World* is considered the definitive work on the subject.

Chapter 2

TRAVEL SMART

Updated by
Alison Roberts

POPULATION
Municipality 545,800, metro area 3,015,000

LANGUAGE
Portuguese

$ CURRENCY
Euro

COUNTRY CODE
351

EMERGENCIES
112

DRIVING
On the right

ELECTRICITY
220–240V; plugs have 2 round prongs

TIME
5 hours ahead of New York (except for periods in March and October when Lisbon is 4 hours ahead)

WEB RESOURCES
www.visitportugal.com
www.visitlisboa.com
www.timeout.com/lisbon

AIRPORT
LIS

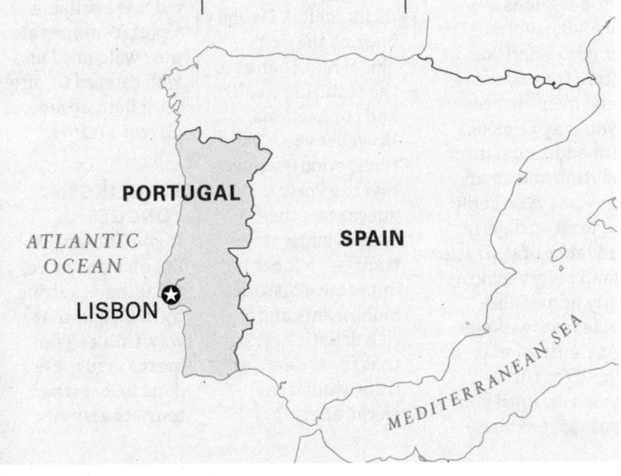

Know Before You Go

What kind of a place is Lisbon? What's the food like? Do the locals speak English? What's the best way to get around? We have the answers to these and other questions to help you prepare for your visit.

NEW VISA RULES
Starting in mid-2025, visa-exempt nationals from 60 countries—including the United States, the United Kingdom, and Canada—must nevertheless pre-register to visit European Union member states such as Portugal, through the new ETIAS (European Travel Information and Authorization System) system. Applications are usually approved in minutes and cost €7 (free for under-18s and over-70s), but you may be asked for additional information and/or an interview, so apply at least 30 days in advance of your trip (and before making any nonrefundable reservations). Authorization is valid for three years (or until your passport expires) and allows multiple entry to participating countries. Visit the official ETIAS website 🌐 *travel-europe.europa.eu/etias_en* for more information and to apply.

KNOW YOUR HISTORY
Portugal may be a tiny country, but it had an outsize role in world history for centuries, during what locals still call the Age of Discovery. As its capital, Lisbon became the first global hub, thanks to the resulting wealth and connections. However you view that period—which saw the Portuguese start the transatlantic slave trade—it left behind impressive historical monuments and a rich artistic heritage that fuses elements from around the world, offering visitors to the city an opportunity to embark on their own voyage of discovery.

FOODIES WELCOME
Portuguese food was long one of Europe's best-kept secrets: fresh fish and shellfish, and hearty meat-based dishes from the interior, served at affordable prices in mainly family-run restaurants. Lisbon is still a great place to sample such delights from across the country, but recent years have seen a step-change in terms of the sophistication of its restaurants and the fare they offer, with a number of Michelin-starred chefs and ever more international cuisine available. Vegetarians are also now welcomed and well catered to, often with flair, by almost all restaurants.

SPEAKING IN TONGUES
If you know a little Spanish and were thinking of getting by in Lisbon that way, think again: most Portuguese don't love it when tourists assume

they would prefer Spanish to English. Many are competent linguists and love to practice their English, but they are always pleased when foreigners make the effort to drop the odd Portuguese word into the conversation. *Por favor* ("please") is the same in both languages, but the odd *obrigado* ("thank you" if you are a man) or *obrigada* (if you are a woman) goes down better than the Spanish equivalent. For more, see the **Helpful Phrases** section.

COFFEE BREAK

Portugal's long dominion over Brazil gave inhabitants of Lisbon a taste for strong coffee that they retain to this day. Meanwhile, sugar shipped in from plantations in the African colonies and in Brazil fostered the manufacture of the kinds of pastries and sweets that you see arrayed in *pastelarias* on every street. To this day, Lisbon's cafés are an important social hub. While Brits and others fond of strong black tea may struggle to find a cuppa to their liking, a range of caffeine-free herbal brews are almost always available.

SAFELY DOES IT

In 2023, Portugal ranked seventh in the Global Peace Index, above nations like Japan and Switzerland. Lisbon's crime rate is low compared with other European capitals, with safety concerns mainly around pickpockets active on streetcars or in crowded areas, rather than violent crime, which in the city center is vanishingly rare. Still, precautions are always a good idea: wandering alone around a deserted Alfama neighborhood with a thousand-dollar camera dangling from your neck is not sensible.

IT'S ALL ABOUT TIMING

Dinner, like lunch, is eaten earlier in Portugal than in Spain, but still rather later than most people from North America or northern Europe are used to. Locals eating out would not normally sit down to order before 8, and on weekends, when they might be planning to go out for a drink or dance afterwards, that would shift to 9 or even 10. Still, city-center restaurants that cater to foreign tourists start serving well before that: from 7 or even earlier.

GO CAR-FREE

Even if you drive into Lisbon, you would be well advised to check in your rental or leave it in the hotel garage or public car park throughout your stay. Traffic in Lisbon is invariably stressful and, at rush hour or during downpours, snarl-ups are common and long-lasting. True, Lisbon's hills are challenging for walkers, but there are funiculars to help with that, plus charming antique streetcars and regular buses, touristy tuk tuks, and e-bikes for rent. But the only way to really get to know this city and its often mazelike neighborhoods is to explore on foot.

Getting Here and Around

Air

From the United States, there are direct flights to Lisbon's Aeroporto Humberto Delgado (LIS) from seven cities, with as many as 44 flights a week from New York alone. The flying time is 6½ hours from New York on a direct flight; it's 10 hours from Chicago and 15 hours from Los Angeles on indirect flights. The flight from London to Lisbon is just under 3 hours.

TAP Air Portugal, the country's national airline, flies nonstop to Lisbon from New York's John F. Kennedy International Airport up to three times daily, and once or twice daily from New Jersey's Newark Liberty International Airport. TAP also flies daily nonstop to Lisbon both from Miami and Washington Dulles, once or twice daily from Boston and Chicago, and several times a week from San Francisco.

United's daily nonstop flights from Newark to Lisbon are scheduled to provide convenient connections from destinations elsewhere in the eastern and southern United States. United also serves Lisbon from Washington Dulles, from late March through October.

Lisbon airport is located about 8 km (5 miles) northeast of the city center. The quickest way to get downtown is the metro, which departs every few minutes from Terminal 1. The 16-minute ride costs €1.80 (including travel on local buses for 60 minutes after validation) loaded onto a reusable €0.50 electronic card, or €1.61 if you load your card with prepaid credit, from €3). Several local buses stop at the airport, taking you to different parts of the city, but the maximum baggage size allowed is 50x40x20 cm. Taxis are available outside Terminal 1 Arrivals; the pickup point for ride-sharing services is upstairs, outside Departures.

Bicycle

Outside the hilly and traffic-choked Old Town—where cycling is a challenging or even perilous pursuit—Lisbon is surprisingly welcoming to bicycles, with dedicated lanes along most of the main avenues and continuously along much of the riverbank. According to city hall, the expanding network already totals 120 km (75 miles), although not all lanes offer as much physical protection from motorized traffic as might be desired. To take advantage of it, you can pick up a conventional or electric bike from one of the docking stations of municipal company Gira after downloading the app and choosing from a daily pass (€2) or one for a longer period. Rival rental outfits for e-bikes and e-scooters—all too often left discarded carelessly on pavements, rather than at designated drop-off points—currently include Bolt (better known as a ride-sharing and takeaway delivery platform), Bird, RideMovi, and Lime.

For longer-term bicycle rentals, there are a number of companies—some of which also offer tours—often based near the river, such as bikeiberia and Biclas.

Boat/Ferry

Lisbon is tucked into a bend on the north bank of the Tagus River, so much of its commuter hinterland is served by ferries: from the Terreiro do Paço boat station for services to and from Barreiro, and from Cais do Sodré (behind the rail station) for other south-bank towns, both by the Transtejo/Soflusa group. Visitors who are in the city for a few days mostly don't venture across the river to these less touristy but still characterful places, but the 10-minute ferry trip from Cais do Sodré to Cacilhas is a great (and cheap) way to escape the city crowds, feel the wind in your hair, and enjoy stunning views of historic Lisbon—even if you don't stay on in Cacilhas for a well-priced seafood lunch at the quayside restaurants or catch a bus up to the Cristo Rei (Christ the King) statue.

Alternatively, for a more leisurely river trip, look up Yellow Bus Tours (an offshoot of city bus company Carris) or, for something a bit different that kids will love, the amphibious HIPPOtrip.

Bus

Lisbon is linked to other Portuguese cities by an extensive network of national and regional bus services that are punctual and comfortable. It's a relatively inexpensive way to get around the country, and the views from your window are often spectacular.

The largest providers include Rede Expressos, which serves much of the country, and EVA Transportes, which covers the south. You can buy tickets for both at the bus station or online (it's always wise to reserve at least a day ahead, particularly in summer when a lot of people are traveling). There are three classes of service: *expressos* are comfortable, fast, direct buses between major cities; *rápidas* are fast regional buses; and *carreiras* stop at every crossroad.

 Car

Driving in Portugal no longer means taking one's life in one's hands, as it frankly once did, with accident rates plummeting in recent decades thanks to improvements in the road network and the quality of both vehicles and drivers. However, in Lisbon itself driving can be quite stressful, due to rush-hour gridlock, narrow streets, confusing one-way systems, and, occasionally, antique trams getting stuck behind badly-parked cars. With taxis and shared bikes plentiful, and much of the city center compact enough to walk, most visitors will find that leaving the car at the hotel or handing in the rental will be best.

Portugal's national highways (labeled "N" with a number) are toll-free, mainly two-lane roads, some of which are identified with "IP" (*Itinerário Principal*) and a number; highways of mainly regional importance have been upgraded to IC (*Itinerário Complementar*). Roads labeled with "E" and a number are routes that connect with the Spanish network.

Commercially operated *autoestradas* (toll roads with two or more lanes in either direction, identified with an "A" and a number) link Lisbon with larger cities, circumventing congested urban centers. The A1 is the quickest drive between Lisbon and Porto, with slower but more scenic routes being the more westerly A8 and then the A17. Heading south, there's good fast access via the A2 to Setúbal and ultimately to the Algarve—or branching off earlier onto the A6 for Évora and other Alentejo towns, ending at the Spanish border near Badajoz. Rush-hour traffic on the Ponte 25 de Abril across the Tagus River can be frustrating; an alternative is taking the 17-km-long (11-mile-long) Ponte Vasco da Gama (Europe's longest bridge) across the Tejo estuary to Montijo; you can then link up with southbound and eastbound roads.

Within the Greater Lisbon area, it's a 30-minute drive (outside of rush hour) along the A5 to Cascais, with exits to the various towns on the Costa do Estoril along the way. The riverside Marginal is far more scenic but takes at least 15 minutes longer, depending on traffic. For Sintra, it takes upwards of 40 minutes, starting off on the A5, exiting to take the N117, and then picking up the IC19 (also known as the A37, but toll free); note that driving in Sintra itself is even more challenging than driving in Lisbon.

Autoestrada tolls are steep—costing, for example, €23.90 between Lisbon and Porto—but time saved by traveling these roads usually makes them worthwhile, as minor roads are often poor and winding, with unpredictable surfaces. If you rent a vehicle, it should come with a Via Verde (Green Lane) electronic transponder that means you can zip past toll booths without stopping, though make sure you take the correct lane.

Some autoestradas in Portugal—including the east–west A22 in the Algarve—now use electronic tolls only, with no method of payment accepted on the roads themselves. To avoid getting fined for not paying the tolls, if you rent a car in Portugal make sure the rental company installs an electronic device that adds the costs of the tolls to your final bill. If you are driving in from Spain, there are four entry points where you can register your license plate and credit card in person; you may also do this beforehand on the Portugal Tolls website.

CAR RENTALS

To rent a car in Portugal you must be a minimum of 18 years old, but many companies have a higher age threshold (19, 21, or even 25) or require at least one or two years of driving experience; they may apply a surcharge for younger drivers. Upper age limits also vary. Your license from home is recognized in Portugal and enables you to drive around for up to six months. However, you should learn the international road-sign system (charts are available to members of most automobile associations).

GASOLINE

Most passenger cars use regular gasoline, but some larger vehicles may take diesel. Make sure to double-check which one your rental car takes before setting off. The cost of either fuel (with prices per liter) is around twice the level in the United States. If you are driving an electric vehicle, research the nearest charging points on your planned voyage beforehand.

Getting Here and Around

PARKING

Most on-street parking is metered; if you don't pay, you will receive a ticket and you'll likely be clamped. You have two hours to phone and pay or your car will be towed, meaning that you will need to go and release it from the impound and also pay a higher fine.

For off-street parking lots or underground car parks, a ticket is issued on entry at a barrier. Before returning to your vehicle, go to the payment machine, insert your ticket, and pay, making sure to retain the ticket to use to exit at the barrier. If you have a rental car with a Via Verde transponder (primarily for automatic payment of autoestrada tolls), you will most likely not need a ticket at most Lisbon off-street parking facilities, as the barrier will automatically open on your arrival and you will be charged virtually based on when you leave.

RULES OF THE ROAD

Driving is on the right. The speed limit on the autoestrada is 120 kph (74 mph); on other roads, it's 90 kph (56 mph), and in built-up areas, 50 kph (30 mph).

At the junction of two roads of equal size, traffic coming from the right has priority. Vehicles already in a traffic circle have priority over those entering from any point. The use of seat belts is obligatory. Horns shouldn't be used in built-up areas, and you should always carry your driver's license, proof of car insurance, a reflective red warning triangle, and EU-approved reflective jacket for use in a breakdown.

Children under 12 years old *must* ride in the back seat in age-appropriate restraining devices (facing backwards for children under 18 months). Motorcyclists and their passengers must wear helmets, and motorcycles must have their headlights on, day and night.

Ⓜ Public Transport

Lisbon's public transportation includes a network of metros, buses, streetcars, funiculars, and elevators, all of which use a single ticketing system. Buy a VIVA Viagem card (€0.50) and either put a Carris/Metro ticket (€1.80) onto it—giving you one hour's travel on the metro and Carris buses, streetcars, and funiculars—or load your card up with cash. A 24-hour ticket for Carris and Metro costs €6.80; for a few euros more you can also travel on cross-Tagus ferries or on suburban trains.

METRO

The city's metro network is not too helpful for many city center sights, which are located on hills where only streetcars and a few buses roam, but it is good for covering longer distances. It is also expanding, with a new circular line to be created from the existing Green and Yellow ones, and two new stations, Estrela and Santos. Further out, there are plans to extend the Red line westwards and south to Alcântara, linking up with the aboveground rail line to Cascais.

BUS

Within the city limits Carris has a comprehensive network of bus routes. Across the wider metropolitan area, myriad municipal companies run local services and routes linking up with the capital, but thankfully all are now under the Carris Metropolitana umbrella, meaning that timetables can be checked on a single website, and you can use a VIVA Viagem card on these buses, too.

FUNICULAR/STREETCAR

Portugal's antique streetcars or *elétricos* are one of the city's best-known attractions but are also used as a means of daily transport by locals—when they can squeeze onto them. Timetables accordingly vary by season, or during school or other holidays, but the last service is generally before midnight.

The downtown streetcar with the longest route is the 28: it starts on Largo Martim Moniz—where there is invariably a long queue of tourists waiting patiently to be assured of a seat—then heads up to hilltop Graça before winding its way down again through Alfama and past Sé Catedral, through downtown Baixa and Chiado and on to the Basílica da Estrela and the bustling Campo de Ourique neighborhood. Other popular streetcars are the 12, which plies a shorter circular route, starting at Praça da Figueira but also traversing Alfama and the Sé; and the 24, whose terminus is in Praça Luís de Camões in Chiado and which runs along the edge of the Bairro Alto and Príncipe Real and Rato. Finally, the more spacious, modern 15 is the best way to reach the monuments and museums of Belém.

Lisbon's venerable funiculars—officially known as *ascensores* but more commonly referred to as *elevadores*—also form part of the Carris network: the Elevador da Glória, which links the western side of Praça dos Restauradores with the Bairro Alto; the Elevador do Lavra,

Getting Here and Around

the city's oldest and mostly used by locals, on the Largo da Anunciada off the eastern side of Praça dos Restauradores; and the Elevador da Bica, which links the increasingly trendy Rua de São Paulo, near Cais do Sodré, with the lower end of the Bairro Alto. Onboard tickets cost €4.10 (for two trips) but, again, just €1.61 on a VIVA Viagem card.

Passes and tickets may also be used on the Elevador da Santa Justa, which unlike its namesakes really is an elevator, carrying passengers from the Baixa to Largo do Carmo, in the upper part of Chiado, via a walkway that affords fabulous views. It's €6 for two trips, but even for this you can use a VIVA Viagem card and be debited just €1.61.

A new funicular opened in March 2024 that links Mouraria (Rua dos Lagares) with Graça.

Ride-Sharing

Uber and Bolt are the two ride-sharing companies operating in Lisbon. The latter is sometimes cheaper, but at busy times both can be more expensive than regular taxis. They are allowed to do pickups at Lisbon airport; note that at Terminal 1 this is outside departures.

Taxi

Lisbon's distinctive black-and-green taxis are safe, cheap, and plentiful (although in a downpour it may be challenging to find one available). They can be ordered by phone, online on the taxi coops' websites, or via apps such as Taxi-Link (which also has digital kiosks in some hotels), or just hailed on the street. Taxi stands are easy to find downtown. The minimum charge is €3.25 (plus 20% from 9 pm to 6 am on weekdays, all day on weekends) and then €0.47 per kilometer. You pay another €1.60 per piece of baggage carried in the trunk.

Train

Portugal's train network, Comboios de Portugal (CP), covers most of the country, though it's thin in the Alentejo region. Lisbon is linked to Coimbra, Aveiro, Porto, Braga, and Faro by fast, extremely comfortable Alfa Pendular trains.

The capital is also served from other major towns by Intercidades trains, which are reliable, although a bit slower and less luxurious than the Alfa trains. Regional services that stop at smaller towns and villages tend to be infrequent and slow.

Advance booking, which may be done online, is recommended for Alfa and Intercidades services, if you want to avoid lines in front of the ticket window on the day of the train.

Travelers aged up to 25 benefit from a 25% reduction in the price of all tickets. Those 65 and over get 50% off. In both cases, just show official ID with proof of your age, such as a driver's license or passport. The CP website details various other discounts, such as 40%–50% off if you travel midweek as a group of three or four.

Around Lisbon, *urbano* services trundle out through the suburbs to Cascais and Sintra (40 minutes, €2.40 one way) to the west and northwest, and to Azambuja via Vila Franca de Xira, to the northeast. To the south, over the Ponte 25 de Abril, private company Fertagus runs commuter services all the way to and from Setúbal, with its Lisbon stations around the northern fringe of the city center at Roma-Areeiro, Entrecampos, and Sete Rios. The price of tickets (loaded onto a €0.50 VIVA Viagem card) vary according to distance but cost €2.40 one-way for Cascais or Sintra.

Essentials

Addresses

Portuguese addresses are written with the name of the street or square first, then the house or building number, then a comma and the floor number. Note that floor numbers are as elsewhere in Europe: 1° is the floor above ground level, ground floor itself is R/C (*rez de chão*), and C/V (c *ave*) is the basement. In buildings where there is more than one unit per floor, there will be a "D" (for *direito*, or right) or "E" (for *esquerdo*, or left) after the floor number: if an apartment is on the right side as you come up the stairs or out of the elevator, it is D; if on the left, E.

Dining

The dining scene in Portugal has changed dramatically over the past few years, with the country's best chefs taking a cue from their counterparts in Spain and around Europe. Above all in Lisbon, it's not hard to find upscale places that have won international awards for their inventive takes on Portuguese fare. But locals will tell you that the best food by far tends be found in more traditional spots, including cheap and cheerful *tascas*. Don't expect much in the way of decor, and if you have trouble squeezing in, remember the rule of thumb: if it's packed, it's probably good.

Restaurants featuring charcoal-grilled meats and fish, called *churrasqueiras*, are also popular (and often economical) options, and Brazilian *rodízio*-type restaurants, where you are regaled with an endless offering of spit-roasted meats, are entrenched in Lisbon.

Shellfish restaurants, called *marisqueiras*, are numerous along the coast; note that lobsters, mollusks, and the like are fresh and good but pricey. Restaurant prices fall appreciably when you leave the city itself (Cascais being the exception), and portion sizes increase the farther out you go.

Portuguese restaurants serve a *menu do dia*, or a set menu of two or three courses, usually including a drink and coffee. This can be a real bargain—usually at least 20% less than the courses ordered separately.

It's easier than it used to be for vegetarians to find suitable options in Portugal: not only is *sopa de legumes* (vegetable soup) often included as a starter, together with the inevitable *salada* (salad) and probably an omelet, but more modern places have at least one decent alternative. The larger cities now have many vegetarian and vegan restaurants, and Chinese, Italian, and Indian restaurants are increasingly common and always have plenty of options.

PAYING

Most restaurants take credit cards, but some smaller places do not. It's worth asking. There is not an established culture of tipping in Portugal, so doing so is seen as a genuine expression of appreciation for good service. However, where foreign visitors are concerned, waiters nowadays may be disappointed if they do not receive a gratuity of 10% or more, particularly at high-end restaurants; a few places now automatically add a tip to the bill, although this is optional and you can ask not to pay it.

RESERVATIONS AND DRESS

Always make a reservation at upscale restaurants when you can. Some are booked weeks in advance, but some popular restaurants don't accept reservations. As unfair as it seems, at more traditional or particularly upscale places, the way you look can influence how you're treated—and where you're seated. Generally speaking, jeans and a button-down shirt will suffice at most restaurants, but some pricier ones require jackets and some insist on ties. In reviews, we mention dress only where men are required to wear a jacket or a jacket and tie. If you have doubts, call the restaurant and ask.

MEALS AND MEALTIMES

Breakfast (*pequeno-almoço*) is the lightest meal, usually consisting of nothing more than a croissant or pastry washed down with coffee. Lunch (*almoço*), the main meal of the day, is served between noon and 3 pm, although nowadays, office workers in cities often grab a house-made soup or *miniprato* (smaller serving of a daily main dish) in a bar instead of stopping for a big meal. Some cafés and snack bars serve light meals throughout the afternoon.

Around 5 pm, people often take a *lanche* break for coffee or tea and a pastry; dinner (*jantar*) is eaten around 8 pm, and restaurants generally serve until about 10 pm—later in the case of more modern places. Monday is a common day for restaurants to close, so check ahead.

Unless otherwise noted, the restaurants listed in this guide are open daily for lunch and dinner.

SMOKING

Smoking is banned in all restaurants and bars.

Essentials

What It Costs in Euros

	$	$$	$$$	$$$$
AT DINNER	under €16	€16–€20	€21–€25	over €25

Health & Safety

There are no specific health concerns for travel in Portugal, but make sure you are up-to-date on all routine vaccines (such as flu or measles, for which cases are on the rise worldwide) before every trip. COVID vaccination is not currently required but is advisable, as new strains of the disease are constantly emerging. If you are thinking of roughing it, hepatitis A might also be good to guard against, and the Center for Disease Control also recommends the hepatitis B vaccine for all unvaccinated travelers under 60 years old, whatever their destination. Portugal's dogs are free of rabies, but some wild species such as bats are not, so if you are likely to be off the beaten track in rural areas, a vaccine would be a good idea.

Portugal's tap water is good to drink, but for reasons of taste you may want to take advantage of the wide range of local fizzy and flat bottled waters, with Pedras Salgadas a particularly pungent one, widely held to have positive digestive effects.

In terms of safety, Portugal regularly ranks in the top five countries in the Global Peace Index, with violent crime relatively rare. Visitors should, however, be alert to the threat posed by skilled pickpockets, particularly in crowded streetcars.

Internet

Hotels invariably have free Wi-Fi for guests, as do most restaurants and many cafés, although other types of hot spots around town are scarce. Some hotels also lend all guests cell phones with prepaid data and local and international calls. But if you want to hit the ground running on arrival at Lisbon airport, head for the Vodafone stall to purchase a prepaid SIM card to insert in your cell. If you are traveling on to other European countries, you can use the card's calls and data there, too, if you activate international roaming on your phone.

Lodging

FACILITIES

There are many different types of lodging options in and around Lisbon, ranging from the ever-expanding short-term rentals sector—known here as *alojamento local*, a category that includes hostels—to B&B-type hotels, many of which still bear the old label of *Residencial*, or international chain hotels with every amenity you can name. Many who travel to the beachfront communities along the Costa do Estoril check themselves into luxurious resorts and never step outside them, taking full advantage of swimming pools, tennis courts, and nearby golf courses.

In the city itself, there are now ever more boutique hotels in period town houses and mansions in central neighborhoods, often with luxurious touches and setting great store on service. But their main advantage is their location: within walking distance of many sights and affording charming views of the river or the local neighborhood. By contrast, the big international chain hotels tend to be in the modern city, further inland, and to reach the main sights you will need to take the metro or taxi.

A unique type of lodging in Portugal is the *pousada*—a term derived from the Portuguese verb *pousar* (to rest). Portugal has several dozen of these, mainly in restored castles, palaces, and monasteries. Two are in Lisbon: one in a former government ministry downtown, the other in a town house in Alfama. There are also pousadas in a sprawling fort in Cascais and attached to the Palace of Queluz. All are tastefully furnished with regional crafts, antiques, and artwork. Make reservations well in advance, especially for stays in summer; visit 🌐 *www.pousadas.pt/en* for details.

PRICES

With summer temperatures high and rising in Lisbon (although nights are often cool), and a growing awareness among foreign visitors of this fact, peak season for city hotels nowadays is May and September, rather than July and August as it once was—at least for those that are not catering to families, such as near the beaches of the Costa do Estoril. Demand now remains strong pretty much all year round, so you will have to hunt around to find bargains and book well in advance. Most tourist accommodations operate on the basis of dynamic pricing—room rates depending on demand at any

Essentials

one time—but a few hotels do make a point of sticking to set prices at given times of year.

What It Costs in Euros			
$	$$	$$$	$$$$
FOR TWO PEOPLE			
under €140	€140–€200	€201–€260	over €260

Money

The most-used notes are €5, €10, and €20; hand a waiter or taxi driver a €50 or €100 and they are sure to grumble, as there is a chronic shortage of change in Portugal that even the country's central bank has never satisfactorily explained. You can pay with plastic (Visa or Mastercard) in most shops and restaurants, but if you make a habit of using cash, try to always keep some coins with you. These range from 1 cent through 2, 5, 10, 20, and 50 cents; there are also €1 and €2 coins.

Note that, across the eurozone, the side of the coin with the number on it is the same everywhere, but every country produces its own design for the other side. As so many foreign tourists pass through Lisbon, you will likely amass quite a collection of these little artworks.

Passport

All non-EU nationals are required to present a passport on arrival in Portugal. (EU nationals have the option of presenting their national ID card.)

Shipping

Specialist stores, such as wine merchants and even small crafts shops, are usually able to arrange to ship your purchases back home and will know what regulations apply, if any. So if you intend to take back something particularly fragile, heavy, or regulated, do ask about the cost of doing so. If you want to arrange the shipping yourself, there are several companies that you can do this with, such as Eurosender.

Taxes

In Lisbon and some other cities, there is a specific levy on tourist accommodation, of €2 per guest per night, up to seven nights. But the main sales levy is the value-added tax (VAT), which applies to most items sold by retailers. The standard rate for goods and services is 23%, but there are two reduced rates, as allowed

Where Should I Stay?

	NEIGHBORHOOD VIBE	PROS	CONS
Baixa	Bustling commercial district with several major sights, now often thronged with tourists	Many new, mid-market hotels, and some posher ones; many dining options	Lots of traffic, very busy during the day but little life at night
Chiado and Bairro Alto	Traditional shops and cafés in Chiado, contrasting with the nightlife of Bairro Alto	Very central, with several charming boutique hotels; several of Lisbon's top restaurants	Chiado very quiet at night, while Bairro Alto is very noisy
Alfama	Warren of narrow alleys and tiny squares, with a medieval feel	Bags of local charm; a choice of restaurants, intimate bars and fado shows	Around half of housing units are now tourist apartments
Graça and São Vicente	Workaday neighborhoods, still retaining signs of local life	Affordable restaurants and cafés, patronized by locals	Few lodging options; a long walk uphill from the city center
Beato and Marvila	Former industrial districts that are now among Lisbon's most happening	Funky bars, eateries, and galleries, with new venues opening all the time	Far from the center, with limited transport links
Avenida da Liberdade	Lisbon's equivalent of the Champs-Élysées, lined with pavement cafés and luxury chain stores	Great central location, with good choice of international chain hotels and boutique properties	Traffic a bit much during rush hour; little nightlife

Essentials

for in EU legislation: 13% on some food products and wine, as well as musical instruments, among other items; and 6% on basic foodstuffs, newspapers and most books, some pharmaceutical products, passenger transport, and hotel accommodations. Some services are VAT exempt, such as health and financial services.

Non-EU residents are entitled to a VAT refund for purchases of €50 or more before tax (not including lodging or meals); look out for the "VAT Refund" or "Tax-Free Shopping" sign in the windows of retailers participating in the tax-free schemes that makes this easy to claim. Let the retailer know that you want to apply for a VAT refund and make sure you have your passport with you; they will then give you a receipt together with a special tax-free form with an electronic registration code on it. You'll need both to get your refund (though note that if Portugal is not the last stop on your trip to the EU, you should wait until the last country before asking for your VAT back). At the airport, visit an E-Taxfree Portugal kiosk to validate your form—before checking your luggage, if you will be putting the purchased item in one of those bags, or after security if it is in your carry-on. Then take the validated form to the desk of the operator of the tax-free scheme in question to get your refund on the spot, or alternatively put your validated form in its drop box, and the refund should be issued to your credit card or sent to your home in the form of a check, as you have specified.

Telephones

Regular landline numbers in Portugal all start with 2 and there are no area codes; although Lisbon numbers invariably start with 21, you must dial the whole number wherever in the country you are calling from. Cell phone numbers start with a 9.

You can buy a local SIM card with calls and data at the Vodafone booth at Lisbon airport, but SIM cards for data and international calls can also be bought in cell phone stores and at stands in locations such as metro stations all over town.

Tipping

Service is not always included in café, restaurant, and hotel bills; when it is included, it is still strictly optional. Waiters and other service people are sometimes poorly paid, and leaving a tip of around 10% will be appreciated (though locals often don't tip at all, or just 5%). If, however, you received bad service, never feel obligated (or intimidated) to leave a tip. Also, if you have something small, such as a sandwich or *petiscos* (appetizers) at a bar, you can leave just enough to round out the bill to the nearest €1.

U.S. Embassy/ Consulate

The U.S. embassy in Portugal is located in Lisbon at ✉ *Avenida das Forças Armadas 133C.*

Visa

Starting in mid-2025, visa-exempt nationals from 60 countries—including the United States, the United Kingdom, and Canada—will need to pre-register through ETIAS (European Travel Information and Authorization System) to visit Portugal and other European Union countries. The ETIAS authorization is valid for three years (or until your current passport expires) and allows multiple visits to any participating country. Most applications should be approved in a few minutes and will cost €7 (free for those under 18 and over 70), but some travelers will have to provide additional information and/or sit for an interview, so be sure to apply at least 30 days in advance of your trip (and before making any nonrefundable reservations). Visit the official ETIAS website at 🌐 *travel-europe.europa.eu/etias_en*to apply. For more helpful information, check out 🌐 *etias.com.* Note that the program's implementation has been delayed several times, so be sure to confirm in advance that ETIAS registration is required at the time of your trip.

Visitor Information

The city tourist board, Turismo de Lisboa, is a public-private joint venture better known to foreign visitors by its Visit Lisboa website (🌐 *www.visitlisboa.com*), which boasts useful tools such as a trip planner and events calendar, as well as hotel listings, themed pages, and promotions. Its main Ask Me Lisboa tourist office is on Praça do Comércio; it also has a desk at the airport, open 7 am–10 pm. As well as these permanent offices, Ask Me Lisboa booths are often staffed inside Baixa-Chiado and São Sebastião metro stations; in Rossio and Campo Pequeno squares; in Cais do Sodré, Santa Apolónia, and Rossio train stations; on the Doca da Marinha quay off Avenida Infante Dom Henrique; in Belém (opposite the Jerónimos Monastery); and at Parque das Nações. At all these places, you can pick up a Lisboa Card (from €22), which gives you free travel on the city's metro network, buses, and streetcars for 24, 48, or 72 hours, plus free or discounted admission to museums and monuments, and other bonuses.

The national tourism authority, Turismo de Portugal, has its own even more comprehensive Visit Portugal website (🌐 *visitportugal.com*).

For tourists who are the victim of a crime or have a security-related query, Portugal's main urban police force, the Polícia de Segurança Pública (PSP), has dedicated officers based at the main cruise ship terminal, located about halfway between Praça do Comércio and Santa Apolónia train station.

High Season: For most of Portugal, June through August is the busiest, hottest, and most expensive time to visit, but in the capital most hotels' rates now peak in May and September. In July and August, when temperatures soar, tourists tend to opt for holidays nearer the beach—so, with the exception of the Costa do Estoril, prices across the region are often a little lower in these summer months.

Low Season: Winter in Portugal is growing in popularity, due to the agreeable year-round temperatures and lower hotel prices. Off-season activities are still varied and plentiful, and while the beach may be off the menu, pleasant strolls and cozy evenings are definitely on it. Don't expect to have the place to yourself, though—these days Lisbon attracts plenty of visitors all year round.

Shoulder Season: April and October are both stunning months in which to visit Portugal, and you may even be lucky enough to enjoy a bracing dip in the pool or sea. Almond and orange blossoms perfume the air, key regions are quieter, and room prices are down from their peaks.

Contacts

Air

AIRLINES TAP Portugal. *800/903–7914 toll-free from U.S., 21/234–400 from Portugal* *www.flytap.com.*

Bicycle Rentals

CONTACTS Biclas. *91/240–3423* *www.biclas.com.* **bikeiberia.** *Largo do Corpo Santo 5, Baixa* *21/347–0347* *www.lisbonhub.com.*

Bus

CONTACTS Carris. *21/361–3000* *carris.pt/en.* **Carris Metropolitana.** *21/041–0400 passenger helpline, 21/041–8800 information line* *www.carrismetropolitana.pt.* **EVA Transportes.** *Lisbon* *21/752–4524* *eva-bus.com.* **Rede Expressos.** *21/752–4524* *rede-expressos.pt/en.*

Public Transportation

CONTACTS Metropolitana de Lisboa. *21/350–0115* *www.metrolisboa.pt/en.*

Train

TRAIN Comboios de Portugal. *808/109–110, 21/090–0032* *www.cp.pt/passageiros/en.* **Fertagus.** *21/106–6363* *www.fertagus.pt/en.*

Visitor Information

VISITOR INFORMATION Ask Me Lisboa Aeroporto. *Aeroporto Humberto Delgado, Lisbon* *21/845–0660, 91/051–7888* *www.visitlisboa.com/en/c/tourist-offices.* **Ask Me Lisboa Terreiro do Paço.** *Praça do Comércio, Baixa* *800/500–503 info line (free within Portugal), 21/031–2810* *www.visitlisboa.com/en.* **Police Tourism Station (PSP).** *Terminal de Cruzeiros de Lisboa, Av. Infante Dom Henrique* *21/880–4030.* **Visit Portugal.** *www.visitportugal.com/en.*

Taxis

Cooptáxis *21/793–2756* *cooptaxis.pt/en.* **Retális** *21/811–9000* *www.retalis.pt.* **Taxi-Link** *21/244–9390* *www.taxisdelisboa.com/en.*

Best Tours

Aside from annoying pick-pockets in many tourist areas (above all on streetcars) Lisbon is safe, compact, and easy to navigate. With a good map and a willingness to get lost, you'll most likely stumble across a few treasures that remind you of why you travel. Still, sometimes it's nice to have a local show you what's what. Aside from the numerous "Free tours" offered by guides in Rossio square, downtown, and Praça Luís de Camões in Chiado—who hope for a generous tip at the end of the walk, and some of whom are quite competent—there are many paying options.

ADVENTURE TOURS

Guincho Aventours. This enduringly popular tour company runs adventure tours in and around Lisbon, including trekking; mountain biking; kayaking; and off-road quad, buggy, and Jeep tours to the most remote areas in the Cascais area, as well as special excursions aimed at kids. ✉ *Rua da Areia 1306, Cascais* ☎ *21/486–9700, 93/447–9075 cell phone* 🌐 *www.guinchotours.com.*

BICYCLE TOURS

bikeiberia. Bike Iberia is a long-established company offering cycling tours all over Portugal; it also leads guided tours by regular and e-bike in and around the capital from its Lisbon Hub near Cais do Sodré train station, including mountain biking in Sintra. ✉ *Largo do Corpo Santo 5, Baixa* ☎ *21/347–0347* 🌐 *www.lisbonhub.com.*

Free Bike Tours Lisbon. This long-established outfit—now with a base behind Santa Apolónia train station—runs daily tours of the historic center and Belém, for which you pay the amount that you feel is appropriate at the end. You will need a bike, of course, which you can bring along if you have rented one already for the day or, if you want the company to supply one (from €14), just check the box when you book online. They also lead regular small-group tours (from €40 per person, e-bike included) of Lisbon's seven hills and of Sintra and Cascais; they organize private tours, too. ✉ *Rua Caminhos de Ferro 62A, Alfama* ☎ *91/952–3068 WhatsApp* 🌐 *www.freebiketourslisbon.com.*

CULTURAL TOURS

Batoto Yetu Portugal. This association based in the Lisbon suburbs works with young locals from less privileged backgrounds who have an interest in African culture, but it is also a pioneer in researching and highlighting the centuries-old African presence in the capital. Its guided tours in English (from €200 for up to four people on foot, or up to five in a tuk tuk) enable visitors to discover this heritage, too, with documented stories of a community whose members played a crucial role in urban life, undertaking the most onerous tasks, yet were consistently undervalued. 🌐 *batotoyetu.pt/guided-tours-african-presence-in-lisbon-bato-to-yetu-portugal.*

FOOD TOURS

Culinary Backstreets. This company specializes in walking food tours around some of the world's best eating cities. The guides are culinary journalists, former chefs and sommeliers, and other gastronomic insiders. In Lisbon, the tours range from a broad overview of the best of the city's dishes, to a journey through ethnic restaurants run by chefs from the former colonies, to a movable seafood feast along the docklands of Alcântara. The tours aren't cheap, but they provide enough food and wine for the entire day. 🌐 *culinary-backstreets.com.*

Food Lover Tour. Established in various European cities, Food Lover guides small groups around traditional Lisbon neighborhoods at different times of day to explore authentic local food stores and eateries, with traditional petiscos, delicious wines, and some classic desserts all included. 🌐 *foodlovertour.com/lisbon.*

WALKING TOURS

Lisbon Walker. Lisbon's longest-established purveyor of walking tours, this company has built up and honed a range of specialties, and all their regular tours—such as the Revelation Tour, Lisbon Old Town, and Lisbon City of Spies (about nefarious goings-on in neutral Portugal during World War II)—are also available as private ones. ☎ *96/357–5635 WhatsApp.*

We Hate Tourism Tours. This quirky tourism company prides itself on knowing the ins and outs of Lisbon, with an emphasis on respecting the city and its inhabitants. Expert guides are happy to share their favorite off-the-beaten track bars, restaurants, and attractions. Its wide range of tours includes dinner at tucked-away eateries only locals know about and walks through "the real Lisbon." ✉ *LxFactory, Rua Rodrigues de Faria 103, Alcântara* ☎ *91/377–6598* 🌐 *www.wehatetourismtours.com* 🎫 *From €17 for walking tours.*

Great Itineraries

Lisbon in 7 Days

You can explore the city center in a couple of days, but it will be a bit of a rush, out of keeping with the city's underlying rhythm, which is slower than that of most European capitals. It is better to take the time to explore beyond the top sights, taking in other neighborhoods for a more local feel.

DAY ONE

A great way to get the measure of the city is to head straight up to the **Castelo de São Jorge** (St. George's Castle) for an overview of its seven hills, with the Ponte 25 de Abril suspension bridge in the distance. This spot harbors remains from pre-Roman times, some of them on show in a small museum. From here, wander downhill for more views from the **Santa Luzia** *miradouro* (viewpoint) and then into the winding alleys of **Alfama**. Enjoy a lunch of grilled fish or meat in a local restaurant, before stepping into the **Sé Catedral** on your way back downtown or, if you are interested in modern history, the **Museu do Aljube**. Take a stroll around **Praça do Comércio**, where there are interactive takes on Portugal's history at the **Lisbon Story Centre** and **Centro Interpretativo da História do Bacalhau** (Interpretive Center of the History of Cod), not to mention the **Wines of Portugal Tasting Room**. To dive into the local musical culture, book a table in a fado house for dinner.

DAY TWO

Start in the Baixa with a stroll around **Largo de São Domingos** and bustling city hub **Rossio square** (official name Praça Dom Pedro IV), before heading up Rua do Carmo into the shopping district of Chiado. There's plenty to catch the eye, with traditional stores boasting elaborate interiors side-by-side with purveyors of fast fashion. Stop for a break at Alcôa, with its jewel-like pastries, or at a famous café like A Brasileira do Chiado. There are some great lunch options around, though you will need to book ahead for top restaurants such as Belcanto or Alma. Continue up to **Largo do Carmo**, where a medieval façade hides a ruined church, behind which a walkway leads to the **Elevador de Santa Justa**, an antique lift whose upper platform affords panoramic views. Further uphill is the **Igreja de São Roque**, a Jesuit church with Lisbon's richest interior. After all this walking, settle into an armchair in the nearby **Solar do Vinho do Porto** to sip a port wine from their extensive list. Afterwards, cross the street for sweeping views from the **Jardim de São Pedro de Alcântara** miradouro before a night out in the Bairro Alto or Príncipe Real neighborhoods.

DAY THREE

Catch the modern n° 15 streetcar to Belém, Lisbon's museum district. The **Mosteiro dos Jerónimos** (Jerónimos Monastery), a 16th-century monastery, is the main draw, along with the **Torre de Belém** (Tower of Belém), built to guard the river. Other sights include Portugal's most visited museum, the **Museu Nacional dos Coches**, with its unrivaled collection of carriages. Art lovers will want to visit the **Museu de Arte Contemporânea** in the Centro Cultural de Belém, with its major permanent collection and changing exhibitions, or the stunning riverside **MAAT** (Museum of Art, Architecture, and Technology). You could spend a whole day in Belém, making sure to sample the famous *pastéis de Belém* (custard tarts), but it's a pleasant 40-minute walk back as far as the Docas de Santo Amaro marina, with its varied restaurants and bars, open until late.

DAY FOUR

Catch the famous n° 28 streetcar up to Graça, a working-class hilltop neighborhood. The trams start in Largo Martim Moniz, setting off when all seats are full, no standing allowed; if you are happy to stand and don't want to join the (usually long) queue, walk up Rua da Palma to the next stop, where you may board regardless. Alighting in Graça, enjoy the views from the miradouro behind the old convent, before heading down to the grand church and monastery of **São Vicente de Fora** (home to Lisbon's Catholic patriarch) and former church of Santa Engrácia, now **National Pantheon**—both with rooftop views that take in the curve of the river. On Tuesdays and Saturdays, the **Feira da Ladra** (flea market) will be in full swing nearby. If you're a fan of ceramic tiles, walk (25 minutes) or take a taxi to the **Museu Nacional do Azulejo** (National Tile Museum), in a former convent whose cloisters and chapel alone are worth the visit. Or, for a dose of high culture, cross town to the **Fundação Calouste Gulbenkian**, set in a delightful landscaped garden, and whose main museum boasts an extensive collection of Western and Asian fine and applied art. For lunch or dinner, the top-floor gourmet food court in the nearby El Corte Inglés department store is a foodies' favorite; there's also an underground one with

Great Itineraries

cheaper options. If it is still light when you are done, climb up to the grassy heights of **Parque Eduardo VII** for an amazing view down over the city center to the river.

DAY FIVE

From downtown, catch the nº 24 streetcar to the **Basílica da Estrela**, an elegant baroque church with a tower to climb for more views. The park across the street is full of life on weekends. From here, walk up to Campo de Ourique, a middle-class neighborhood that is one of the few flat places in the city and a great place to potter or shop. The cemetery at the end of the tram route, **Cemitério dos Prazeres**, with its carved stone tombs of prominent local families, is an evocative place. For lunch, the small food court in the local covered market is an excellent option. Afterwards, it's a 25-minute walk down through the pretty embassy district of Lapa to the **Museu Nacional de Arte Antiga**, the city's principal art museum, and the best place to appreciate the fusions resulting from Portugal's maritime voyages. End your day at **Time Out Market Lisboa** in Cais do Sodré, where everything from pizza slices to gourmet dishes is served. The area's many bars stay open until the early hours.

DAY SIX

Take the metro out to the Parque das Nações—former site of Expo 98, which retains many of its original attractions. The **Oceanário de Lisboa**, an architecturally spectacular aquarium, has sharks, rays, otters, penguins, and countless other aquatic species, while the Pavilhão do Conhecimento offers an interactive experience for kids. Other draws include a cable car and a mall with a wide range of local and international chains. Both it and the wider area afford a range of lunch options, often with river views. As the afternoon wears on, you might head for Marvila, currently Lisbon's hippest neighborhood and home to cutting-edge art galleries, trendy restaurants, and bars selling craft beer, plus the **Fábrica Braço da Prata**, a cultural center whose programming ranges from dance classes to late-night live music.

DAY SEVEN

Make the most of a longer stay in the region to visit Cascais or Sintra—or both, taking in Cabo da Roca, Europe's westernmost point—or spend the day on a beach on the Estoril or Caparica coasts. Alternative trips out include the former royal palaces at Queluz and Mafra.

On the Calendar

February

Carnaval. The Shrove Tuesday festival (which normally falls in February, occasionally in March) in Lisbon isn't as elaborate as some outside the capital (including in Montijo, a ferry ride away across the Tagus, or in Torres Vedras, an hour's drive) but there are always parades and parties around town, with locals donning colorful costumes.

March

Lisbon Half Marathon. More than 30,000 runners from around the world compete in this event, one of the fastest half marathons in the world and also perhaps the most beautiful—this is the only time that pedestrians are allowed on Lisbon's iconic Ponte 25 de Abril. The rest of the course follows the waterfront, with lots of fans turning up to cheer on the runners. 🌐 *www.maratonaclubedeportugal.com*

ModaLisboa. Lisbon's main fashion show takes place twice yearly (the other is in October), in this case showcasing the fall/winter collections of locally based designers. 🌐 *modalisboa.pt*

Monstra Festival de Animação de Lisboa. Also known as the Lisbon Animation Festival, Monstra is the first of a long season of themed film festivals, based mostly at the city-owned Cinema São Jorge on Avenida da Liberdade. 🌐 *monstrafestival.com/en*

April

Estoril Open. The only Portuguese stop on the ATP World Tour calendar, this tournament draws millions of tennis fans each year. 🌐 *millenniumestorilopen.com*

Lisbon Art & Antiques Fair. The LAAF is the event to find the widest range of authentic art and design—ancient, modern, and contemporary—in one place. 🌐 *apa.pt/index.php/en/fairs-and-events*

Mafra International Organ Festival. It's worth the trip out to the vast Palace-Convent of Mafra, northwest of Lisbon, for this series of concerts in its basilica—the only space in the world with six organs, though they are rarely played all together—and other local churches and chapels.

25 de Abril. The anniversary of the 1974 Revolution sees official and informal celebrations, including a march down Avenida da Liberdade and a major event on Praça do Comércio with music and fireworks or videomapping.

On the Calendar

May–June

ARCOlisboa International Contemporary Art Fair. Organized annually since 2018 by the people behind ARCOmadrid, this is Lisbon's largest showcase for Portuguese galleries and artists. 🌐 *ifema.es/en/arco/lisboa*

Feira do Livro de Lisboa. The Lisbon Book Fair sees the city's booksellers and publishers set up stalls in Parque Eduardo VII for several weeks, offering books at reduced prices and hosting readings and author chats. Locals turn out in droves, creating a party-like atmosphere with food and drink vendors. 🌐 *feiradolivrodelisboa.pt*

Festival de Música dos Capuchos. One of Portugal's most interesting festivals, with classical and Renaissance music performed in the delightful 16th-century Convento dos Capuchos in Almada, on the south bank of the Tagus. 🌐 *festivalcapuchos.com*

Festival Internacional da Máscara Ibérica. The International Festival of the Iberian Mask—several days of processions, concerts, dances, workshops, and handicrafts and regional products fairs—celebrates Portugal and Spain's shared culture.

Festival Internacional de Marionetas e Formas Animadas. The International Festival of Puppets and Animated Forms brings marionettes of all kinds from around the world for a month of shows.

IndieLisboa International Film Festival. An annual feast of nonmainstream cinematic works from around the world. The festival includes several competitive sections and an IndieJúnior spinoff for kids. 🌐 *indielisboa.com/en*

Jardins Abertos. A relatively new initiative, in which dozens of gardens around town that are usually closed to the public open their doors, with guided tours, workshops, and activities linked to art, botany, and sustainability. 🌐 *www.jardinsabertos.com/en*

Open House Lisboa. As part of the international Open House movement to invite the public into intriguing private spaces, volunteers unlock the city's secret spaces and inform visitors about one of Europe's greatest urban environments. 🌐 *www.trienaldelisboa.com/ohl/en*

Rock in Rio. Every other year (next in 2026) Lisbon hosts its own mammoth local version of Brazil's biggest music festival, with lots of global stars as well as artists from

Portuguese-language countries. It's more of a family event than most rock fests. *rockinriolisboa.pt*

Santos Populares. Hands-down the biggest, most important festival in Lisbon is Santos Populares, when the city celebrates its most popular saints by throwing giant street parties. Everyone eats grilled sardines, drinks sangria, sings, dances, and generally makes merry. The party goes all month in various historic neighborhoods, but the main event is June 12, the night before the saint's day of Santo António. Squads from each neighborhood dress up and compete in a procession down Avenida da Liberdade, before dispersing back home to those street parties. On the 13th, a figure of Santo António is taken on a street procession and then, because he is known as the patron saint of lovers, a procession of dozens of brides and grooms heads to the Sé Catedral to make their vows en masse.

July

Festival ao Largo. This free outdoor festival celebrates music, singing, theater, and dance in one of the main squares of Chiado. Performers include the National Ballet Company and the Portuguese Symphony Orchestra. *festivalaolargo.pt*

NOS Alive. Lisbon's most consistently successful popular music festival hosts leading indie bands and a few big-name veterans, plus top DJs. *nosalive.com*

Super Bock Super Rock. One of Portugal's longest-running festivals, now back at Meco, a boho beach area south of Lisbon with on-site camping. *superbocksuperrock.pt*

August

Jazz em Agosto. Internationally renowned contemporary jazz musicians perform in the open-air amphitheater of the Fundação Calouste Gulbenkian for a series of outdoor concerts. *gulbenkian.pt*

O Sol da Caparica. South of the river at the Parque Urbano in Caparica Coast, O Sol da Caparica is a celebration of sand, surf, and music, aimed at a young, mainly local crowd. The performers include musicians from Portugal, Africa, and Brazil, playing everything from hip-hop and rock to fado and samba. There are also other performance art venues for dance and animated cinema, plus options for skateboarding, surfing, and windsurfing. 🌐 *www.facebook.com/osoldacaparica*

September

Festa do Avante! Since 1976, this festival, named after the newspaper of the Portuguese Communist Party, has taken place over the first weekend in September. It's more party than politics (though those do remain), with three days of concerts by well-known Portuguese and international artists, as well as other festivities. Hundreds of thousands of people attend, many of whom camp. There's food, venues for debates, book and music fairs, theater, cinema, and sports events. 🌐 *www.festadoavante.pcp.pt*

Festival Santa Casa Alfama. This event sponsored by the charity that runs the national lottery brings together Portugal's premier fado artists for a weekend of dozens of concerts in various venues. 🌐 *santacasaalfama.com*

MOTELX. Organized by fans for fans, the Lisbon International Horror Film Festival promotes the best of the genre from around the world. 🌐 *www.motelx.org/en*

Queer Lisboa. Lisbon's longest-established film festival, with international pulling power and featuring myriad themed sections and side events. 🌐 *queerlisboa.pt*

October

doclisboa. Perhaps Lisbon's highest-profile genre festival champions indie documentary films from around the world and with competitive sections. 🌐 *doclisboa.org*

Lisbon Marathon. This event is famed for the beauty of its course. Runners start in Cascais, follow the coast through towns like Carcavelos and Oeiras, pass the Jerónimos Monastery, and finish downtown at Praça do Comércio square. 🌐 *maratonalisboa.com*

November

Alkantara Festival. For a quarter of a century, this festival has championed cutting-edge performance arts. The programs includes a good deal of dance and other nonlinguistic performances. 🌐 *alkantarafestival.pt*

Web Summit. The largest, most prestigious tech and start-up conference in Europe takes place in Lisbon every November. 🌐 *websummit.com*

Chapter 3

BAIXA

Updated by
Alison Roberts

Sights	Restaurants	Hotels	Shopping	Nightlife
★★★★★	★★★☆☆	★★★★☆	★★★★★	★★★★★

NEIGHBORHOOD SNAPSHOT

TOP EXPERIENCES

- **Sip a coffee on Rossio square.** Praça Dom Pedro IV (as only maps call it) has been a hub since medieval times.
- **Delve into an ancient past.** Discover Roman fish-salting tanks and other remains in a bank basement.
- **Check out traditional retail.** The "Lojas com História" sign on facades identifies fast-disappearing "shops with history."
- **Sample local tipples.** Stop at a tiny bar selling ginjinha (wild-cherry liqueur) or book a tasting at the Wines of Portugal Tasting Room.
- **Lounge by the river at sunset.** Join canoodling couples on the stone wall at Terreiro do Paço or head west to the waterfront steps and drinks stalls of Ribeira das Naus.

GETTING HERE

Baixa is a near-perfect base for sightseeing. Attractions are within easy walking distance, and the area is almost entirely flat. There are three metro stations—Rossio, Baixa-Chiado, and Terreiro do Paço—and overground trains depart Rossio station for Sintra. If you do arrive by car, it's best to leave it in one of the area's underground parking facilities.

PLANNING YOUR TIME

Baixa bustles from the moment commuters pour off ferries and trains in the morning. It quiets down at night, though nowadays it is rarely completely deserted, thanks to the many hotels and restaurants.

OFF THE BEATEN PATH

- **Terminal Fluvial Sul e Sueste.** The eateries on Terreiro do Paço square draw hordes of tourists. To escape, head for this ferry terminal serving south-bank commuter towns; a terrace café affords river views and, at rush hour, people-watching opportunities. ✉ *Av. Infante Dom Henrique 1B.*

PAUSE HERE

- **Igreja de São Domingos.** Locals often step into Baixa churches to get away from the clamor or to light a candle. The most popular is this former monastery church, ravaged by fire in 1959, giving its cavernous interior a fantastical feel. ✉ *Largo de São Domingos.*

Baixa literally means "downtown," and this area has served as Lisbon's commercial center for centuries. Many banks and other businesses have moved to more modern premises further inland, but recent years have seen urban renewal thanks to the city's tourism boom.

A tributary of the Tagus once flowed through this low-lying terrain outside the city walls built by the Romans. But over the centuries ever more marshy land was reclaimed and built on, and by the Middle Ages it had become a mass of narrow streets and winding alleys, opening out at its northern end onto Rossio square. A key moment was the decision by King Manuel I to move down from the castle hill in 1503 to a new riverside palace, the Paço da Ribeira, in order to keep tabs on the burgeoning maritime trade. Ships were already being built next door at the Ribeira das Naus, where today the former boatyards are again visible after being buried for centuries.

The earthquake of 1755 destroyed the palace and reduced most of Lisbon to rubble, killing thousands of its inhabitants in the process. Within a decade, frantic rebuilding under the direction of the king's chief minister, later ennobled as the Marquês de Pombal, had given the Baixa a neoclassical look, with its grid of streets lined with grand stone buildings made quake-proof by wooden *gaiola* (cage) structures.

The Baixa stretches from Rossio—which has retained its medieval status as both a place of passage and a gathering place—to the riverfront Praça do Comércio, which is still known locally as Terreiro do Paço, after the long-vanished palace.

Pombal intended the arteries to house workshops for various trades, something that's still reflected in street names such as Rua dos Sapateiros (Cobblers' Street) and Rua da Prata (Silver Street). The central axis was given the grand name of Rua Augusta; today this traffic-free avenue is dominated by touristy restaurants and chain stores, but as elsewhere in the Baixa the odd traditional retail holdout or old-style café survives—look for the metal "Loja com História" sign jutting from the façade. At crossroads along Rua Augusta and at its southern end—in the shadow of the neoclassical arch that was the last part of the Baixa master plan to be completed—street entertainers often draw crowds.

Northeast of Rossio, the Rua das Portas de Santo Antão has pricey seafood restaurants, but the area is also known for its surviving ginjinha bars—cubbyholes where local characters throw down shots of the wild-cherry liqueur.

Baixa

Sights

Arco da Rua Augusta

NOTABLE BUILDING | FAMILY | Capping the post-earthquake restoration of Lisbon's downtown, the Arco Triunfal, as it's also known, was planned almost 50 years before the Parisian Arc de Triomphe. Its rooftop offers a splendid viewpoint from which to admire the handsome buildings around Praça do Comércio; on the terrace children delight in ringing a giant bell, while grown-ups can stand at the foot of the giant sculptures of Glory crowning Genius and Valour. In the square, you can identify other statues on the main facade by António Víctor de Figueiredo Bastos: from the left, a reclining figure representing the Tagus, followed by Viriato, native scourge of the Romans, and Vasco da Gama; and on the right, the Marquês de Pombal, medieval national hero Nuno Álvares Pereira, and the Douro River. ✉ *Rua Augusta 2, Baixa* 🌐 *www.visitlisboa.com/en/places/arco-da-rua-augusta* 🎫 *€3.50* Ⓜ *Blue Line to Terreiro do Paço.*

Elevador de Santa Justa (*Santa Justa Elevator*)

VIEWPOINT | The Santa Justa Elevator is one of Lisbon's more extraordinary structures. Designed by Raoul Mesnier du Ponsard, who studied under French engineer Gustave Eiffel, the Gothic-style tower was built in 1902. Queues are often frustratingly long in high season, but it's an enjoyable ride up to the top. The return ticket sold on board is a poor value—instead, get a 24-hour public transportation pass, which is valid on the elevator as well as all of the city's buses, trams, and metro lines. To skip the queues and the fare, you can access the upper walkway from Largo do Carmo. ✉ *Rua do Ouro, Baixa* 🎫 *€6 (return fare)* Ⓜ *Blue or Green Line to Baixa-Chiado, Green Line to Rossio.*

★ Lisboa Story Centre

HISTORY MUSEUM | FAMILY | This family-friendly museum uses multimedia exhibits to bring Lisbon's history to life. Over the course of an hour, the story is broken down into chapters, with a focus on the country's golden age of maritime adventures. Midway through, a small cinema shows dramatic reenactment of the 1755 earthquake and the fiery aftermath. ✉ *Praço do Comércio 78–81, Baixa* ☎ *211/941027* 🌐 *www.lisboastorycentre.pt/en* 🎫 *€7* Ⓜ *Blue Line to Terreiro do Paço.*

★ Núcleo Arqueológico da Rua dos Correeiros

RUINS | More than 2,500 years of history is on display at this archaeological treasure trove. The buried network of tunnels occupies almost a whole block in Lisbon's historic center and was unearthed in the 1990s during excavation works carried out by the bank Millennium BCP. The digs revealed homes and artifacts from the Roman, Visigoth, Islamic, medieval, and Pombaline periods. Free 50-minute guided tours in English or Portuguese lead visitors through underground walkways and around the foundations of ancient buildings. ✉ *Rua dos Correeiros 9, Baixa* ☎ *21/113–1070* 🌐 *www.fundacaomillenniumbcp.pt/en/nucleo-arqueologico* ⏲ *Closed Sun.* *Reservations necessary* Ⓜ *Blue or Green Line to Baixa-Chiado, Blue Line to Terreiro do Paço.*

★ Praça do Comércio

PLAZA/SQUARE | **FAMILY** | Known to locals as the Terreiro do Paço after the royal palace that once stood on this spot, this square is lined with 18th-century colonnaded buildings fronted by expansive esplanades. Down by the river, steps and slopes—once used by occupants of the royal barges that docked here—lead up from the water, and sunbathers strip down to catch rays during the summer. The equestrian statue in the center is of Dom José I, king at the time of the earthquake and subsequent rebuilding. In the summer, there are often live music events in the square and sunset pop-up drink stands sell potent caipirinhas. ✉ *Praça do Comércio, Baixa* Ⓜ *Blue Line to Terreiro do Paço.*

★ Rossio

PLAZA/SQUARE | **FAMILY** | The formal name for this grand public square is Praça Dom Pedro IV, but locals stick to its previous name, Rossio. A gathering place since at least Roman times, it was formally laid out in the 13th century as Lisbon's main public space. It remains a bustling social hub, where crowds socialize beside baroque fountains beneath a statue of Dom Pedro atop a towering column. Visitors can admire the dramatic wave-pattern cobblestones, famously reconstructed on the beach promenades of Rio de Janeiro. On nearby Largo de São Domingos, there's a memorial to Jewish victims of a massacre in 1506; three decades later centuries of more organized persecution began with the creation of the Portuguese Inquisition, headquartered where the Teatro Nacional Doña Maria II now stands, on the north side of

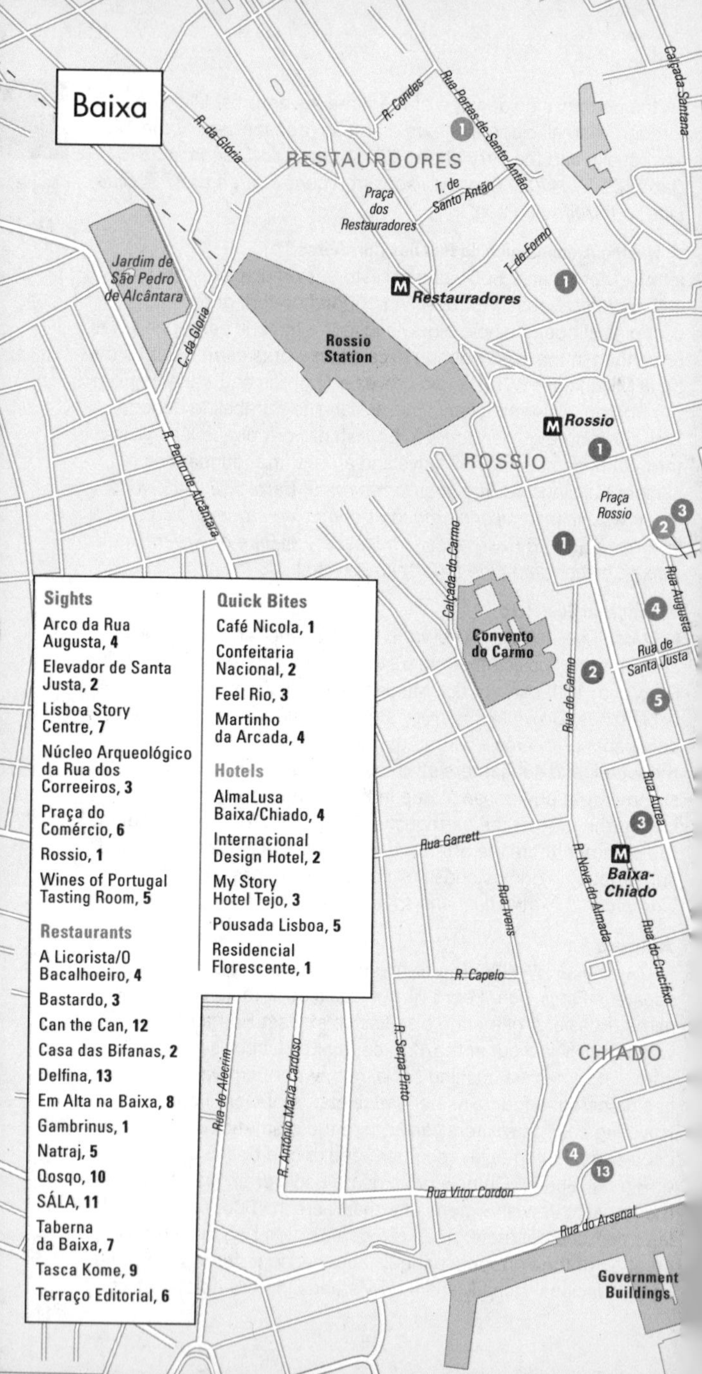

Baixa
RESTAURDORES
R. Condes
Rua Portas de Santo Antão
Calçada Santana
R. da Glória
Praça dos Restauradores
T. de Santo Antão
T. do Forno
Restauradores
Jardim de São Pedro de Alcântara
C. da Gloria
Rossio Station
Rossio
ROSSIO
R. Pedro de Alcântara
Praça Rossio
Calçada do Carmo
Rua Augusta
Convento do Carmo
Rua do Carmo
Rua de Santa Justa
Rua Áurea
Rua Garrett
Baixa-Chiado
Rua Ivens
R. Nova do Almada
Rua do Crucifixo
R. Capelo
R. Serpa Pinto
CHIADO
Rua do Alecrim
R. António Maria Cardoso
Rua Vitor Cordon
Rua do Arsenal
Government Buildings
Sights
Arco da Rua Augusta, 4
Elevador de Santa Justa, 2
Lisboa Story Centre, 7
Núcleo Arqueológico da Rua dos Correeiros, 3
Praça do Comércio, 6
Rossio, 1
Wines of Portugal Tasting Room, 5
Restaurants
A Licorista/O Bacalhoeiro, 4
Bastardo, 3
Can the Can, 12
Casa das Bifanas, 2
Delfina, 13
Em Alta na Baixa, 8
Gambrinus, 1
Natraj, 5
Qosqo, 10
SÁLA, 11
Taberna da Baixa, 7
Tasca Kome, 9
Terraço Editorial, 6
Quick Bites
Café Nicola, 1
Confeitaria Nacional, 2
Feel Rio, 3
Martinho da Arcada, 4
Hotels
AlmaLusa Baixa/Chiado, 4
Internacional Design Hotel, 2
My Story Hotel Tejo, 3
Pousada Lisboa, 5
Residencial Florescente, 1

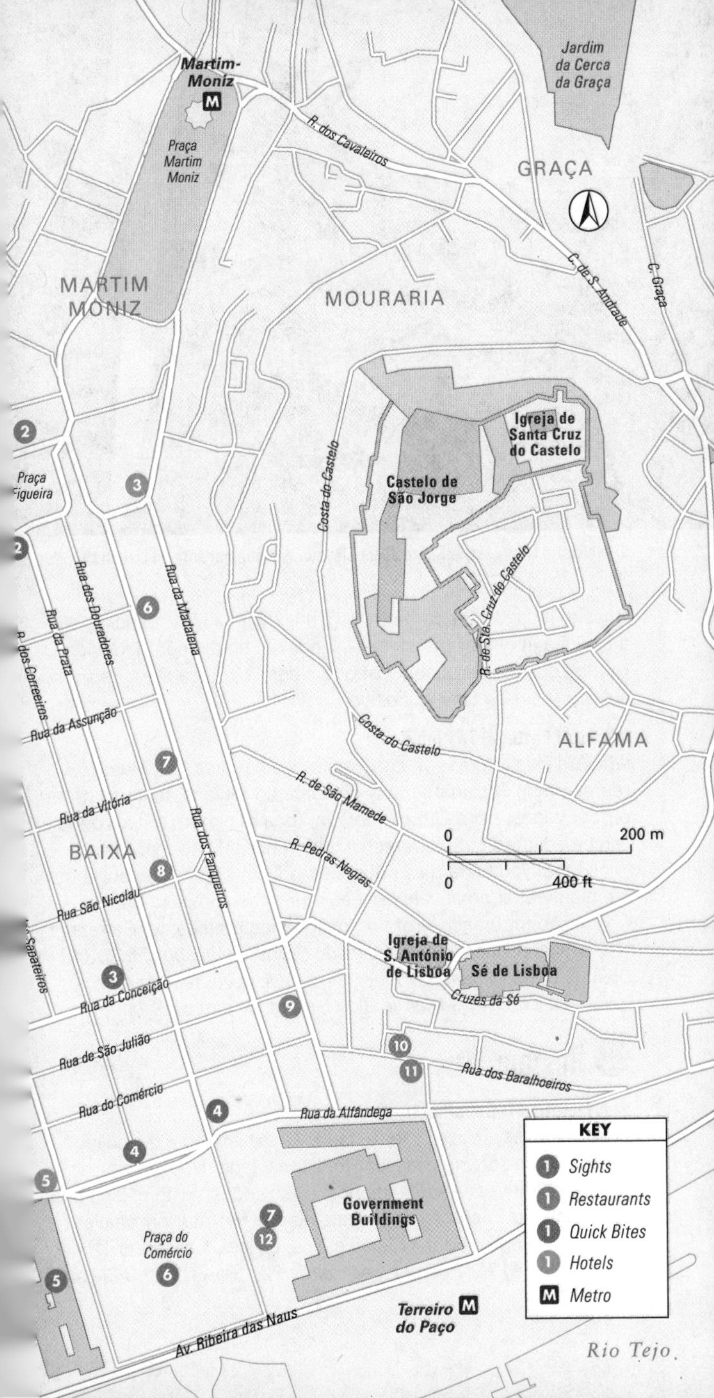

Martim-Moniz
M
Jardim da Cerca da Graça
R. dos Cavaleiros
GRAÇA
Praça Martim Moniz
C. de S. Andrade
C. Graça
MARTIM MONIZ
MOURARIA
Igreja de Santa Cruz do Castelo
Costa do Castelo
Castelo de São Jorge
Praça Figueira
R. de Sta. Cruz do Castelo
Rua dos Douradores
Rua da Madalena
Rua da Prata
R. dos Correeiros
Rua da Assunção
Costa do Castelo
ALFAMA
R. de São Mamede
Rua da Vitória
Rua dos Fanqueiros
0
200 m
R. Pedras Negras
BAIXA
0
400 ft
Rua São Nicolau
Sapateiros
Igreja de S. António de Lisboa
Sé de Lisboa
Rua da Conceição
Cruzes da Sé
Rua de São Julião
Rua dos Baralhoeiros
Rua do Comércio
Rua da Alfândega
KEY
Sights
Restaurants
Quick Bites
Hotels
Metro
Government Buildings
Praça do Comércio
Terreiro do Paço
Av. Ribeira das Naus
Rio Tejo

The historic Gothic-style Santa Justa Elevator is a popular stop on Lisbon's tourist trail.

Rossio. Today locals come here to relax with a newspaper or sip a ginjinha at one of the bars—A Tendinha, on the southern side of the square, is probably Lisbon's oldest. ✉ *Praça Dom Pedro IV, Rossío* Ⓜ *Green Line to Rossio.*

Wines of Portugal Tasting Room

WINERY | This impressive showroom has hundreds of wines representing Portugal's many demarcated regions. Tastings (three or four wines, from €15 per person, for a minimum of two people) can be adapted to suit personal preferences. Note that the wines that you taste may not necessarily all be on sale, but there are plenty of alternatives; or head round the corner to Rua da Conceição for branches of two major wine merchants, Garrafeira Nacional and Napoleão. ✉ *Praça do Comércio, Lisbon* ☎ *21/342–0690* 🌐 *www.winesofportugal.com/en/discover/tasting-rooms* ⏲ *Closed Sun. Nov.–Mar.* Ⓜ *Blue Line to Terreiro do Paço.*

Restaurants

★ A Licorista/O Bacalhoeiro

$ | **PORTUGUESE** | These twin restaurants are among a dwindling band in Baixa serving excellent traditional food. House specialties include *bacalhau à minhota* (fried codfish with onions and potatoes) and fresh fish and meats. **Known for:** informal efficient service; reliably good traditional mains; delicious desserts. 💲 *Average main: €13* ✉ *Rua dos Sapateiros 220, Baixa* ☎ *21/343–1415* www.facebook.com/alicoristaobacalhoeiro Closed Sun. Green Line to Rossio.

★ Bastardo

$$$ | **CONTEMPORARY** | The cool colorful restaurant of the Internacional Design Hotel is as cheeky and irreverent as its name suggests. The menu takes Portugal's culinary traditions on fantastic flights of fancy using the freshest of local seafood and sushi. **Known for:** innovative menu; playful interior design; potent cocktails. *Average main: €25 Internacional Design Hotel, Rua da Betesga 3, Rossío 21/324–0993 restaurantebastardo.com/en Green Line to Rossio.*

Can the Can

$$ | **PORTUGUESE** | **FAMILY** | The Portuguese take their canned fish seriously. Find out what the fuss is about at this funky restaurant where canned goods turn up in all manner of *petiscos* (small plates)—it sounds gimmicky, but the results are delicious. **Known for:** sophisticated tidbits from canned foods; prime location on Terreiro do Paço; artsy ambience and great cocktails. *Average main: €19 Praça do Comércio 82–83, Baixa 21/885–1392 www.canthecan.net Blue Line to Terreiro do Paço.*

★ Casa das Bifanas

$ | **PORTUGUESE** | The humble *bifana* (pork steak), braised in a sauce flavored with garlic, bay leaf, and wine (or beer) and then served in a rustic roll, is a lunch favorite. This bustling eatery on Praça da Figueira, Rossio's smaller twin, is one of the best places to try it—even if they don't bother to put it on the menu! **Known for:** sunny terrace; affordable Portugese cuisine; historical engravings. *Average main: €8 Praça da Figueira 6, Baixa 21/342–1637 Closed Sun. Green Line to Rossio.*

★ Delfina

$$ | **PORTUGUESE** | Delfina is the house restaurant at the chic AlmaLusa boutique hotel, but all are welcome to enjoy small plates such as *peixinhos da horta* (crispy tempura green beans, served with ginger-and-lemon tartare) or mains such as a magnificently creamy house bacalhau. The cut-price à la carte lunch menu draws locals, but dinner is a good value, too. **Known for:** great location overlooking a monumental square; selection of vegetarian dishes; deliciously rich flour-free chocolate cake. *Average main: €18 AlmaLusa, Praça do Município 23, Baixa 21/269–7445 www.almalusahotels.com/delfina Blue or Green Line to Baixa-Chiado, Green Line to Cais do Sodré.*

Em Alta na Baixa

$$$ | PORTUGUESE | Contemporary Portuguese restaurant Em Alta na Baixa delivers genuinely high-quality food and service. The menu spans local classics and international fare such as duck magret and *moqueca,* a Brazilian fish stew made with coconut milk. **Known for:** delicious risottos and pastas; satisfying hamburgers; extensive wine list. Ⓢ *Average main: €21* ✉ *Rua de São Nicolau 16, Baixa* ☎ *21/887–0250* 🌐 *fullest.pt/en/espacos/em-alta-na-baixa* Ⓜ *Blue or Green Line to Baixa-Chiado.*

Gambrinus

$$$$ | SEAFOOD | In business for almost nine decades, Gambrinus has plenty of historical drama in its decor, including arched wooden ceilings and stained-glass depictions of beer-swilling royals. Prawns, lobster, and crab are always available, and seasonal choices like sea bream, sea bass, and sole are offered grilled or garnished with clam sauce. **Known for:** eye-catching mural; special occasion dishes like caviar and partridge pie; top quality seafood and meat. Ⓢ *Average main: €34* ✉ *Rua das Portas de Santo Antão 23–25, Baixa* ☎ *21/342–1466* 🌐 *www.gambrinuslisboa.com* Ⓜ *Blue Line to Restauradores, Blue or Green Line to Rossio.*

Natraj

$ | INDIAN | This offshoot of a long-established uptown restaurant is worth seeking out if you yearn for classic Mughlai food. There's a huge range of dishes, with plenty of vegetarian options, all excellent value. **Known for:** welcoming staff; well-priced Indian classics; vegetarian options. Ⓢ *Average main: €10* ✉ *Rua dos Sapateiros 171, Baixa* ☎ *21/346–8113* Ⓜ *Green Line to Rossio, Blue or Green Line to Baixa-Chiado.*

★ Qosqo

$$ | PERUVIAN | Fans are adamant that this longtime favorite serves the best ceviche outside Peru. Unusual mains include beef ribs with black beer and *chaufa* (Peruvian fried rice with chicken). **Known for:** South American favorites; vegetarian options; attention to detail. Ⓢ *Average main: €17* ✉ *Rua dos Bacalhoeiros 26A, Baixa* ☎ *21/241–8058* 🌐 *www.facebook.com/ceviche.portugal* Ⓜ *Blue Line to Terreiro do Paço.*

SÁLA

$$$$ | PORTUGUESE | It's not easy to find genuinely excellent food in Baixa, but this restaurant—so small you can see into the kitchen from the entrance—has put the area on the map thanks to João Sá, whose modern Portuguese cuisine won him a Michelin star in 2024. He draws on Asian cuisines to create tasting menus that excite both visually and in their combinations of flavors and textures. **Known for:** amazing taste combinations; the best

Portuguese ingredients; cozy atmosphere. *Average main: €110* ✉ *Rua dos Bacalhoeiros 103, Baixa* ☎ *21/887–3045* 🌐 *restaurantesala.pt* ⏲ *Closed Sun. and Mon. No lunch Tues.* Ⓜ *Blue Line to Terreiro do Paço.*

★ Taberna da Baixa

$$ | PORTUGUESE | This family-run restaurant serves truly traditional Portuguese dishes. The *pataniscas* (cod fritters) with bean rice, the baked cod, and the pork cheeks are among the specialties, and there's an extensive list of Portuguese wines. **Known for:** daily specials; range of petiscos; hearty traditional dishes. *Average main: €18* ✉ *Rua dos Fanqueiros 161–163, Baixa* ☎ *21/887–0290* 🌐 *tabernadabaixa.mdig.pt* ⏲ *No lunch Sat.* Ⓜ *Blue or Green Line to Baixa-Chiado.*

★ Tasca Kome

$$ | JAPANESE | This unassuming restaurant serves authentic Japanese cuisine, from squid sashimi to chashu braised pork belly, plus the odd fusion dish—all at very affordable prices. To drink, there are sakes, beers, and Portuguese wines, plus house-made nonalcoholic drinks, and some fabulous desserts. **Known for:** good-value lunch menu; authentic Japanese dishes; sake pairings. *Average main: €17* ✉ *Rua da Madalena 57, Baixa* ☎ *21/134–0117* 🌐 *facebook.com/tascakome* ⏲ *Closed Sun. and Mon.* Ⓜ *Blue Line to Terreiro do Paço, Blue or Green Line to Baixa-Chiado.*

Terraço Editorial

$ | EUROPEAN | Sate an appetite for Lisbon's dramatic panoramic views at this chic restaurant-bar, which sits on the top floor of a storied department store. It's a sophisticated spot for salads and finger foods, as well as more substantial, more traditional dishes. **Known for:** reasonable prices; sunset cocktails; contemporary cuisine with vegetarian options. *Average main: €15* ✉ *Pollux, Rua dos Fanqueiros 276, 8th fl., Baixa* ☎ *91/202–7876* 🌐 *terracoeditorial.pt/en* Ⓜ *Green Line to Rossio.*

 Coffee and Quick Bites

Café Nicola

$$$ | PORTUGUESE | The distinctive 1930s facade and tables right on Rossio square make Nicola a memorable spot for a coffee or bite to eat while sightseeing. Breakfasts and brunches here are good, with lots of eggs, meaty sausages, and strong Nicola-brand coffee (or fresh fruit and juices, should you prefer). **Known for:** prime location; historic building; good steaks. *Average main: €22* ✉ *Praça Dom Pedro IV 24–25, Rossío* ☎ *21/346–0579* Ⓜ *Green Line to Rossio.*

★ Confeitaria Nacional

$ | **CAFÉ** | **FAMILY** | Serving *pastéis de nata* and other sweetly delicious treats since 1829, Confeitaira Nacional is the oldest *pastelaria* in Lisbon. The handsome antique decor competes for attention with the glass cabinets packed with mouthwatering cakes, pastries, and chocolates. **Known for:** beautiful Pombaline architecture; Christmas fruitcake sold year-round; tearoom serving light meals. *Average main: €15 ✉ Praça da Figueira 18B, Baixa ☎ 21/342–4470 🌐 confeitarianacional.com Ⓜ Green Line to Rossio.*

Feel Rio

$ | **BRAZILIAN** | Members of Lisbon's large Brazilian community flock to this all-day snack bar for tasty generously sized *pastéis de vento* (deep-fried meat or cheese patties), *coxinhas* (chicken croquettes), and *pão de queijo* (cheese rolls made with cassava flour); various menus with cassava fries or tapioca are available. Sugarcane is among the fresh juices on offer, as well as detox blends, and there are sweets, too. **Known for:** Brazilian snacks; fresh juices; pão de queijo. *Average main: €8 ✉ Rua do Crucifixo 108, Baixa ☎ 21/346–0654 🌐 www.facebook.com/FeelRioPT Ⓜ Blue or Green Line to Baixa-Chiado.*

Martinho da Arcada

$$$ | **PORTUGUESE** | Open since the 1700s, this café under the arches overlooking Praça do Comércio is thought to be the oldest in the city and was a favorite of archetypal Lisbon poet Fernando Pessoa. There's a formal dining space inside, with plenty of well-prepared traditional dishes on offer, but the real appeal is sipping a coffee on the flagstones and watching Lisbon life go by. **Known for:** grand 18th-century building; rich history of hosting poets and intellectuals; great people-watching. *Average main: €22 ✉ Praça do Comércio 3, Baixa ☎ 21/887–9259 🌐 martinhodaarcada.pt Ⓜ Blue Line to Terreiro do Paço.*

Hotels

AlmaLusa Baixa/Chiado

$$$$ | **HOTEL** | In an artfully restored 18th-century showplace, this chic boutique hotel retains many original features, including medieval flagstones, rough-hewn wooden beams, and original antique tiles. **Pros:** on the historic Praça do Município; comprehensive concierge service; guest cell phones. **Cons:** no spa or fitness area; not all rooms have views; some small rooms. *Rooms from: €300 ✉ Praça do Munícipio 21, Baixa ☎ 21/269–7440 🌐 www.almalusahotels.com/baixachiado 28 rooms 🍽 Free Breakfast Ⓜ Blue or Green Line to Baixa-Chiado.*

A Short History of Lisbon

Sitting alongside the wide and natural harbor of the Tagus River, Lisbon has been a strategically important trading seaport throughout the ages. The city was probably founded around 1200 BC by the Phoenicians, who called it Alis-Ubbo. The Greeks came next, naming it Olisipo. In 205 BC the Romans, calling it in their turn Felicitas Julia, linked it by road to the great Spanish cities of the Iberian Peninsula. The Visigoths followed in the 5th century and built the earliest fortifications on the site of the Castelo de São Jorge, but it was with the arrival of the Moors in AD 714 that Lisbon, then renamed Al-Ušbūna, came into its own.

The city flourished as a trading center during the four centuries of Moorish rule, and Alfama—Lisbon's oldest residential district—retains its intricate Arab-influenced layout. In 1147 a Christian army led by Dom Afonso Henriques (with the assistance of Crusaders from northern Europe) took the city after a ruthless siege. Then in 1255 Afonso III transferred the royal seat of power from Coimbra, making Lisbon the capital of Portugal.

The next great period—that of the Discoveries—began with the 15th-century voyages of the great Portuguese navigators, first to the islands of the Azores, Madeira, and the Canaries; then down the west coast of Africa; and to Brazil, India, and ultimately Japan. The wealth realized by these expeditions was phenomenal and helped finance grand buildings and impressive commerce. Late-Portuguese Gothic architecture assumed a rich individualistic style, characterized by elaborate sculptural details, often with a maritime motif; the Torre de Belém and the Mosteiro dos Jerónimos are supreme examples.

On November 1, 1755, Lisbon's prosperity was interrupted by a huge earthquake, whose tremors were felt as far north as Scotland. Two-thirds of Lisbon was destroyed, with 40,000 people killed and entire neighborhoods swept away by the ensuing tidal wave or ravaged by fires that burned for days afterwards.

Lisbon was rebuilt quickly and ruthlessly, with buildings fortified to withstand future earthquakes. The medieval quarters were leveled and replaced with broad boulevards; a new commercial center, the Baixa, was laid out in a grid; and the great Praça do Comércio was planned. Downtown Lisbon was left with an elegant 18th-century layout that remains as pleasing today as it was centuries ago.

The waterfront Praça do Comércio is one of Lisbon's most spectacular squares.

Internacional Design Hotel

$$ | **HOTEL** | Rooms at this fun and funky design hotel overlooking the Rossio are themed by design and by scent—take your pick from Urban, Tribal, Pop, and Zen. All of the rooms have unique designs with playful modern artworks, and some have private terraces with views of the bustling square and the shopping street of Rua Augusta, including three spacious superior suites that are among five lodgings added in a 2023 revamp. **Pros:** double-glazed windows to keep out the noise; stylishly decorated common areas; trendy restaurant and bar. **Cons:** not all rooms have great views; street-facing rooms still get some noise; no exercise facilities. *Rooms from: €198* *Rua da Betesga 3, Baixa* *21/324–0990* *www.idesignhotel.com* *60 rooms* *Free Breakfast* *Green Line to Rossio.*

My Story Hotel Tejo

$$ | **HOTEL** | Just steps away from the busy Praça da Figueira, this hotel offers smart modern rooms in a nicely restored 19th-century building. **Pros:** central location; renovations have preserved period details; atmospheric restaurant. **Cons:** busy in high season; some rooms tucked into odd spaces; some rooms lack views. *Rooms from: €167* *Rua dos Condes de Monsanto 2, Baixa* *96/642–1589 WhatsApp, 21/886–6182 landline* *www.mystoryhotels.com/en/my-story-hotel-tejo* *135 rooms* *Free Breakfast* *Green Line to Rossio.*

★ Pousada Lisboa

$$$$ | **HOTEL** | Lisbon's downtown *pousada*—part of a national network of hotels in historic buildings—this former government ministry, whose presidential suite was the office of the dictator Salazar, has been overhauled with a view to elegance and comfort. **Pros:** historic building in unbeatable central location; friendly staff; works by leading artists on display. **Cons:** guest rooms lack balconies; small spa, gym, and pool; gloomy common areas. *Rooms from: €390 Praça do Comércio 31–34, Baixa 21/040–7640 pousadas.pt/en/hotel/pousada-lisboa 90 rooms Free Breakfast Blue Line to Terreiro do Paço.*

Residencial Florescente

$ | **HOTEL** | **FAMILY** | If you're looking for a great location for sightseeing, check into one of the bright and cheerful rooms on the five azulejo-lined floors of the Residencial Florescente. **Pros:** central location; pool with sun terrace and bar; good breakfast. **Cons:** some very small rooms; standard rooms a little lacking in flair; some noise. *Rooms from: €120 Rua das Portas de Santo Antão 95, Baixa 21/342–6609 www.residencialflorescente.com 67 rooms Free Breakfast Blue Line to Restauradores.*

Nightlife

BARS

Brew

BARS | The craft beer revolution is here in force: of the ever-changing list of 23 beers Brew has on tap, half a dozen are local. New York–style pizzas, whole or by the slice, accompany. *Rua Nova do Almada 14, Baixa 21/589–4928 www.brewportugal.pt Blue or Green Line to Baixa-Chiado.*

The George

PUB | The only British pub in Lisbon, The George is a popular meeting point for locals and homesick Brits alike. A mutual love of gin (or perhaps the televised soccer and rugby) could be a factor in the long-standing friendship between the two. *Rua do Crucifixo 58–66, Baixa 91/196–5630 www.facebook.com/thegeorgepublisbon Blue or Green Line to Baixa-Chiado.*

Trobadores

BARS | Drink mead from a ceramic mug, eat flaming chouriço sausage, and pretend you're back in medieval times at this offbeat tavern. There are flickering candles and live folk performances. *Calçada de São Francisco 6A, Baixa 21/346–2105 www.facebook.com/TrobadoresBar Closed Sun. and Mon. Blue or Green Line to Baixa-Chiado.*

Ginjinha

One cannot visit Portugal without trying its delicious, sweet cherry liqueur, ginjinha.

It's made from the ginja sour cherry, whose origin is difficult to establish, but which supposedly originated on the banks of the Caspian River and was gradually dispersed among the Mediterranean countries via trade routes.

The liqueur has a deep dark red color, with an intense flavor and aroma perfumed by the fermented cherries. It's produced and sold in two distinct varieties: the liqueur on its own or the liqueur with actual ginja fruits inside, sometimes flavored with vanilla or cinnamon.

The best thing to have with ginjinha is chocolate, and some touristy places serve it in little chocolate cups. Or eat a big slice of chocolate cake with your cordial.

Shopping

CRAFTS AND SOUVENIRS

★ Amatudo

CRAFTS | This cute arts-and-crafts store sells traditional and contemporary Portuguese products like handcrafted ceramics and colorful homewares, beautifully presented in a vintage-chic setting. ✉ *Rua da Madalena 76/78* ☎ *91/960–4834* Ⓜ *Blue Line to Terreiro do Paço, Blue or Green Line to Baixa-Chiado.*

Toranja

SOUVENIRS | "Presents with art" is the offer at this shop showcasing colorful prints, cushions, handicrafts, and accessories designed by dozens of Portugal-based artists. ✉ *Rua Augusta 231, Baixa* 🌐 *toranja.com* Ⓜ *Blue or Green Line to Baixa-Chiado, Green Line to Rossio.*

CLOTHING

★ A Outra Face da Lua

CLOTHING | Prepare to be completely engaged by the eclectic mix of vintage clothes, needlepoint purses, and boxes of costume jewelry. There's also a retro-chic café and cocktail bar (with vegan treats). ✉ *Rua da Assunção 22, Baixa* ☎ *21/886–3430* 🌐 *aoutrafacedalua.com* Ⓜ *Blue or Green Line to Baixa-Chiado.*

Achega

CLOTHING | You won't find knitwear in Lisbon of a better quality than at Achega, one of the city's best-loved retailers. The family-owned company—founded in 1957—still designs its own

A historic and still-popular meeting place, Rossio is an ideal spot for people-watching while sipping on ginjinha.

classic lambswool and merino pieces. ✉ *Rua da Prata 240, Baixa* ☎ *21/887–8415* 🌐 *achega.com* Ⓜ *Green Line to Rossio.*

Ás de Espadas

SECOND-HAND | Stepping into this store is traveling back in time, to when colorful patterns and pleated skirts were the latest styles. Ás de Espadas is a treasure chest filled with vintage wear that looks good in the new millennium and encourages shoppers to show off their individuality. ✉ *Rua da Conceição 117–119, Baixa* Ⓜ *Blue or Green Line to Baixa-Chiado.*

★ Azevedo Rua

HATS & GLOVES | Whether it's a Panama, a traditional golfing hat, or the wide-brimmed Portuguese style worn by modernist poet Fernando Pessoa, you can find it here; they also stock many elegant walking sticks and umbrellas. ✉ *Praça Dom Pedro IV 69 and 72–73, Baixa* ☎ *21/342–7511* 🌐 *azevedorua.pt* Ⓜ *Green Line to Rossio.*

FOOD AND WINE

Conserveira de Lisboa

FOOD | This tiny canned goods store is one of the few in Baixa with the fittings and layout typical of a century ago. Tuna may no longer be soaked in brine on the premises, but the vintage packaging of the store's own brands—Tricana, Prata do Mar, and Minor—means their cans make for charming gifts. ✉ *Rua dos Bacalhoeiros 34, Baixa* ☎ *21/886–4009* 🌐 *conserveiradelisboa.pt* Ⓜ *Blue Line to Terreiro do Paço.*

★ Garrafeira Nacional

WINE/SPIRITS | This respected wine merchant has been in business for almost a century, and the knowledgeable English-speaking staff will let you know everything about the vintage you've selected. It's known for its selection of Portuguese spirits and fortified wines, as well as foreign whiskies. ✉ *Rua de Santa Justa 18, Baixa* ☎ *21/887–9080* 🌐 *www.garrafeiranacional.com* Ⓜ *Green Line to Rossio.*

Manuel Tavares

FOOD & DRINK | This enticing shop dating back to 1860 stocks cheeses, preserves, vintage port, and other fine Portuguese products. ✉ *Rua da Betesga 1AB, Baixa* ☎ *21/342–4209* 🌐 *www.manueltavares.com* Ⓜ *Green Line to Rossio.*

Mercearia dos Açores

FOOD & DRINK | This well-stocked store is the best place in Lisbon to sample some of the Azores' top products, including creamy cheeses, spicy sausages, ultra-sweet pastries and liqueurs, and green and black teas. ✉ *Rua da Madalena 115, Baixa* ☎ *21/888–0070* 🌐 *merceariadosacores.pt* Ⓜ *Blue or Green Line to Baixa-Chiado.*

HEALTH AND BEAUTY

Ervanária Rosil

HEALTH & BEAUTY | Herbal remedies have always been popular in Portugal, and since 1950 Ervanária Rosil has built up a thriving business with its own-brand tisanes for everything from coughs to ailments of the stomach, kidneys, or other vital organs, with white-coated staff happy to offer advice and recommendations. ✉ *Rua da Madalena 210, Baixa* ☎ *21/887–2097* 🌐 *www.ervanaria-rosil.pt* Ⓜ *Green Line to Rossio.*

HOUSEWARES

Pollux

HOUSEWARES | Of most interest to foreign visitors in this department store is the first floor featuring ceramics from Vista Alegre, crystal from Atlantis, and flatware from Cutipol and other cutlery manufacturers from northern Portugal. ✉ *Rua dos Fanqueiros 276, Baixa* ☎ *21/881–1200* 🌐 *www.pollux.pt/en* Ⓜ *Green Line to Rossio.*

JEWELRY

★ W. A. Sarmento

JEWELRY & WATCHES | One of the city's oldest goldsmiths, W. A. Sarmento first opened its doors in 1870 and remains famous for its characteristic Portuguese gold and silver filigree work. ✉ *Rua Áurea 251, Baixa* ☎ *21/342–6774* 🌐 *ourivesariasarmento.pt* Ⓜ *Blue or Green Line to Baixa-Chiado.*

Chapter 4

CHIADO AND BAIRRO ALTO

Updated by
Alison Roberts

Sights	Restaurants	Hotels	Shopping	Nightlife
★★★★☆	★★★★★	★★★★★	★★★★★	★★★★★

NEIGHBORHOOD SNAPSHOT

TOP EXPERIENCES

- **Drink in the views.** Stop for a coffee or aperitif as you absorb the panorama at some of the city's best miradouros.
- **Shop for unique souvenirs.** From handmade gloves, hats, and shoes to beautiful azulejo tiles, there's something for everyone in Chiado.
- **Savor Portugal's finest.** These neighborhoods have been central to the rise of modern Portuguese cuisine, with a cluster of restaurants overseen by top chefs.
- **Barhop in the Bairro Alto.** This grid of streets turns into a sprawling outdoor party on weekend nights.

GETTING HERE

Baixa-Chiado metro station, where the Blue and Green lines intersect, is downtown's busiest. The vintage 28 tram also runs through Chiado, skirting the southern edge of Bairro Alto on its way to São Bento, while the 24 tram runs along the eastern side of Bairro Alto on its way between Cais do Sodré train station down by the river and the Príncipe Real neighborhood uphill.

PLANNING YOUR TIME

Chiado is Lisbon's prime traditional shopping district, and in daytime its streets and cafés draw locals and tourists alike. The neighboring Bairro Alto beats the rest of Lisbon for its sheer concentration of restaurants and bars; here things only get going in the evening.

VIEWFINDER

- **Elevador de Santa Justa walkway.** For a unique (and free) view of the whole city center, walk past the Convento do Carmo and up a small flight of stairs to the walkway atop the Elevador de Santa Justa. You'll miss the thrill of taking the antique lift up from Baixa, but also save yourself the price of a ticket—and a long wait—at the bottom. *Travessa Dom Pedro de Menezes (off Largo do Carmo).*

OFF THE BEATEN PATH

- **Lower terrace of Jardim de São Pedro de Alcântara.** The upper part of the famous miradouro draws crowds round the clock, but down just a few steps is a terrace that is rarely busy and is ideal for a quiet break with the same gorgeous view. ✉ *Rua de São Pedro de Alcântara.*

The twin neighborhoods of Chiado and Bairro Alto are two of the city's most historic districts, yet they have much to keep visitors entertained from morning to night.

Draped over the broad hill on the western side of Baixa—in some parts gently sloping, in others impossibly steep—Chiado is Lisbon's most elegant neighborhood, home to Belle Epoque–style stores and cafés. Here you will also find some of the city's most sophisticated restaurants, several of them opened by internationally famed chefs in recent years to join the area's historic theaters, baroque churches, and old bookstores.

The old-world retail offerings span everything from a unique glove specialist to handmade shoes and fine woolen clothing from northern Portugal, as well as stunning traditional jewelry and world-famous ceramics.

Away from the busy shopping streets, quiet oases remain, such as tree-shaded Largo do Carmo, overlooked by a medieval ruin that was left shattered by the 1755 earthquake but which many still see as Lisbon's most beautiful church. Nearby are a couple of great viewpoints.

At the top of the neighborhood's main axis, Rua Garrett, is Largo do Chiado and then, across a busy junction, Praça Luís de Camões, named for Portugal's national poet, whose statue stands at its center. Spreading up the hillside to the north of this square is Bairro Alto (literally "high neighborhood"), the city's first rationally planned grid of streets, laid out in 1513. They may seem like narrow alleys today but they were designed to be wide enough for carriages to pass through.

Originally overseen by the Jesuits—whose lavishly decorated church, the Igreja de São Roque, is one of the area's main draws—by the 19th century, Bairro Alto had become a bohemian district, home to several newspapers and also to countless bars, *tascas* (cheap eateries), fado houses, and brothels. When, in the 1980s, Lisbon had its *movida* (a countercultural movement), it inevitably took off here, with many venues known for welcoming members of the LGBTQ+ community.

Only a very few bars from those times remain today. But Bairro Alto remains a popular destination for a night out, despite competition from the increasing number of bars in the riverside Cais do Sodré district. It can still boast the biggest variety of places to eat of any city neighborhood—including some of Lisbon's most distinguished fado venues—and groups of all ages still gather, drinks in hand, outside wine bars and tiny DJ-driven clubs. There's a street party atmosphere on Friday and Saturday night, as locals and tourists hop from bar to bar.

Chiado and Bairro Alto

Sights

Convento de São Pedro de Alcântara

CHURCH | This convent from 1670 opened to the public in 2014 after the last nuns moved out. The church and chapel are free to visit any day, while the rest of the building can be seen on guided tours (in Portuguese), which usually take place on the second Sunday of the month. The baroque church stands between two wings of the convent; most of its interior dates from 1758, after the 1755 earthquake left it slightly damaged. The older paintings were originally in the colossal convent and palace of Mafra, while the tile panels were added in the late 1700s and illustrate scenes from the life of St. Peter of Alcántara. ✉ *Rua Luísa Todi 1–11, Lisbon* ☎ *21/323–5065* 🎫 *Free for church; €3 for guided tour* Ⓜ *Blue or Green Line to Baixa-Chiado, Blue Line to Restauradores then Elevador da Glória.*

Convento do Carmo (*Carmelite Convent*)

RUINS | The Carmelite Convent was built in 1389 in thanks for battlefield victories over Castile but was all but ruined by the earthquake in 1755. The shell of the church is hauntingly beautiful; its sacristy houses a small collection of carved stone, ceramic tiles, ancient coins, and other city finds. The tree-shaded square outside—linked via a walkway to the top of the Elevador de Santa Justa—is a good spot to dawdle over a coffee or a cocktail. Hard to imagine that it was the scene of one of the most dramatic moments of Portugal's 1974 revolution, when the prime minister took refuge in the Republican National Guard headquarters next to the church as rebellious troops amassed outside. ✉ *Largo do Carmo, Lisbon* ☎ *21/346–0473* 🌐 *museuarqueologicodocarmo.pt* 🎫 *€7* ⏲ *Closed Sun.* Ⓜ *Blue or Green Line to Baixa-Chiado.*

Elevador da Glória

TRANSPORTATION | **FAMILY** | One of the finest approaches to Bairro Alto is via this funicular railway. It was inaugurated in 1888, taking just a few minutes to run from the western side of Avenida da Liberdade up a steep hill to the Jardim de São Pedro de Alcântara miradouro on the edge of Bairro Alto. The funicular is included in public transportation day passes. ✉ *Calçada da Glória 6, Lisbon* 🎫 *€4.10 round-trip* Ⓜ *Blue Line to Restauradores.*

★ Galeria Zé dos Bois

ARTS CENTER | This gallery-cum-performing arts venue is one of the hippest addresses in the city. The exhibition space hosts stimulating contemporary art shows and cutting-edge talks, often in English, from 6–10 pm. After that, there are usually concerts of experimental music in a rather claustrophobic performance space. On warm nights, head up to the rooftop bar, which occasionally serves as an open-air cinema. ✉ *Rua da Barroca 59, Lisbon* ☎ *21/343–0205* 🌐 *zedosbois.org* 🎫 *Concerts from €6* ⏲ *Closed Sun.* Ⓜ *Bule or Green Line to Baixa-Chiado.*

★ Igreja and Museu de São Roque (*Sao Roque Church and Museum*)

CHURCH | This church, completed in 1574, was one of the earliest Jesuit buildings in the world; the attached museum is home to one of Portugal's most comprehensive collections of religious art. While the church's exterior is somewhat plain and austere, the inside is dazzling, with abundant use of gold and marble—the only remaining example in Lisbon of the painted ceilings from the mannerist period. Eight side chapels have statuary and art dating from the early 17th century. ✉ *Largo Trindade Coelho, Lisbon* ☎ *21/323–5065* 🌐 *museusaoroque.scml.pt/en* 🎫 *Church free; museum €10* ⏲ *Museum closed Mon.* Ⓜ *Blue or Green Line to Baixa-Chiado.*

Igreja de Santa Catarina

CHURCH | This is one of Lisbon's richest and most beautiful churches but one of the least visited, despite its central location. The baroque and rococo interior is a monumental mix of gilded wood carvings and stucco decoration, added in 1727 to a building that dates from 1647. The organ is considered a masterpiece of gilded woodwork, while the altar is a highlight of the art commissioned during the wealthy reign of King João V, with sculptures brought from Flanders. ✉ *Calçada do Combro 82, Lisbon* 🎫 *Free for church; €2 for museum* ⏲ *Closed Sun. except for mass* Ⓜ *Blue or Green Line to Baixa-Chiado, Tram 28.*

★ Jardim de São Pedro de Alcântara

VIEWPOINT | **FAMILY** | Arguably Lisbon's most romantic miradouro, this landscaped promenade is split into two levels, each offering a wonderful view across the city center to the castle on its hill on the other side. On the upper level, a large kiosk serves refreshments and light meals, while down the steps is another, more secluded kiosk with a smaller range of offerings. ✉ *Rua de São Pedro de Alcântara, Lisbon* Ⓜ *Blue or Green Line to Baixa-Chiado, Blue Line to Restauradores then Elevador da Glória.*

Sights

Convento de São Pedro de Alcântara, **2**

Convento do Carmo, **5**

Elevador da Glória, **1**

Galeria Zé dos Bois, **6**

Igreja and Museu de São Roque, **4**

Igreja de Santa Catarina, **7**

Jardim de São Pedro de Alcântara, **3**

Miradouro de Santa Catarina, **9**

Museu da Farmácia, **8**

Restaurants

Afuri Izakaya, **26**

Água pela Barba, **4**

Alfaia Restaurant, **10**

Alma, **28**

Aqui Há Peixe, **17**

As Salgadeiras, **22**

Bairro do Avillez, **16**

Belcanto, **27**

Bistro 100 Maneiras, **14**

Boa-Bao, **18**

Cantinho da Paz, **1**

Casanostra, **11**

The Decadente, **9**

EPUR, **30**

Faz Frio, **6**

Grapes & Bites, **12**

Honorato, **20**

Jardim das Cerejas, **19**

La Paparrucha, **7**

Lisboa à Noite, **13**

100 Maneiras, **8**

Palácio Chiado, **25**

Pharmacia Felicidade, **2**

Rocco Gastrobar, **29**

Sea Me Peixaria Moderna, **23**

Suba Restaurante, **3**

Taberna da Rua das Flores, **24**

Tágide, **31**

Tasca do Manel, **21**

Toma Lá Dá Cá, **5**

Trindade, **15**

Quick Bites

A Brasileira do Chiado, **5**

A Carioca/ Vegan Nata, **4**

Alcôa, **6**

Aloma, **2**

Café no Chiado, **9**

Kaffeehaus, **10**

Landeau Chocolate, **8**

Manteigaria, **3**

Noobai, **1**

Santini Chiado, **7**

Hotels

Bairro Alto Hotel, **5**

Hotel do Chiado, **8**

The Ivens, **7**

Lisboa Carmo Hotel, **6**

The Lumiares, **2**

Palácio das Especiarias, **4**

Palácio Ludovice Wine Experience Hotel, **1**

Verride Palácio Santa Catarina, **3**

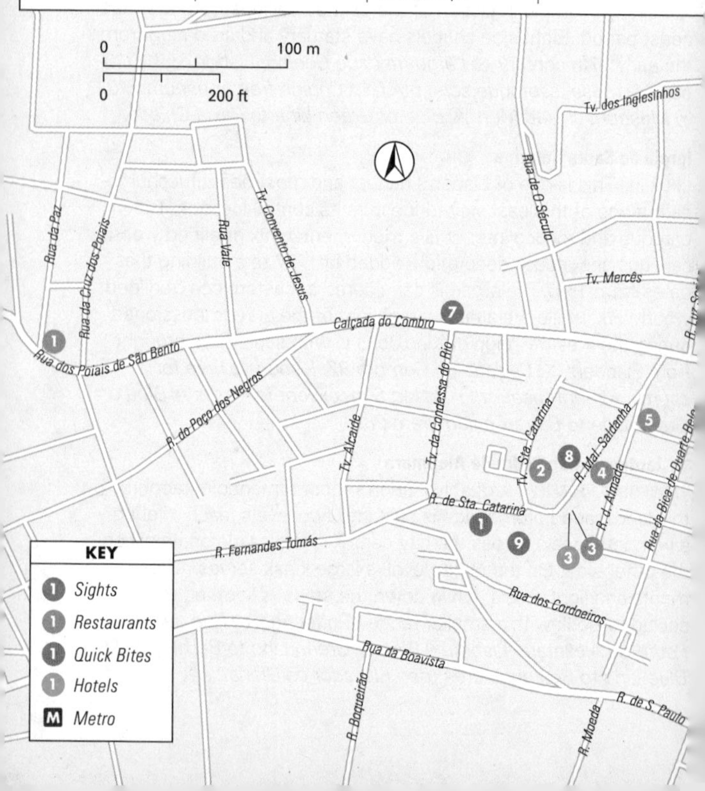

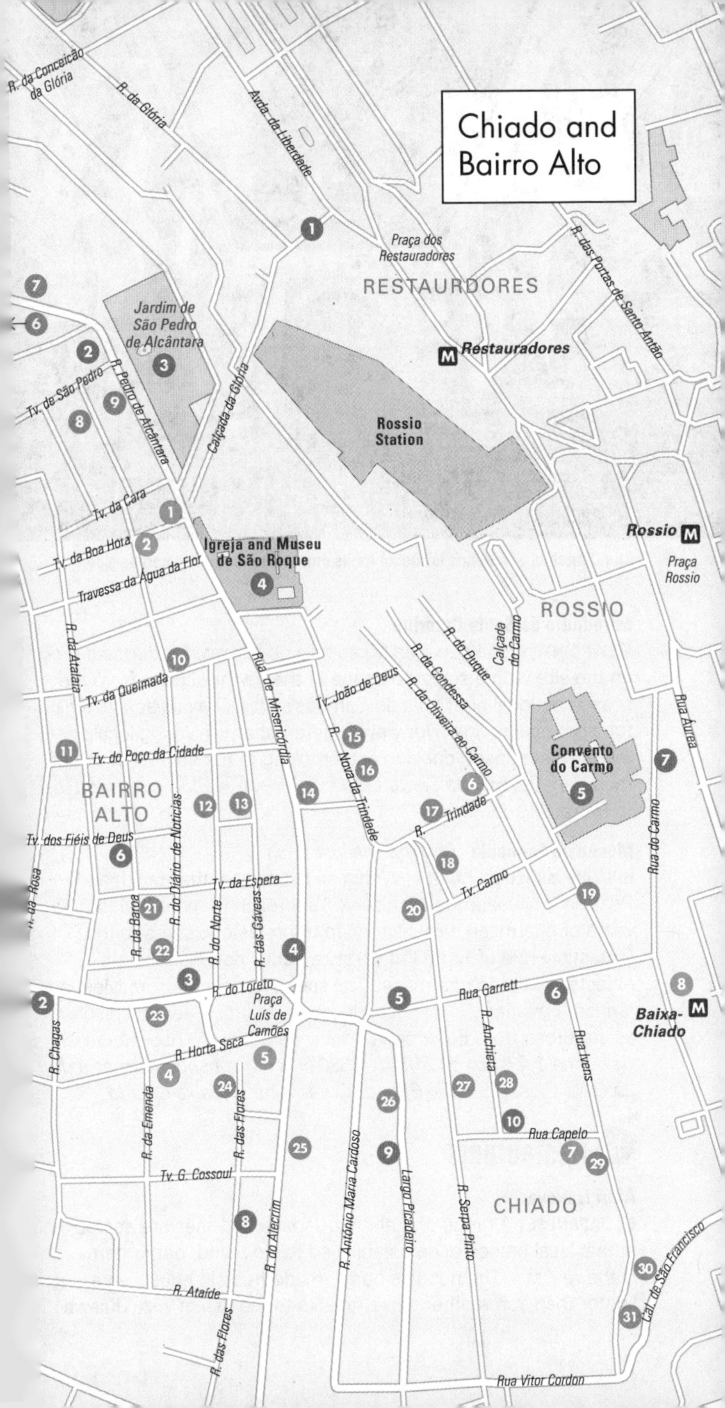
Chiado and Bairro Alto
RESTAURDORES
Praça dos Restauradores
Restauradores
Rossio Station
Rossio
Praça Rossio
ROSSIO
Jardim de São Pedro de Alcântara
Igreja and Museu de São Roque
Convento do Carmo
BAIRRO ALTO
CHIADO
Baixa-Chiado
Praça Luís de Camões
R. da Conceição da Glória
R. da Glória
Avda. da Liberdade
R. das Portas de Santo Antão
Tv. de São Pedro
R. Pedro de Alcântara
Calçada da Glória
Tv. da Cara
Tv. da Boa Hora
Travessa da Água da Flor
R. da Atalaia
Tv. da Queimada
Rua de Misericórdia
Tv. João de Deus
R. da Condessa
R. da Oliveira ao Carmo
R. do Duque
Calçada do Carmo
Rua Áurea
Tv. do Poço da Cidade
R. Nova da Trindade
R. Trindade
Rua do Carmo
Tv. dos Fiéis de Deus
R. da Rosa
R. do Diário de Notícias
Tv. da Espera
R. da Barroa
R. do Norte
R. das Gáveas
Tv. Carmo
R. do Loreto
Rua Garrett
R. Anchieta
Rua Ivens
R. Chagas
R. Horta Seca
R. da Emenda
R. das Flores
Rua Capelo
Tv. G. Cossoul
R. do Alecrim
R. António Maria Cardoso
Largo Picadeiro
R. Serpa Pinto
Cal. de São Francisco
R. Ataíde
Rua Vitor Cordon

The Church of São Roque is known for its ornate interior and numerous side chapels.

Miradouro de Santa Catarina

VIEWPOINT | Also known as Miradouro do Adamastor due to a rock on the site with a sculpted image of the mythical giant from the seas in national poet Luís de Camões's epic *The Lusiads*, this hill-top spot boasts fine river views. Here bohemian young locals get together at sunset, drinking and smoking to the sounds of street musicians. ✉ *Rua de Santa Catarina, Lisbon* Ⓜ *Blue or Green Line to Baixa-Chiado.*

Museu da Farmácia (*Pharmacy Museum*)

HISTORY MUSEUM | **FAMILY** | Within an old palace, the Health and Pharmacy Museum takes a playful approach to more than 5,000 years of pharmaceutical history, from prehistoric cures to the fantastic world of Harry Potter–style fictive potions. Ancient objects related to pharmaceutical science and art—from Mesopotamian, Egyptian, Roman, and Incan civilizations—are on display, as are those from Europe over many centuries. ✉ *Rua Marechal Saldanha 1, Lisbon* ☎ *21/340–0680* 🌐 *www.museudafarmacia.pt* 🎫 *€6* ⏲ *Closed Sun.* Ⓜ *Blue or Green Line to Baixa-Chiado.*

Restaurants

Afuri Izakaya

$ | **JAPANESE** | A range of authentic Japanese dishes are served at this local branch of an established Tokyo brand, but ramen is the real star. The noodles here—made fresh in-house—are lighter than some other types, thanks to the use of yuzu. **Known**

for: house-made noodles; ultra-fresh ingredients; gluten-free versions available. *Average main: €14 Rua Paiva de Andrade 7–13, Lisbon 96/871–0555 afuri.pt Blue or Green Line to Baixa-Chiado.*

Água pela Barba
$$ | **SEAFOOD** | Imaginative small plates are the main attraction at this trendy seafood-focused spot, which also has nice vegan options. The ceviche is hugely popular, and for good reason. **Known for:** range of Portuguese wines; regional dishes; vegan "ceviche." *Average main: €17 Rua do Almada 29–31, Lisbon 21/346–1376 www.facebook.com/aguapelabarbarestaurante No lunch Mon. Blue or Green Line to Baixa-Chiado, Tram 28.*

Alfaia Restaurant
$$ | **PORTUGUESE** | **FAMILY** | In this traditional restaurant, one of the oldest in Lisbon, the courteous staff serve up Portuguese classics and pair them with one of the 600 choices on the wine list. **Known for:** late-night spot; excellent wine-pairing advice; expertly grilled fish. *Average main: €16 Travessa da Queimada 22, Lisbon 21/346–1232 www.restaurantealfaia.com/alfaia-restaurant Blue or Green Line to Baixa-Chiado.*

Alma
$$$$ | **PORTUGUESE** | Henrique Sá Pessoa is one of Portugal's leading chefs, known for drawing on both traditional Portuguese cuisine and Asian influences. At this flagship venture he has applied "refined taste, perfect technique, and excellent product" to gain his first Michelin star in 2016 and a second in 2022. **Known for:** fish and seafood; some dishes finished by the chef at the table; tasting menus and à la carte options. *Average main: €60 Rua Anchieta 15, Lisbon 21/347–0650 www.almalisboa.pt/en Closed Mon. Blue or Green Line to Baixa-Chiado.*

★ **Aqui Há Peixe**
$$$ | **SEAFOOD** | This restaurant's name translates to "There's Fish Here," and indeed it's one of the top places in town to savor the catch of the day, served fried, grilled, or roasted. Dinner attracts a youngish crowd, who enjoy options like cuttlefish with black rice and saffron mayonnaise. **Known for:** fresh fish; affordable lunch specials; boozy desserts. *Average main: €26 Rua da Trindade 18A, Lisbon 21/134–4228 aquihapeixe.pt/en Closed Sun. and Mon. No lunch Sat. Blue or Green Line to Baixa-Chiado.*

As Salgadeiras
$$$ | **PORTUGUESE** | This rustic restaurant was established in a former bakery and has kept the building's original large brick baking oven and stone arches. It serves well-presented classic

Portuguese cuisine and a few original dishes from a menu evenly divided between meat and fish options. **Known for:** variety of cod dishes; chocolate chiffon dessert; excellent service by friendly staff. $ *Average main: €25* ✉ *Rua das Salgadeiras 18, Lisbon* ☎ *21/342–1157* 🌐 *www.as-salgadeiras.com* ⏲ *No lunch. Closed Mon.* Ⓜ *Blue or Green Line to Baixa-Chiado.*

★ Bairro do Avillez

$$$ | PORTUGUESE | José Avillez, Portugal's most distinguished chef, has created his own foodie "neighborhood" incorporating a range of dining styles. For formal meals, there's the airy Páteo, serving classic Portuguese dishes, while at the more casual Taberna, where haunches of ham hang over the bar, you can choose from a wide range of fine local cheeses or sample intensely flavored small plates, presented with flair. **Known for:** showcase for Lisbon's most renowned chef; great attention to detail; only the best local ingredients used. $ *Average main: €25* ✉ *Rua Nova da Trindade 18, Lisbon* ☎ *21/583–0290* 🌐 *bairrodoavillez.pt* Ⓜ *Tram 24, Blue Line to Restauradores then Elevador da Glória.*

★ Belcanto

$$$$ | PORTUGUESE | A fixture in the World's 50 Best list and boasting two Michelin stars, Belcanto is the jewel in the crown of celebrity chef José Avillez and Lisbon's most celebrated culinary haven. Widely credited with putting modern Portuguese cuisine on the global map, Avillez and his team deconstruct traditional dishes and remake them in startling form, in a panoply of colors, flavors, and textures, with Portugal's outstanding seafood given its full due. **Known for:** delightfully inventive amuse-bouches and dishes; huge list of fine regional wines; witty and evocative presentations. $ *Average main: €200* ✉ *Rua Serpa Pinto 10A, Lisbon* ☎ *21/342–0607* 🌐 *www.belcanto.pt* ⏲ *Closed Sun. and Mon.* Ⓜ *Blue or Green Line to Baixa-Chiado.*

★ Bistro 100 Maneiras

$$$$ | ECLECTIC | Celebrated Sarajevo-born chef Ljubomir Stanisic, whose flagship restaurant boasts a Michelin star, is known not only for his unorthodox approach but also for the slick design of his venues. Expect to be wowed by both the tasteful redesign of a handsome art deco building and the ever-changing roster of small plates—and, at weekends, all-in roasts. **Known for:** Lisbon's famous "rock-and-roll" chef; small plates made with the finest ingredients; prize-winning cocktails. $ *Average main: €35* ✉ *Largo da Trindade 9, Lisbon* ☎ *91/030–7575* 🌐 *100maneiras.com* ⏲ *No lunch weekdays* Ⓜ *Blue or Green Line to Baixa-Chiado.*

Boa-Bao

$$ | **ASIAN** | This restaurant takes you on a trip around Asia, with a wide selection of dishes that go from Thailand to Indonesia. There are also vegan and gluten-free options. **Known for:** spicy food; fancy cocktails; lively atmosphere. *Average main: €19 Largo Rafael Bordalo Pinheiro 30, Lisbon 91/902–3030 en.boabao.pt/lisboa Blue or Green Line to Baixa-Chiado.*

Cantinho da Paz

$ | **INDIAN** | **FAMILY** | The cozy wood-paneled "little corner of peace" specializes in cuisine from Portugal's former colony of Goa, resulting in unique Portuguese-Indian fusion dishes. The menu includes traditional desserts such as *bebinca*, a sort of Goan tiramisu. **Known for:** delicious vegetable samosas; attentive service; perfectly-spiced meat, fish, and vegetable curries. *Average main: €13 Rua da Paz 4, Lisbon Off Rua dos Poiais de São Bento 96/501–4667 www.facebook.com/Ana74Fernandes Closed Sun. and Mon. Tram 28.*

Casanostra

$$ | **ITALIAN** | One of the first truly Italian restaurants in Lisbon is still one of the best. On the menu are the Italian owner's favorite dishes, including meat, fish, and pasta options. **Known for:** retro-minimalist interior; Italian desserts; daily specials. *Average main: €18 Travessa do Poço da Cidade 60, Lisbon 21/342–5931 www.casanostra.pt No lunch Sat. Tram 28 to Praça de Luis de Camões.*

The Decadente

$$$$ | **PORTUGUESE** | A lively crowd gathers in the chic dining room of this contemporary restaurant (once the Swiss ambassador's residence), packs into the backyard terrace, and jostles for a spot at the cocktail bar. The zero-waste menu, which changes regularly, focuses on fresh seasonal ingredients, all sourced from Portuguese shores. **Known for:** all-Portuguese wine list; trendy bar with excellent craft cocktails; imaginative dishes, presented with flair. *Average main: €26 Rua de São Pedro de Alcântara 81, Lisbon 91/118–3459 thedecadente.pt No lunch Tram 24 to S. Pedro Alcântara.*

EPUR

$$$$ | **INTERNATIONAL** | After many years in the kitchens of some of the top restaurants in Portugal, French chef Vincent Farges opened his own spot in Lisbon, where he presents creative seasonal tasting menus that since 2022 have earned him a Michelin star. His cuisine is inspired by different parts of the world and is accompanied by Portuguese wine. **Known for:** beautiful view over downtown Lisbon; tiled 18th-century interior with

modern touches; daily fish or shellfish specials. $ *Average main: €120 ✉ Largo da Academia Nacional das Belas Artes 14, Lisbon ☎ 21/346–0519 🌐 www.epur.pt ⏲ Closed Sun. and Mon.* Ⓜ *Blue or Green Line to Baixa-Chiado, Tram 28.*

Faz Frio

$$$ | PORTUGUESE | Today it's a lively spot for petiscos and cocktails, but Casa Faz Frio was once the location for secret political meetings (and romantic trysts), thanks to its secluded *gabinetes* (booths). It's been given a top-to-toe overhaul, but retains its paneled booths, tiled floors, and other details from its more than 150 years of history. **Known for:** social atmosphere; tapas-style plates; cozy booths. $ *Average main: €23 ✉ Rua Dom Pedro V 96–98, Lisbon ☎ 21/581–4296 🌐 www.facebook.com/restaurantefazfrio ⏲ Closed Sun.* Ⓜ *Tram 24E to Príncipe Real.*

Grapes & Bites

$$ | PORTUGUESE | There's an enormous array of top-quality Portuguese cheeses, wines, and petiscos on the menu at Grapes & Bites. **Known for:** vegetarian options like mushroom or asparagus risotto; renowned shellfish and octopus dishes; huge range of small plates for sharing. $ *Average main: €20 ✉ Rua do Norte 85, Lisbon ☎ 92/445–7494 🌐 grapesandbites.eatbu.com ⏲ Closed Tues.* Ⓜ *Blue or Green Line to Baixa-Chiado.*

Honorato

$ | BURGER | Named after the Brazilian chef who came up with the recipes for this restaurant's original hamburgers, Honorato is a minichain of trendy burger joints. The branch in Chiado is the most popular—it has a lively atmosphere and large windows looking out to one of the neighborhood's main squares. **Known for:** a face sculpted on a wall by famous street artist Vhils; variety of gins and cocktails; homestyle fries. $ *Average main: €15 ✉ Largo Rafael Bordalo Pinheiro 12, Lisbon ☎ 91/028–5425 🌐 www.honorato.pt* Ⓜ *Blue or Green Line to Baixa-Chiado.*

★ Jardim das Cerejas

$ | VEGAN | FAMILY | Vegans in the know head to this little place off Rua Garrett, which has a well-priced varied buffet of salads, hot entrées, sides, and sauces for both lunch and dinner. **Known for:** all-in vegan buffet; cozy place with friendly staff; range of fresh juices. $ *Average main: €13 ✉ Calçada do Sacramento 36, Lisbon ☎ 21/346–9308 ⏲ Closed Sun.* Ⓜ *Blue or Green Line to Baixa-Chiado.*

La Paparrucha

$$$$ | ARGENTINE | FAMILY | The inspiration for this restaurant's food comes from Argentina, so expect a steak-heavy menu that has long made it a favorite among Lisbon's carnivores. You'll also find fish dishes borrowed from traditional Portuguese cuisine and a couple of vegetarian options, too. **Known for:** panoramic views and some tables on the terrace; affordable set lunch menus that change daily; family-friendly vibe. *Average main: €28 Rua Dom Pedro V 18–20, Bairro Alto 21/342–5333 lapaparrucha.com Tram 24, Blue Line to Restauradores then Elevador da Glória.*

★ Lisboa à Noite

$$$$ | PORTUGUESE | One of Bairro Alto's most successful restaurants since opening in 2003, Lisboa à Noite serves imaginative cuisine that manages to be both traditional and contemporary, mostly following Portuguese recipes but adding a few international touches. The arched interior was once a stable, and you can still see the ring chains used to tie the horses. **Known for:** beautiful dining room with blue-and-white tile panels; variety of cod dishes; traditional dessert cart. *Average main: €27 Rua das Gáveas 69, Lisbon 96/718–1296, 21/346–8557 www.lisboanoite.com Closed Sun. No lunch Blue or Green Line to Baixa-Chiado.*

★ 100 Maneiras

$$$$ | MEDITERRANEAN | A native of Bosnia, Ljubomir Stanisic made his name in Portugal as a young chef full of flair, fronting TV shows, writing books, and, above all, experimenting with food (and wine). When he reopened this industrial-chic foodie haven in Bairro Alto, it made the 50 Best Discovery list within months, and in 2024 it secured a Michelin star. **Known for:** tasting menus, including vegetarian; unusual Portugese ingredients; innovative dishes reflecting pan-European influences. *Average main: €140 Rua do Teixeira 39, Lisbon 91/091–8181 100maneiras.com No lunch Blue or Green Line to Baixa-Chiado.*

★ Palácio Chiado

$$$$ | INTERNATIONAL | The 18th-century Quintela Palace—once taken over by one of Napoléon's generals—now welcomes diners to a gastronomic experience in a space like no other in the city. Climb the grand staircase to dine in one of four airy elegant rooms, where you can enjoy Portuguese and international cuisine (and where there are well-priced lunch menus). **Known for:** grand interior; signature cocktails; traditional Portuguese desserts. *Average main: €28 Rua do Alecrim 70, Lisbon 21/010–1184 www.facebook.com/palaciochiado Blue or Green Line to Baixa-Chiado.*

Pharmacia Felicidade

$ | PORTUGUESE | Sharing the building of the Pharmacy Museum, this smart restaurant with a large terrace faces one of the city's most popular viewpoints and is open throughout the day for meals and drinks—including medicinal-themed cocktails. Chef Susana Felicidade, known as a judge on the Portuguese edition of the *MasterC hef* television show, gives a twist to traditional Portuguese cuisine, featuring dishes from her native Algarve such as gazpacho and carob cake. **Known for:** small plates to share; decor re-creating the atmosphere of an old pharmacy; "therapeutic cocktails." $ *Average main: €14* ✉ *Rua de Santa Catarina 2, Lisbon* ☎ *21/346–2146* 🌐 *www.facebook.com/restaurantepharmacia* Ⓜ *Blue or Green Line to Baixa-Chiado, Tram 28.*

★ Rocco Gastrobar

$$$$ | **ITALIAN** | You don't need to be a guest at snazzy Chiado hotel The Ivens in order to snag a table in its glamorous downstairs bar, but you are advised to book in advance. Perch yourself on one of the high seats for communal dining and watch the talented mixologists create the perfect cocktail to accompany light sharing dishes like tuna tartare with wasabi pearls and avocado, or order a heartier Portuguese or Italian-style main dish such as beef tagliata. **Known for:** wide range of cocktails; huge wine collection and excellent advice on pairings; DJ sets in the evenings. $ *Average main: €26* ✉ *The Ivens Hotel, Rua Ivens 14, Lisbon* ✥ *Separate entrance from hotel* ☎ *21/054–3168* 🌐 *www.rocco.pt* Ⓜ *Blue or Green Line to Baixa-Chiado.*

★ Sea Me Peixaria Moderna

$$$$ | **JAPANESE FUSION** | This restaurant is a modern spin on Lisbon's traditional fish markets and beer halls, with a dash of Japanese flair in the form of ultra-fresh sushi and sashimi. Take your pick from vast glass display cabinets of fish and crustaceans, and have it prepared on the spot in a variety of ways, whether it's dunked whole into the cooking pot or filleted and tossed onto the grill. **Known for:** seafood platters; day's catch displayed on ice; famous prego steak sandwich. $ *Average main: €29* ✉ *Rua do Loreto 21, Lisbon* ☎ *21/346–1564* 🌐 *peixariamoderna.com* Ⓜ *Blue or Green Line to Baixa-Chiado.*

Suba Restaurante

$$$$ | **PORTUGUESE** | The view from this prize-winning hotel restaurant in the hilltop Santa Catarina district is extraordinary, but your attention will soon be drawn to the delicious food—Portuguese with a contemporary twist, made from ingredients sourced from across the country and its chilly coastal waters—exquisitely presented by chef Fábio Alves and his team. For the full experience opt for one of the tasting menus; with the eight-course menu, you can choose between a 100% Portuguese wine pairing and a global tour that includes wines from Oregon to Georgia, via

Andalusia. **Known for:** updated Portuguese cuisine; sophisticated vegetarian options; jaw-dropping river view. $ *Average main: €40* ✉ *Verride Palácio Santa Catarina, Rua de Santa Catarina 1, Lisbon* ☎ *21/157–3055 Verride Hotel* 🌐 *subarestaurante.com* ⏲ *No lunch Tues.–Fri.* Ⓜ *Blue or Green Line to Baixa-Chiado.*

Taberna da Rua das Flores
$ | **PORTUGUESE** | Following time-tested recipes of traditional Portuguese dishes, this small restaurant has become a mecca for those looking for an old-school experience. Some recipes have fallen out of fashion and even been forgotten by locals, so many dishes are unique to Taberna da Rua das Flores. **Known for:** traditional decor recalling Lisbon's old taverns; freshly baked bread; wines from the Lisbon region. $ *Average main: €14* ✉ *Rua das Flores 103, Lisbon* ☎ *21/347–9418* ▭ *No credit cards* ⏲ *Closed Sun.* Ⓜ *Blue or Green Line to Baixa-Chiado.*

Tágide
$$$$ | **PORTUGUESE** | Named after the mythical water nymphs of the Tagus River, this place is divided into two parts: a sleek modern dining room serving refined versions of Portuguese dishes upstairs and a more relaxed wine-and-tapas bar downstairs. Both spaces face the river, and the tables by the windows are some of the most coveted in town. **Known for:** spectacular views and elegant interiors; excellent fish and seafood dishes; tasting menu with optional wine pairings. $ *Average main: €33* ✉ *Largo da Academia Nacional de Belas Artes 18–20, Lisbon* ☎ *21/340–4010* 🌐 *www.restaurantetagide.com* ⏲ *Closed Sun. and Mon.* Ⓜ *Tram 28, Blue or Green Line to Baixa-Chiado.*

Tasca do Manel
$ | **PORTUGUESE** | **FAMILY** | An unpretentious traditional *tasca* (cheap eatery) hidden among Bairro Alto's many noisy cocktail bars and tourist traps, Tasca do Manel serves hearty portions of excellent Portuguese food at fair prices. Game on offer includes stewed pheasant and boar, served either grilled or in a bean stew, and there are rarely found local fish dishes such as fried shad with *açorda* bread soup. **Known for:** more locals than tourists; good grilled meats and fish; lively atmosphere. $ *Average main: €14* ✉ *Rua da Barroca 24, Lisbon* ☎ *21/346–3813* ▭ *No credit cards* ⏲ *Closed Sun.* Ⓜ *Blue or Green Line to Baixa-Chiado.*

Toma Lá Dá Cá
$ | **PORTUGUESE** | Locals and tourists who don't show up early often wait for as much as an hour for a table, knowing this is where you can still eat the good old-fashioned Lisbon way. Staff rush from table to table, serving doses of reasonably priced standards like grilled tuna and garlic prawns accompanied by a good house wine.

Known for: fresh-grilled fish; steak with mushroom sauce; delicious cheesecake or strawberry mousse (you have to ask). *Average main: €11* *Travessa do Sequeiro 38, Lisbon* *21/347–9243* *Closed Sun.* *Tram 28, Blue or Green Line to Baixa-Chiado.*

★ Trindade

$$$$ | **PORTUGUESE** | A visit to this eatery—in a space that probably was once the refectory of a 13th-century monastery—is a quintessential Lisbon experience, although these days it's a pricey one. Transformed into a beer hall in 1836, and recently completely refurbished, it's one of the city's most popular seafood restaurants, packing in locals and tourists under the vaulted ceiling to sample dishes from a menu devised by Michelin-starred chef Alexandre Silva. **Known for:** huge variety of shellfish; feels like traveling back in time; a recent slick renovation. *Average main: €35* *Rua Nova da Trindade 20, Lisbon* *21/342–3506* *www.cervejariatrindade.pt/en* *Blue or Green Line to Baixa-Chiado, Tram 24.*

Coffee and Quick Bites

★ A Brasileira do Chiado

$$$ | **CAFÉ** | Dating from 1905, Lisbon's most famous café maintains its dazzling art deco interior, though you'll probably prefer to take a quick peek and then settle in at one of the tables outside to watch the lively street scenes unfold. The coffee no longer comes exclusively from the former colony that gave the place its name, but it still serves some of the best in town (it even features in the sauce on the house steak) alongside tasty cakes, pastries, and artfully presented seafood dishes. **Known for:** prime location for people-watching; long history of serving excellent coffee and snacks; tasty sharing plates. *Average main: €25* *Rua Garrett 120–122, Lisbon* *21/346–9541* *www.abrasileira.pt* *Blue or Green Line to Baixa-Chiado.*

A Carioca/Vegan Nata

$ | **VEGAN** | Portugal's first vegan *pastéis de nata* (custard tarts) are available at this long-established coffee merchant, with its vintage facade and wood-and-glass interior. Nonvegans, too, will love these egg- and dairy-free treats. **Known for:** vegan custard tarts; lovely vintage interior; sells coffee by the bag. *Average main: €1.30* *Rua da Misericórdia 9, Lisbon* *Blue or Green Line to Baixa-Chiado.*

★ Alcôa

$ | **PORTUGUESE** | This pastry shop opened in 1957 in the city of Alcobaça, and six decades later it expanded to the capital. You can now try the tarts together with "monastic pastries" that follow age-old recipes by Cistercian monks, all in this small shop on Chiado's busiest street. **Known for:** beautiful interior decorated with contemporary tiles by renowned artist Querubim Lapa; mouthwatering window displays; eggy custard pastries. $ *Average main: €4 ✉ Rua Garrett 37, Lisbon ☎ 21/136–7183 Ⓜ Blue or Green Line to Baixa-Chiado.*

Aloma

$ | **CAFÉ** | More of a local option than some cafés in the area, Aloma is known for its prize-winning pastéis de nata, whose fame has helped it build up a small chain and even go into the export business. This outlet also offers a range of other pastries, plus sandwiches and quiches. **Known for:** prize-winning pastries; traditional Portuguese coffees; local haunt in a touristy area. $ *Average main: €1.20 ✉ Largo Calhariz 3, Lisbon ☎ 21/346–2730 🌐 www.aloma.pt Ⓜ Blue or Green Line to Baixa-Chiado.*

Café no Chiado

$$ | **CAFÉ** | The tables outside this long-established haven are the perfect place to watch the old trams go by, while an interior reading room offers a quiet space to relax with a book and a snack or meal (the two-course set lunches are a good value at €15). Less touristy than some other cafés nearby, it still attracts artists from the neighboring theaters who stop for a drink. **Known for:** shaded terrace; creative salads and small plates; perfect spot for an afternoon glass of wine. $ *Average main: €19 ✉ Largo do Picadeiro 10–12, Lisbon ☎ 21/346–0501 🌐 www.cafenochiado.com Ⓜ Blue or Green Line to Baixa-Chiado.*

Kaffeehaus

$ | **AUSTRIAN** | This long-established Austrian-style café is popular with most locals and tourists, with its combination of bottled and draft beers (including their very own brand) and hearty central European dishes such as Wiener schnitzel, homemade sausages, and spätzle, along with vegan and vegetarian options. The dessert menu includes apple strudel and Sacher torte. **Known for:** good range of beers; great place for coffee and cake; cheerful atmosphere. $ *Average main: €14 ✉ Rua Anchieta 3, Lisbon ☎ 21/095–6828 🌐 www.kaffeehaus-lisboa.com Ⓜ Blue or Green Line to Baixa-Chiado.*

Landeau Chocolate

$ | **DESSERTS** | Ever since the *New York Times* described it as "devilishly good," Landeau's chocolate cake has been reason enough to head to Chiado (or one of their three other Lisbon shops). Here you can buy an entire cake to enjoy at home or sit for a slice with some tea. **Known for:** relaxing, dimly lit interior; reasonably priced drinks; welcoming staff. $ *Average main: €4* ✉ *Rua das Flores 70, Lisbon* ☎ *91/181–0801* 🌐 *www.landeau.pt* Ⓜ *Blue or Green Line to Baixa-Chiado.*

Manteigaria

$ | **CAFÉ** | The custard tarts at this tiny shop rival those of the famous shop in Belém for the title of the best pastéis de nata in town. A bell is rung every time a batch emerges warm from the oven. **Known for:** glassed-in kitchen showing the baking process; art nouveau facade; traditional Portuguese drinks, such as ginjinha and port wine. $ *Average main: €1.30* ✉ *Rua do Loreto 2, Lisbon* ☎ *21/347–1492* 🌐 *manteigaria.com* Ⓜ *Blue or Green Line to Baixa-Chiado.*

Noobai

$$ | **PORTUGUESE** | **FAMILY** | With two terraces, this very popular café is located in a corner of the Santa Catarina viewpoint, so expect bird's-eye views over the port and the city. There are well-priced daily specials for light meals and refreshing drinks, but it's the weekend brunch that attracts most locals. **Known for:** colorful space with a small play area for kids; small plates of traditional Portuguese dishes; cocktails. $ *Average main: €19* ✉ *Miradouro de Santa Catarina, Lisbon* ☎ *21/346–5014* 🌐 *noobaicafe.com* Ⓜ *Blue or Green Line to Baixa-Chiado, Tram 28.*

Santini Chiado

$ | **ICE CREAM** | **FAMILY** | For some of the best ice cream and sorbets in town, drop into this branch of a family-run chain founded in 1949. New flavors are introduced regularly, but all stick to the tradition of using only fresh fruit and all-natural ingredients. **Known for:** genuine Italian-style gelato; delicious milkshakes; perfect pastries. $ *Average main: €5.40* ✉ *Rua do Carmo 88, Lisbon* ☎ *21/346–8431* 🌐 *www.santini.pt* Ⓜ *Blue or Green Line to Baixa-Chiado.*

Hotels

★ Bairro Alto Hotel

$$$$ | **HOTEL** | Lisbon's first boutique hotel was treated to a top-to-toe redesign courtesy of Pritzker Prize–winning Portuguese architect Eduardo Souto de Moura, making it one of the finest places to stay in the heart of the city. **Pros:** rooftop terrace is a photographer's dream; close to the city's best nightlife; thoughtful design. **Cons:** some small rooms; terrace is often packed; books up fast in high season. $ *Rooms from: €450* ✉ *Praça de Luís de Camões 2, Lisbon* ☎ *21/340–8288* 🌐 *www.bairroaltohotel.com* *87 rooms* *Free Breakfast* Ⓜ *Blue or Green Line to Baixa-Chiado.*

Hotel do Chiado
$$$$ | **HOTEL** | Occupying the sixth to eighth floors of the Grandes Armazéns do Chiado shopping complex, this boutique hotel blends elements of 16th-century Portugal with 21st-century amenities. **Pros:** beautifully restored historic building; perfect location for shopping and sightseeing; private terraces with gorgeous views. **Cons:** terrace bar can get crowded; staid design; breakfast not included in cheapest room rates. *Rooms from: €323 Rua Nova do Almada 114, Lisbon 21/325–6100 www.hoteldochiado.pt 38 rooms No Meals Blue or Green Line to Baixa-Chiado.*

★ **The Ivens**
$$$$ | **HOTEL** | **FAMILY** | Urban explorers will love this vibrant design-led boutique hotel, which opened in 2021 on a charming Chiado side street. **Pros:** storied building; ample free parking on-site; upscale bathroom amenities from Acqua di Parma. **Cons:** staff uniforms can feel over-the-top; no pool or spa; major-brand parent company. *Rooms from: €690 Rua Capelo 5, Lisbon 21/054–3135 www.theivenshotel.com 87 rooms No Meals Blue or Green Line to Baixa-Chiado.*

Lisboa Carmo Hotel
$$$$ | **HOTEL** | Located on beautiful Largo do Carmo in the hilly Chiado neighborhood, this boutique charmer has amazing views of the historic square, the red rooftops of the city, and the Tagus River. **Pros:** prime location for sightseeing and barhopping; facing one of the city's most charming squares; extremely comfortable room furnishings. **Cons:** some small rooms; not all views are created equal; street noise at night. *Rooms from: €300 Rua da Oliveira ao Carmo 1–3, Lisbon 21/326–4710 www.lisboacarmohotel.pt 45 rooms No Meals Blue or Green Line to Baixa-Chiado.*

★ **The Lumiares**
$$$$ | **HOTEL** | Just a few steps from the São Pedro de Alcântara viewpoint, The Lumiares is a chic boutique hotel in an 18th-century former palace in the heart of bustling Bairro Alto. **Pros:** very central location; castle views from the rooftop bar; dazzling design. **Cons:** lower-level rooms look directly onto the busy street; spa is small; noisy neighborhood. *Rooms from: €450 Rua do Diário de Notícias 142, Lisbon 21/116–0200 www.thelumiares.com 53 rooms Free Breakfast Tram 24, Blue Line to Restauradores then Elevador da Glória.*

Palácio das Especiarias
$$$$ | **HOTEL** | A characterful boutique hotel in the heart of Chiado, Palácio das Especiarias occupies a beautifully restored

16th-century mansion hiding a wealth of intriguing detail behind its low-key facade. **Pros:** lovely details, like ornate azulejo tiles and beautiful bed canopies; lots of light in rooms and communal areas; on-site wellness center and spa with Roman baths. **Cons:** decor won't appeal to minimalists; books up early in high season; no on-site parking. *Rooms from: €350 Rua da Horta Seca 11, Lisbon 93/048–0337 www.palaciodasespeciarias.com/pt/casinhasdelisboa/palacio-das-especiarias 42 rooms Free Breakfast Blue or Green Line to Baixa-Chiado.*

Palácio Ludovice Wine Experience Hotel
$$$$ | **HOTEL** | If you want to feel utterly pampered amid the hectic pace of Bairro Alto, this beautifully restored 18th-century mansion is the place. **Pros:** good spa and chic wine bar; central location; gorgeous building. **Cons:** service may not always match luxurious feel; breakfast is extra; surrounding area is rowdy at night. *Rooms from: €360 Rua de São Pedro de Alcântara 39, Lisbon 21/151–3850 www.palacioludovice.com 61 rooms No Meals Tram 24, Blue Line to Restauradores then Elevador da Glória.*

Verride Palácio Santa Catarina
$$$$ | **HOTEL** | It's hard to imagine a more stunning location in Lisbon for a hotel, and the interior of this painstakingly refurbished hilltop mansion isn't too shabby, either. **Pros:** beautiful and unique decor; central location with amazing views; highly attentive staff. **Cons:** children ages eight and up only; no pool, spa, or gym; on a square with a sometimes heavy late-night scene. *Rooms from: €800 Rua de Santa Catarina 1, Lisbon 21/157–3055 19 rooms Free Breakfast Blue or Green Line to Baixa-Chiado.*

Performing Arts

★ Teatro Nacional de São Carlos
THEATER | Inaugurated in 1793, this grand neoclassical theater was inspired by Venice's opera house, La Fenice. You have to see the main hall to appreciate the building's splendor. The stage itself is rather plain, but the five tiers of private boxes on either side draw the eye to the domed royal box, awash with gold leaf and held aloft by soaring columns. Two cherubs hold aloft the royal coat of arms. The theater has its own choir, is home to the Portuguese Symphonic Orchestra, and hosts music and dance performances, as well as opera. Book guided tours in advance by email. *Rua Serpa Pinto 9, Lisbon 21/325–3045 visitas@saocarlos.pt tnsc.pt Blue or Green Line to Baixa-Chiado.*

Home to the Orquestra Sinfónica Portuguesa, the Teatro Nacional de São Carlos is a grand sight in its own right.

Shopping

ART GALLERIES

Galeria Graça Brandão

ART GALLERY | Founded in Porto, this gallery moved to Lisbon and took over an old printing house. It presents works by Portuguese and Brazilian artists. ✉ *Rua dos Caetanos 26, Lisbon* ☎ *21/342–1819* 🌐 *www.galeriagracabrandao.pt* Ⓜ *Blue or Green Line to Baixa-Chiado.*

BOOKS

★ Bertrand Livreiros

BOOKS | Founded in 1732, this is the world's oldest operating bookstore—a certificate near the door from Guinness World Records attests to that—and nowadays the flagship of a nationwide chain. Here, current bestsellers welcome you to the first room, before you continue into the vaulted interior to find different sections divided by theme, finishing with a small café that is also accessible from Rua Serpa Pinto. In particular, the store has a small English-language selection of works by the major Portuguese authors and Lisbon-related books. You can also buy international newspapers and magazines. ✉ *Rua Garrett 73–75, Lisbon* ☎ *21/030–5590* 🌐 *www.bertrand.pt* Ⓜ *Blue or Green Line to Baixa-Chiado.*

CERAMICS

★ Fábrica Sant'Anna

CERAMICS | This is the downtown showroom for a company established in 1741 that continues to use centuries-old techniques in its workshop in Ajuda (uphill from Belém), including painting and glazing entirely by hand, to create contemporary designs and reproductions of antique azulejo tiles. ✉ *Largo Barão de Quintela 4, Lisbon* ☎ *21/342–2537* 🌐 *santanna.com.pt* Ⓜ *Blue or Green Line to Baixa-Chiado.*

Luza Portugal

CERAMICS | From ornate azulejo tiles to kitsch designs (think dishes shaped like giant lettuce leaves), Portuguese ceramics are much sought after by visitors from around the world. Hidden slightly off the main shopping strip in upscale Chiado, Luza offers beautiful pieces at very affordable prices, with some items priced by weight. Smaller items, like Portuguese cockerel wine stoppers, make cute mementos and gifts. ✉ *Rua Capelo 16, Lisbon* ☎ *21/598–4813* 🌐 *www.luzaportugal.pt* Ⓜ *Blue or Green Line to Baixa-Chiado.*

★ Vista Alegre

CERAMICS | Originally a royal factory founded in 1817, Vista Alegre is now one of Europe's most prestigious porcelain manufacturers. Prestigious glassware and crystal maker Atlantis is also now part of the group. This flagship store presents the companies' ever-changing collections, which are often signed by national and international artists. ✉ *Largo do Chiado 20–23, Lisbon* ☎ *21/346–1401* 🌐 *vistaalegre.com* Ⓜ *Blue or Green Line to Baixa-Chiado.*

CLOTHING AND SHOES

A Fábrica dos Chapéus

HATS & GLOVES | The stylish proprietor of this funky hat store stocks a huge range of their own designs for men, women, and children and also makes exclusive items to order. ✉ *Rua da Rosa 118, Lisbon* ☎ *91/717–8919* 🌐 *www.afabricadoschapeus.com* Ⓜ *Tram 24, Blue Line to Restauradores then Elevador da Glória.*

Cantê

SWIMWEAR | If you're looking for chic beachwear for the whole family, this is the place to visit. This stylish store stocks limited-edition Portuguese-made swimsuits, bikinis, and comfy but stylish clothing and accessories for women, men, and kids. ✉ *Calçada Nova de São Francisco 10, Lisbon* ✥ *Entrance via Galerias Páteo Garrett, from Rua Garrett 19* ☎ *21/138–0136* 🌐 *www.cantelisboa.com* Ⓜ *Blue or Green Line to Baixa-Chiado.*

The Feeting Room

SHOES | This offshoot of a Porto-based retailer, housed in a minimalist former industrial bakery, The Feeting Room offers Portuguese-made and international independent fashion brands—both footwear and clothes—not otherwise available in the capital.

It also stocks accessories, home design, and lifestyle pieces, mostly produced in Portugal. ✉ *Calçada do Sacramento 26, Lisbon* ☎ *21/246–4700* 🌐 *thefeetingroom.com* Ⓜ *Blue or Green Line to Baixa-Chiado.*

Sapataria do Carmo

SHOES | In business since 1904, this charming old shoe store features an interior that hasn't changed much since the 1950s. Customers still sit on velvet sofas to try on shoes that are stored in vintage boxes, and it still specializes in handmade Portuguese shoes, finished in the workshop next door. You can expect top quality at reasonable prices, with some classic and some trendy models, as well as a few exclusive pieces. There's another branch in the lower part of Chiado, at Rua do Carmo 89. ✉ *Largo do Carmo 26, Lisbon* ☎ *21/342–3386, 93/578–2559 WhatsApp* 🌐 *sapatariadocarmo.com* Ⓜ *Blue or Green Line to Baixa-Chiado.*

Soulmood

CLOTHING | This small minimalist concept store offers the avant-garde fashions of lesser-known European designers. It's laid out almost like a gallery, with the curated collections on color-coordinated display. In addition to fashion and accessories, you may find jewelry by local designers like Valentim Quaresma, whose pieces have been featured in Lady Gaga videos. ✉ *Travessa do Carmo 1, Lisbon* ☎ *21/346–3179* 🌐 *soulmood.pt* Ⓜ *Blue or Green Line to Baixa-Chiado.*

★ Storytailors

CLOTHING | For some fairy-tale shopping, browse the racks here filled with fantastical frocks, capes, and more. Madonna is whispered to be among the celeb customers to have done so. ✉ *Calçada do Ferragial 8, Lisbon* ☎ *21/343–2306* 🌐 *www.storytailors.pt* Ⓜ *Tram 28, Blue or Green Line to Baixa-Chiado.*

CRAFTS AND SOUVENIRS

★ Burel Factory

SPECIALTY STORE | The mountains of Serra da Estrela in central Portugal are in the one of the country's coldest regions, so locals have a centuries-old tradition of using sheep's fleece in a variety of ways. This store has taken that regional product and given it even more uses by creating modern design items, such as handbags, backpacks, blankets, and even chairs. The colorful products are mostly by young Portuguese designers, but all are recognized for their innovation, sustainability, and functionality. Next-door, a separate store stocks rolls of the fabric in a wide range of colors and patterns for you to make up at home, as well as ready-made cushions. ✉ *Rua Serpa Pinto 15B, Lisbon* ☎ *91/473–9164* 🌐 *burelfactory.com* Ⓜ *Blue or Green Line to Baixa-Chiado.*

Cork & Company

CRAFTS | Portugal's abundance of cork oaks are the basis for all the products showcased here. Look for eye-catching designs for homeware, office supplies, handbags, jewelry, and accessories for men and women. ✉ *Rua das Salgadeiras 6, Lisbon* ☎ *21/609–0231, 96/013–7485* 🌐 *corkandcompany.pt* ⏲ *Closed Sun.* Ⓜ *Blue or Green Line to Baixa-Chiado.*

Fabrica Features

CRAFTS | Overlooking the the busiest part of Chiado, above a Benetton store, this shop has a particularly Instagram-worthy view of the cobblestone pavement from above. The collection of bags, stationery, ceramics, and other products designed in Portugal and abroad are worth the trip up to the top floor for more than just a photograph. ✉ *Rua Garrett 83, 4th fl., Lisbon* ☎ *21/342–0596* 🌐 *www.facebook.com/fabricalisboa* Ⓜ *Blue or Green Line to Baixa-Chiado.*

FOOD AND WINE

Casa dos Ovos Moles em Lisboa

FOOD | Just down the street from Convento do Carmo, this store offers sweets that originated in convents all over Portugal. Nuns used to make a living by selling their confections, invariably using lots of sugar and egg yolks (since the nuns used the whites to starch their collars and wimples). This store is named after the extra-sweet "soft eggs" in wafer-thin pastry from the city of Aveiro, but you can buy many other specialties from around the country. ✉ *Calçada do Sacramento 25, Lisbon* ☎ *91/811–6513* 🌐 *www.casadosovosmolesemlisboa.pt* Ⓜ *Blue or Green Line to Baixa-Chiado.*

HOUSEWARES

★ Caza das Vellas Loreto

SPECIALTY STORE | Fans of artisanal candles will be charmed by this historic place (founded in the year of the French Revolution and George Washington's election as U.S. president), with its selection of traditional and updated designs in a dazzling range of shapes and colors—every one unique and all made by hand. You can choose from purely decorative or aromatic, ecological, and rustic lines; they also specialize in baptismal and other religious candles. ✉ *Rua do Loreto 53/5, Lisbon* Ⓜ *Blue or Green Line to Baixa-Chiado.*

Cutipol

HOUSEWARES | Portugal is the only western European country aside from Germany with a thriving cutlery-making industry (in and around the northern city of Guimarães), and Cutipol is one of its most prestigious representatives. It is known for its smart contemporary designs, which are showcased here along with tableware and other fine goods from top brands in Portugal and abroad. ✉ *Rua do Alecrim 105, Lisbon* ☎ *21/322–5075* 🌐 *www.cutipol.pt/en* Ⓜ *Blue or Green Line to Baixa-Chiado.*

JEWELRY

Joalharia do Carmo

JEWELRY & WATCHES | In business since 1924, this is one of Lisbon's oldest and most beautiful shops. Behind its historic art nouveau facade, it displays museum-worthy gold and silver pieces, plus exclusive Portuguese jewelry. It's also an excellent place to find the traditional handmade filigree from the north of the country. ✉ *Rua do Carmo 87B, Lisbon* ☎ *21/342–4200* 🌐 *www.joalhariado-carmo.pt/en* Ⓜ *Blue or Green Line to Baixa-Chiado.*

★ Leitão & Irmão

JEWELRY & WATCHES | Founded in Porto more than two centuries ago, this shop moved to Lisbon after it was appointed jewellers to the Portuguese Crown in 1887. Its atelier in Bairro Alto (where it also has another, smaller store, at ✉ *Travessa da Espera 8–14*) turns out traditional and contemporary pieces in silver, gold, and platinum, employing up-to-date design and manufacturing techniques along with traditional production processes. At this, its main showroom, you'll find everything from engagement rings to art deco cutlery, table centerpieces, and religious figures; they also do bespoke and customized items. ✉ *Largo do Chiado 16, Lisbon* ☎ *91/222–8817 WhatsApp, 21/325–7870* 🌐 *www.leitao-irmao.com/en* Ⓜ *Blue or Green Line to Baixa-Chiado.*

LEATHER GOODS

★ Luvaria Ulisses

HATS & GLOVES | Lisbon's smallest shop is one of its most charming, selling nothing but custom-made, finely crafted gloves since 1925. It's the last place in Portugal where you can get these exclusive gloves, and it's recognized as one of the best stores of its kind in Europe. The well-preserved neoclassical interior fits two customers at a time, who go through the process of trying on the different sizes and colors by placing their elbows on a small cushion and letting the fitter make the perfect adjustments. ✉ *Rua do Carmo 87A, Lisbon* ☎ *21/342–0295* 🌐 *www.luvariaulisses.com* Ⓜ *Green Line to Rossio, Blue or Green Line to Baixa-Chiado.*

MALLS

★ Armazéns do Chiado

DEPARTMENT STORE | It calls itself "Lisbon's meeting point" for a reason: this chic former department store is where people of all ages meet before a night out on the town. Inside are 50 national and international stores—including a branch of the Fnac chain, stocking a large range of books, music, and computers—offering everything you could need to look and feel fabulous, and there are 15 restaurants in the smart food court on the top floor, with views of Chiado. The building itself is worth a visit, having been painstakingly restored after a fire consumed much of the centuries-old building in 1988. ✉ *Rua do Carmo 2, Lisbon* ☎ *21/321–0600* 🌐 *www.armazensdochiado.com* Ⓜ *Blue or Green Line to Baixa-Chiado.*

PERFUMES

Claus Porto

FRAGRANCES | This Portuguese brand dates back to 1887, but this is its first flagship store, opened as recently as 2016. It took over the space of a former pharmacy, meeting the increasing demand for its fragrances that are now available in more than 60 countries. There are luxurious soaps, colognes, and scented candles, all beautifully wrapped in retro art nouveau packages. Photographs on the walls tell the history of the brand. There's another branch in the lower part of Chiado, on Rua do Carmo 82. ✉ *Rua da Misericórdia 135, Lisbon* ☎ *91/721–5855* 🌐 *clausporto.com* Ⓜ *Tram 24, Blue or Green Line to Baixa-Chiado.*

Bairro Alto, long the center of Lisbon's nightlife, is one of the best places in the city for barhopping. There's a street-party vibe on weekends, when revelers take their drinks outdoors. A number of bars here have a predominately gay clientele but invariably welcome all.

BARS

Duque Brewpub

BREWPUBS | A group of friends got together in 2015 and created their own craft beer, which resulted in Lisbon's first brewpub. It's found on a steep street with steps linking downtown to Chiado and Bairro Alto and has tables outside for afternoon or after-dark drinks and snacks. In addition to its own brand, it offers five other made-in-Portugal craft beers on tap. ✉ *Calçada do Duque 49–51, Lisbon* 🌐 *www.facebook.com/DuqueBrewpub* Ⓜ *Blue or Green Line to Baixa-Chiado.*

Lumi Rooftop

BARS | For a sophisticated sundowner before a night out in Bairro Alto, head to this leafy roof terrace with sweeping city views. The cocktails are excellent across the board, whether you order a classic margarita or a signature drink like the Lumi Negroni (made with infused gin, Portuguese vermouth, and Madeira wine). Soak up the alcohol with light meals and snacks, which are prepared with seasonal ingredients by Chef João Silva. ✉ *The Lumiares, Rua de São Pedro de Alcântara 35, Lisbon* 🌐 *www.thelumiares.com/eat-and-drink/lumi-rooftop* Ⓜ *Tram 24, Blue Line to Restauradores then Elevador da Glória.*

★ Maria Caxuxa

BARS | Recently revamped, this fun and funky bar retains the giant wood-fired oven that harks back to the building's previous life as a bakery. There's now a spacious rooftop terrace, but the interior of the bar is still reliably packed with young hipsters who've turned out to hear the hottest local DJs. The lengthy cocktail menu and famous shots of strong spirits can ramp up a night on the town. ✉ *Rua da Barroca 6–12, Lisbon* ☎ *21/346–1311* 🌐 *www.facebook.com/mariacaxuxabar* Ⓜ *Blue or Green Line to Baixa-Chiado.*

Mini Bar

BARS | Tucked away in the back of Bairro do Avillez—the "neighborhood" of eateries overseen by top local chef José Avillez—is this fun burlesque-themed gastrobar. Here you'll find a menu of small plates with some of his greatest hits, divided into different "acts." You may choose to just have a drink and enjoy the "opening act," or stay on for live music and/or DJs and dancing on Wednesday and Thursday nights—and on weekends a show, too. ✉ *Bairro do Avillez, Rua Nova da Trindade 18, Lisbon* ☎ *21/130–5393* 🌐 *www.minibar.pt* Ⓜ *Blue or Green Line to Baixa-Chiado.*

O Purista - Barbière

BARS | A bar that doubles as a barbershop, or vice versa, this is where Lisbon's coolest guys come to ensure they look sharp for a night on the town. The interior is classically decorated, a comfortable space for men (and women) to relax with a gin at any time of the day or night. ✉ *Rua Nova da Trindade 16C, Lisbon* ☎ *91/152–5750* 🌐 *www.instagram.com/opuristabar* ⏲ *Closed Mon.* Ⓜ *Blue or Green Line to Baixa-Chiado.*

Park

BARS | Take the elevator and ramp to the top of an unassuming multilevel car park to emerge onto a leafy terrace where a trendy crowd sips cocktails and DJs spin tunes to the early hours, against the backdrop of Lisbon's stunning skyline. There are several bars and seating areas, but it's standing room only as soon as sunset approaches. ✉ *Calçada do Combro 58, Lisbon* ✥ *Elevator best accessed from Travessa André Valente* ☎ *21/591–4011* 🌐 *www.facebook.com/parklisboaofficial* ⏲ *Closed Sun.* Ⓜ *Tram 28.*

Whether performed in fancy venues or neighborhood bars, the soulful sounds of fado music captivate audiences throughout Lisbon.

Portas Largas

BARS | Partiers spill out into the street from the massive front doors of this former old-world tavern, now a gay-friendly bar, one of the busiest in the area, whose dance floor attracts a lively crowd keen to dance to Brazilian beats. Shots and cocktails keep the party spirits flowing until the early hours. ✉ *Rua da Atalaia 105, Lisbon* Ⓜ *Tram 28, Blue or Green Line to Baixa-Chiado.*

★ Solar do Vinho do Porto

BARS | A refined place in Bairro Alto to start off your evening (it is open during the day, until 7 pm) is the relaxed Solar do Vinho do Porto, on the first floor of a grand former palace, the rest of which is now an upscale hotel. Here you can sink into an armchair and sample port wines from a list of several hundred. You can also buy bottles to take away. ✉ *Rua de São Pedro de Alcântara 45, Lisbon* ☎ *22/207–1693* Ⓜ *Tram 24, Blue Line to Restauradores then Elevador da Glória.*

DANCE CLUBS

Incognito

DANCE CLUB | Hidden on a mostly residential street not far from the noisier lanes of Bairro Alto, one of Lisbon's oldest clubs is true to its name—there's no sign at the door and you have to ring a bell to enter. Inside, on the small dance floor, the crowd dances to alternative sounds and pop hits from the present and the past, going all the way back to the 1980s. ✉ *Rua dos Poiais de São Bento 37, Lisbon* ☎ Ⓜ *Tram 28.*

Silk

DANCE CLUB | Dress to impress (no sneakers) if you want to get past the door staff at this fancy rooftop hangout, which caters to a well-heeled crowd with serious cash to splash. The terrace offers panoramic views over Lisbon, and glass walls mean that even those who make a reservation to drink and dine indoors can appreciate stunning vistas in all directions. There's a refined Japanese restaurant attached, and a weekend bottle service for those who want wines and spirits brought directly to their table. It's open until 4 am on Friday and Saturday, when the space takes on a clubbier vibe than during the week. ✉ *Rua da Misericórdia 14, 6th fl., Lisbon* ☎ *91/300–9193* 🌐 *silk-club.com* Ⓜ *Blue or Green Line to Baixa-Chiado.*

FADO CLUBS

★ Adega Machado

LIVE MUSIC | Bairro Alto is home to several of Lisbon's leading fado houses—venues where singers belt out soulful standards, accompanied by both the lute-like Portuguese *guitarra* and Spanish guitar—and Adega Machado is one of the best. Its artistic director is Marco Rodrigues, a leading member of the current generation of *fadistas*, who regularly performs here, along with Isabel Noronha, Bárbara Santos, and Pedro Moutinho. To attend the evening show at 9 pm, you must make a dinner reservation, so arrive in good time to choose from the range of traditional dishes (à la carte with mains at €30, or a €47 set menu, one of which is vegetarian). For just a taster, drop in for their daily 5 pm Fado Inside the Box 45-minute session (€17 including wine and snacks). Nearby Café Luso, at ✉ *Travessa da Queimada 10*, is another famous old venue, part of the same group. ✉ *Rua do Norte 91, Lisbon* ☎ *21/322–4640* 🌐 *www.adegamachado.pt/en* Ⓜ *Blue or Green Line to Baixa-Chiado.*

Tasca do Chico

LIVE MUSIC | The fado-loving owner of this informal space—once used to store olives and sausages, now lined with photos of famous fadistas—opened this bar serving simple food almost three decades ago; it has established itself as the city's best-known venue for *fado vadio*, or "vagabond fado," with mainly amateur singers, on Monday and Wednesday. Performers put their heart and soul into it (some even have half-decent voices), and the very competent musicians hold things together. Later on, professionals often turn up to do a turn when nearby fancier fado houses close. Tasca do Chico has an offshoot in the Alfama neighborhood, at ✉ *Rua dos Remédios 83*, where there's fado Thursday through Sunday. ✉ *Rua do Diário de Notícias 39, Lisbon* ☎ *96/505–9670* Ⓜ *Blue or Green Line to Baixa-Chiado.*

LGBTQ+ CLUBS

★ Purex Clube

DANCE CLUB | Thursday through Saturday, DJs pack the dance floor at this local favorite, a tiny space that's nevertheless more of a club than a bar. It's usually quite crowded, so many patrons grab a drink and enjoy it on the street. ✉ *Rua das Salgadeiras 28, Lisbon* ☎ *93/394–8764* 🌐 *www.facebook.com/purexclube* Ⓜ *Blue or Green Line to Baixa-Chiado.*

WINE BARS

Artis Wine Bar

WINE BAR | The intimate, dimly lit space and musical backdrop of tinkling jazz make a memorable setting for savoring a glass of wine, while sampling delicious and inexpensive versions of traditional Portuguese food. Bring cash, as international cards are not accepted. ✉ *Rua do Diário de Notícias 95, Lisbon* ☎ *21/342–4795* 🌐 *www.artiswinebar.pt/en* ⏲ *Closed Mon. No lunch* Ⓜ *Blue or Green Line to Baixa-Chiado.*

By the Wine

WINE BAR | Stepping into this bar is like entering a wine cellar; hundreds of bottles cover the stone-arch interior. It's owned by Portugal's largest producer, Sogrape, and serves as a showcase for its wines from across the country (and from its estates in New Zealand, Argentina, Chile, and Spain). ✉ *Rua das Flores 41–43, Lisbon* ☎ *21/342–0319* 🌐 *bythewine.pt/en* Ⓜ *Blue or Green Line to Baixa-Chiado.*

The Old Pharmacy

WINE BAR | The name says it all: this space used to be a pharmacy, and you'd just need to take a peek inside to know that. All the wines on offer are from Portugal and can be poured by the glass, to be accompanied by cheese and meat platters. Other choices change daily, to be enjoyed at the barrel tables. ✉ *Rua do Diário de Notícias 83, Lisbon* ☎ *92/023–0989* ⏲ *Closed Tues.* Ⓜ *Blue or Green Line to Baixa-Chiado.*

The Sandeman Chiado

WINE BAR | Unlike most other wine bars in town, this one is open from midday. It has inviting outdoor seating and a tastefully designed interior that tells the story of Sandeman, one of the best-known port wine labels. Since 2016 this outpost has been offering all of its different types of wine—plus port wine cocktails—along with desserts and a couple of food options. ✉ *Largo Rafael Bordalo Pinheiro 28, Lisbon* ☎ *93/785–0068* 🌐 *www.facebook.com/thesandemanchiado* Ⓜ *Blue or Green Line to Baixa-Chiado.*

Chapter 5

AVENIDA DA LIBERDADE, PRÍNCIPE REAL, AND RESTAURADORES

Updated by
Joana Taborda

Sights	Restaurants	Hotels	Shopping	Nightlife
★★★☆☆	★★★★☆	★★★★★	★★★★★	★★★★★

NEIGHBORHOOD SNAPSHOT

TOP EXPERIENCES

■ **Avenida da Liberdade.** Luxury shops, hotels, and kiosks line this Parisian-style boulevard connecting the Old Town to the new town.

■ **Catch a show.** Make the most of the city's entertainment scene by visiting one of the cinemas, theaters, and concert halls in this neighborhood.

■ **Convento dos Cardaes.** This little-known 17th-century convent is one of the few places that survived the earthquake and features original tiles from that era.

■ **Shop independent.** All along Príncipe Real, you'll find a variety of indie boutiques. Head to EmbaiXada for a selection of products designed by Portuguese makers.

GETTING HERE

Avenida da Liberdade is best reached by metro and is accessible from three stations on the Blue Line: Marquês de Pombal, Avenida, and Restauradores. Príncipe Real can be reached by walking up the hill from Avenida da Liberdade or by taking the metro (Rato station on the Yellow Line) or Tram 24 that departs from Praça de Luís de Camões in Chiado. Alternatively, take the Elevador da Glória by Praça dos Restauradores that ends up in Bairro Alto and is just a few feet from Príncipe Real's main street (Rua Dom Pedro V).

PLANNING YOUR TIME

Visit in the early evening, when locals gather around the neighborhood's kiosks and bars for an after-work drink.

VIEWFINDER

■ **Jardim do Torel.** For a view over Avenida da Liberdade and toward Príncipe Real, head up the hill to one of Lisbon's quietest viewpoints. It can be reached by taking Lisbon's oldest funicular, hidden around the corner from the Avenida. ✉ *Rua Júlio de Andrade* 🚊 *Elevador do Lavra or Bus 723/760 to Campo dos Mártires da Pátria.*

PAUSE HERE

■ **Miradouro de São Pedro de Alcântara.** Just before the start of Rua Dom Pedro V, this viewpoint is a great place to recharge on your way up to Príncipe Real. Beyond the panoramic views of the Castelo de São Jorge and the river, you'll often hear buskers playing music. ✉ *Rua de São Pedro de Alcântara* 🚊 *Tram 24 or Bus 758 to Elevador da Glória.*

Fill your bags with luxury goods or independent brands, stroll monumental squares and gardens, and savor a cocktail from the city's trendiest bars.

Tree-lined Avenida da Liberdade was modeled after Paris's Champs-Élysées and is covered with some of Lisbon's most beautifully designed cobblestone pavements. It's home to most of the city's luxury stores, and down its central lanes are food kiosks open throughout the day. Like the Parisian boulevard, it ends at a square with a traffic circle, Praça do Marquês de Pombal, named after the man who oversaw downtown Lisbon's reconstruction following the Great Earthquake of 1755 and whose statue stands at the center. Behind him is Parque Eduardo VII, laid out in the 19th century and home to a beautiful greenhouse garden. Bookworms head here around May and early June, when the park hosts the city's annual book fair, known as Feira do Livro.

While there are only a handful of monuments on this stretch, the lush gardens and the cluster of theaters and concert halls attract locals here. Indeed this has been the city's entertainment hub since the 1930s, when Parque Mayer staged the first revue shows (*teatro de revista*) and welcomed the dance parades that would inspire the Marchas Populares, now a staple of the city's summer festivities.

At the other end of the avenue is Praça dos Restauradores, with an obelisk commemorating the restoration of the Portuguese crown in 1640, ending 60 years of the Iberian Union, when Portugal and Spain shared the same king. Surrounding it are a number of attractive buildings, most notably Palácio Foz, built in 1777 with an interior inspired by the Palace of Versailles.

Rising up the hill to the west of the Avenida is romantic Príncipe Real, a neighborhood of stately mansions, trendy restaurants, concept stores, antique traders, and green spaces. It's also known as Lisbon's "gayborhood," with discreet LGBTQ+ bars and clubs on quiet residential streets. It was in one of these that queer Portuguese singer António Variações performed for the first time. Many people head here for the nightlife, but Príncipe Real is just as nice during the day, when you can tour hidden gems like the 17th-century Convento dos Cardaes, sample artisanal chocolate, or browse through independent bookshops along Rua da Escola Politécnica.

A stroll along tree-lined Avenida da Liberdade treats visitors to sights of historic buildings, luxury shops, and monuments to writers and composers.

Avenida da Liberdade, Príncipe Real, and Restauradores

Sights

Avenida da Liberdade (*Liberty Avenue*)
STREET | Liberty Avenue was laid out in 1879 as an elegant Parisian-style boulevard modeled on the Champs-Élysées. It has since lost some of its allure: many of the late-19th-century mansions and art deco buildings that once graced it have been demolished; others have been turned into soulless office blocks. There are, however, still some notable survivors of the original boulevard, now turned into luxury hotels and international fashion outlets. It's worth a leisurely stroll up the 1½-km (1-mile) length of the avenue, past ponds, fountains, and statues, from Praça dos Restauradores to Parque Eduardo VII, at least once, if only to cool off with a drink in one of the *quiosques* (refreshment kiosks) beneath the trees and to admire the iconic designs of the cobblestone pavements. ✉ *Avenida da Liberdade* Ⓜ *Blue Line to Avenida.*

★ **Cinemateca Portuguesa** (*Portuguese Cinema Museum*)
SPECIALTY MUSEUM | With a beautiful Moorish-style atrium, the city's movie museum hosts exhibitions on film history and screens classics from all over the world, usually in the original language and with Portuguese or English subtitles. Arrive early

to check out the treasures displayed around the building, like the first Lumière projector used in the country. There's a café with a pleasant terrace. ✉ *Rua Barata Salgueiro 39, Avenida da Liberdade* ☎ *21/359–6200* 🌐 *www.cinemateca.pt* ⏲ *Closed Sun.* Ⓜ *Blue Line to Avenida.*

Convento dos Cardaes

RELIGIOUS BUILDING | One of Lisbon's hidden treasures, the exterior of this 17th-century convent belies the riches inside. Still inhabited by nuns and women in need, it opens for visits every day except Tuesday, starting in the beautiful church lined with Portuguese and Dutch tile panels. They're found below paintings framed by gilded wood carvings, which, together with the gold-and-marble altar, make it one of Lisbon's most notable examples of Portuguese baroque. ✉ *Rua do Século 123, Príncipe Real* ☎ *21/342–7525* 🌐 *www.conventodoscardaes.com* 🎫 *€7* ⏲ *Closed Tues.* Ⓜ *Yellow Line to Rato.*

Jardim Botânico de Lisboa (*Lisbon Botanical Garden*)

GARDEN | FAMILY | Lisbon's main botanical garden was first laid out in 1874 to teach students about botany, and it is still part of the University of Lisbon. Hidden behind the small Museu de História Natural, about 2 km (1 mile) north of Bairro Alto, the garden has 10 acres of paths through nearly 15,000 species of subtropical plants. ✉ *Rua da Escola Politécnica 58, Príncipe Real* ☎ *21/392–1808* 🌐 *museus.ulisboa.pt/jardim-botanico-de-lisboa* 🎫 *€5; €8 with museum* Ⓜ *Yellow Line to Rato.*

Jardim do Torel

GARDEN | Also known as Miradouro do Torel, this garden-viewpoint is accessed through a gate at the top of a hill above Avenida da Liberdade. Unlike the other famous viewpoints in the city, it gets very few visitors, except for young couples and older folks from the neighborhood, who sit in the shade admiring the view, walk their dogs, or stop for coffee. The café is found down a few steps that lead to an 18th-century fountain and a terrace. That fountain often becomes a pool used by local children in the summer, when the terrace becomes a small "urban beach." ✉ *Travessa do Torel, Avenida da Liberdade* Ⓜ *Elevador do Lavra.*

Movimento Arte Contemporânea

ART GALLERY | Founded in 1993 with the aim of fostering cultural exchange between artists in Portugal and Portuguese-speaking countries such as Brazil, Angola, and Mozambique, this gallery displays contemporary paintings, sculptures, ceramics, and jewelry. ✉ *Av. Álvares Cabral 58/60, Príncipe Real* ☎ *21/385–0789* 🌐 *www.movimentoartecontemporanea.com* Ⓜ *Yellow Line to Rato.*

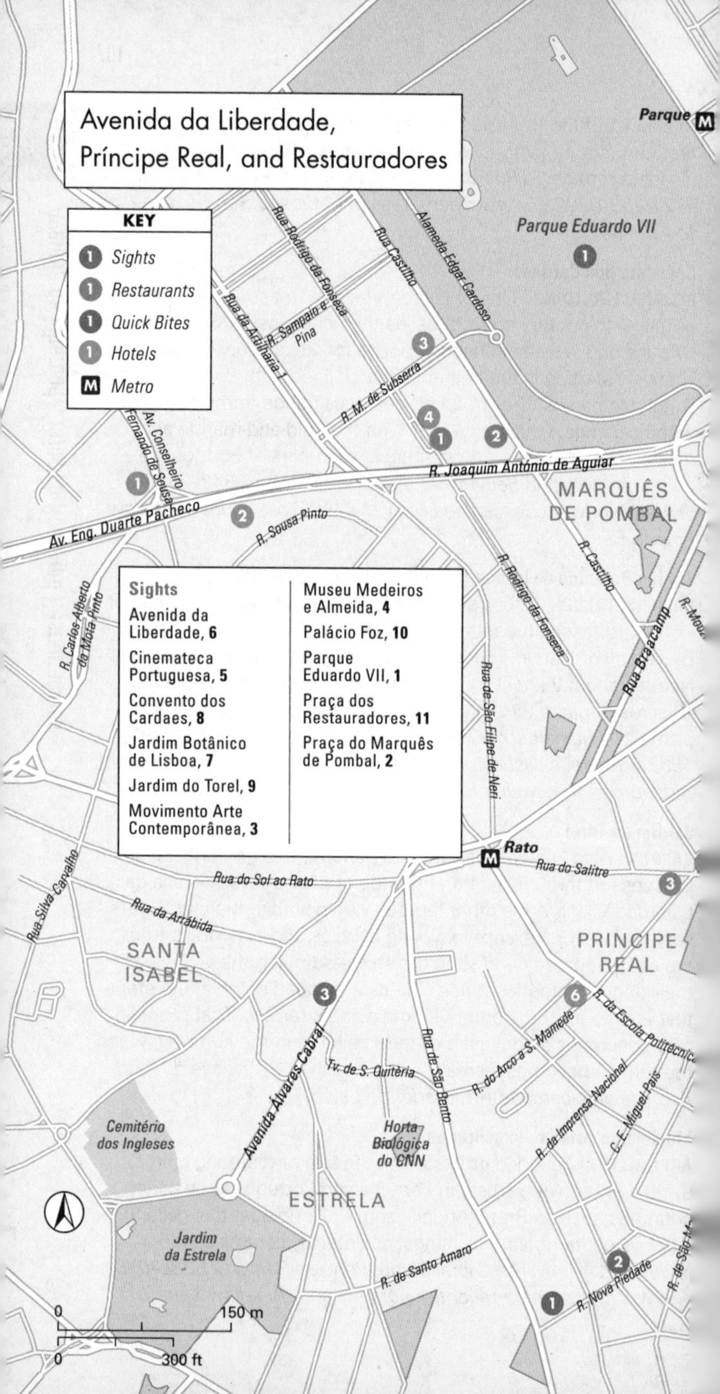

Avenida da Liberdade, Príncipe Real, and Restauradores
KEY
Sights
Restaurants
Quick Bites
Hotels
Metro
Sights
Avenida da Liberdade, 6
Cinemateca Portuguesa, 5
Convento dos Cardaes, 8
Jardim Botânico de Lisboa, 7
Jardim do Torel, 9
Movimento Arte Contemporânea, 3
Museu Medeiros e Almeida, 4
Palácio Foz, 10
Parque Eduardo VII, 1
Praça dos Restauradores, 11
Praça do Marquês de Pombal, 2
Parque
Parque Eduardo VII
Rua Rodrigo da Fonseca
Rua Castilho
Alameda Edgar Cardoso
Rua da Artilharia 1
R. Sampaio e Pina
R. M. de Subserra
Av. Conselheiro Fernando de Sousa
R. Joaquim António de Aguiar
MARQUÊS DE POMBAL
Av. Eng. Duarte Pacheco
R. Sousa Pinto
R. Castilho
R. Rodrigo da Fonseca
R. Carlos Alberto da Mota Pinto
Rua de São Filipe de Neri
Rua Braacamp
Rato
Rua do Salitre
Rua do Sol ao Rato
Rua da Arrábida
Rua Silva Carvalho
SANTA ISABEL
PRINCIPE REAL
R. da Escola Politécnica
R. do Arco a S. Mamede
Avenida Álvares Cabral
Tv. de S. Quitéria
Rua de São Bento
R. da Imprensa Nacional
C.-E. Miguel Pais
Cemitério dos Ingleses
Horta Biológica do CNN
ESTRELA
Jardim da Estrela
R. de Santo Amaro
R. Nova Piedade
0
150 m
0
300 ft

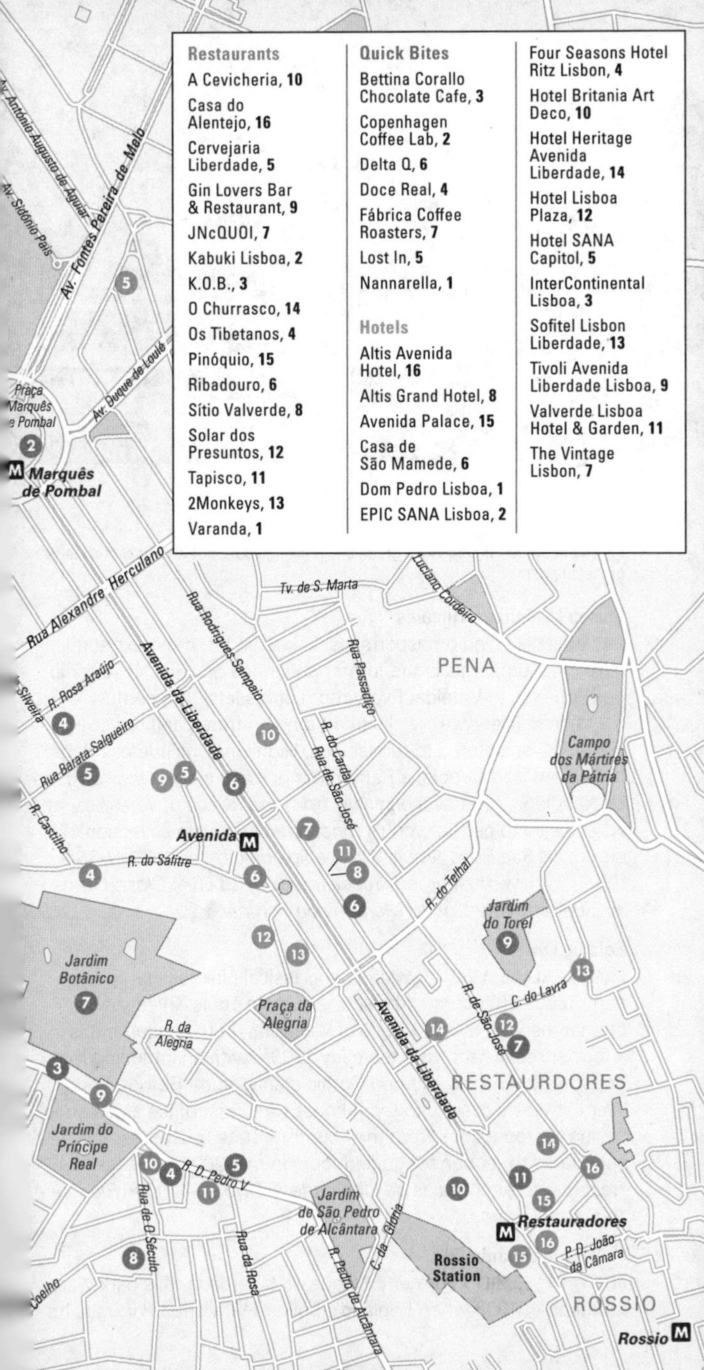
Restaurants
A Cevicheria, 10
Casa do Alentejo, 16
Cervejaria Liberdade, 5
Gin Lovers Bar & Restaurant, 9
JNcQUOI, 7
Kabuki Lisboa, 2
K.O.B., 3
O Churrasco, 14
Os Tibetanos, 4
Pinóquio, 15
Ribadouro, 6
Sítio Valverde, 8
Solar dos Presuntos, 12
Tapisco, 11
2Monkeys, 13
Varanda, 1
Quick Bites
Bettina Corallo Chocolate Cafe, 3
Copenhagen Coffee Lab, 2
Delta Q, 6
Doce Real, 4
Fábrica Coffee Roasters, 7
Lost In, 5
Nannarella, 1
Hotels
Altis Avenida Hotel, 16
Altis Grand Hotel, 8
Avenida Palace, 15
Casa de São Mamede, 6
Dom Pedro Lisboa, 1
EPIC SANA Lisboa, 2
Four Seasons Hotel Ritz Lisbon, 4
Hotel Britania Art Deco, 10
Hotel Heritage Avenida Liberdade, 14
Hotel Lisboa Plaza, 12
Hotel SANA Capitol, 5
InterContinental Lisboa, 3
Sofitel Lisbon Liberdade, 13
Tivoli Avenida Liberdade Lisboa, 9
Valverde Lisboa Hotel & Garden, 11
The Vintage Lisbon, 7
Av. António Augusto de Aguiar
Av. Sidónio Pais
Av. Fontes Pereira de Melo
Av. Duque de Loulé
Praça Marquês de Pombal
Marquês de Pombal
Rua Alexandre Herculano
Tv. de S. Marta
Luciano Cordeiro
Rua Rodrigues Sampaio
Avenida da Liberdade
Rua Passadiço
PENA
R. Rosa Araújo
Rua Barata Salgueiro
R. Castilho
R. do Cardal
Rua de São José
Campo dos Mártires da Pátria
Avenida
R. do Salitre
R. do Telhal
Jardim do Torel
Jardim Botânico
Praça da Alegria
C. do Lavra
R. de São José
R. da Alegria
RESTAURDORES
Jardim do Príncipe Real
R. D. Pedro V
Rua de O Século
Rua da Rosa
Jardim de São Pedro de Alcântara
R. Pedro de Alcântara
C. da Glória
Rossio Station
Restauradores
P. D. João da Câmara
ROSSIO
Rossio
Coelho

Parque Eduardo VII provides a green and relaxing oasis, but with beautiful views of the city center.

Museu Medeiros e Almeida

ART MUSEUM | One of Lisbon's lesser-known but most extraordinary museums, this is the former residence of collector António de Medeiros e Almeida. Every room of his late-19th-century mansion is filled with works of art ranging from paintings to ceramics, sculptures to furnishings. Highlights include paintings by Rubens and Tiepolo, a Rembrandt portrait, a silver tea set used by Napoléon, fountains originally from the Palace of Versailles, and what's said to be the world's most notable private collection of clocks. ✉ *Rua Rosa Araújo 41, Avenida da Liberdade* ☎ *21/354–7892* 🌐 *www.museumedeirosealmeida.pt* 🎫 *€6* ⏲ *Closed Sun.* Ⓜ *Blue or Yellow Line to Marquês de Pombal.*

Palácio Foz

CASTLE/PALACE | With a striking neoclassical pink facade, this sumptuous 18th-century palace features a Louis XIV–style interior inspired by the Palace of Versailles. In the basement is a former restaurant from the early 1900s, with an intriguing mix of esoteric symbols and neo-Gothic architecture. Before World War I, it was a casino. Today, it houses a tourist office and a shop selling reproductions from the country's state museums. It is scheduled to reopen for guided tours in mid-2025. ✉ *Praça dos Restauradores, Avenida da Liberdade* ☎ *21/322–1200* Ⓜ *Blue Line to Restauradores.*

★ Parque Eduardo VII

CITY PARK | **FAMILY** | Formerly Parque da Liberdade, this park was renamed in 1903 when England's Edward VII visited Portugal. Its large central promenade has manicured lawns featuring traditional Portuguese cobblestone pavement with geometric designs and views of the city center. The beautifully kept Estufa Fria is a sprawling 1930s greenhouse garden whose various habitats are arranged around a pretty pool. It's a romantic oasis in the middle of the city. ✉ *Praça do Marquês de Pombal, Avenida da Liberdade* *Free for park; €3.50 for Estufa Fria* *Estufa Fria closed Mon.* Ⓜ *Blue Line to Parque or Marquês de Pombal.*

Praça do Marquês de Pombal (*Marquês de Pombal Square*)
PLAZA/SQUARE | Dominating the center of Marquês de Pombal Square is a statue of the marquis himself, the man responsible for the design of the "new" Lisbon that emerged from the ruins of the 1755 earthquake. On the statue's base are representations of both the earthquake and the tidal wave that engulfed the city; a female figure with outstretched arms signifies the joy at the emergence of the refashioned city. The square is effectively a large roundabout and a useful orientation point, since it stands at the northern end of Avenida da Liberdade. ✉ *Praça do Marquês de Pombal, Avenida da Liberdade* Ⓜ *Blue or Yellow Line to Marquês de Pombal.*

Praça dos Restauradores (*Restauradores Square*)
PLAZA/SQUARE | Adjacent to Rossio train station, this square marks the beginning of modern Lisbon. Here the broad tree-lined Avenida da Liberdade starts its northwesterly ascent. *Restauradores* means "restorers," and the square commemorates the 1640 uprising against Spanish rule that restored Portuguese independence. An 1886 obelisk commemorates the event. Note the elegant pink-hued 18th-century Palácio Foz (under renovation into mid-2025) on the square's west side. The only building to rival the palace is the restored Éden building, just to the south. This art deco masterpiece of Portuguese architect Cassiano Branco now contains a hotel. You'll also see the Elevador da Glória, the funicular that travels up to Bairro Alto and its famous viewpoint. ✉ *Praça dos Restauradores, Avenida da Liberdade* Ⓜ *Blue Line to Restauradores.*

Restaurants

A Cevicheria
$$$ | **LATIN AMERICAN** | This trendy spot draws the attention of passersby as much for the number of people drinking at the door as for the gigantic octopus hanging from the ceiling inside. Chef Kiko Martins, who is behind a handful of restaurants in town, was influenced by Peruvian cuisine but incorporates Portuguese and global flavors. **Known for:** creative ceviche; Latin American–inspired

desserts; pisco sours. *Average main: €25 Rua Dom Pedro V 129, Príncipe Real 21/803–8815 www.acevicheria.pt Yellow Line to Rato, Tram 24 to Príncipe Real.*

★ Casa do Alentejo

$ | **PORTUGUESE** | Originally a social club for people hailing from the region of Alentejo, this hidden restaurant is found on the upper floor of a Moorish-style building from the 1800s. There's a formal dining room serving classic northern Portuguese dishes like *carne de porco à alentejana* (pork with clams), and a relaxed terrace specializing in *petiscos* (snacks) and very affordable jugs of house wine. **Known for:** local favorite; beautiful tiled interior courtyard; pleasant outdoor area. *Average main: €15 Rua das Portas de Santo Antão 58, Avenida da Liberdade 21/340–5140 casa-doalentejo.pt Blue Line to Restauradores.*

★ Cervejaria Liberdade

$$$$ | **SEAFOOD** | Lisbon's beer halls tend to be noisy crowded places, but those looking for a more sophisticated atmosphere should head to this upscale eatery with towering murals and handsome wood paneling tucked inside the Tivoli Avenida Liberdade Hotel. You'll find traditional fish or meat dishes on the menu, served with flair by an attentive staff. **Known for:** local oysters; impressive list of local wine and beer; juicy steak in a house-made sauce. *Average main: €32 Tivoli Avenida Liberdade Hotel, Av. da Liberdade 185, Avenida da Liberdade 21/319–8620 www.tivolihotels.com/en/tivoli-avenida-liberdade-lisboa/restaurants Blue Line to Avenida.*

Gin Lovers Bar & Restaurant

$$ | **INTERNATIONAL** | The Moorish-style courtyard of Palacete Ribeiro da Cunha (now the EmbaiXada shopping gallery) was turned into a bar and restaurant. It serves contemporary Portuguese cuisine, as well as lighter snacks such as salads and burgers. **Known for:** variety of gin; huge cocktail list; reasonably priced tasting menu. *Average main: €18 Praça do Príncipe Real 26, Príncipe Real 21/347–1341 ginlovers.pt/bar-restaurant/ Yellow Line to Rato, Tram 24 to Príncipe Real.*

★ JNcQUOI

$$$$ | **INTERNATIONAL** | A room inside the Tivoli Theater, designed in the 1920s, is now this upscale restaurant featuring a classy decor that somehow includes a life-size skeleton of a dinosaur. It's actually a three-in-one (a restaurant, bar, and gourmet store), open throughout the day. **Known for:** international cuisine with classics from Portugal, France, and Italy; French Ladurée desserts; attracts the local elite. *Average main: €40 Av. da Liberdade 182–184,*

Avenida da Liberdade ☎ 21/936–9900 🌐 www.jncquoi.com Ⓜ Blue Line to Avenida.

★ Kabuki Lisboa

$$$$ | **JAPANESE** | Japan meets the Mediterranean at this Michelin-starred restaurant behind the Four Seasons Hotel. Despite the title, the food is relatively affordable, more so at lunchtime when business folks take over the tables on the top floor. **Known for:** bento boxes; dishes with toro (fatty tuna); vegan degustation menu. *Ⓢ Average main: €50 ✉ Rua Castilho 77B, Avenida da Liberdade ☎ 21/249–1683 🌐 www.kabukilisboa.pt ⊙ Closed Sun. and Mon. No lunch Sat. Ⓜ Blue or Yellow Line to Marquês de Pombal.*

K.O.B.

$$$$ | **STEAK HOUSE** | Local celebrity restaurateur Olivier has several spots in town, and this one is all about meat. The name is an acronym for "Knowledge of Beef," and there are cuts from different origins, from Portugal to Argentina. **Known for:** Black Angus dishes; long list of Portuguese wines; classic and original cocktails. *Ⓢ Average main: €40 ✉ Rua do Salitre 169, Avenida da Liberdade ☎ 93/400–0949 🌐 restaurantesolivier.com/en/kob Ⓜ Yellow Line to Rato.*

O Churrasco

$ | **PORTUGUESE** | **FAMILY** | On a street lined with tourist traps, O Churrasco is a local favorite and deservedly so. The paneled dining room serves top-notch piri-piri chicken, sizzling steaks, and perfectly grilled fish. **Known for:** ideal location near all of the major sights; scattering of tables on the street; house-made desserts. *Ⓢ Average main: €14 ✉ Rua das Portas de Santo Antão 83–85, Lisbon ☎ 21/342–3059 🌐 restauranteochurrasco.business.site Ⓜ Blue Line to Restauradores, Green Line to Rossio.*

Os Tibetanos

$ | **VEGETARIAN** | Delicious meat-free dishes (think mango-and-tofu curry, seitan steak, and spinach-filled Tibetan momo dumplings) ensure that there's always a line for a table in this restaurant's extremely colorful dining room or on the pleasant patio. It's part of a Buddhist center where a small shop stocks books, incense, homeopathic medicines, and other products, and yoga and meditation classes take place upstairs. **Known for:** serving vegan food since before it was trendy in Lisbon; good-value lunch menu; casual atmosphere. *Ⓢ Average main: €12 ✉ Rua do Salitre 117, Avenida da Liberdade ☎ 21/314–2038 🌐 www.facebook.com/OsTibetanosRestaurante 💳 No credit cards Ⓜ Blue Line to Avenida.*

★ Pinóquio

$$$$ | SEAFOOD | Although it's quite spacious and comfortable inside, most people choose to sit at one of this restaurant's many tables outside facing Praça dos Restauradores. Waiters rush from table to table, mostly serving super fresh seafood and grilled fish and meats. **Known for:** friendly and professional staff; rich fish and seafood stews; outdoor seating overlooking Praça dos Restauradores. *Average main: €28* *Praça dos Restauradores 79–80, Restauradores* *21/346–5106* *www.restaurantepinoquio.pt* *Blue Line to Restauradores.*

Ribadouro

$$$ | SEAFOOD | What you see is what you get at Ribadouro, one of Lisbon's best-known seafood spots: take your pick of the lobster, mantis shrimp, tiger shrimp, whelks, oysters, and clams on display and the staff will create a seafood platter to your specifications. You can dine inside or at tree-shaded tables and chairs set out at a kiosk on the Avenida, opposite the main restaurant. **Known for:** crowds on evenings and weekends; seafood and grilled steaks; late-night dinners. *Average main: €25* *Av. da Liberdade 155, Avenida da Liberdade* *21/354–9411* *www.cervejariaribadouro.pt* *Blue Line to Avenida.*

★ Sítio Valverde

$$$ | PORTUGUESE | This restaurant facing the courtyard of the Hotel Valverde focuses on contemporary Portuguese cuisine reinterpreted by the chef. Its weekly lunch menu is popular among locals who work nearby and those looking for a more intimate spot. **Known for:** different menus for different times of the day; sophisticated vintage decor; signature cocktails. *Average main: €25* *Hotel Valverde, Av. da Liberdade 164, Avenida da Liberdade* *21/094–0310* *www.valverdehotel.com/restaurante.html* *Blue Line to Avenida.*

★ Solar dos Presuntos

$$$ | PORTUGUESE | Framed photographs of celebrities who've visited (from singer Adele to soccer star Cristiano Ronaldo) cover every inch of the walls at this bustling eatery. In business since 1947, it's known for the dry-cured ham that gave the place its name, but there are also many meat and seafood dishes on the menu. **Known for:** authentic dishes from the Minho region; lobster rice and other seafood standouts; terrace for petiscos and drinks. *Average main: €25* *Rua das Portas de Santo Antão 150, Avenida da Liberdade* *21/342–4253* *solardospresuntos.com* *Closed Sun.* *Blue Line to Restauradores.*

Tapisco

$$ | **PORTUGUESE** | This restaurant is a gastronomic trip through Portugal and Spain, serving traditional Iberian specialties with the touch of local celebrity chef Henrique Sá Pessoa. Dishes are beautifully presented and meant to be shared in a relaxing and informal environment. **Known for:** Iberian hams; modern riffs on traditional dishes; vermouth cocktails. *Average main: €20 Rua Dom Pedro V 81, Príncipe Real 21/342–0681 tapisco.pt Yellow Line to Rato, Tram 24 to Príncipe Real.*

2Monkeys

$$$$ | **INTERNATIONAL** | Chef Vitor Matos has managed restaurants all over the country, but this is his first venture in the capital to win a Michelin star. Here he is joined by Francisco Quintas, the young chef who welcomes you at the 14-seat counter facing the kitchen. **Known for:** Portuguese wine pairings; various types of caviar; delicious braised fish. *Average main: €100 Torel Palace Lisbon, Rua Câmara Pestana 45, Avenida da Liberdade 21/826–2927 2monkeys.com.pt Closed Sun. and Mon. Blue Line to Restauradores.*

Varanda

$$$$ | **PORTUGUESE** | One of several notable restaurants at the Four Seasons Hotel Ritz, Varanda is consistently at the top of its game. There's a seasonally changing tasting menu at dinner and a wide range of à la carte dishes throughout the day. **Known for:** Lisbon's best weekend brunch buffet; stellar views of Parque Eduardo VII; desserts from in-house pastry chef. *Average main: €50 Four Seasons Hotel Ritz, Rua Rodrigo da Fonseca 88, Avenida da Liberdade 21/381–1400 www.fourseasons.com/lisbon/dining Blue or Yellow Line to Marquês de Pombal.*

Coffee and Quick Bites

Bettina Corallo Chocolate Cafe

$ | **CAFÉ** | Coffee addicts and chocolate lovers stop at this small store across from the Jardim do Príncipe Real, drawn by the scent of the beans that arrive straight from a family plantation in the former Portuguese colony of São Tomé and Príncipe in Africa. **Known for:** chocolate sorbets; variety of coffee; 100% cocoa bars. *Average main: €4 Rua da Escola Politécnica 4, Príncipe Real 21/386–2158 bettinacorallo.com Closed Sun. Yellow Line to Rato, Tram 24 to Príncipe Real.*

Copenhagen Coffee Lab

$ | **INTERNATIONAL** | The roasted coffee beans come from Copenhagen, as did the inspiration for the minimalist decor. The Coffee Lab has become a favorite, both for the different types on the menu and the welcoming and relaxed atmosphere. **Known for:** filter coffees; breakfast plates; Danish pastries. Ⓢ *Average main: €7* ✉ *Rua Nova da Piedade 10, Príncipe Real* ☎ *21/604–7980* 🌐 *copenhagencoffeelab.com* Ⓜ *Yellow Line to Rato.*

Delta Q

$ | **INTERNATIONAL** | The flagship store of this Portuguese coffee brand faces Avenida da Liberdade and offers more than just its coffee. Come here for a light meal, brunch, or a cocktail in the wood-clad interior or at the tables outside. **Known for:** freshly brewed coffee; reasonably priced menus; refreshing teas. Ⓢ *Average main: €10* ✉ *Av. da Liberdade 144–156, Avenida da Liberdade* ☎ *21/342–7351* 🌐 *deltacoffeehouse.com* Ⓜ *Blue Line to Avenida.*

Doce Real

$ | **PORTUGUESE** | This tiny corner café might not look like much, but step inside, and you'll find a stunning art nouveau interior with tiled facades and marble tables. It specializes in *salgados* (savory treats), but it also has a few sweet options, like the ubiquitous *pastéis de nata* (custard tarts). **Known for:** handmade pies; historic interior; affordable lunch deals. Ⓢ *Average main: €6* ✉ *Rua Dom Pedro V 119, Príncipe Real* ☎ *21/346–5923* ⊙ *Closed Sun.* Ⓜ *Yellow Line to Rato.*

Fábrica Coffee Roasters

$ | **CAFÉ** | Hidden just a few feet from the Elevador do Lavra, this was one of the first places in the city to offer specialty coffee, roasted and ground on the premises. Sandwiches and pastries are also available. **Known for:** inviting terrace; industrial and vintage-style interior; coffee merch and beans. Ⓢ *Average main: €4* ✉ *Rua das Portas de Santo Antão 136, Avenida da Liberdade* ☎ *21/139–9261* 🌐 *fabricacoffeeroasters.com* Ⓜ *Blue Line to Avenida.*

★ Lost In

$$ | **INTERNATIONAL** | A curious Indian-inspired decor welcomes you to this café/bar/restaurant, but your attention immediately goes to the view of Avenida da Liberdade. Despite the decor, the menu lists international dishes. **Known for:** colorful terrace; diverse Sunday brunch; large selection of petiscos. Ⓢ *Average main: €18* ✉ *Rua Dom Pedro V 56D, Príncipe Real* ☎ *91/775–9282* 🌐 *lostinrestaurante.com* ⊙ *No lunch Mon.–Wed.* Ⓜ *Yellow Line to Rato, Tram 24 to Príncipe Real.*

Nannarella

$ | **ICE CREAM** | **FAMILY** | An Italian family opened this small ice-cream shop around the corner from the Parliament building (and just a short walk from the Jardim do Príncipe Real), and it immediately drew locals who don't mind waiting in line to try the variety of flavors. They're served in a cup or cone, with or without whipped cream on top. **Known for:** Sicilian cannoli; ice-cream cakes; flavors that change daily. *Average main: €5 Rua Nova da Piedade 64, Príncipe Real 92/687–8553 www.nannarella.pt Tram 28 to Rua de São Bento/Calçada da Estrela.*

 Hotels

★ Altis Avenida Hotel

$$$$ | **HOTEL** | Occupying an elegant art deco building that has been classified as a historic landmark, the monumental Altis Avenida offers glamour and luxury in a central location that makes it ideal for sightseeing. **Pros:** upstairs eatery serves delicious small plates; sunny rooftop terrace; pleasant staff and excellent service. **Cons:** some rooms are rather small; no on-site swimming pool; can be pricey. *Rooms from: €280 Rua 1° de Dezembro 120, Restauradores 21/044–0000 www.altishotels.com/altis-avenida-hotel/ 118 rooms Free Breakfast Blue Line to Restauradores.*

★ Altis Grand Hotel

$$$ | **HOTEL** | This upscale lodging is every bit as refined and stately as you'd expect, from the welcoming lounge in the lobby area to the lively rooftop terrace bar where you can gaze out over the city. **Pros:** impeccable service; large spa area with heated pool; lavish buffet breakfast. **Cons:** dark fitness center; some lower-floor rooms lack views; location is not particularly scenic. *Rooms from: €240 Rua Castilho 11, Marquês de Pombal 21/310–6000 www.altishotels.com/altis-grand-hotel/ 295 rooms Free Breakfast Blue or Yellow Line to Marquês de Pombal.*

Avenida Palace

$$$$ | **HOTEL** | Built in 1892, the city's first luxury hotel combines regal elegance, modern comforts, and a romantic Belle Époque style. **Pros:** British-inspired bar serves delicious cocktails; suites decorated to reflect historic period; regal lobby. **Cons:** formal atmosphere; no restaurant on the premises; no swimming pool. *Rooms from: €280 Rua 1° de Dezembro 123, Restauradores 21/321–8100 www.hotelavenidapalace.pt 82 rooms Free Breakfast Blue Line to Restauradores.*

Casa de São Mamede

$ | **HOTEL** | **FAMILY** | One of the first private houses to be built in Lisbon after the 18th-century earthquake, Casa de São Mamede has been transformed into a relaxed boutique guesthouse endowed with a tiled dining room, a grand staircase, and stained-glass windows. **Pros:** 10-minute walk from Bairro Alto; affordable room rate includes generous breakfast; family-friendly vibe. **Cons:** a little staid; no pool or fitness facilities; no parking available. *Rooms from: €105* *Rua da Escola Politécnica 159, Rato* *21/396–3166* *www.casadesaomamede.pt* *26 rooms* *Free Breakfast* *Yellow Line to Rato.*

Dom Pedro Lisboa

$$ | **HOTEL** | The guest rooms at this gleaming five-star high-rise are decked out with the kind of stately wooden desks and ornate drapes that appeal to the prosperous business executives who make up a big part of the clientele. **Pros:** upper floors have expansive views; spa has indoor pool, sauna, hot tub, and treatment rooms; cheaper than other luxury hotels. **Cons:** 15-minute walk to subway station; dated decor; extra charge for breakfast. *Rooms from: €180* *Av. Engenheiro Duarte Pacheco 24, Amoreiras* *21/389–6600* *lisboa.dompedro.com* *263 rooms* *No Meals* *Yellow Line to Rato.*

EPIC SANA Lisboa

$$$ | **HOTEL** | **FAMILY** | With a heated infinity pool on the rooftop, an indoor pool in the enormous spa, and a well-equipped fitness center that looks out onto a beautiful botanical garden, this slick hotel draws an active crowd. **Pros:** great rooftop pool; good location for shopping; Sunday brunch buffet. **Cons:** far from most of the city's sights; some rooms a little cramped; lacks local flavor. *Rooms from: €255* *Av. Engenheiro Duarte Pacheco 15, Marquês de Pombal* *21/246–8688* *www.sanahotels.com/hotel/epic-sana-lisboa* *311 rooms* *Free Breakfast* *Blue or Yellow Line to Marquês de Pombal.*

★ **Four Seasons Hotel Ritz Lisbon**

$$$$ | **HOTEL** | **FAMILY** | The feeling of luxury starts the minute you step into the Four Seasons Hotel Ritz Lisbon's marbled reception area and continues through to the lounge, whose terrace overlooks one of the city's prettiest parks. **Pros:** rooftop gym and full-size running track; stunning spa; outstanding restaurants on-site including Michelin-starred CURA. **Cons:** some of the most expensive rooms in Lisbon; extra charge for breakfast; decor may feel stuffy. *Rooms from: €1,050* *Rua Rodrigo da Fonseca 88, Marquês de Pombal* *21/381–1400* *www.fourseasons.*

com/lisbon 282 rooms No Meals Blue or Yellow Line to Marquês de Pombal.*

★ **Hotel Britania Art Deco**

$$$$ | **HOTEL** | Impeccable service and historic design details are the key selling points of this well-located hotel. **Pros:** complimentary afternoon tea; courteous and friendly staff; plenty of architectural flourishes. **Cons:** most rooms lack views; missing amenities like a gym; no on-site restaurant. *Rooms from: €306 Rua Rodrigues Sampaio 17, Avenida da Liberdade 21/315–5016 lisbonheritagehotels.com/hotel-britania 33 rooms Free Breakfast Blue Line to Avenida.*

★ **Hotel Heritage Avenida Liberdade**

$$$ | **HOTEL** | With an excellent location on the Avenida da Liberdade, this style-conscious boutique hotel is located in an 18th-century town house styled by the Portuguese architect Miguel Câncio Martins. **Pros:** inviting common areas; excellent location for sightseeing; bright and sunny rooms with good soundproofing. **Cons:** some rooms lack views; small indoor swimming pool; design details won't appeal to everybody. *Rooms from: €220 Av. da Liberdade 28, Avenida da Liberdade 21/340–4040 lisbonheritagehotels.com/heritage-avenida-liberdade-hotel 42 rooms Free Breakfast Blue Line to Restauradores.*

Hotel Lisboa Plaza

$$ | **HOTEL** | **FAMILY** | Just a few steps from stylish Avenida da Liberdade, Hotel Lisboa Plaza recalls the glamour of Lisbon in the 1950s. **Pros:** lots of nice extras like free decanter of port in suites; large and relaxing common areas; excellent location. **Cons:** many rooms lack views; some rooms are small; design won't appeal to all tastes. *Rooms from: €160 Travessa do Salitre 7, Avenida da Liberdade 21/321–8218 lisbonheritagehotels.com/lisbon-plaza-hotel 112 rooms No Meals Blue Line to Avenida.*

Hotel SANA Capitol

$ | **HOTEL** | **FAMILY** | Facing a quiet backstreet near Praça do Marquês de Pombal, SANA Capitol offers a central location, lots of creature comforts, and high-tech touches. **Pros:** great value; modern attractive decor; good breakfast. **Cons:** lacks a gym and other usual amenities; paid parking; restaurant only serves breakfast. *Rooms from: €135 Rua Eça de Queiroz 24, Marquês de Pombal 21/353–6811 www.sanahotels.com/en/hotel/sana-capitol 59 rooms Free Breakfast Blue or Yellow Line to Marquês de Pombal.*

InterContinental Lisboa

$$$$ | **HOTEL** | Business travelers and vacationers like this upscale hotel's location near Parque Eduardo VII, as well as its smartly renovated rooms with plush furnishings and the latest tech amenities. **Pros:** high-end fixtures and fittings; pet-friendly; excellent service. **Cons:** not the best location for most of the city's sights; can be busy with business convention visitors; chain-hotel feel. *Rooms from: €270 Rua Castilho 149, Marquês de Pombal 21/381–8700 www.iclisbonhotel.com 331 rooms No Meals Blue or Yellow Line to Marquês de Pombal.*

Sofitel Lisbon Liberdade

$$$$ | **HOTEL** | Facing bustling Avenida da Liberdade, the opulent Sofitel has comfortably appointed rooms decorated in sophisticated variations of black, white, and gold and outfitted with high-tech touches. **Pros:** spacious rooms; walking distance to many major sites; luxurious feel. **Cons:** very pricey; small gym; a little impersonal. *Rooms from: €400 Av. da Liberdade 127, Avenida da Liberdade 21/322–8300 www.sofitel-lisbon-liberdade.com 163 rooms No Meals Blue Line to Avenida.*

Tivoli Avenida Liberdade Lisboa

$$$$ | **HOTEL** | There's enough marble in the public areas of this grande dame to make you fear for the future supply of the stone, but the grandness gives way to comfort in the rooms, which are characterized by stylish dark wood and plush furnishings. **Pros:** relaxing leafy garden; top-notch spa and outdoor swimming pool; outstanding rooftop views. **Cons:** rooftop bar and restaurant often packed; some decor is a bit basic; impersonal feel. *Rooms from: €445 Av. da Liberdade 185, Avenida da Liberdade 21/319–8900 www.tivolihotels.com/en/tivoli-avenida-liberdade-lisboa 285 rooms No Meals Blue Line to Avenida.*

★ **Valverde Lisboa Hotel & Garden**

$$$$ | **HOTEL** | In a handsome 19th-century town house on Lisbon's grandest boulevard, Valverde exudes a sense of understated luxury. **Pros:** unbeatable location; pool and leafy garden; even the mini rooms are spacious. **Cons:** pricey; awkward TV placement; busy area. *Rooms from: €300 Av. da Liberdade 164, Avenida da Liberdade 21/094–0300 www.valverdehotel.com 48 rooms Free Breakfast Blue Line to Avenida.*

★ **The Vintage Lisbon**

$$$$ | **HOTEL** | The discreet entrance to The Vintage Lisbon hotel and spa masks a wealth of chic treats inside, from a luxurious spa to a rooftop bar and even complimentary in-room gin and tonic trays. **Pros:** leafy rooftop bar; lovely spa with pool and gym;

fabulous mid-century modern design. **Cons:** it's not cheap; a bit far from major sights; some street noise at night. *Rooms from: €290* *Rua Rodrigo da Fonseca 2, Príncipe Real* *21/040–5400* *www.thevintagelisbon.com* *56 rooms* *Free Breakfast* *Yellow Line to Rato.*

Nightlife

BARS

Ático

BARS | From this bar on the rooftop of the NH Collection Lisboa Liberdade Hotel you can look over Avenida da Liberdade and see the castle at the top of the hill. It's found next to a pool that's open to everyone (for a fee, if you're not staying at the hotel), and on warmer days it attracts a mix of locals and hotel guests enjoying cocktails with the views. *Av. da Liberdade 180B, Avenida da Liberdade* *21/351–4060* *www.nh-hotels.com/en/hotels/lisbon* *Closed Nov.–Mar.* *Blue Line to Avenida.*

★ CINCO Lounge

COCKTAIL BARS | With moody lighting, rococo furnishings, and creations that look (almost) too good to drink, this spot is frequently cited as Lisbon's best cocktail bar. It's an intimate space, so book in advance. CINCO Lounge also runs cocktail workshops for those who want to learn how to shake and stir their own boozy showstoppers at home. *Rua Ruben a Leitão 17A, Príncipe Real* *21/342–4033* *www.cincolounge.com* *Yellow Line to Rato.*

Foxtrot

COCKTAIL BARS | In business since the 1970s, this bar feels like it could have opened in the early 20th century thanks to the art deco interior. Inspired by English pubs and Prohibition-era speakeasies, you must ring a bell to enter the dimly lit rooms. There's a cozy fireplace for chilly evenings and a pleasant open-air patio for warmer nights. In addition to a long list of creative cocktails, Foxtrot serves small bites and larger plates, perfect for late-night snacking. *Travessa Santa Teresa 28, Príncipe Real* *21/395–2697* *www.barfoxtrot.pt* *Closed Sun.* *Yellow Line to Rato, Tram 28 to Calçada da Estrela.*

Monkey Mash

COCKTAIL BARS | Cited as one of the world's 50 best cocktail bars, Monkey Mash is a playful younger brother bar to the sophisticated celebrated Red Frog speakeasy (housed behind a secret door inside Monkey Mash). Although the decor and atmosphere here are more flamboyant and tropical than Red Frog, the fruit-forward designer cocktails—many of which feature sugarcane rum—are prepared with every bit as much care and attention. ✉ *Praça da Alegria 66B, Avenida da Liberdade* ☎ *21/136–4241* 🌐 *www.monkeymash.pt* ⏲ *Closed Sun. and Mon.* Ⓜ *Blue Line to Avenida.*

★ Pavilhão Chinês

BARS | For a quiet drink in an intriguing setting, you can't beat this speakeasy-style lounge. Its five rooms are filled to the brim with fascinating junk collected over the years—from old toys to miniature statues—and it has two snooker tables where locals just might challenge you to a game. Cocktails and service are spot-on, and you may be reluctant to leave once you've settled into one of the comfy chairs. ✉ *Rua Dom Pedro V 89, Príncipe Real* ☎ *21/342–4729* Ⓜ *Yellow Line to Rato.*

★ Red Frog

COCKTAIL BARS | Reservations are essential at this intimate speakeasy bar, which is famed for its inventive cocktails and its air of secrecy. Post-pandemic, Red Frog made the puddle jump from its previous spot on Rua do Salitre to a new home within the confines of hipster hangout Monkey Mash (they're both under the same ownership). Alongside inventive small plates for sharing, the signature drink is the Spiced Rusty Cherry, ranked among the best cocktails in the world. ✉ *Monkey Mash, Praça da Alegria 66B, Avenida da Liberdade* ☎ *21/583–1120* 🌐 *www.redfrog.pt* ⏲ *Closed Sun. and Mon.* Ⓜ *Blue Line to Avenida.*

★ Sky Bar by SEEN

COCKTAIL BARS | The largest rooftop bar in town sits at the top of the Tivoli Avenida Liberdade Hotel. It looks over Avenida da Liberdade and the castle and serves predinner drinks and late-night cocktails to a mix of locals and hotel guests. ✉ *Tivoli Avenida Liberdade Hotel, Av. da Liberdade 185, 9th fl., Avenida da Liberdade* ☎ *21/096–5775* 🌐 *www.skybarrooftop.com* ⏲ *Closed Nov.–Mar.* Ⓜ *Blue Line to Avenida.*

LGBTQ+ CLUBS

★ Finalmente Club

DANCE CLUB | Open since 1976, the city's oldest gay club remains a popular hangout, thanks in no small part to the wonderfully flamboyant drag shows. The biggest star is Deborah Kristall, who regularly calls on audience members to join in the onstage singing and dancing. In addition to its famously packed dance floor, the club now has a restaurant and table service. Book in advance if you want to catch the show. ✉ *Rua da Palmeira 38, Príncipe Real* ☎ *21/347–9923* 🌐 *www.finalmenteclub.com* Ⓜ *Yellow Line to Rato.*

★ Trumps

DANCE CLUB | One of Lisbon's most iconic gay clubs, Trumps has attracted the city's trendiest crowds since it opened in the early 1980s. Two separate dance floors pack with partiers dancing to everything from reggaeton and Brazilian funk to pop hits, EDM, and house. ✉ *Rua da Imprensa Nacional 104B, Príncipe Real* ☎ *91/593–8266* 🌐 *trumps.pt* Ⓜ *Yellow Line to Rato.*

MUSIC CLUBS

★ Hot Clube de Portugal

LIVE MUSIC | Europe's oldest jazz club started in a tiny basement in 1948, and all these decades later Hot Clube de Portugal remains the place for live jazz performances. It features local and international acts and has almost daily performances. ✉ *Praça da Alegria 48, Avenida da Liberdade* ☎ *21/361–9740* 🌐 *hcp.pt* Ⓜ *Blue Line to Avenida.*

Shopping

ANTIQUES

Solar Antiques

ANTIQUES & COLLECTIBLES | One of Lisbon's best-known antiques shops, Solar specializes in azulejo panels and also stocks 16th- to 18th-century Portuguese furnishings and paintings, many of them salvaged from old mansions, churches, and palaces. ✉ *Rua Dom Pedro V 68–70, Príncipe Real* ☎ *21/346–5522* 🌐 *www.solar.com.pt* ⏲ *Closed Sun.; Closed Sat. in July and Aug.* Ⓜ *Yellow Line to Rato.*

CLOTHING

Fashion Clinic

CLOTHING | Dozens of luxury labels (from Christian Louboutin to Stella McCartney to YSL) are represented at this store, which caters to the city's fashionable elite. In addition to chic clothing and accessories, there's a stylish bar and restaurant. ✉ *Tivoli Forum, Av. da Liberdade 180, Avenida da Liberdade* ☎ *96/669–2066* 🌐 *www.fashionclinic.com* Ⓜ *Blue Line to Avenida.*

JEWELRY

Maria João Bahia

JEWELRY & WATCHES | Designer Maria João Bahia has been creating jewelry since 1985; after two successful decades, she opened this store, where she presents her exclusive jewels together with silverware, crystals, and handbags. ✉ *Av. da Liberdade 102, Avenida da Liberdade* ☎ *21/324–0018* 🌐 *mariajoaobahia.com* ⏲ *Closed Sun.* Ⓜ *Blue Line to Avenida.*

SHOES AND ACCESSORIES

Luis Onofre

SHOES | Famous women like Michelle Obama, Naomi Watts, and Paris Hilton have worn Portuguese designer Luis Onofre's shoes, and here you can try on his latest creations. Next to the luxurious footwear that he now mostly exports worldwide are his collections of bags and clutches. ✉ *Av. da Liberdade 247, Avenida da Liberdade* ☎ *21/131–3629* 🌐 *luisonofre.com* 🕓 *Closed Sun.* Ⓜ *Blue or Yellow Line to Marquês de Pombal.*

SHOPPING CENTERS

★ EmbaiXada

SHOPPING CENTER | Shopping doesn't get any more stylish than at this grand 18th-century mansion, which has been transformed into a gallery showcasing some of the best of Portuguese design and even a few international brands. The restaurant-bar in the inner Moorish-style courtyard is an attractive place for a meal or a gin drink. Head here on Sunday evenings when the gallery hosts alternative fado concerts hosted by Real Fado (🌐 *www.realfadoconcerts.com*). ✉ *Praça do Príncipe Real 26, Príncipe Real* ☎ *96/530–9154* 🌐 *embaixadalx.pt* Ⓜ *Yellow Line to Rato.*

Performing Arts

Cinema São Jorge

FILM | This movie theater from 1950 is now the stage for most of the city's annual film festivals. A renovation in 2001 kept the original interior and facade and brought its three screening rooms back into operation. The popular independent film festival IndieLisboa happens here in the spring; the gay and lesbian film festival Queer Lisboa is every September; and documentary, Italian, and French film festivals are scheduled at other times throughout the year. From its balcony on the top floor you have a view of Avenida da Liberdade's famous pavement designs. ✉ *Av. da Liberdade 175, Avenida da Liberdade* ☎ *21/310–3400* 🌐 *www.cinemasaojorge.pt* Ⓜ *Blue Line to Avenida.*

Coliseu dos Recreios

PERFORMANCE VENUES | Constructed in 1890, this circular concert hall is a Lisbon cultural landmark. The great acoustics have made it one of the city's most important venues for performances ranging from classical music to rock. The smaller Sala hosts more intimate events like stand-up comedy. ✉ *Rua das Portas de Santo Antão 96, Restauradores* ☎ *21/324–0585* 🌐 *www.coliseulisboa.com* Ⓜ *Blue Line to Restauradores.*

Chapter 6

ALFAMA, GRAÇA, AND SÃO VICENTE

Updated by
Joana Taborda

Sights ★★★★★ Restaurants ★★★★★ Hotels ★★★☆☆ Shopping ★★☆☆☆ Nightlife ★★☆☆☆

NEIGHBORHOOD SNAPSHOT

TOP EXPERIENCES

■ **Listen to fado.** As the birthplace of fado, Alfama is the perfect spot to catch live performances.

■ **Sé de Lisboa.** Get a glimpse of medieval Lisbon by visiting the city's oldest cathedral.

■ **Party with the locals.** Visit around June and you'll find crowds of locals and tourists seeking out plates of grilled sardines and dancing the night away to pimba, a popular music style famous for its cheeky innuendos.

GETTING HERE

Alfama is a relatively easy walk from Praça do Comércio and other major sites. The famous Tram 28 runs right through the heart of it, but the area can also be accessed by taking the metro to Terreiro do Paço or Santa Apolónia or via the 734 bus.

You can access Graça and São Vicente via the Santa Apolónia or the Martim Moniz metro stations. A 5-minute walk from Martim Moniz is the Rua dos Lagares, where you can catch a funicular straight to the Miradouro da Graça. You can also reach this hilltop neighborhood by taking Trams 12 and 28 or Buses 712 and 734.

PLANNING YOUR TIME

Get to Alfama early in the morning to avoid the big tourist groups and wander the maze of streets on your own. Head to Graça around sunset and join the locals at one of the neighborhood viewpoints.

VIEWFINDER

■ **Alfama's miradouros.** Alfama is an Instagrammer's dream, between the colorful azulejos that adorn the historic homes and the many *miradouros* that give postcard-perfect views of the city and the river below. Miradouro de Santa Luzia and the Miradouro das Portas do Sol are excellent spots to relax with a coffee or a glass of wine while snapping your photos. ✉ *Largo de Santa Luzia / Largo das Portas do Sol* 🚊 *Tram 12 and 28.*

PAUSE HERE

■ **Teatro de Garagem.** There are also fantastic vistas from the casual café of the Teatro da Garagem. Once a pre- and post-theater hangout, it's now become an Instagrammer's delight, with postcard-perfect views of the city center. ✉ *Costa do Castelo 75* 🚊 *Tram 12 to R. Lagares.*

History unfolds with each step you take here as you witness the city's oldest monuments, its soulful music, and unforgettable sunsets from its numerous hilltop viewpoints.

Alfama is the oldest part of the city, and it remains a charming warren of narrow streets and alleyways. The neighborhood miraculously survived the devastating earthquake of 1755 that destroyed much of Lisbon, so its historic architecture is largely intact. Indeed, you'll find remains here that go as far back as the Roman era, when the city was known as Olisipo. The Romans established themselves here in 138 BC and stayed for seven centuries until the Moors took their place, setting up the walls of the Castelo de São Jorge that still surveils the city today. When Afonso Henriques, Portugal's first king, and his crusaders reclaimed the city in 1147, it was this castle they went for first, creating the foundations of what would become the kingdom's capital.

It's no surprise then that Alfama has become one of the city's most visited neighborhoods. It's a capsule of Lisbon's history and culture, where you'll find iconic landmarks like the 12th-century Sé Catedral, hear singers pour their hearts out in traditional fado houses, and sip shots of *ginjinha* (sour cherry liqueur) at a local's doorstep.

Venture further up the hill, and you'll end up in Graça and São Vicente. Monks and nuns have paraded the streets of these neighborhoods since the 13th century, when the first convent emerged here, though only a few stand today. After the earthquake, this area transformed into an industrial hub, as folks left the countryside to set up shop here and help build the city's railway line. These days, the Santa Apolónia station is a jumping-off point for anyone looking to explore Lisbon's east side.

Many people hop on the historic Tram 28 to traverse Alfama and Graça in one go, but it's worth getting on your own two feet to uncover its monuments, hidden bars, and breathtaking miradouros. Given its perch higher up the hill from Alfama, Graça has more lookouts with dramatic sunset views over the city. Catching this daily phenomenon is a must-do while in Lisbon, as crowds gather around for a shot of the city's cotton-candy skies over a glass of wine or beer—the typical precursor to dinner and a night out.

Alfama

Sights

Casa dos Bicos (*House of Spikes*)

HISTORIC HOME | This Italianate dwelling is one of Alfama's most distinctive buildings. It was built in 1523 for Brás de Albuquerque, the son of Afonso, who became the viceroy of India and conquered Goa and Malacca. The name translates as "House of Spikes," and it's not hard to see why—it has a striking facade studded with pointed white stones in diamond shapes. The building now houses the José Saramago Foundation, a cultural institute memorializing the only Portuguese-language winner of the Nobel Prize in Literature. ✉ *Rua dos Bacalhoeiros 10, Alfama* ☎ *21/099–3811* 🌐 *www.museudelisboa.pt/en/sites/casa-dos-bicos* 🎫 *€3* ⏲ *Closed Sun.* ☞ *Free access to the archaeological ruins on the ground floor* Ⓜ *Blue Line to Terreiro do Paço.*

★ **Castelo de São Jorge** (*St. George's Castle*)

CASTLE/PALACE | **FAMILY** | Although St. George's Castle was constructed by the Moors, the site had previously been fortified by Romans and Visigoths. To your left as you pass through the main entrance is a statue of Dom Afonso Henriques, whose forces in 1147 besieged the castle and drove the Moors from Lisbon. A residence of the kings of Portugal until the 16th century, the palace remnants now house a small museum showcasing archaeological finds. Beyond the keep, traces of pre-Roman and Moorish houses are visible thanks to recent archaeological digs, as well as the remains of a palace founded in the 15th century. The castle's outer walls encompass a small neighborhood (Castelo) and the medieval church of Santa Cruz (with its lookout tower). ✉ *Rua de Santa Cruz do Castelo, Castelo* ☎ *21/880–0620* 🌐 *castelodesaojorge.pt* 🎫 *€15* Ⓜ *Tram 12 and 28 to Miradouro de Santa Luzia, Bus 737 to Castelo.*

Igreja de Santo António

CHURCH | This church, constructed in 1767, sits on the site where Lisbon's patron saint was born. Although it's fairly compact, the interior is stunning, with ornately painted walls, abundant natural light, and stone carvings. The altarpiece representing Saint Anthony on the side of the nave's gospel is thought to be from the 16th century, and locals still come to express their devotion. ✉ *Largo de Santo António da Sé, Alfama* ☎ *21/886–9145* 🌐 *stoantoniolisboa.com* Ⓜ *Blue Line to Terreiro do Paço.*

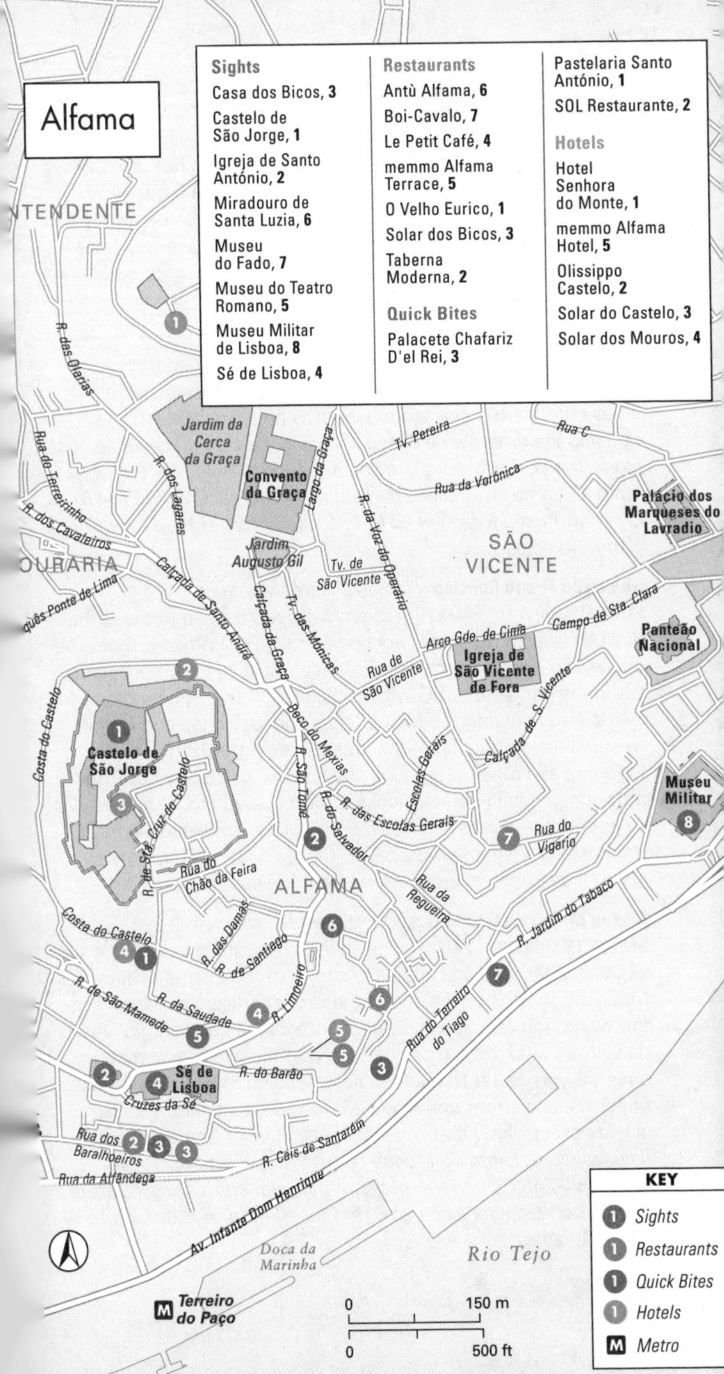
Alfama
Sights
Casa dos Bicos, 3
Castelo de São Jorge, 1
Igreja de Santo António, 2
Miradouro de Santa Luzia, 6
Museu do Fado, 7
Museu do Teatro Romano, 5
Museu Militar de Lisboa, 8
Sé de Lisboa, 4
Restaurants
Antù Alfama, 6
Boi-Cavalo, 7
Le Petit Café, 4
memmo Alfama Terrace, 5
O Velho Eurico, 1
Solar dos Bicos, 3
Taberna Moderna, 2
Quick Bites
Palacete Chafariz D'el Rei, 3
Pastelaria Santo António, 1
SOL Restaurante, 2
Hotels
Hotel Senhora do Monte, 1
memmo Alfama Hotel, 5
Olissippo Castelo, 2
Solar do Castelo, 3
Solar dos Mouros, 4
INTENDENTE
MOURARIA
SÃO VICENTE
ALFAMA
Jardim da Cerca da Graça
Convento da Graça
Jardim Augusto Gil
Palácio dos Marqueses do Lavradio
Panteão Nacional
Igreja de São Vicente de Fora
Castelo de São Jorge
Museu Militar
Sé de Lisboa
R. das Olarias
Rua do Terreirinho
R. dos Cavaleiros
R. dos Lagares
Calçada de Santo André
Largo da Graça
Calçada da Graça
Tv. das Mónicas
Tv. de São Vicente
R. da Voz do Operário
Tv. Pereira
Rua C
Rua da Verónica
Campo de Sta. Clara
Arco Gde. de Cima
Rua de São Vicente
Calçada de S. Vicente
Escolas Gerais
Beco do Mexias
R. São Tomé
R. do Salvador
R. das Escolas Gerais
Rua do Vigario
Rua da Regueira
R. Jardim do Tabaco
Costa do Castelo
R. de Sta. Cruz do Castelo
Rua do Chão da Feira
R. das Damas
R. de Santiago
R. Limoeiro
R. de São Mamede
R. da Saudade
R. do Barão
Cruzes da Sé
Rua dos Baralhoeiros
Rua da Alfândega
R. Cais de Santarém
Rua do Terreiro do Tiago
Av. Infante Dom Henrique
Doca da Marinha
Rio Tejo
Terreiro do Paço
0 150 m
0 500 ft
KEY
Sights
Restaurants
Quick Bites
Hotels
Metro

Miradouro de Santa Luzia (*St. Lucy's Overlook*)

VIEWPOINT | FAMILY | Notable for its pretty terrace with blue-and-yellow azulejo tiles, the Miradouro de Santa Luzia has great views of the rooftops of Alfama and the boats along the Tagus River. Street musicians draw crowds with jazz and samba performances, and artists sell reasonably priced etchings of the scene. A pleasant kiosk serves coffee, cocktails, and snacks. ✉ *Largo de Santa Luzia, Alfama* Ⓜ *Blue Line to Terreiro do Paço.*

Museu do Fado

SPECIALTY MUSEUM | Visitors intrigued by the haunting sounds of fado can learn about the celebrated Portuguese music at this small but carefully curated museum. A permanent exhibition outlines the emergence of the style and its key artists, while occasional live performances provide a chance to hear modern day stars. ✉ *Largo do Chafariz de Dentro 1, Alfama* ☎ *21/882–3470* 🌐 *www.museudofado.pt* 🎫 *€5* 🕒 *Closed Mon.* Ⓜ *Blue Line to Santa Apolónia.*

Museu do Teatro Romano (*Roman Theater Museum*)

HISTORY MUSEUM | FAMILY | This small museum close to the cathedral displays some of the few visible traces of Roman Lisbon. The space was once a Roman amphitheater built by Emperor Augustus in the 1st century BC with capacity for 4,000 spectators. It fell into disrepair during the Middle Ages and lay buried and forgotten until reconstruction of the area began in the 18th century. Columns and other interesting artifacts are on display here, and multilingual touch-screen kiosks explain everything. ✉ *Rua de São Mamede 3A, Alfama* ☎ *21/581–8530* 🌐 *www.museudelisboa.pt/en/sites/roman-theatre* 🎫 *€3* 🕒 *Closed Mon.* Ⓜ *Blue Line to Terreiro do Paço, Blue or Green Line to Baixa-Chiado.*

Museu Militar de Lisboa (*Lisbon Military Museum*)

SPECIALTY MUSEUM | FAMILY | The spirit of heroism is palpable in the sprawling barracks and arsenal complex of the Lisbon Military Museum, which houses one of the largest artillery collections in the world. You can ogle a 20-ton bronze cannon and admire Vasco da Gama's sword in a room dedicated to the explorer and his voyages. As you clatter through endless echoing rooms of weapons, uniforms, and armor, you may be followed by a guide who can convey exactly how that bayonet was jabbed or that gruesome flail swung. ✉ *Largo do Museu da Artilharia, Santa Apolónia* ☎ *21/884–2453* 🌐 *www.exercito.pt/pt/quem-somos/organizacao/ceme/vceme/dhcm/lisboa* 🎫 *€3* 🕒 *Closed Mon.* Ⓜ *Blue Line to Santa Apolónia.*

The distinctive "House of Spikes" now houses the José Saramago Foundation, memorializing the Nobel Prize-winning author of novels like *"Blindness"*.

★ **Sé de Lisboa** *(Lisbon Cathedral)*
RELIGIOUS BUILDING | Lisbon's austere Romanesque cathedral was founded in 1150 to commemorate the defeat of the Moors three years earlier. To rub salt in the wound, the conquerors built the sanctuary on the spot where Moorish Lisbon's main mosque once stood. Be sure to visit the rooftop terrace and the treasure-filled sacristy, which contains the relics of the martyr Saint Vincent. According to legend, the relics were carried from the Algarve to Lisbon in a ship piloted by ravens; the saint became Lisbon's official patron. **■ TIP→ Visitors are expected to dress respectfully.** ✉ *Largo da Sé, Alfama* ☎ *21/886–6752* 🌐 *www.sedelisboa.pt* 🎫 *€5* 🕓 *Closed Sun.* Ⓜ *Blue Line to Terreiro do Paço.*

Restaurants

Antù Alfama
$ | ECLECTIC | Take a seat beneath twisting grapevines for drinks and snacks at one of the most inviting terraces in Alfama. The menu is strong on fresh ingredients and healthier versions of fast-food favorites, prepared with care. **Known for:** good cocktails; popular Saturday brunch; free coworking room upstairs. $ *Average main: €14* ✉ *Beco de São Miguel, Alfama* ☎ *21/887–0649* 🌐 *antueurope.com* Ⓜ *Blue Line to Terreiro do Paço.*

Boi-Cavalo
$$$$ | ECLECTIC | Known as a wild child among the relentlessly traditional neighborhood dining spots, you'll hear indie rock

The Roots of Fado

Fado is a haunting music that emerged in Lisbon from hotly disputed roots: African, Brazilian, and Moorish are among the contenders. A lone singer—male or female—is accompanied by a Spanish guitar and the 12-string Portuguese *guitarra*, a closer relative of the lute. The lyrics often embody the feeling of *saudade*, which loosely translates as "longing." Amália Rodrigues, Lisbon's beloved fadista, made fado famous around the world.

The neighborhoods of Mouraria and Alfama (where Amália was born) are said to be the birthplace of fado, and that's where you'll find most *casas de fado* today. These serve traditional Portuguese food (it's rarely anything special), and the singing usually starts at 9 or 10 pm, often continuing until 2 am Reservations for dinner are essential, but if you want to go along later just to listen, most establishments will let you in if you buy drinks, usually around €10 minimum.

Although fado is always performed in Portuguese, you don't have to speak the language to feel the emotion in classic fado songs like "Uma Casa Portuguesa" and "Ai, Mouraria," which celebrate Portuguese life and Lisbon's historic neighborhoods. In fact you shouldn't say anything, as it's considered rude to talk during a fado performance. *Silêncio, que se vai cantar o fado!*

instead of fado at Boi-Cavalo and experience a menu that features unusual Portuguese products like mackerel with pickles and green beans–rice with pine nuts. The chef uses his kitchen as a lab for experiments with these oddball products, pairing them with Asian and other international influences. **Known for:** creative tasting menus; intimate environment; celebration of forgotten Portuguese ingredients. *Average main: €35* *Rua do Vigário 70B, Alfama* *93/875–2355* *boi-cavalo.pt* *Closed Mon. and Tues.* *Blue Line to Santa Apolónia.*

Le Petit Café

$$ | PORTUGUESE | Don't let the name fool you: this sophisticated restaurant serves a menu that is largely Portuguese—there's plenty of codfish, octopus, and grilled Portuguese meats—but also includes Italian appetizers and pastas (and the occasional head-scratcher like chicken samosas). **Known for:** romantic atmosphere; eclectic wine list; good pasta. *Average main: €20* *Largo de São Martinho 6, Alfama* *21/888–1304* *lepetitcaferesto.wixsite.com/lepetitcafe* *Blue Line to Terreiro do Paço.*

A stunning sunset view of Castelo de São Jorge, which dominates the historic Alfama neighborhood.

★ memmo Alfama Terrace

$$ | **PORTUGUESE** | The terrace at the chic Memmo Alfama Hotel has some of the neighborhood's best views. The menu centers around tapas-style small plates—the selection of Portuguese cheeses and meats, served with a basket of fresh-baked bread, is a good place to start. **Known for:** house-made desserts; fantastic sunset views; creative house cocktails. *Average main: €20* *memmo Alfama Hotel, Travessa das Merceeiras 27, Alfama* *96/415–0453* *www.memmohotels.com/alfama/the-terrace* *Blue Line to Terreiro do Paço.*

★ O Velho Eurico

$ | **PORTUGUESE** | A group of young locals took over this traditional *tasca* in 2019 and gave it a second life, adding O Velho to the name as a nod to the old man who used to run the place. They still specialize in homemade Portuguese dishes but with a contemporary touch. **Known for:** friendly service; petiscos (small dishes meant to share); house-made moonshine to end the meal. *Average main: €15* *Largo São Cristóvão 3, Castelo* *www.instagram.com/ovelhoeurico* *Closed Sun. and Mon.* *Green Line to Rossio.*

Solar dos Bicos

$$ | **PORTUGUESE** | Huge stone arches and a beautiful mural made of azulejo tiles grace this charming restaurant. Light Portuguese dishes are prepared with love and beautifully presented, and the cocktail list is impressive, too. **Known for:** great terrace; light dishes like octopus salad; friendly service. *Average main: €18*

✉ *Rua dos Bacalhoeiros 8A–8B, Alfama* ☎ *21/886–9447* 🌐 *www.solardosbicos.pt* Ⓜ *Blue Line to Terreiro do Paço.*

Taberna Moderna

$$$ | **PORTUGUESE** | This updated version of the traditional Portuguese *tasca* (tavern) is an informal space where everyone seems to start off with a gin and tonic—there are 80 gins on the list. The kitchen turns out delicious plates like black rice with cuttlefish or braised tuna that are the perfect size to share. **Known for:** one of the city's best places to go for a cocktail; table dining or petiscos at the bar; umbrella-shaded tables on the street. 💲 *Average main: €25* ✉ *Rua dos Bacalhoeiros 18, Alfama* ☎ *21/886–5039* 🌐 *tabernamoderna.com* ⏲ *Closed Sun. No lunch weekdays* Ⓜ *Blue Line to Terreiro do Paço.*

Coffee and Quick Bites

Palacete Chafariz D'el Rei

$$ | **INTERNATIONAL** | One of the most eye-catching buildings in Alfama also houses one of its best refined hideaways. The tearoom in this lavish palace-turned-hotel is open to the public, and it's a great place for a spot of tea—the real deal, from Gorreana in Portugal's Azores—or a brunch fit for royalty with cheeses, fruits, eggs, cakes, and house-made marmalades. **Known for:** elegant location; afternoon tea; weekend brunch. 💲 *Average main: €20* ✉ *Travessa Chafariz del Rei 6, Alfama* ☎ *21/888–6150* 🌐 *chafarizdelrei.com* Ⓜ *Blue Line to Terreiro do Paço.*

Pastelaria Santo António

$ | **PORTUGUESE** | You'll likely walk past this pastry shop on your way to the castle; step inside to see bakers whipping up a fresh batch of *pastéis de nata.* **Known for:** artisanal ice cream; sweet and savory croissants; award-winning custard tarts. 💲 *Average main: €4* ✉ *Rua do Milagre de Santo António 10, Alfama* ☎ *21/887–1717* Ⓜ *Blue Line to Terreiro do Paço.*

SOL Restaurante

$ | **INTERNATIONAL** | Head to this spot for light meals and cocktails against a jaw-droppingly beautiful backdrop. The menu is split between sunrise and sunset, though this is one for the late risers, as breakfast only starts at 10 am. **Known for:** airy indoor space; simple fare like toasts and salads; good selection of cocktails and mocktails. 💲 *Average main: €14* ✉ *Largo das Portas do Sol, Beco de Santa Helena, Alfama* ☎ *21/885–1299* 🌐 *www.portasdosol.pt* Ⓜ *Blue Line to Terreiro do Paço, Tram 12 or 28.*

Hotels

memmo Alfama Hotel

$$$ | **HOTEL** | With a lofty location at the top of historic Alfama, this stylish boutique hotel scores major points for its detail-driven design, carefully restored 19th-century building, and friendly staff. **Pros:** stunning views; excellent rooftop pool and bar; minimalist chic design. **Cons:** infinity pool isn't heated; kids under 16 not allowed; some rooms lack views. *Rooms from: €235 Travessa das Merceeiras 27, Alfama 21/049–5660 www.memmo-hotels.com/alfama 42 rooms Free Breakfast Blue Line to Terreiro do Paço.*

Hotel Senhora do Monte

$$ | **HOTEL** | **FAMILY** | If you want expansive views of the castle and the entire neighborhood, book a room on one of the upper floors of this small modern hotel perched atop the tallest of Lisbon's seven hills. **Pros:** amazing views from many rooms; quiet residential neighborhood; friendly service. **Cons:** a long climb up a steep hill; not too many amenities; small breakfast selection. *Rooms from: €170 Calçada do Monte 39, Graça 21/886–6002 www.hotelsenhoradomonte.com 28 rooms Free Breakfast Tram 28 and Bus 13B.*

Olissippo Castelo

$$ | **HOTEL** | This small elegant hotel near Castelo de São Jorge pampers guests with luxurious linens, elegant furnishings, and marble bathrooms. **Pros:** great views; feels miles from the hustle and bustle; small bar serves light meals. **Cons:** up a steep hill; very limited parking; decor is a bit basic. *Rooms from: €170 Rua Costa do Castelo 120, Castelo 21/882–0190 www.olissippo-hotels.com/en/Hotels/Castelo/The-Hotel.aspx 24 rooms Free Breakfast Green Line to Martim Moniz.*

★ **Solar do Castelo**

$$$ | **B&B/INN** | Located in an 18th-century mansion within the walls of Castelo de São Jorge, this boutique hideaway has been lovingly restored. **Pros:** archaeological finds from the site on display; beautiful breakfast area in the courtyard; guests who book through hotel website get free taxi service from the airport. **Cons:** up a steep cobblestone road; no car access; no restaurant. *Rooms from: €382 Rua das Cozinhas 2, Castelo 21/880–6050 lisbonheritagehotels.com/solar-do-castelo 20 rooms Free Breakfast Green Line to Rossio.*

Solar dos Mouros

$$ | **HOTEL** | Cool and serene, this handsome boutique hotel's location near the Castelo de São Jorge makes it perfectly placed

for admiring the city from up high. **Pros:** suites have their own spacious terraces; lovely views from just about everywhere; well placed for Alfama sightseeing. **Cons:** up a steep hill with stairs to climb; extra charge for breakfast; no gym or pool. *Rooms from: €180 Rua do Milagre de Santo António 6, Alfama 21/885-4940 www.solardosmouroslisboa.com 13 rooms No Meals Blue Line to Terreiro do Paço, Tram 28.*

Nightlife

BARS

Outro Lado

BARS | For a taste of Lisbon's artisanal brews, head to this craft beer bar in the heart of Alfama. All of Portugal's major breweries are represented, along with others from around the world. If you want to try a beer (or cider or barley wine) from Warsaw or Tallinn in Lisbon, this is your place. *Beco do Arco Escuro 1, Alfama 96/006-1470 outrolado.beer Closed Tues. Blue Line to Terreiro do Paço.*

Ulysses Lisbon Speakeasy

COCKTAIL BARS | This tiny five-seat bar, named one of the Top 50 World's Best Bars, serves only classic and bespoke cocktails catered to each guest. It also has one of the largest bourbon collections in Lisbon. Reservations (via Instagram or WhatsApp) are a must. *Rua da Regueira 16A, Alfama 92/769-6684 www.instagram.com/ulysseslisbon Blue Line to Terreiro do Paço.*

FADO CLUBS

★ A Baiuca

LIVE MUSIC | The quality of both the food and the singing is reliably great at this family-run establishment, and the setting—which calls to mind the dining room of a well-traveled older relative—is always welcoming. It's a fado *vadio* (vagabond) spot, meaning the night often ends with amateur singers lined up outside, raring to perform. *Rua de São Miguel 20, Alfama 93/945-7098 abaiuca@sapo.pt Blue Line to Terreiro do Paço.*

A Travessa do Fado

LIVE MUSIC | Prominent fadistas, both traditional singers and next-generation artists who are expanding the boundaries of the form, perform most nights in this modern café attached to the Museu do Fado. Reservations are essential in the evening. *Largo do Chafariz de Dentro 1, Alfama 21/887-0144 www.museudofado.pt Closed Mon. and Tues. Blue Line to Santa Apolónia.*

Casa de Linhares

LIVE MUSIC | Some of the biggest names in modern-day fado—Jorge Fernando, Fábia Rebordão, Vânia Duarte, and André Baptista—are in residence at this establishment. The dark candlelit dining room is located in the remains of a Renaissance building; the atmospheric location matches the melancholy and strong emotion of the music. ✉ *Beco dos Armazéns do Linho 2, Alfama* ☎ *91/018–8118* 🌐 *casadelinhares.com* Ⓜ *Blue Line to Terreiro do Paço.*

Clube de Fado

LIVE MUSIC | An international crowd flocks to this spot to hear established performers and rising stars take turns at the microphone. Dinner is pricey, but music fans arriving from around 10:30 pm can skip the food and concentrate on the music. ✉ *Rua de São João da Praça 86–94, Alfama* ☎ *21/885–2704* 🌐 *www.clubedefado.pt/en* Ⓜ *Blue Line to Terreiro do Paço, Tram 28.*

★ **Mesa de Frades**

LIVE MUSIC | All the rage among local fado lovers, this performance space is housed in a tiny azulejo-lined former chapel. The traditional Portuguese food is perfectly palatable, and the music and atmosphere are always top rate. You can slip in at the end of the night, order a drink or two, and enjoy the show. ✉ *Rua dos Remédios 139A, Alfama* ☎ *91/702–9436* 🌐 *mesadefrades.pt* 🕒 *Closed Sun.* Ⓜ *Blue Line to Santa Apolónia.*

★ **Parreirinha de Alfama**

LIVE MUSIC | This little club was founded by late fado legend Argentina Santos in the 1950s. Over the centuries, it has welcomed many fadistas, including the acclaimed Amália. The food, which includes rich seafood stews, is as appealing as the music. ✉ *Beco do Espírito Santo 1, Alfama* ☎ *21/886–8209* 🌐 *www.parreirinhadealfama.com* 🕒 *Closed Mon.* Ⓜ *Blue Line to Santa Apolónia.*

Páteo de Alfama

LIVE MUSIC | There is more entertainment than authenticity in the 30-minute fado shows at this restaurant, although the performers are first-rate and include a number of the genre's current famous names. A theme traces the evolution of fado from the 19th century to the present, and folklore shows feature dancers in old-fashioned costumes. ✉ *Rua São João da Praça 18, Alfama* ☎ *21/587–3415* 🌐 *pateodealfama.pt* Ⓜ *Blue Line to Terreiro do Paço.*

Sr. Fado

LIVE MUSIC | This long-running fado house was first established by fado singer Ana Marina and fado violist Duarte Santos, who had the idea of serving guests home-cooked Portuguese food before their performances. They specialize in *cataplana* (a dish cooked in a copper pan) of seafood or pork, but there's also a bean and vegetable stew for vegetarians. ✉ *Rua dos Remédios 168, Alfama* ☎ *96/317–9419* 🌐 *www.sr-fado.com* ⏲ *Closed Mon.* Ⓜ *Blue Line to Santa Apolónia.*

Tasca da Bela

LIVE MUSIC | This homey fado tavern is also known for the high quality of its typical Portuguese dishes that are meant to be shared, such as tempura green beans, codfish cakes, and bell pepper salad. ✉ *Rua dos Remédios 190, Alfama* ☎ *92/607–7511* ⏲ *Closed Mon. and Tues.* ☞ *Reservations recommended* Ⓜ *Blue Line to Santa Apolónia.*

MUSIC VENUES

Tejo Bar

LIVE MUSIC | This tiny, somewhat divey music bar has a cozy living-room vibe. The concerts tend to be informal, often more like jam sessions (not just fado) among local and touring musicians who head here after their own performances; things really start rolling around midnight. ✉ *Beco do Vigário 1A, Alfama* ☎ *96/975–6148* ⏲ *Closed Sun.* Ⓜ *Blue Line to Santa Apolónia.*

WINE BARS

The CorkScrew Wine Bar

WINE BAR | This is a pretty straightforward wine bar—a wide array of Portuguese vintages are complemented with local cheese, charcuterie, and even main dishes. Come for a glass of a unique varietal you've never tried in a cozy room. ✉ *Rua dos Remédios 95, Alfama* ☎ *96/956–3664* Ⓜ *Blue Line to Santa Apolónia.*

Shopping

CERAMICS

Loja dos Descobrimentos

CERAMICS | You can often see artists at work in this shop specializing in hand-painted tiles. They ship worldwide, so there's no need to haul any breakables home in your bags. ✉ *Rua dos Bacalhoeiros 12A, Alfama* ☎ *21/886–5563* 🌐 *www.loja-descobrimentos.com* Ⓜ *Blue Line to Terreiro do Paço.*

CRAFTS AND SOUVENIRS

Chi Coração - Museu

TEXTILES | Part of the name means "heart," and that's exactly what the family behind this wool shop has put into their business. Since the 1960s, they have been saving and restoring old mills and tools used for wool production, and re-creating typical Portuguese designs. The top-quality products range from blankets to coats for women and men, as well as children's puppets. This branch in the cathedral's former stables also has a rotating display of Portuguese crafts for sale, including ceramics, cork, and basketry. *Rua Augusto Rosa 40, Alfama* *91/495–2499* *chicoracao.com* *Blue Line to Terreiro do Paço.*

O Passeio da D. Sardinha e do Sr. Bacalhau

SOUVENIRS | This family-owned shop sells locally made souvenirs; expect lots of cork and items shaped like sardines. The quality is high and the prices fair. *Rua dos Remédios 169, Alfama* *91/739–3675* *alfamashop.blogspot.com* *Closed Sun.* *Blue Line to Santa Apolónia.*

FOOD

★ Conserveira de Lisboa

FOOD | There's a feast for the eyes at this shop, whose walls are lined with colorful tins of sardines and other seafood combos like octopus stew or mackerel with curry. *Rua dos Bacalhoeiros 34, Alfama* *21/886–4009* *www.conserveiradelisboa.pt* *Closed Sun.* *Blue Line to Terreiro do Paço.*

Performing Arts

★ Chapitô

CIRCUSES | A good way to break the language barrier is to see a show at this vibrant venue, where contemporary clowning, circus acts, and physical theater dominate. There's also the pleasant Chapitô à Mesa restaurant with fine views of the city and the bohemian Bartô bar with a mix of live music and DJs. *Costa do Castelo 1–7, Castelo* *21/885–5550* *chapito.org* *Blue Line to Terreiro do Paço.*

Teatro da Garagem

THEATER | Also known as the Teatro Taborda, the resident company at this historic theater has spent three decades exploring and performing new, historic, and experimental works. Although Portuguese is the primary language, many performances incorporate dance and multimedia elements that make them entertaining to visitors. *Costa do Castelo 75, Castelo* *21/885–4190* *teatrodagaragem.com* *Green Line to Martim Moniz.*

The Monastery of of St. Vincent is known for its abundant azulejos, Baroque altar, and vibrant sacristy (shown here).

Graça and São Vicente

Sights

Mosteiro de São Vicente de Fora

RELIGIOUS BUILDING | The Italianate facade of the twin-towered St. Vincent's Monastery heralds an airy church with a barrel-vault ceiling. It's the work of three architects including Spaniard Juan de Herrera (1530–1597) and Italian Filippo Terzi (1520–97) and was completed in 1704. Its superbly tiled cloister depicts the fall of Lisbon to the Moors. The monastery also serves as the pantheon of the Bragança dynasty, which ruled Portugal from the restoration of independence from Spain in 1640 to the declaration of the republic in 1910. Guided tours of around 90 minutes are available for a modest extra charge, but must be booked in advance. ✉ *Largo de São Vicente, São Vicente* ☎ *21/881–0559* 🌐 *mosteirodesaovicentedefora.com* 🎫 *€8* Ⓜ *Blue Line to Santa Apolónia, Tram 28.*

★ **Panteão Nacional** (*National Pantheon*)

TOMB | The large domed edifice is the former church of Santa Engrácia. It took 285 years to build, hence the Portuguese phrase "a job like Santa Engrácia." Today, the building doubles as Portugal's National Pantheon, housing the tombs of the country's former presidents as well as cenotaphs dedicated to its most famous explorers and writers. A more recent arrival is fado diva Amália Rodrigues, whose tomb is invariably piled high with

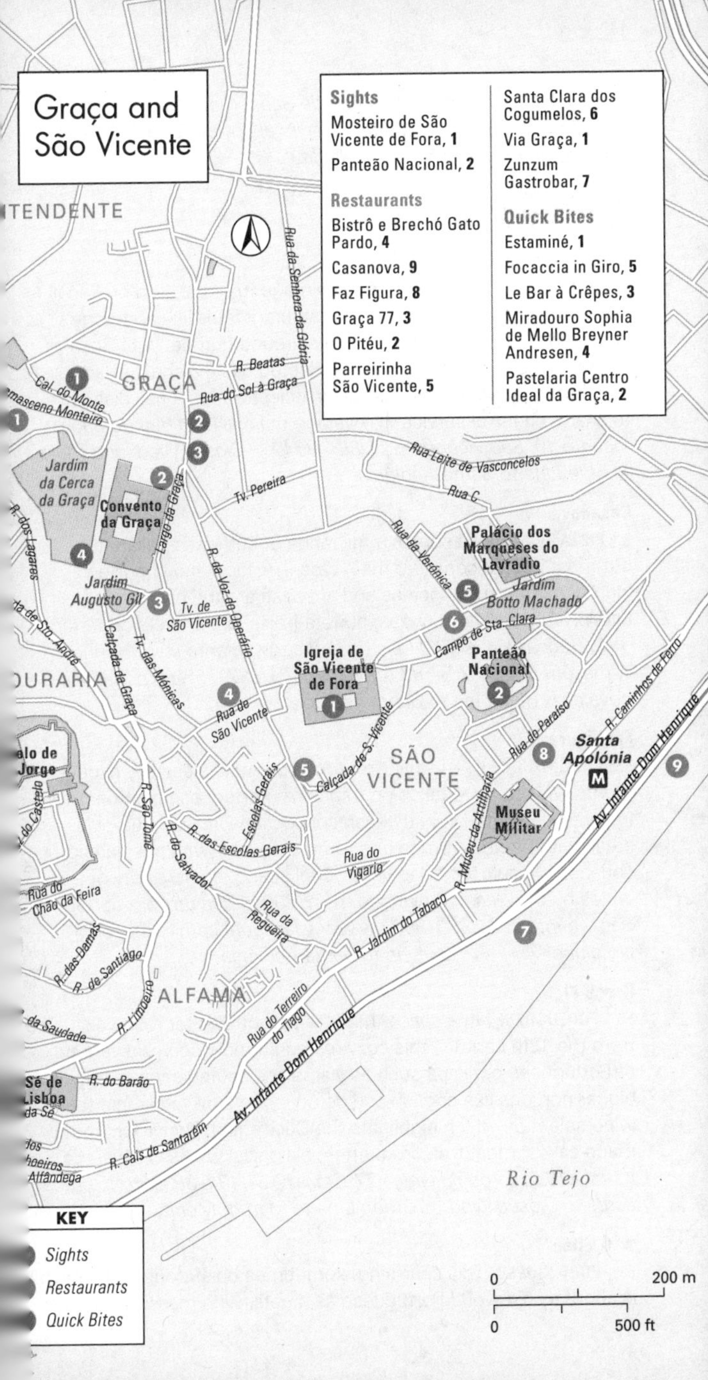

Graça and São Vicente
Sights
Mosteiro de São Vicente de Fora, 1
Panteão Nacional, 2
Restaurants
Bistrô e Brechó Gato Pardo, 4
Casanova, 9
Faz Figura, 8
Graça 77, 3
O Pitéu, 2
Parreirinha São Vicente, 5
Santa Clara dos Cogumelos, 6
Via Graça, 1
Zunzum Gastrobar, 7
Quick Bites
Estaminé, 1
Focaccia in Giro, 5
Le Bar à Crêpes, 3
Miradouro Sophia de Mello Breyner Andresen, 4
Pastelaria Centro Ideal da Graça, 2
GRAÇA
SÃO VICENTE
ALFAMA
Convento da Graça
Jardim da Cerca da Graça
Jardim Augusto Gil
Igreja de São Vicente de Fora
Palácio dos Marqueses do Lavradio
Jardim Botto Machado
Panteão Nacional
Museu Militar
Santa Apolónia
Rio Tejo
KEY
Sights
Restaurants
Quick Bites
0
200 m
0
500 ft

flowers from admirers. ✉ *Campo de Santa Clara, São Vicente* ☎ *21/885–4820* 🌐 *www.panteaonacional.gov.pt* 🎟 *€8* ⏲ *Closed Mon.* Ⓜ *Blue Line to Santa Apolónia.*

Restaurants

Bistrô e Brechó Gato Pardo

$ | **ECLECTIC** | With its stone walls, vintage furniture, and broken-in leather chairs and couches, this restaurant feels like someone's living room. The menu hopscotches around Europe, with Spanish-style padrón peppers, Italian-inflected pasta dishes, salads, and Portuguese classics. **Known for:** eclectic vibe; small dishes to share; cheerful service. $ *Average main: €12* ✉ *Rua de São Vicente 10, São Vicente* ☎ *21/887–3647* ⏲ *Closed Wed. and Thurs.* Ⓜ *Blue Line to Santa Apolónia.*

Casanova

$ | **PIZZA** | Casanova serves a full range of authentic Italian fare, but most people come for the pizzas. The local and imported ingredients for the toppings and antipasti are the best available. **Known for:** wood-fired pizzas; burrata from Puglia; riverside terrace. $ *Average main: €15* ✉ *Cais da Pedra, Av. Infante Dom Henrique, Armazém B, Loja 7, Santa Apolónia* ☎ *21/887–7532* 🌐 *pizzeriacasanova.pt* Ⓜ *Blue Line to Santa Apolónia.*

Faz Figura

$$$$ | **PORTUGUESE** | This riverfront restaurant successfully experiments with creative takes on traditional Portuguese gastronomy. Innovative vegetarian and vegan concoctions include pumpkin steak with beetroot puree and tomato ceviche with piri-piri and coriander. **Known for:** killer views; cool scene; great variety of wines by the glass. $ *Average main: €30* ✉ *Rua do Paraíso 15B, São Vicente* ☎ *21/886–8981* 🌐 *www.fazfigura.com* ⏲ *Closed Mon. No dinner Sun.* Ⓜ *Blue Line to Santa Apolónia.*

Graça 77

$$ | **PORTUGUESE** | In a space that was part of a water reservoir from the 12th century, this cozy restaurant now serves a variety of Portuguese petiscos such as clams and sautéd shrimp, but also bigger portions like codfish and octopus. Be sure to sample their wine selection which highlights the Dão region. **Known for:** homemade cakes; meat-free croquettes; biological wines. $ *Average main: €16* ✉ *Largo da Graça 77, Graça* ☎ *21/134–8839* 💳 *No credit cards* ⏲ *Closed Wed.* Ⓜ *Green Line to Martim Moniz.*

★ **O Pitéu**

$$ | **PORTUGUESE** | This charming, sometimes boisterous restaurant is about as old-world Portuguese as it gets, with massive portions

of grilled meat, seafood, and fish in a no-nonsense, brightly lit room. It's especially popular with neighborhood families. **Known for:** fish fillets; fresh ingredients; good wine cellar. *Average main: €17 Largo da Graça 95–96, Graça 21/887–1067 No credit cards Closed Sun. Green Line to Martim Moniz.*

Parreirinha São Vicente

$ | **PORTUGUESE** | The food at this wood-paneled restaurant is expertly prepared and comes in portions big enough to share. It's a popular choice in the neighborhood, especially in the summer when they bring out the grilled fish. **Known for:** handful of tables on the street; favorite with locals; inexpensive lunch menu. *Average main: €15 Calçada de São Vicente 54–58, São Vicente 21/886–8893 parreirinhasaovicente.eatbu.com No credit cards Blue Line to Santa Apolónia.*

Santa Clara dos Cogumelos

$$ | **ECLECTIC** | An Italian living in Lisbon had the odd but surprisingly successful idea of opening a restaurant that would serve only mushroom-based dinners. The chefs here have certainly managed to find a lot of ways to use mushrooms: in tartare, pâté, or croquettes, and even in ice cream. **Known for:** portobello steak; porcini and black trumpet risotto with walnuts; Thai-style coconut soup with Pleurotus. *Average main: €20 Mercado de Santa Clara, Campo de Santa Clara 7, São Vicente 91/304–3302 santaclaracogumelos.wixsite.com/santaclaracogumelos No lunch Sun.–Fri. Blue Line to Santa Apolónia.*

Via Graça

$$$$ | **PORTUGUESE** | This hilltop restaurant has "date night" (or at least "big splurge") written all over it. The city views are so spectacular that what lands on the plate is almost an afterthought. **Known for:** sunset views; customized menus (with advance notice); romantic mood. *Average main: €50 Rua Damasceno Monteiro 9B, Graça 21/887–0830 restauranteviagraca.pt Green Line to Martim Moniz.*

★ Zunzum Gastrobar

$$$ | **PORTUGUESE** | Chef Marlene Vieira is one of the few female chefs at the forefront of Lisbon's fine dining scene. At Zunzum she has a more relaxed approach, but still with cutting-edge dishes like Portuguese stew gyozas or cockle fritters in *bulhão pato*, a garlicky white wine and coriander sauce. **Known for:** Portuguese produced Wagyu; pataniscas de bacalhau (codfish fritters); popcorn tart with salted caramel. *Average main: €22 Av. Infante D. Henrique, Santa Apolónia 91/550–7870 www.zunzum.pt No dinner Sun. Blue Line to Santa Apolónia.*

The National Pantheon houses the tombs and cenotaphs of some of Portugal's most prominent presidents, explorers, writers, and other notables.

Coffee and Quick Bites

Estaminé

$$ | BRAZILIAN | Everything is made with love at this tiny Brazilian-owned café, from the collection of art on the walls to the fresh juices and French-press coffee. Simple snacks include cheese and charcuterie boards, bruschetta, and toasts with tapenade. **Known for:** juices made with Brazilian fruits, like maracujá and cupuaçu; French-press coffee; Brazilian cheese bread. *Average main: €16* *Calçada do Monte 86A, Graça* *91/058–4194* *No credit cards* *Closed Tues. and Wed.* *Blue Line to Santa Apolónia.*

Focaccia in Giro

$ | ITALIAN | Focaccia sandwiches, made according to traditional Italian recipes but with high-quality Portuguese ingredients, are the draw at this small shop in the Feira da Ladra market. **Known for:** authentic Italian flavors; organic Portuguese ingredients; easy snacks while on the go. *Average main: €10* *Campo de Santa Clara 141, São Vicente* *21/598–2367* *www.focacciaingiro.com* *Closed Wed. and Thurs.* *Blue Line to Santa Apolónia.*

Le Bar à Crêpes

$ | FRENCH | A slice of Brittany in Lisbon, this French-owned café specializes in buckwheat crepes, or *galettes bretonnes*, with sweet or savory fillings and cheeky names. **Known for:** authentic French flavors; friendly waitstaff; gluten-free options. *Average main: €10* *Largo da Graça 18–19, Graça* *91/150–0259* *Blue Line to Santa Apolónia.*

Miradouro Sophia de Mello Breyner Andresen

$ | CAFÉ | Perhaps the best place in the city to watch the sunset, the menu here is like at every other kiosk in the city, but there's friendly table service and great people-watching. **Known for:** city views; speedy service; lively scene. *Average main: €5* ✉ *Calçada da Graça, Graça* Ⓜ *Green Line to Martim Moniz.*

Pastelaria Centro Ideal da Graça

$ | BAKERY | The cakes and pastries in this shop, from the classic pastéis de nata to croissants and Christmas miniatures, are high quality and made fresh daily. **Known for:** pastéis de nata; strong Portuguese coffee; holiday cakes. *Average main: €3* ✉ *Largo da Graça 5/7, Graça* ☎ *21/886–1673* *No credit cards* Ⓜ *Blue Line to Santa Apolónia.*

Nightlife

★ Bom Bom Bom

WINE BAR | You may come for a glass of wine (sourced from small producers), but it's the music and the food that will make you stay. Dishes feature everything from fresh oysters to slow-cooked pork cheek and even some vegetarian alternatives (the roasted butternut squash is to die for). ✉ *Rua Angelina Vidal 5, Graça* ☎ *93/532–7446* *Closed Tues.* Ⓜ *Green Line to Intendente.*

★ Botequim

BARS | This homey bar serves bottles from Lisbon's major craft breweries, Portuguese wines, competent cocktails, and a handful of typical Portuguese snacks, as well as some atypical ones like seitan *prego* (typically a small beef sandwich) on sweet-potato bread. ✉ *Largo da Graça 79–80, Graça* ☎ *21/888–8511* Ⓜ *Green Line to Martim Moniz.*

Clube Ferroviário de Portugal

GATHERING PLACE | This warehouse space has many personalities. The large rooftop terrace, with unobstructed views of the Tagus River, is the most popular. After sunset, there can be a diverse range of entertainment, such as street performers, small concerts, and alfresco cinema. ✉ *Rua de Santa Apolónia 59–63, Santa Apolónia* ☎ *21/765–1869* *clubeferroviario.pt/espacos/#main* *Closed Mon.–Wed.* Ⓜ *Blue Line to Santa Apolónia.*

★ Damas

LIVE MUSIC | This cool restaurant, bar, and concert venue is one of the best spots in Lisbon for live music. Local and international bands and DJs take the stage around 11 pm most nights. ✉ *Rua da Voz do Operário 60, Graça* ☎ *96/496–4416* *www.facebook.com/damaslisboa* *Closed Mon.* Ⓜ *Blue Line to Santa Apolónia.*

Graça do Vinho

WINE BAR | There are just a handful of barstools and tables at this quaint colorful wine bar featuring a number of notable Portuguese wines. ✉ *Calcada da Graça 10A/B, Graça* ☎ *21/011–8041* ⏲ *Closed Sun.* Ⓜ *Green Line to Martim Moniz.*

LuxFrágil

DANCE CLUB | Lisbon's most famous club has two dance floors favored by big-name local and foreign DJs. A young stylish crowd comes to dance until dawn. The doormen are selective and there can be a long line. ✉ *Av. Infante Dom Henrique, Armazém A, Santa Apolónia* ☎ *21/882–0890* 🌐 *www.luxfragil.com* ⏲ *Closed Sun.–Wed.* Ⓜ *Blue Line to Santa Apolónia.*

O Vinhaça

WINE BAR | This hole-in-the-wall looks like a Portuguese grandma's kitchen with copper pots hanging on the walls. There's a good selection of Portuguese wine and craft beers, and the tapas-style snacks are just as traditional. ✉ *Rua do Salvador 53, São Vicente* ☎ *91/572–5435* 🌐 *www.ovinhaca.pt* ⏲ *Closed Sun. and Mon.* Ⓜ *Blue Line to Santa Apolónia.*

Shopping

Campo Santa Clara Cerâmicas

CERAMICS | This shop specializes in ceramics from various Portuguese factories and artisans' workshops. Crockery, tableware, and decorative pieces take the form of pumpkins, frogs, lizards, sardines, and hanging codfish. Prices are more than fair. ✉ *Campo de Santa Clara 112, São Vicente* ✥ *Near Feira da Ladra market* 🌐 *www.instagram.com/campo_santa_clara* ⏲ *Closed Sun., Mon., and Wed.–Fri.* Ⓜ *Blue Line to Santa Apolónia.*

★ **Feira da Ladra**

MARKET | The so-called "thieves" market is now the most famous flea market in Portugal. You'll need a few hours to browse all the stalls selling everything from vintage clothes to antique furnishings, with plenty of colorful treasures in between. It runs until about 2 pm on Tuesday and a little later into the afternoon on Saturday. ✉ *Campo de Santa Clara, São Vicente* Ⓜ *Blue Line to Santa Apolónia.*

Garbags

ACCESSORIES | This stylish boutique specializes in handmade messenger bags, backpacks, wallets, and small cases that are upcycled from materials that would normally be found in the trash. ✉ *Calçada da Graça 16–16A, Graça* ☎ *93/798–1772* 🌐 *www.garbags.com* Ⓜ *Blue Line to Santa Apolónia.*

Chapter 7

BEATO AND MARVILA

Updated by
Ann Abel

Sights	Restaurants	Hotels	Shopping	Nightlife
★★☆☆☆	★★★☆☆	★☆☆☆☆	★☆☆☆☆	★☆☆☆☆

NEIGHBORHOOD SNAPSHOT

TOP EXPERIENCES

■ **Sipping craft beer.** The large warehouses and (formerly) low rents in Marvila encouraged an artisanal brewing scene to take root here.

■ **Cutting-edge contemporary art.** Some of Lisbon's best art galleries and art spaces have set up shop here.

■ **Alternative nightlife.** While the bars in Bairro Alto and clubs along Pink Street draw a cross section of revelers, the "underground" spaces in these edgier neighborhoods draw a local mix of artists and hipsters.

■ **Riverside rambles.** Less crowded than most of the city's waterfront, the eastern reaches of Beato and Marvila offer wide promenades with a small but growing number of restaurants and cafés.

GETTING HERE

Given their history as working-class and warehouse districts, Beato and Marvila are not well served by public transportation. The closest metro stop is the Blue Line terminus in Santa Apolónia, but that's just the starting point for a 30-minute (or longer) walk that's not terribly interesting. The 728, 759, and 781 buses make various stops in both neighborhoods.

PLANNING YOUR TIME

Beato and Marvila come to life on weekends and during the evening. Many establishments don't open until the afternoon; the sweet spot tends to be around sunset, as these neighborhoods can feel deserted as the night goes on.

PAUSE HERE

■ **Prata Riverside Village.** Anchoring the northern end of Marvila is a new mixed-use project by noted Italian architect Renzo Piano. While luxury real estate is certainly part of it, the blocks-long complex has other draws including cafés, restaurants, and a—literally—underground art gallery. The park in front is perfect for a walk or a bike ride.

OFF THE BEATEN PATH

■ **Matinha.** The groovy abandoned towers of Matinha became known locally as the backdrop for one of the city's must cutting-edge music and arts festivals. Even with no performances, they're worth a look for anyone who appreciates gently decaying infrastructure.

The lazy shorthand for the newly gentrifying districts of Beato and Marvila is a comparison to Bushwick in Brooklyn or the East End of London, and these aren't far off the mark.

These neighborhoods, which used to be composed predominantly of working-class residences or large-scale industrial warehouses, had some of the last affordable rents in Lisbon. That's changing now, thanks to artists and risk-takers who have been capitalizing on that affordability.

It's easy to see the migration, as businesses from elsewhere in the city—a cultural hub in Bairro Alto, a chain of brunch restaurants in Santos, a restaurant at the edge of Chiado—are opening spin-offs in Marvila. Meanwhile, creative international entrepreneurs have snapped up palaces in Beato and transformed them into interactive dining experiences.

Still, Beato and Marvila, which are physically off the beaten path—northeast of the historic center but south of the posh and contemporary Parque das Nações district that was manufactured for a World Expo in the 1990s—have a feeling of being places that are on the verge of discovery.

And they retain their alternative democratic soul. A group of largely young, local risk-takers are reinventing derelict factories and turning them into multiconcept cultural venues offering everything from yoga classes to storytelling evenings, or turning old warehouses into coworking spaces and cultural organizations.

Of course, if your interests lean more toward pleasures of the glass and the plate, these bohemian neighborhoods also have an appeal. The big spaces made them appealing for the city's first craft breweries, and although some have already moved on, new ones have taken their place. Along with restaurant concepts that have already made their name elsewhere in the city, new fully local projects are offering up new takes on Portuguese gastronomy.

Outside the formal neighborhood confines, there are a handful of other institutions that have stood the test of time and added indelible color to the city of Lisbon, including a museum dedicated to the art of Portuguese tile-making and one of the most iconic places to dine on salted cod.

Beato and Marvila

Sights

★ 8 Marvila

PEDESTRIAN MALL | In early 2024, the opening of the cultural and commercial center 8 Marvila cemented the district's reputation as the capital of alternative cool. Occupying several of Marvila's old warehouses, the multiuse space encompasses shops for artisanal furniture, vintage clothing, cultivated plants, contemporary art, tarot readings, and wordy tattoos. Restaurants and food trucks serve vegetarian pizza, smash burgers, ramen, and tacos. ✉ *Praça David Leandro da Silva 8, Marvila* 🌐 *www.8marvila.com* ⏲ *Closed Mon.–Wed.* Ⓜ *Blue Line to Santa Apolónia.*

Galeria Filomena Soares

ART GALLERY | Housed in a former warehouse not far from the Museu Nacional do Azulejo, this gallery is owned by, and bears the name of, one of Europe's leading female art dealers. Her roster includes leading Portuguese and international artists like Sara Bichão and Dan Graham. ✉ *Rua da Manutenção 80, Beato* ☎ *21/862–4122* 🌐 *www.gfilomenasoares.com* ⏲ *Closed Sun. and Mon.* Ⓜ *Blue Line to Santa Apolónia.*

Galeria Francisco Fino

ART GALLERY | After five years as a nomadic gallery, presenting exhibitions in other museums and commercial establishments, this art space opened in its permanent home in Marvila in 2017. It continues to show the work of artists such as Helena Almeida, Diogo Evangelista, and Tris Vonna-Michell, among many others. Their genres range from video art to sculpture installations, meaning there's always something thought-provoking to see. ✉ *Rua Capitão Leitão 76, Marvila* ☎ *21/584–2211* 🌐 *www.franciscofino.com* ⏲ *Closed Sun. and Mon.* Ⓜ *Blue Line to Santa Apolónia.*

Marvila Art District

ARTS CENTER | One of the most beautiful old mansions on Marvila's main square has become a combination of artists' open studios and exhibition spaces. The rooms of the house serve as individual gallery spaces for Portuguese and international artists, and sometimes you can watch some of them at work. ✉ *Rua Fernando Palha 1, Marvila* ☎ *92/673–0023* 🌐 *madmarvila.pt* ⏲ *Closed Sun.* Ⓜ *Blue Line to Santa Apolólnia.*

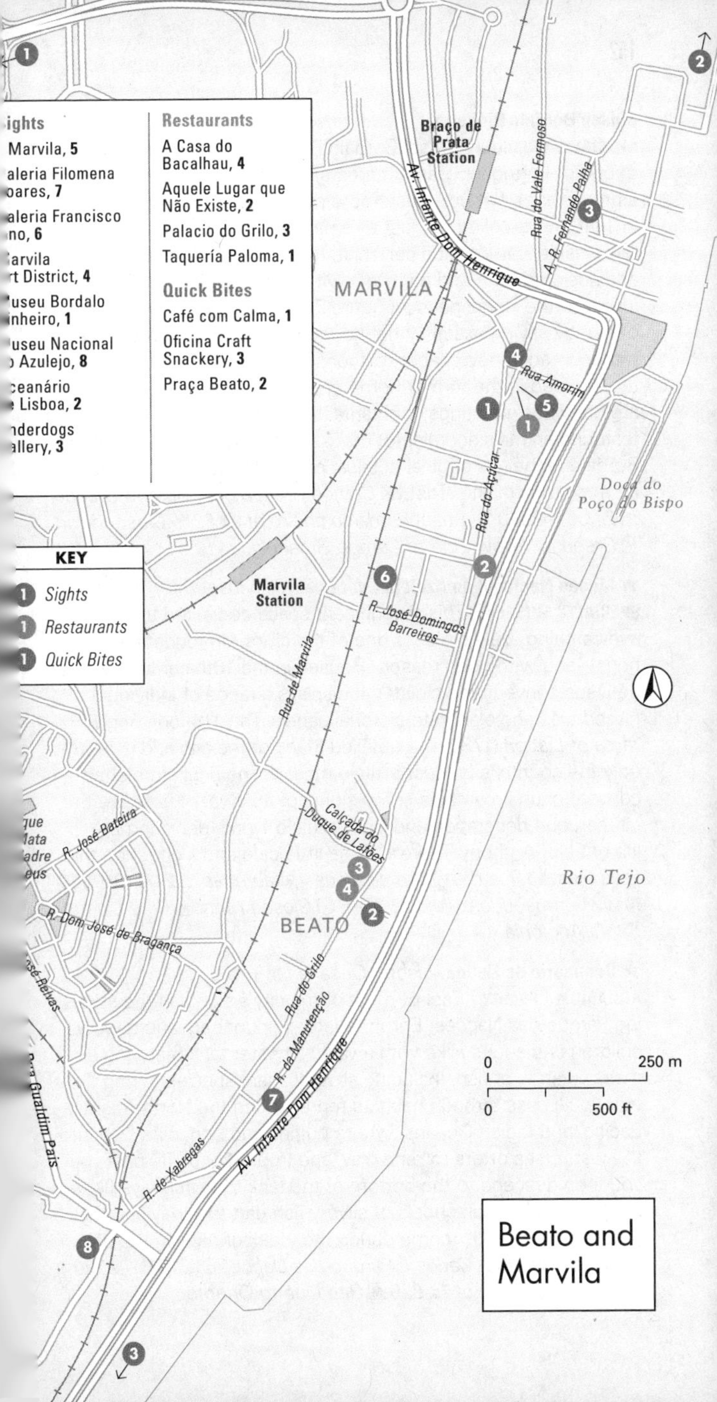

ights
Marvila, 5
aleria Filomena
oares, 7
aleria Francisco
no, 6
arvila
rt District, 4
useu Bordalo
inheiro, 1
useu Nacional
Azulejo, 8
ceanário
Lisboa, 2
nderdogs
allery, 3
Restaurants
A Casa do Bacalhau, 4
Aquele Lugar que Não Existe, 2
Palacio do Grilo, 3
Taquería Paloma, 1
Quick Bites
Café com Calma, 1
Oficina Craft Snackery, 3
Praça Beato, 2
KEY
Sights
Restaurants
Quick Bites
Braço de Prata Station
Marvila Station
MARVILA
BEATO
Av. Infante Dom Henrique
Rua do Vale Formoso
A. R. Fernando Palha
Rua Amorim
Rua do Açúcar
Doca do Poço do Bispo
R. José Domingos Barreiros
Rua de Marvila
Calçada do Duque de Lafões
Rua do Grilo
R. da Manutenção
R. de Xabregas
R. José Bateira
R. Dom José de Bragança
Rua Gualdim Pais
Rio Tejo
0
250 m
0
500 ft
Beato and Marvila

Museu Bordalo Pinheiro

SPECIALTY MUSEUM | Rafael Bordalo Pinheiro was the older brother of one of Portugal's greatest artists, Columbano, and was himself a prominent artist but much more multifaceted. Born in Lisbon in 1846, he excelled not just as a painter but above all as an outrageous caricaturist and ceramist. He satirized Portugal's political and social climate and put great wit into everything he did. He invented the iconic peasant figure Zé Povinho, who had the habit of bluntly saying exactly what he thought and who came to be represented in newspaper cartoons and ceramics. At this museum, housed in the former home of an admirer of the artist, there are drawings, paintings, and fantastically designed ceramics, often featuring animals and plants. There's also a library with some of Bordalo Pinheiro's original publications and a video explaining the art and times of the artist. ✉ *Campo Grande 382, Campo Grande* ☎ *21/581–8540* 🌐 *museubordalopinheiro.pt* 🎫 *€2* ⏲ *Closed Mon.* Ⓜ *Green or Yellow Line to Campo Grande.*

★ **Museu Nacional do Azulejo** (*National Tile Museum*)

SPECIALTY MUSEUM | This magnificent space dedicated to the city's eye-catching azulejo tiles is one of the city's top tourist attractions—and with good reason. Housed in the 16th-century Madre de Deus convent and cloister, it displays a range of individual glazed tiles and elaborate pictorial panels. The 118-foot-long *Panorama of Lisbon* (1730) is a detailed study of the city and is reputedly the country's longest azulejo mosaic. The richly furnished convent church contains some sights of its own: of note are the gilt baroque decoration and lively azulejo works depicting the life of Saint Anthony. There's also a little café and a gift shop that sells tiles. ✉ *Rua da Madre de Deus 4, Xabregas* ☎ *21/810–0340* 🌐 *www.museudoazulejo.pt* 🎫 *€5* ⏲ *Closed Mon.* Ⓜ *Blue Line to Santa Apolónia.*

★ **Oceanário de Lisboa** (*Lisbon Oceanarium*)

AQUARIUM | **FAMILY** | East of most of the city's sights in the sprawling Parque das Nações, Europe's largest indoor aquarium wows children and adults alike with a vast saltwater tank featuring a massive array of fish, including several shark species. Along the way you'll pass through habitats representing the North Atlantic, Pacific, and Indian Oceans, where puffins and penguins dive into the water, sea otters roll and play, and tropical birds flit past you. You then descend to the bottom of the tank to watch rays float past gracefully and schools of silvery fish dart this way and that. To avoid the crowds, come during the week or early in the day. ✉ *Esplanada Dom Carlos I, Parque das Nações* ☎ *21/891–7000* 🌐 *www.oceanario.pt* 🎫 *€25* Ⓜ *Red Line to Oriente.*

The "Panorama of Lisbon," housed in the Museu Nacional do Azulejo, depicts 18th century Lisbon over a 118-foot span of tiles.

★ Underdogs Gallery

ART GALLERY | One of Lisbon's most important contemporary art galleries, Underdogs, founded in 2010, works with some of the most renowned urban-inspired contemporary artists from around the world. Not only are there several solo and group shows in the warehouse-type space, but the founders formed a partnership with the city to give local, international, well-known, and up-and-coming artists spaces to create street art. They had a hand in some of the city's most iconic murals, including pieces by local hero Vhils and American artist Shepard Fairey; a map of pieces they commissioned is on their website. ✉ *Rua Fernando Palha, Armazém 56, Marvila* ☎ *21/868–0462* 🌐 *www.under-dogs.net* ⏲ *Closed Sun. and Mon.* Ⓜ *Blue Line to Santa Apolónia.*

Restaurants

A Casa do Bacalhau

$$$ | **PORTUGUESE** | Just as the 90-seat dining room sits below a vaulted brick ceiling that dates from the 18th century, many of the dishes are based on archival recipes. As the name suggests, the emphasis is on *bacalhau* (salted codfish), which is served in 25 different ways, ranging from the typical *à Brás* (with eggs and potatoes) to curried cod with asparagus risotto. **Known for:** wine list with more than 100 labels; mix of classic and contemporary cod dishes; historic site. $ *Average main: €24* ✉ *Rua do Grilo 54, Beato* ☎ *21/862–0007* 🌐 *casadobacalhau.pt* Ⓜ *Blue Line to Santa Apolónia.*

Beyond Marvila in the Parque das Nações, Lisbon's Oceanarium provides an entertaining and enlightening getaway for families.

Aquele Lugar que Não Existe

$ | **ECLECTIC** | The name means "that place that doesn't exist" in Portuguese, and that's a clue (along with its lack of online presence) that this restaurant aims to have an insider, underground vibe. However, it does exist, and the main restaurant is a stylish room with that serves an eclectic menu of Indian dishes, pizza, and soup. **Known for:** eccentric design using found objects; river views from the rooftop; vegetarian and vegan options. $ *Average main: €15* ✉ *Rua do Açucar 89, Marvila* ☎ *96/001–6208* Ⓜ *Blue Line to Santa Apolónia.*

Palacio do Grilo

$$$ | **INTERNATIONAL** | The passion project of a French theater director, Palacio do Grilo is an immersive theater experience that also happens to serve good food. The restaurant occupies an 18th-century palace in what was then the far outskirts of Lisbon, built as a palace of dreams for a noble family. **Known for:** surrealist theater pieces; historic palace architecture with whimsical touches; museum-like curated rooms. $ *Average main: €22* ✉ *Calçada do Duque de Lafões 1, Beato* ☎ *91/044–0942* 🌐 *palaciogrilo.com* Ⓜ *Blue Line to Santa Apolónia.*

Taquería Paloma

$ | **MEXICAN** | A lively but no-frills dining hall is the setting for authentic tacos inspired by the street-side stalls in Mexico City. The menu includes old-school classics like pork *al pastor* (slow-roasted) and chorizo verde (with a tomatillo sauce), as well as vegan fare like quesadillas with avocado, black beans, and mixed vegetables. **Known for:** late-night hours; meat tacos; customizable margaritas. $ *Average main: €10* ✉ *Praça David Leandro da Silva 9A, Marvila* ☎ *96/374–5573* 🌐 *www.instagram.com/taqueriapaloma* ⏲ *Closed Mon. and Tues.* Ⓜ *Blue Line to Santa Apolónia.*

 Coffee and Quick Bites

Café com Calma

$ | **CAFÉ** | Mismatched chairs, old plates used as wall art, and a simple menu of quality coffees and small meals are the order of the day at this neighborhood café. The menu includes healthy and vegan options. **Known for:** house-made cakes and other sweets; Brazilian savory snacks; homey but hip vibe. $ *Average main: €12* ✉ *Rua do Açúcar 10, Marvila* ☎ *21/868–0398* 🌐 *www.facebook.com/cafecomcalmamarvila* ⏲ *Closed weekends* Ⓜ *Blue Line to Santa Apólonia.*

Oficina Craft Snackery

$ | **BURGER** | A highlight among the food trucks in the hipster venue 8 Marvila, Oficina Craft Snackery specializes in "decadent," artisanal smashed-patty burgers. The menu is brief but hits all the bases, ranging from a double beef burger with bacon and cheddar to a portobello burger with red coleslaw and lime sauce. **Known for:** gloriously messy burgers; French fries with cheddar sauce; hipster ambience. $ *Average main: €11* ✉ *8 Marvila, Praça David Leandro da Silva 8, Marvila* 🌐 *www.facebook.com/oficinacrafts-nackery* ⏲ *Closed Mon.–Wed.* Ⓜ *Blue Line to Santa Apolónia.*

Praça Beato

$ | **CAFÉ** | This new combination gourmet market and food hall also serves as a laptop-friendly all-day café. Different stalls sell coffee, snacks, cheese, sausages, and various light bites. **Known for:** indoor-outdoor seating; weekend brunch; cheese and sausage from small producers around the country. $ *Average main: €9* ✉ *Hub Criativo do Beato, Travessa do Grilo 1, Beato* ☎ *21/050–7569* 🌐 *apraca.pt* Ⓜ *Blue Line to Santa Apólonia.*

 Nightlife

★ Dois Carvos Marvila Taproom

BREWPUBS | One of Lisbon's first craft breweries and its first taproom, Dois Corvos is a brewer-owned outfit known for its range of beers, from dependable session beers and IPAs to big barrel-aged stouts, experimental ales, and mixed fermentations. The taproom is a place where you can quaff with other beer lovers and brewers. All the core beers are on tap, along with seasonal experiments and a guest tap for other breweries. ✉ *Rua Capitão Leitão 94, Marvila* ☎ *21/138–4366* 🌐 *www.doiscorvos.pt* ⏲ *Closed Mon.* Ⓜ *Blue Line to Santa Apolónia.*

Fermentage

BREWPUBS | The newest brewpub in Marvila's nightlife lineup, Fermentage not only takes its name from the process of brewing beer but also offers a snack menu that celebrates fermented foods. Come here for the beer—there are more than a dozen hyperspecific varieties on tap—and the table games and occasional live entertainment. ✉ *Rua Capitão Leitão 1B, Marvila* ☎ *21/584–6678* 🌐 *www.fermentage.com* Ⓜ *Blue Line to Santa Apolónia.*

★ MUSA de Marvila

BREWPUBS | MUSA makes a range of small-batch artisanal beer using traditional methods and archival recipes. The taproom here is less a cathedral of hops and more a place to have a good time. After a few location changes, the brewing equipment is still visible inside, but on sunny days, the action is outside, on the colorful terrace. There's a roster of live music and a menu of beer-friendly snacks. ✉ *Rua do Vale Formoso 9, Marvila* ☎ *92/423–6447* 🌐 *cervejamusa.com* Ⓜ *Blue Line to Santa Apolónia.*

Performing Arts

★ Fábrica Braço de Prata

PERFORMANCE VENUES | In a former armaments factory, this multiconcept cultural space encompasses exhibition rooms, a bookstore, shops, conferences, film screenings, and concerts ranging from jazz to rock, funk, and world music. Although everything is now up to code, it still retains some of the feeling of a half-abandoned building, with rooms that artists might take over from time to time. One of the more popular residencies is a storytelling series that takes place in English and in Portuguese. ✉ *Rua Fábrica de Material de Guerra 1, Marvila* ☎ *93/049–7484* 🌐 *www.fabricabracodeprata.com* Ⓜ *Blue Line to Santa Apolónia.*

Teatro Meridional

THEATER | This experimental theater company is one of the most highly regarded in Portugal. While many of the productions are dramas performed in Portuguese, the programming also includes adaptations of major theatrical works (Shakespeare et al.), opera, dance, and other performances in which the spoken word isn't the main form of communication. ✉ *Rua do Açúcar 64, Beco da Mitra - Poço do Bispo, Marvila* ☎ *91/999–1213* 🌐 *www.teatromeridional.net* Ⓜ *Blue Line to Santa Apolónia.*

Chapter 8

ALCÂNTARA, CAIS DO SODRÉ, AND SANTOS

Updated by
Ann Abel

Sights	Restaurants	Hotels	Shopping	Nightlife
★☆☆☆	★★★★☆			

NEIGHBORHOOD SNAPSHOT

TOP EXPERIENCES

■ **Lively nightlife.** Cais de Sodré and its famous Pink Street are an epicenter of Lisbon's nightlife scene.

■ **Sipping natural wines.** The main drag in Santos is lined with small bars specializing in seasonal small plates and natural and low-intervention wines.

■ **Gourmet extravaganza.** One of Lisbon's most visited spots, the Time Out Market in Mercado da Ribeira collects the culinary vision of the city's top chefs under one roof.

GETTING HERE

Trains, metros, buses, and ferries arrive at and depart from Cais do Sodré, making it one of the best spots in the city for transportation. Trains from Cais do Sodré stop at Santos and Alcântara on their way to Belém and the beaches of the Costa do Estoril. A bus stop in Alcântara serves destinations south of the Tagus River. Santos has no metro stop (although one is being constructed) and parts of the neighborhood are hilly with narrow streets that are impossible to reach by car—something to bear in mind if you're laden down with luggage.

PLANNING YOUR TIME

There's no bad time of day to visit here. In the morning, a slew of cafés serve specialty coffee and avocado toast; by the time they close, the wine bars and casual bistros are opening up. After dinner, the bars of Pink Street and clubs along the river come to life, with the party really getting started after midnight.

VIEWFINDER

■ **Miradouro da Rocha de Conde de Óbidos.** While these riverside neighborhoods lack the dramatic viewpoints of their hilltop counterparts, this small park in Santos has benches along a nice river overlook. A restaurant called Catch Me shares the same view, as does the garden at Museu Nacional de Arte Antiga. ✉ *Rua Presidente Arriaga.*

OFF THE BEATEN PATH

■ **Tapada das Necessidades.** This somewhat abandoned garden was once a royal residence, with exotic plants, historic statuary, and a beautifully decaying crystal palace. Unlike most parks, it doesn't have cafés or concessions (for now, at least), so it tends to be quieter and a good spot for picnics. ✉ *Largo Necessidades.*

Although Lisbon's cool kids have largely moved on to less expensive bohemian enclaves away from the historic city center, this trio of neighborhoods beside the Tagus River has largely retained its hipster appeal.

An influx of foreign residents has changed the fabric of the districts—you're likely to hear more English than Portuguese in many establishments—but they're still home to destination dining, nightlife, and artsy shopping. The whole stretch from the Cais de Sodré train station westward toward Belém is awash in ndependent bars, cafés, and boutique stores. Anchored by the nega-successful Time Out Market food hall and the booming Pink Street on one end, and the manufactured bohemia of LxFactory nd Village Underground on the other, the area appeals to those vho appreciate a low-key good meal or good time. While it's not place for checklist travel—no must-see monuments or famous ity views—it draws a good number of visitors who like the "slice f life" feeling of its small independent businesses.

ormerly a working-class neighborhood alongside the city's fishing nd industrial ports, Alcântara played a starring role in Lisbon's ebirth as Europe's Capital of Cool almost a decade ago. That was hanks in large part to the revamped warehouses at LxFacto- y—now a miniature village with boho-chic bars, boutiques, and ookshops. Nearby Village Underground is a late-night party spot rgely made of disused shipping containers and double-decker uses. But apart from those party places, the neighborhood is still ome to old-school seafood joints where the tables are covered ith white paper, waiters serve tiny cold beers faster than you can rder them, and a Benfica football match always seems to be on e television.

stroll along the banks of the Tagus River takes visitors to Santos, here natural wine bars, specialty coffee shops, and sushi joints side by side with traditional homes. Although many apartments ve been taken over by Airbnb and resident foreigners, some ighborhood old-timers still grill sardines on the cobblestone eets during June's famous street parties. Santos is also home a number of universities, including an arts and design school, awing a lot of young Portuguese creatives and international idents.

To get a feel for cool, happening modern Lisbon, head to the bars, shops, and workspaces of LxFactory.

Nightlife steps it up a level along the Santos waterfront and in nearby Cais do Sodré. Partiers pack the bars of Pink Street until dawn, and tucked away behind the ferry terminal, large riverside nightclubs—many with a strong Brazilian accent—throb through the night.

A stroll along the riverfront takes you from one neighborhood to the next, although the people-watching and snack opportunities improve significantly if you move away from the river and walk along Rua de São Paulo, Rua da Boavista, and Rua das Janelas Verdes (all essentially one street, following Lisbon's convention of changing its street names every couple of blocks). Alternatively, you can jump on a bus, tram, or train to save time and energy; each of these hot spots is on the railway line to Cascais.

Alcântara, Cais do Sodré, and Santos

Sights

★ LxFactory

NEIGHBORHOOD | A former industrial area that was transformed into a symbol of Lisbon's creative spirit, LxFactory is a colorful collection of cafés, bars, and boutiques. There's an excellent bookshop, Ler Devagar ("Read Slowly") with its own bar, plus a rooftop bar atop a hostel that serves cocktails to a young laid-bac crowd. There's notable art to admire, too, and fans line up to snap pictures of the giant bee by Bordalo II, one of Lisbon's most celebrated street artists. ✉ *Rua Rodrigues de Faria 103, Alcântara* 🌐 *lxfactory.com* Ⓜ *Cascais Line to Alcântara-Mar.*

Museu da Carris

TRANSPORTATION MUSEUM | FAMILY | This museum celebrating Lisbon's public transport past and present is next to the creative hub Village Underground and donated the distinctive double-decker buses that now house that attraction's café. It's worth taking the opportunity to climb aboard a classic tram that trundles from one converted warehouse to another, allowing visitors to admire vintage buses, streetcars, uniforms, and other artifacts from Lisbon's public transport history. A gift shop sells cute miniature buses and trams. ✉ *Rua 1 de Maio 101–103, Alcântara* ☎ *21/361–3087* 🌐 *museu.carris.pt* 🎫 *€4.50* ⏲ *Closed Sun.* Ⓜ *Tram 15E or 18E to Estação Santo Amaro.*

Museu Nacional de Arte Antiga (*National Museum of Ancient Art*)

ART MUSEUM | Portugal's National Museum of Ancient Art is housed in an opulent 17th-century palace, built at the behest of the Count of Alvor and later occupied by the brother of the Marquês de Pombal. Try not to spend too much time gaping at the dramatic painted ceilings, stucco detailing, and baroque doorways or you'll miss the collection of more than 40,000 works, including the unsettling circa-1500 triptych *Temptations of Saint Anthony* by Hieronymous Bosch, one of the most important pieces in the country. A cafeteria with seating in lovely gardens is the perfect place for a post-viewing drink or meal. ✉ *Rua das Janelas Verdes, Santos* ☎ *21/391–2800* 🌐 *www.museudearteantiga.pt* 🎫 *€10* ⏲ *Closed Mon.* Ⓜ *Tram 15E or 18E to Cais Rocha.*

Pilar 7 Bridge Experience

VIEWPOINT | FAMILY | At this innovative interactive attraction you'll be whisked up to a glass-floored viewing platform alongside the beautiful Ponte 25 de Abril. You'll learn how this engineering marvel was constructed, get a glimpse inside one of the massive pillars, and take a virtual-reality tour of parts that nobody can otherwise reach. ✉ *Ponte 25 de Abril, Av. da Índia, Alcântara* ☎ *21/111–7880* 🌐 *www.visitlisboa.com/en/places/pilar-7-bridge-experience* 🎫 *€5.50* Ⓜ *Cascais Line to Alcântara-Mar.*

Ponte 25 de Abril (*25th of April Bridge*)

BRIDGE | Lisbon's first bridge across the Tagus River, linking the Alcântara and Almada districts, is a double-decker suspension bridge that stands 230 feet above the water and stretches more than 2 km (1½ miles). Reminiscent of San Francisco's Golden Gate Bridge, it's slightly shorter but still a spectacular sight from any direction. Cars and buses cross on the top tier while trains

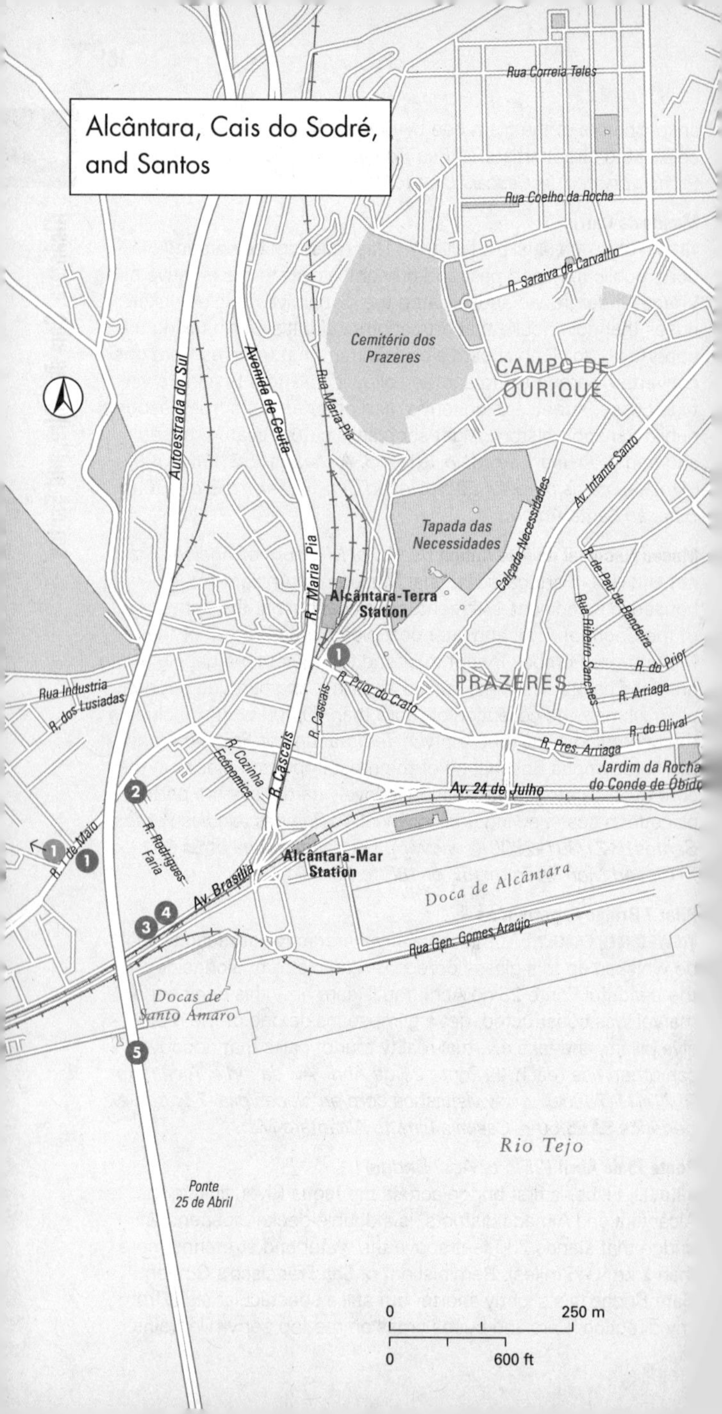
Alcântara, Cais do Sodré, and Santos
Rua Correia Teles
Rua Coelho da Rocha
R. Saraiva de Carvalho
Cemitério dos Prazeres
CAMPO DE OURIQUE
Autoestrada do Sul
Avenida de Ceuta
Rua Maria Pia
Av. Infante Santo
Tapada das Necessidades
Calçada Necessidades
R. de Pau de Bandeira
R. Maria Pia
Alcântara-Terra Station
Rua Ribeiro Sanches
R. do Prior
PRAZERES
R. Arriaga
R. Prior do Crato
R. Cascais
Rua Industria
R. dos Lusiadas
R. do Olival
R. Pres. Arriaga
Jardim da Rocha do Conde de Óbidos
R. Cozinha Económica
R. Cascais
Av. 24 de Julho
R. 1 de Maio
R. Rodrigues Faria
Alcântara-Mar Station
Av. Brasília
Doca de Alcântara
Rua Gen. Gomes Araújo
Docas de Santo Amaro
Rio Tejo
Ponte 25 de Abril
0
250 m
0
600 ft

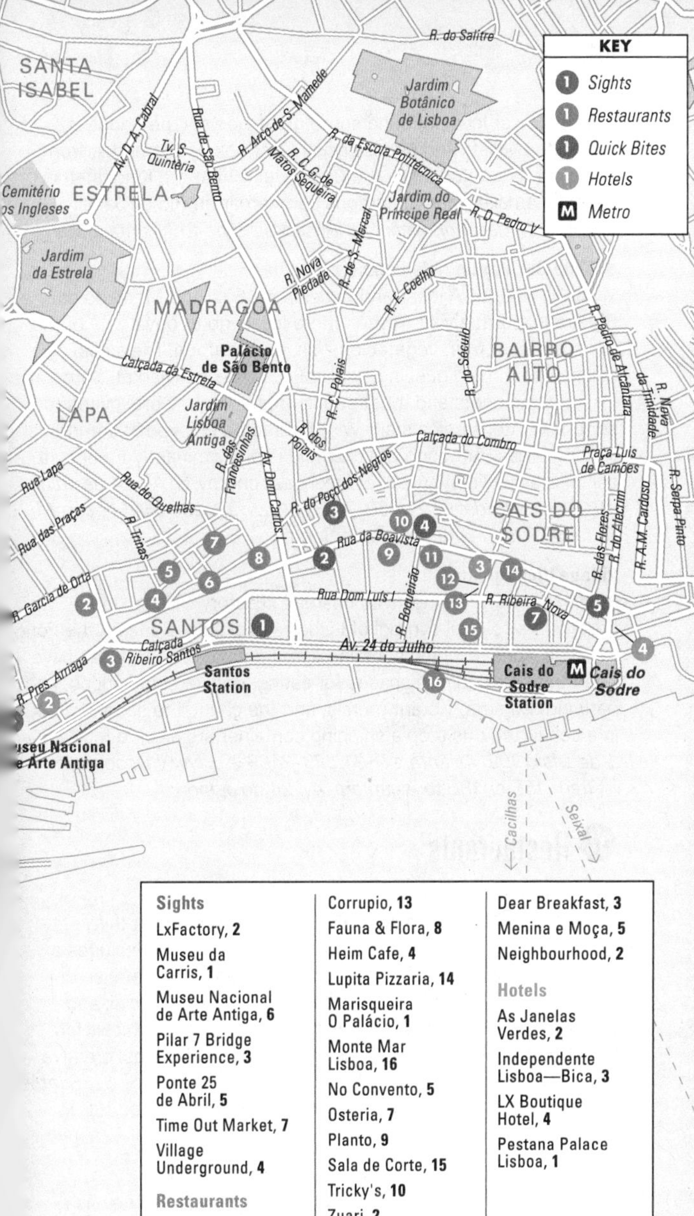

Sights

LxFactory, **2**

Museu da Carris, **1**

Museu Nacional de Arte Antiga, **6**

Pilar 7 Bridge Experience, **3**

Ponte 25 de Abril, **5**

Time Out Market, **7**

Village Underground, **4**

Restaurants

Black Trumpet, **3**

Boca Linda, **6**

Brilhante, **12**

Cav 86, **11**

Corrupio, **13**

Fauna & Flora, **8**

Heim Cafe, **4**

Lupita Pizzaria, **14**

Marisqueira O Palácio, **1**

Monte Mar Lisboa, **16**

No Convento, **5**

Osteria, **7**

Planto, **9**

Sala de Corte, **15**

Tricky's, **10**

Zuari, **2**

Quick Bites

A Merendeira, **1**

Comoba, **4**

Dear Breakfast, **3**

Menina e Moça, **5**

Neighbourhood, **2**

Hotels

As Janelas Verdes, **2**

Independente Lisboa—Bica, **3**

LX Boutique Hotel, **4**

Pestana Palace Lisboa, **1**

use the lower level, offering some great views. (The bridge is closed to cyclists and pedestrians.) Overlooking the bridge from a hill on the south bank is the Cristo Rei (Christ the King) statue, which is smaller than its famous counterpart in Rio de Janeiro. ✉ *Ponte 25 de Abril, Alcântara* Ⓜ *Cascais Line to Alcântara-Mar.*

★ **Time Out Market** (*Mercado da Ribeira*)
MARKET | **FAMILY** | A local landmark since 1892, the Mercado da Ribeira is worth a visit to see where locals go to buy some of the city's freshest fruit, vegetables, fish, and seafood. The adjoining hall has become a bustling food court, Time Out Market. Some of Lisbon's top chefs and most popular restaurants were invited to set up counter-service stalls with food to be enjoyed at communal seating areas. Although the clientele is predominantly tourists, it still offers a solid overview of local gastronomy. ✉ *Av. 24 de Julho 49, Cais do Sodré* ☎ *21/060–7403* 🌐 *www.timeoutmarket.com/lisboa* Ⓜ *Green Line to Cais do Sodré.*

Village Underground
PLAZA/SQUARE | Together with nearby LxFactory, Village Underground is a colorful symbol of Lisbon's cool side. Beneath the Ponte 25 de Abril, shipping containers and double-decker buses have been transformed into spaces for eating, drinking, coworking, and partying. DJ sets, vibrant murals, and the chance to eat and drink in a converted bus atop a shipping container are all on offer. ✉ *Rua 1 de Maio 103, Alcântara* ☎ *21/583–2469* 🌐 *www.vulisboa.com* Ⓜ *Tram 15E or 18E to Alcântara–Av. 24 de Julho.*

Restaurants

Black Trumpet
$$$ | **ECLECTIC** | Mushrooms are the star of the show at this stylish, low-lit new eatery in Santos. While the menu includes a few fish and meat plates, most of the dishes are vegetarian or vegan, spotlighting enoki, lamb's foot, portobello, porcini, and the restaurant's namesake black truffle mushrooms. **Known for:** live DJs; mushroom workshops and cultural gatherings; creative brunch. $ *Average main: €25* ✉ *Calçada Ribeiro Santos 31, Santos* ☎ *91/505–9586* 🌐 *www.blacktrumpet.pt* Ⓜ *Tram 15E or 18E to Santos.*

Boca Linda
$$$ | **MEXICAN** | Virtually everyone in the kitchen at this new-ish restaurant in Santos is from Mexico, making Boca Linda a more authentic alternative to some of the trendier taco joints sprouting up around town. The guacamole comes with *chapulines* (grasshoppers), the green *aguachile* is properly spicy, and the tacos

come with fillings like *cochinita pibil* (suckling pig) and *barbacoa* (slow-cooked meat). **Known for:** great margaritas; authentic tacos; lively atmosphere. *Average main: €22 Calçada Marquês Abrantes 92–94, Santos 93/704–1918 www.bocalindarestaurante.com Closed Mon. Tram 15E or 18E to Santos.*

Brilhante

$$$$ | FRENCH FUSION | This French-accented restaurant brings a big dose of old-school glamour to a neighborhood increasingly populated with Instagrammable brunch spots and sharable small plates. The kitchen occupies the center of the dining room, surrounded by a gleaming bar counter where patrons can dine and watch the show; alternatively, diners can tuck themselves away on red-velvet banquettes to dig into classic dishes like sole meunière and steak à la Marrare, a century-old Lisbon classic brought by a Neapolitan chef. **Known for:** glamorous bar seating; 19th-century-inspired cocktails; beef tenderloin with a secret sauce. *Average main: €30 Rua da Moeda 1G, Cais do Sodré 21/054–7981 www.restaurantebrilhante.pt Green Line to Cais do Sodré.*

Cav 86

$$$ | ECLECTIC | While the main street linking Cais de Sodré and Santos seems to be one natural wine bar after another, Cav 86 stands out from the crowd for the quality of its wine selection and for the sophistication of its food menu. There's not a perfunctory snack in sight; rather, the long menu of sharable plates includes dishes like duck rillettes, pumpkin arancini, and beef tartare with mussels escabeche. **Known for:** long-fermentation sourdough bread; good selection of wines by the glass; thoughtful vegetarian options. *Average main: €25 Rua da Boavista 86, Cais do Sodré 21/346–0629 www.cav86.com Green Line to Cais do Sodré.*

★ Corrupio

$$ | PORTUGUESE | A U-shaped dining counter takes center stage at this laid-back restaurant in the heart of Cais do Sodré. The menu offers twists on typical Portuguese dishes—octopus salad comes with dollops of purple potato puree, for instance, and a bacalhau dish sweetened with persimmon—in a relaxed sharable-plates format. **Known for:** all-Portuguese soundtrack; fresh oysters at the bar; stylish but relaxed design. *Average main: €18 Rua da Moeda 1, Cais do Sodré 21/396–1585 www.corrupio.pt Green Line to Cais do Sodré.*

auna & Flora

| **ECLECTIC** | **FAMILY** | This all-day brunch spot does a roaring trade n pancakes, avocado toast, smoothie bowls, and other breakfast

The ever-busy Time Out Market lets you sample cuisine from some of Lisbon's best chefs—from the traditional to the cutting-edge—under one roof.

favorites. Lines are virtually inevitable at any time of day, but the flower-filled café is a pleasant place to wait. **Known for:** healthy menu with lots of fresh fruit and vegetables; good smoothies, coffee, and cocktails; bright interior and attractively presented dishes. *Average main: €12* *Rua da Esperança 33, Santos* *96/164–5040* *www.faunafloralisboa.com* *Tram 15E or 18E to Santos.*

Heim Cafe

$ | **ECLECTIC** | This bright and breezy Ukrainian-owned café was a pioneer in bringing trendy Instagrammable brunches to Santos's main drag. Its pretty, tasty meals made it famous, so there's usually a line, but the avocado toast on house-baked sourdough is worth the wait. **Known for:** trendy crowd; choice of set brunches; gluten-free and vegan options. *Average main: €11* *Rua de Santos-o-Velho 2–4, Santos* *93/577–5833* *www.facebook.com/heim.lisbon* *Tram 25E to Santos-o-Velho.*

Lupita Pizzaria

$ | **PIZZA** | Widely considered one of Lisbon's best pizzerias, Lupita is the product of a Brazilian chef turning out Italian-style pies. The dining room is no-frills—guests sit on tiny stools at low tables, and the line is usually down the block—and the pizzas are both simple and playful. **Known for:** light, naturally leavened crust; Basque-style cheesecake; daring topping choices. *Average main: €14* *Rua de São Paulo 79, Cais do Sodré* *93/500–2182* *www.facebook.com/lupita.pizzaria* *Green Line to Cais do Sodré.*

Marisqueira O Palácio

$$ | **SEAFOOD** | **FAMILY** | Staunchly traditional amid the flurry of modernization in the surrounding streets, this old-school *marisqueira* (seafood hall) is the best of several local spots specializing in shellfish. Priced by the kilo, the day's offer varies according to season and what the anglers have hauled in, but expect enormous, perfectly fresh crustaceans year-round. **Known for:** loyal local clientele; vast array of fresh fish and seafood; simple traditional design. *Average main: €20* *Rua Prior do Crato 142, Alcântara* *21/396–1647* *www.facebook.com/marisqueirapalacio* *Closed Thurs.* *Tram 15E or 18E to Alcântara–Av. 24 de Julho.*

Monte Mar Lisboa

$$$$ | **SEAFOOD** | A city-smart sister to the celebrated Monte Mar restaurant in Cascais, Monte Mar Lisboa offers the same superior seafood with a more relaxed riverfront ambience. Occupying one of the formerly disused warehouses along a lightly revitalized stretch of the waterfront, Monte Mar has a terrific view of the river, the Ponte 25 de Abril, and the Cristo Rei on the other side, while indoors it's all industrial-chic black and chrome. **Known for:** tasty spider crab, lobster, and other crustaceans; signature dish of hake fillet with cockle rice; set lunch menu weekdays. *Average main: €26* *Rua da Cintura do Porto de Lisboa, Armazém 65, Cais do Sodré* *96/334–2983* *www.montemar.pt* *Green Line to Cais do Sodré.*

No Convento

$$$$ | **FRENCH FUSION** | The name means "in the convent" in Portuguese, because this new date-night spot occupies a 17th-century convent tucked away on a side street in Santos. The food combines Portuguese ingredients with French traditions. **Known for:** romantic candlelit atmosphere; luxury ingredients like foie gras and Wagyu beef; historic setting. *Average main: €40* *Travessa do Convento das Bernardas 12, Santos* *91/538–9532* *www.noconvento.com* *Closed Mon.* *Tram 15E or 18E to Santos.*

Osteria

$ | **ITALIAN** | This tiny welcoming Italian restaurant serves small plates designed to be shared among friends. There are excellent imported cheeses, sausages, and wines alongside mains and desserts typical of the Sardinia region. **Known for:** warm welcome and homestyle cooking; affordable wine list and Italian liqueurs; cozy decor with lots of Italian flags and film posters. *Average main: €12* *Rua das Madres 52, Santos* *21/396–0584* *Tram 25E to Rua da Esperança.*

Planto

$$ | **PORTUGUESE** | Chef Vitor Adão made his name across town at the fine-dining Plano, but at this casual all-day spin-off, you can find the same quality without the commitment of a tasting menu. The plates here are simple Portuguese classics—tempura green beans, octopus rice, and Alentejo black pork—but with top-notch ingredients and technique. **Known for:** quality ingredients from top Portuguese producers; pretty plant-filled dining room; creative cocktails. *Average main: €20* ✉ *Rua da Boavista 68A, Cais do Sodré* ☎ *93/838–1922* Ⓜ *Green Line to Cais de Sodré.*

Sala de Corte

$$$$ | **STEAK HOUSE** | Sala de Corte is all about the meat, notably prime cuts of beef, grilled to perfection and accompanied by a savory dipping sauce, like Stilton, chimichurri, black truffle mayo, or béarnaise. Sip a cocktail at the stylishly lit long bar before taking a table. **Known for:** dry-aged beef cooked in a Josper oven; sophisticated contemporary style; classic steak-house sides like creamed spinach. *Average main: €36* ✉ *Praça de Dom Luis I 7, Cais do Sodré* ☎ *21/346–0030* 🌐 *saladecorte.pt* Ⓜ *Green Line to Cais do Sodré.*

★ Tricky's

$$$ | **ECLECTIC** | One of the hippest tables in town, Tricky's is a collaborative project between natural wine sommeliers and creative next-gen chefs. Cooks in the open kitchen—the best seats are at the counter right in front of it—create a menu of sharable small plates with Portuguese, Italian, and Asian influences, and they're matched with low-intervention wines from across Europe. **Known for:** creative small plates; eclectic international list of natural wines; festive vibe. *Average main: €21* ✉ *Rua da Boavista 112, Cais do Sodré* ☎ *93/958–8019* 🌐 *www.cometotrickys.com* ⊙ *Closed weekends* Ⓜ *Green Line to Cais de Sodré.*

Zuari

$ | **INDIAN** | **FAMILY** | Serving spicy samosas, curries, and other spicy treats since the 1970s, Zuari was one of the first Goan restaurants to open in Lisbon (and many would argue it's still the best). It's a wonderful introduction to the flavors of the former Portuguese colony, and the very fair prices mean culinary adventures here won't break the bank. **Known for:** traditional Goan cuisine; excellent shrimp curries; light and crispy samosas. *Average main: €11* ✉ *Rua São João da Mata 41, Santos* ☎ *21/397–7149* 🌐 *www.facebook.com/restaurantezuari* ⊙ *Closed Mon.* Ⓜ *Tram 25E to Santos-o-Velho.*

Coffee and Quick Bites

A Merendeira

$ | **PORTUGUESE** | The late-night fueling stop of choice for many a hard-partying Lisboeta, A Merendeira's specialty is as simple as it is delicious: *pão com chouriço* (sausage baked into a bread roll). Grab one to go, or sit down and enjoy it with a bowl of *caldo verde* (cabbage soup). **Known for:** late-night grub; affordable prices; traditional Portuguese savory snacks. *Average main: €5 ✉ Av. 24 de Julho 54G, Santos ☎ 21/397–2726 ⊕ amerendeira.com Ⓜ Yellow Line to Santos, Tram 15E or 18E to Santos.*

Comoba

$ | **ECLECTIC** | This eco-conscious café sources all its ingredients from local independent producers. There's abundant use of matcha, quinoa, and spirulina, and as there's no refined sugar in any of the cakes, cookies, and other sweet treats, they make a perfect guilt-free pick-me-up when combined with a cup of Comoba's excellent coffee. **Known for:** lots of vegan and gluten-free options; bright rustic-chic interior; excellent small-batch-roasted coffee. *Average main: €13 ✉ Rua da Boavista 90, Cais do Sodré ⊕ www.comoba-lisboa.com Ⓜ Green Line to Cais do Sodré.*

Dear Breakfast

$ | **CONTEMPORARY** | However you like your eggs in the morning (or afternoon), Dear Breakfast will cook them to perfection, alongside a cheerful range of house-baked breads, fresh juices, and jams. Eat them any which way, from omelets and eggs Benedict to chipotle shakshuka. **Known for:** minimalist interior; style mags to flick through; organic juices. *Average main: €10 ✉ Rua das Gaivotas 17, Santos ☎ 21/228–1082 ⊕ www.dearbreakfast.com Ⓜ Tram 25E to Conde Barão.*

Menina e Moça

$ | **CAFÉ** | Offering a little respite from the rowdy nightlife of Pink Street, this cute café-bar doubles as a bookstore, and it's not unusual to see live jazz or jam sessions. The bright primary colors and painted ceiling give it the look of a cozy kids' corner, but the coffees and cocktails are strictly for grown-ups. **Known for:** live music; late hours; subdued vibe. *Average main: €6 ✉ Rua Nova do Carvalho 40–42, Cais do Sodré ☎ 21/827–2331 ⊕ www.facebook.com/livrariabarmeninaemoca Ⓜ Green Line to Cais do Sodré.*

Neighbourhood

$ | **COFFEE** | Neighbourhood was a pioneer in Lisbon's specialty coffee scene when it opened in 2019, and it still offers a wide selection of top-quality caffeinated drinks, including batch brew and V60. There are also snacks like banana bread, and bigger meals like breakfast burritos and Turkish eggs. **Known for:** high-quality coffee selection; craft beer and hard kombucha; evening burger menu. *Average main: €9 Largo Conde-Barão 25, Cais do Sodré 21/406–8809 www.neighbourhoodlisbon.com Green Line to Cais do Sodré.*

Hotels

★ As Janelas Verdes

$$$$ | HOTEL | A member of the Lisbon Heritage collection of storied small hotels, this late-18th-century town house maintains its period furnishings, paintings, and tile in the common areas, and the guest rooms have been individually furnished with the same care and taste. **Pros:** romantic setting; free tea and coffee all day in the lounge; location far from tourist crowds. **Cons:** no subway station nearby; no pool; classic rooms on the small side. *Rooms from: €370 Rua das Janelas Verdes 47, Santos 21/396–8143 lisbonheritagehotels.com/as-janelas-verdes 29 rooms Free Breakfast Green Line to Santos.*

Independente Lisboa—Bica

$$$$ | HOTEL | The newest hotel from Lisbon's boho-chic Independente group occupies a 150-year-old building on a lively block near Cais de Sodré. **Pros:** great location near nightlife, transit, and cafés; unique set-menu Asian breakfast; state-of-the-art appliances and tech. **Cons:** basic rooms are small; built-in furniture limits floor space; twin and triple rooms have bunk beds. *Rooms from: €295 Rua de São Paulo 93, Cais do Sodré 91/230–2197 independente.eu/lisboa-bica/ 41 rooms Free Breakfast Green Line to Cais de Sodré.*

LX Boutique Hotel

$$ | HOTEL | With a location in one of Lisbon's liveliest neighborhoods, the duck-egg-blue LX Boutique Hotel is perfect if you're looking forward to a night on the town, want to visit the historic sights at Belém, or spend some time at the beach. **Pros:** close transport links; chic design; at the heart of the nightlife action. **Cons:** "classic" rooms are small; breakfast not included in base rate; can be noisy at night. *Rooms from: €180 Rua do Alecrim 12, Cais do Sodré 21/347–4394 www.lxboutiquehotel.com 61 rooms No Meals Green Line to Cais do Sodré.*

★ Pestana Palace Lisboa

$$$$ | HOTEL | Madonna based herself at this restored 19th-century palace while house hunting in Lisbon, and it's not hard to see why the Queen of Pop fell in love with the place: the former home of the Marquis of Valle Flôr and its gardens are classified as national monuments, and the elegant property harbors a collection of fine art. **Pros:** elegant Valle Flôr restaurant; beautiful outdoor and indoor swimming pools; spa offers an exclusive range of treatments. **Cons:** some distance from major attractions; outdoor pool area busy in summer; luxury comes at a price. *Rooms from: €330* *Rua Jau 54, Ajuda* *21/361–5600* *www.pestanacollection.com/en/hotel/pestana-palace* *194 rooms* *Free Breakfast.*

Nightlife

BARS

A Tabacaria

COCKTAIL BARS | Killer cocktails are served with flair at this tiny former tobacconist (dating back to the 1880s) that feels a world away from the big bold sidewalk bars nearby. Don't expect a seat—space is tight, and it's usually standing room only. *Rua de São Paulo 75–77, Cais do Sodré* *91/916–2674* *Green Line to Cais do Sodré.*

★ Collect

BARS | On Lisbon's famously rowdy Pink Street, Collect is a space for those who take their music as seriously as their eating and drinking. With an on-site vinyl store and its own radio station, the spacious bar attracts a hip clientele keen to discuss their latest film and music obsessions over a craft beer, hard seltzer, or cocktail. The burgers are crowd-pleasers, too. *Rua Nova do Carvalho 60–62, Cais do Sodré* *91/716–9796* *linktr.ee/collect.pt* *Green Line to Cais do Sodré.*

★ Matiz Pombalina

COCKTAIL BARS | An upmarket cocktail bar whose decor is inspired by the Pombaline architecture of downtown Lisbon, Matiz Pombalina feels like the living room of an exceptionally stylish friend. The main focus is on gin, but every cocktail on the extensive list can be customized; live jazz provides the perfect soundtrack to your sipping. The space is quite small, so it's worth reserving a table in advance. *Rua das Trinas 25, Santos* *93/728–2684* *matiz-pombalina.pt* *Closed Sun. and Mon.* *Tram 15E or 18E to Santos.*

★ O Bom O Mau e O Vilão

BARS | This film-themed bar (the name comes from the Portuguese title of *The Good, the Bad, and the Ugly*) attracts an artsy young crowd thanks to its lengthy cocktail list and vintage-chic decor. DJs spin vinyl while patrons loaf in comfy armchairs or prop up the bar. *Rua do Alecrim 21, Cais do Sodré* *96/398–2094* *www.obomomaueovilao.pt* *Green Line to Cais do Sodré.*

★ Pensão Amor

COCKTAIL BARS | Housed in a former bordello, this offbeat hangout recalls its decadent past with velvet armchairs, tassled curtains, and a huge mural across the ceiling. Its warren of rooms houses an erotic bookshop, a bar, a café, and a dance floor. Burlesque shows add to the racy appeal, but it's more suggestive than sordid. ✉ *Rua Nova do Carvalho 38, Cais do Sodré* 🌐 *pensaoamor.pt* Ⓜ *Green Line to Cais do Sodré.*

★ Quimera Brewpub

BREWPUBS | If you choose just one craft beer spot in Lisbon, make it this one. Where else could you drink artisanal *cervejas* in a cavernous tunnel that served as a passageway for the 18th-century royal cavalry? Substantial sandwiches and a series of live music events add to the considerable appeal. ✉ *Rua Prior do Crato 6, Alcântara* ☎ *91/707–0021* 🌐 *www.quimerabrewpub.com* Ⓜ *Cascais Line to Alcântara-Mar.*

Sol e Pesca

BARS | This former fishing-tackle shop kept much of the original decor—including fishing rods and life preservers—when it reopened as a bar. The lively spot specializes in canned fish and seafood served alongside cocktails and draft beers. Arrive early to catch one of the outdoor tables on the famous Pink Street. ✉ *Rua Nova do Carvalho 44, Cais do Sodré* ☎ *21/346–7203* 🌐 *www.facebook.com/solepesca* Ⓜ *Green Line to Cais do Sodré.*

DANCE CLUBS

Dock's Club

DANCE CLUB | Arrive after midnight and be prepared to dance until dawn at this dressy nightclub in a converted warehouse by the docks of Alcântara. Expect mainstream R&B and EDM, with some Angolan beats and Brazilian funk thrown in. Weekends are packed after 1 am, and Ladies Night drinks offers on Tuesday attract a decent crowd. ✉ *Rua da Cintura do Porto de Lisboa 226, Alcântara* ☎ *96/588–2581* 🌐 *www.thedocksclub.pt* Ⓜ *Tram 15E or 18E to Cais Rocha.*

Lounge

DANCE CLUB | This hip joint is where twenty- and thirtysomething vinyl lovers gather to chat (or shout) above the pumping sound of dance music. DJs take turns on the decks, and live music performances (think hip-hop, punk, and Brazilian funk) draw crowds on weekends. ✉ *Rua da Moeda 1, Cais do Sodré* ☎ *21/397–3730* 🌐 *www.facebook.com/loungelisboa* Ⓜ *Green Line to Cais do Sodré.*

LIVE MUSIC

★ Água de Beber

LIVE MUSIC | This under-the-radar spot draws an extremely enthusiastic crowd for live Brazilian music. The excellent caipirinhas help get the party spirit flowing, and traditional meals and snacks from Brazil keep energy levels from flagging. ✉ *Rua Poiais de São Bento 73, Cais do Sodré* ☎ *91/158–1413* 🌐 *aguadebeber.pt* Ⓜ *Green Line to Cais do Sodré.*

★ B.Leza Clube

LIVE MUSIC | Playing African beats for more than 20 years, B.Leza really packs them in at this riverfront warehouse. It has a strong Angolan influence, with *kizomba* dance workshops and regular live music and dance shows. ✉ *Cais da Ribeira Nova, Armazém B, Cais do Sodré* ☎ *21/010–6837* 🌐 *www.facebook.com/blezaclube* Ⓜ *Green Line to Cais do Sodré.*

★ MusicBox

LIVE MUSIC | Under the arches on the famous Pink Street—you can find it by the enormous mural overhead—MusicBox is one of the best spots in Lisbon to catch well-known bands and popular DJs. The musical menu is quite eclectic, so check listings in advance and be prepared to dance until dawn. ✉ *Rua Nova do Carvalho 24, Cais do Sodré* ☎ *21/343–0107* 🌐 *musicboxlisboa.com* Ⓜ *Green Line to Cais do Sodré.*

Quiosque Ribeira das Naus

LIVE MUSIC | Grab a seat—or a sunlounger—at this riverfront kiosk and listen to live pop, rock, or samba as the sun sets over the Tagus. Musicians gather here on sunny evenings to entertain the totally chillaxed crowds. ✉ *Avenida Ribeira das Naus, Cais do Sodré* ☎ *91/214 088 889* Ⓜ *Green Line to Cais do Sodré.*

Titanic Sur Mer

LIVE MUSIC | Live music comes with a dash of Brazilian panache at this popular late-night dance spot. The famous Sunday-night Roda da Samba (musicians take turns to play) attracts artists from across the city. Hip-hop, rock, and Cuban jazz take the stage as well. Check listings in advance as this popular spot has one of the most eclectic musical menus in Lisbon. ✉ *Cais da Ribeira Nova, Armazém B, Cais do Sodré* 🌐 *www.facebook.com/titanicsurmer* Ⓜ *Green Line to Cais do Sodré.*

FOOD AND DRINK

★ Gleba—Moagem e Padaria

FOOD | Sourdough loaves made by talented and passionate young baker Diogo Amorim attract carb-craving Lisboetas from across the city. Amorim learned his trade in some of the world's top kitchens, and here he perfects the art, using flour prepared in an on-site stone mill. There are now several outposts of Gleba in and around Lisbon, but this is where it all began. ✉ *Rua Prior do Crato 16, Lisbon* ☎ *96/606–4697* 🌐 *mygleba.com* Ⓜ *Tram 15E or 18E to Alcântara–Av. 24 de Julho.*

Loja das Conservas

FOOD | Shop and sample more than 300 beautifully packed varieties of canned fish at this store/museum. Maps and other artifacts illuminate the Portuguese craft of conserving fish in tins, and you can guess the star ingredient of the adjoining café. ✉ *Rua do Arsenal 130, Cais do Sodré* ☎ *91/118–1210* 🌐 *www.facebook.com/lojadasconservas* Ⓜ *Green Line to Cais do Sodré.*

CLOTHING

+351

CLOTHING | This made-in-Portugal shop celebrates life between the city and the sea. The boutique offers a selection of colorful, unisex post-surf and streetwear basics in high-quality cotton T-shirts and sweatshirts, sometimes printed with laid-back slogans, and cozy fleece pullovers. ✉ *Rua da Boavista 81C, Cais do Sodré* 🌐 *plus351.pt* Ⓜ *Green Line to Cais de Sodré.*

Chapter 9

ESTRELA, CAMPO DE OURIQUE, AND LAPA

Updated by
Joana Taborda

Sights	Restaurants	Hotels	Shopping	Nightlife
★★★☆☆	★★★★☆	★★☆☆☆	★★★☆☆	★★★☆☆

NEIGHBORHOOD SNAPSHOT

TOP EXPERIENCES

■ **Local crafts.** Browse through the stalls of Estrela's craft and design market, held every first weekend of the month (except January) at the Jardim da Estrela.

■ **Sightseeing tours.** Hop on Tram 25 or 28 and enjoy a slow-paced ride.

■ **Mercado de Campo de Ourique.** Renovated in 2013, this is one of Lisbon's first gourmet food markets.

■ **Go tile hunting.** Have your camera handy to capture the picturesque tile facades adorning the neighborhood's streets.

GETTING HERE

Estrela, Campo de Ourique, and Lapa are about a 15-minute walk up Avenida Álvares Cabral from the Rato metro station, but the best way to reach this part of town is by tram. Trams 25 and 28 both go from the city center past the basilica in Estrela, ending their journey in Campo de Ourique.

VIEWFINDER

Torres das Amoreiras. Just a few feet from Campo de Ourique's grid of streets are the imposing and modern Amoreiras Towers. They are mostly home to offices and luxury apartments, but downstairs is Lisbon's first major mall, which opened in 1985. That's where you'll find an elevator that takes you to the top of the towers and the tallest observation deck in the city. Once there, take in the gorgeous 360-degree views. ✉ *Av. Engenheiro Duarte Pacheco* 🌐 *www.amoreiras360view.com* 🚊 *Tram 24 to Rua Amoreiras.*

PLANNING YOUR TIME

■ Some restaurants and shops close on Sunday and/or Monday, so plan your visit accordingly to make the most of the sights.

OFF THE BEATEN PATH

■ **Aqueduto das Águas Livres.** About a 15-minute walk from Campo de Ourique is Lisbon's remarkable aqueduct, one of the few structures left standing after the Great Earthquake of 1755. Still considered one of the greatest hydraulic and engineering works of all time, it had the world's tallest stone arches when it was built in 1732. You can now walk over the 14 largest arches while enjoying views of the city. ✉ *Calçada da Quintinha 6* 🚊 *Tram 24 to Campolide.*

Lisbon's historic trams snake through these quiet residential neighborhoods, but it's worth jumping off to explore streets lined with rare tiled facades, family-friendly gardens, and a hidden reservoir-turned-art-gallery.

The affluent district of Lapa was laid out shortly after the Great Earthquake of 1755, on what was then the outskirts of the city. It was where the wealthier classes built their mansions, most of which have since been turned into embassies or hotels (the most notable examples are down Rua do Sacramento à Lapa). Other buildings follow a neoclassical style, with many featuring beautiful decorative tiles on their facades.

In the middle of these three neighborhoods is Jardim da Estrela, a semitropical garden which is a beloved meeting spot for locals. It's a popular hangout for expat families, as many private schools like the Lycée Français are located nearby. The British have been coming here since the 18th century; many of them, including writer Henry Fielding, are now buried in the English Cemetery opposite the garden.

On the other end is the Basilica da Estrela, a neoclassical church with an iconic dome that can be spotted across the city. With Lisbon's metro network set to extend to Estrela in 2025, this area will likely become even more popular.

Those who prefer the nostalgic feel of the tram can continue to ride it across the neighborhood all the way up to Campo de Ourique. This area is very much tied to Portugal's Republican uprising, as it was established in 1910 when the monarchy was overthrown. Portuguese engineer Frederico Ressano Garcia designed the neighborhood following a modern grid layout. During the First Republic, which lasted until 1926, several protests and strikes took place here, and there were regular literary gatherings at the neighborhood's cafés. Indeed, this would become the living grounds for many Portuguese cultural figures like writer Fernando Pessoa, whose house has been converted into a museum.

For the most part, this is still a residential area where neighbors linger over a coffee at the local kiosk, stock up on fresh produce from small grocery stores, and peruse endless shops dedicated to home decor and kids' clothing.

Estrela, Campo de Ourique, and Lapa

Sights

Aqueduto das Águas Livres (*Aqueduct of Free Waters*)
NOTABLE BUILDING | Stretching for more than 18 km (11 miles), the Aqueduct of Free Waters began providing Lisbon with clean drinking water in 1748. The most imposing section is the 35 arches—the largest of these is said to be the highest ogival (pointed) arch in the world—that stride across the Alcântara River Valley. Nearer the city center, another 14 arches run 200 feet along the Praça das Amoreiras, ending in the Mãe d'Agua reservoir. ✉ *Calçada da Quintinha 6, Campolide* ☎ *21/810–0215* 🌐 *www.epal.pt/EPAL/en/menu/water-museum* 🎟 *€4* 🕒 *Closed Mon.* Ⓜ *Tram 24 to Campolide.*

Basílica da Estrela (*Estrela Basilica*)
RELIGIOUS BUILDING | A standout on Lisbon's skyline, this gleaming white basilica was built in the baroque and neoclassical styles. Its location at the top of one of Lisbon's seven hills makes for dramatic views from its rococo *zimbório* (dome). It was built at the end of the 18th century under the command of Queen Maria I. The interior is striking, with black-and-pink marble walls and floors and an elaborate nativity scene displayed year-round. ✉ *Praça da Estrela, Estrela* ☎ *21/396–0915* 🎟 *Free for basilica; €4 for dome* Ⓜ *Yellow Line to Rato, Tram 25 or 28 to Estrela.*

Casa Fernando Pessoa
HISTORIC HOME | Writer Fernando Pessoa spent his last 15 years (1920–35) living in this house. Visitors can see Pessoa's personal items, including the typewriter where he wrote many of his last works and his personal library, with more than 1,000 handwritten notebooks and a collection of Portuguese and international poetry. The site is also a cultural center that organizes literary debates and exhibitions. ✉ *Rua Coelho da Rocha 16–18, Campo de Ourique* ☎ *21/391–3270* 🌐 *www.casafernandopessoa.pt* 🎟 *€5* 🕒 *Closed Mon.* Ⓜ *Tram 25 or 28 to Rua Saraiva Carvalho.*

English Cemetery
CEMETERY | The English Cemetery is where Lisbon's once-sizeable English community was laid to rest over the years. Thanks to the Anglo-Portuguese alliance in the 14th century, the kingdoms of Portugal and England maintained close relationships, and a considerable number of British merchants settled in Lisbon. The cemetery, found behind a gate across from Jardim da Estrela, is filled with tombstones mixing English and Portuguese surnames,

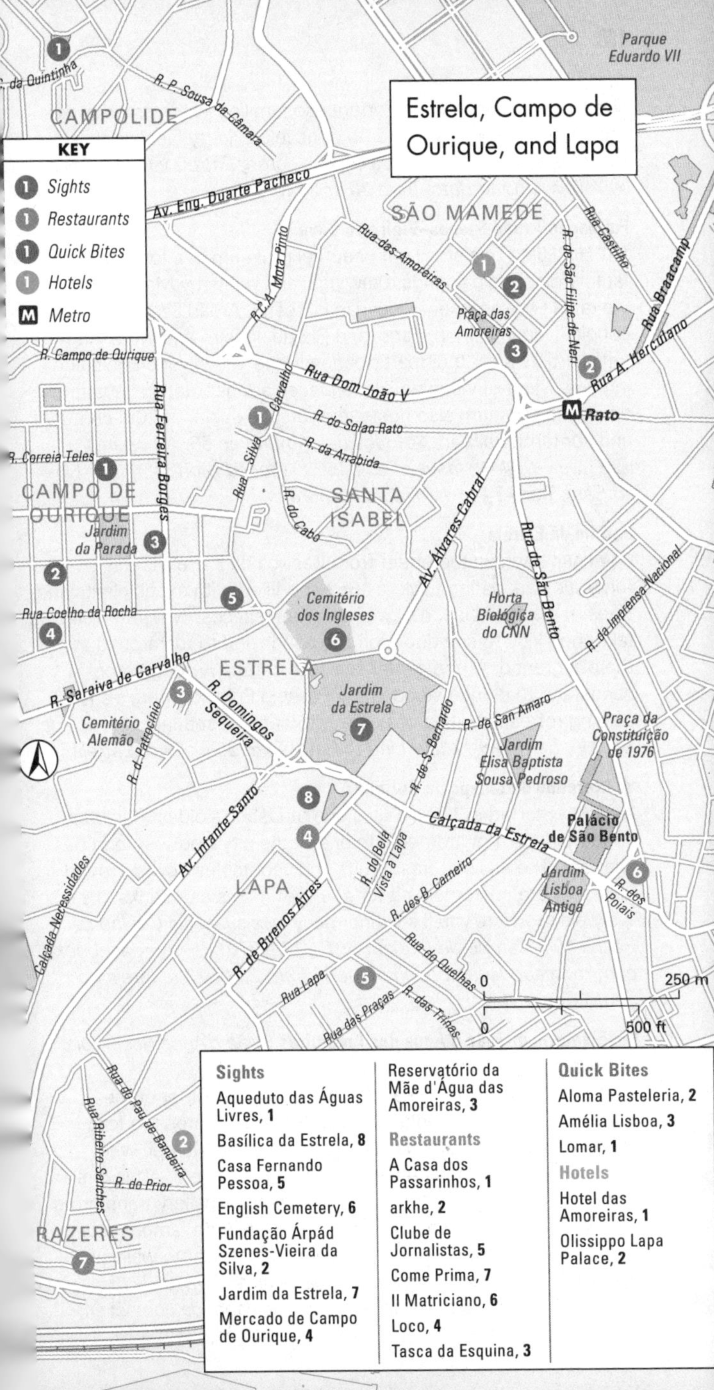

Sights

Aqueduto das Águas Livres, **1**

Basílica da Estrela, **8**

Casa Fernando Pessoa, **5**

English Cemetery, **6**

Fundação Árpád Szenes-Vieira da Silva, **2**

Jardim da Estrela, **7**

Mercado de Campo de Ourique, **4**

Reservatório da Mãe d'Água das Amoreiras, **3**

Restaurants

A Casa dos Passarinhos, **1**

arkhe, **2**

Clube de Jornalistas, **5**

Come Prima, **7**

Il Matriciano, **6**

Loco, **4**

Tasca da Esquina, **3**

Quick Bites

Aloma Pasteleria, **2**

Amélia Lisboa, **3**

Lomar, **1**

Hotels

Hotel das Amoreiras, **1**

Olissippo Lapa Palace, **2**

showing how British and Portuguese families intermarried over the centuries, but it's the tomb of novelist Henry Fielding that most visitors look for. ✉ *Rua de São Jorge, Estrela* ⏲ *Closed Sat.* Ⓜ *Yellow Line to Rato, Tram 25 or 28 to Estrela.*

Fundação Árpád Szenes–Vieira da Silva

ART MUSEUM | This small but beautiful museum in a former silk factory displays paintings, drawings, and prints by Maria Helena Vieira da Silva and her Hungarian husband, Árpád Szenes. The couple lived in Lisbon, Paris, and Rio de Janeiro and were influential artists after their participation in the 1937 World Exhibition in Paris. Most of Vieira da Silva's pieces are geometrical abstractions; the museum also hosts temporary exhibits of 20th-century and contemporary art. ✉ *Praça das Amoreiras 56, Amoreiras* ☎ *21/388–0044* 🌐 *fasvs.pt* 🎟 *€7.50* ⏲ *Closed Mon.* Ⓜ *Yellow Line to Rato, Tram 24 to Jardim das Amoreiras.*

Jardim da Estrela

CITY PARK | Across the street from Basílica da Estrela is this romantic park dating back to 1852 and filled with exotic plants and trees. It's one of Lisbon's loveliest green spaces, where families take their kids to see ducks on the ponds and to run around on the playground. At the center is a 19th-century wrought-iron bandstand that once stood in the Passeio Público. There's a kiosk serving refreshments and a café with outdoor seating. ✉ *Praça da Estrela, Estrela* Ⓜ *Yellow Line to Rato, Tram 25 or 28 to Estrela.*

★ Mercado de Campo de Ourique

MARKET | Started in 1934, this is one of Lisbon's oldest neighborhood markets, now turned into one of the city's hottest food destinations. The stalls of fresh fruits and vegetables now surround tables where customers sit for gourmet meals and drinks. It's a lively place where you'll still find many locals. ✉ *Rua Coelho da Rocha 104, Campo de Ourique* ☎ *21/132–3701* 🌐 *www.facebook.com/mercadodecampodeourique* Ⓜ *Tram 25 or 28 to Igreja do Santo Condestável.*

Reservatório da Mãe d'Água das Amoreiras (*Mãe d'Agua Reservoir and Water Museum*)

NOTABLE BUILDING | The Mãe d'Agua—literally "Mother of the Water"—is a centuries-old reservoir that's an impressive feat of engineering from Hungarian architect Carlos Mardel, who designed the enormous Aqueduto das Águas Livres. Art lovers are in for a treat, too: the ultramodern Immersivus gallery transforms the walls of the reservoir into a giant canvas, with famous works by artists like Monet, Klimt, and Kahlo projected onto walls and water. ✉ *Praça das Amoreiras 8, Amoreiras* ☎ *21/810–0215, 91/065–8479 Immersivus gallery* 🌐 *portugalagenda.com* 🎟 *€4;*

The Mãe d'Água reservoir is worth visiting as both an engineering feat and a place for artistic reflection.

€12.50 for Immersivus ⏲ Closed Mon. Ⓜ Yellow Line to Rato, Tram 24 to Jardim das Amoreiras.

Restaurants

A Casa dos Passarinhos

$ | PORTUGUESE | In business for nearly a century, "The House of the Little Birds" is a favorite for neighborhood locals and nearby office workers. Come for the house specialties, which include the famous *naco na pedra* (steak cooked on a hot stone), *vitela barrosã* (tender veal), and *açorda de gambas* (shrimp and bread stew). **Known for:** charming dining rooms; dishes served in the pots they were cooked in; affordable set lunches. $ *Average main: €14 ✉ Rua Silva Carvalho 195, Campo de Ourique ☎ 21/388–2346 🌐 www.facebook.com/acasadospassarinhos ⏲ Closed Sun. Ⓜ Yellow Line to Rato.*

★ arkhe

$$$$ | VEGETARIAN | When arkhe opened in 2019, it was one of the first fine-dining vegetarian restaurants in town. With Brazilian and Portuguese roots, Chef João Ricardo Alves has classic Italian and French training, but it was when he lived in Asia that he got a taste for plant-based cuisine. **Known for:** range of mushroom dishes; superb wine pairing; organic chocolate. $ *Average main: €75 ✉ Rua de São Filipe Néri 14, Amoreiras ☎ 21/139–5258 🌐 arkhe.pt ⏲ Closed weekends Ⓜ Yellow Line to Rato.*

★ Clube de Jornalistas

$$$ | INTERNATIONAL | Although the name suggests it's only open to the press, this restaurant welcomes everyone. The menu features innovative dishes like eggplant drizzled with miso caramel or white fish ceviche topped with spicy popcorn. **Known for:** classic 18th-century interior; creative menu incorporating European and pan-Asian influences; tempting desserts and house-made ice creams. *Average main: €23* *Rua das Trinas 129, Lapa* *21/397–7138* *restauranteclubedejornalistas.com* *Closed Wed.* *Tram 25 to Rua de São Domingos à Lapa.*

Come Prima

$$ | ITALIAN | Come Prima occupies a low-lit space split into two levels and is always packed with locals who love its distinguished Italian cuisine. If you're looking for a romantic place off the beaten path, this is a good choice. **Known for:** tasty Alba truffles; wood-oven pizzas; gigantic Parmigiano-Reggiano cheese used for pastas. *Average main: €16* *Rua do Olival 258, Santos* *21/390–2457* *www.comeprima.pt* *Closed Sun. No lunch* *Tram 15 or 18 to Avenida Infante Santo.*

Il Matriciano

$$ | ITALIAN | One of Lisbon's most authentic Italian restaurants, Il Matriciano faces the Palácio de São Bento and is owned by a couple from Rome. Diners are greeted like family and presented with a menu made from ingredients brought in twice a month from Italy. **Known for:** cheese from Italy's different regions; rustic-style interior; fruit-shaped Italian ice cream. *Average main: €16* *Rua de São Bento 107, São Bento* *21/395–2639* *Closed Sun.* *Tram 28 to Rua de São Bento/Calçada da Estrela.*

★ Loco

$$$$ | PORTUGUESE | This slick Michelin-starred restaurant offers tantalizing tasting menus by chef Alexandre Silva, who changes them frequently so he can take advantage of the freshest seasonal ingredients. Occasionally, he invites other top chefs from Lisbon and beyond to create special one-night-only menus in the dramatic open kitchen. **Known for:** tasting menus only; high-quality yet little-known Portuguese wines; gorgeous interior design. *Average main: €156* *Rua dos Navegantes 53B, Lapa* *21/395–1861* *www.loco.pt* *Closed Sun. and Mon. No lunch* *Tram 25 or 28 to Estrela.*

Tasca da Esquina

$$$$ | PORTUGUESE | Vítor Sobral, one of the country's most famous chefs, has brought together the vibe of a traditional neighborhood eatery and sophisticated dishes that appeal to modern palates. Expect to see fast-food favorites like *bitoque* (lean steak topped with an egg) given a slick modern twist. **Known for:** sharing plates; traditional cod dishes served with flair; takeaway option. $ *Average main: €29* ✉ *Rua Domingos Sequeira 41C, Campo de Ourique* ☎ *91/983–7255* 🌐 *tascadaesquina.com* ⏲ *Closed Tues. and Wed.* Ⓜ *Tram 25 or 28 to Rua Saraiva Carvalho.*

Coffee and Quick Bites

Aloma Pastelaria

$ | **PORTUGUESE** | This neighborhood pastry shop has receiving accolades for its excellent custard tarts, which stand out for being creamier than most and for always being served cold. $ *Average main: €2* ✉ *Rua Francisco Metrass 67, Campo de Ourique* ☎ *21/396–3797* 🌐 *www.aloma.pt* Ⓜ *Tram 25 or 28 to Igreja do Santo Condestável.*

Amélia Lisboa

$ | **INTERNATIONAL** | Amélia Lisboa attracts not only the people of the neighborhood but also Lisbon's young and trendy, who love the fun decor and the colorful healthy meals (which include power bowls and plenty of gluten-free and vegan options). $ *Average main: €8* ✉ *Rua Ferreira Borges 101, Campo de Ourique* ☎ *21/385–0863* 🌐 *www.ilovenicolau.com/en/our-locations/amelia* Ⓜ *Tram 25 or 28 to Rua Saraiva Carvalho.*

Lomar

$ | **PORTUGUESE** | Locals head to this small pastry shop whenever they crave something sweet. It's around the corner from the Jardim da Parada, and not far from the Mercado de Campo de Ourique. **Known for:** good-value menus for light meals; brioche croissants; sugary pastries. $ *Average main: €5* ✉ *Rua Tomás da Anunciação 72, Campo de Ourique* ☎ *21/385–8417* 💳 *No credit cards* ⏲ *Closed Sun.* Ⓜ *Tram 25 or 28 to Igreja do Santo Condestável.*

Hotels

Hotel das Amoreiras

$$$ | **HOTEL** | Facing the peaceful Jardim das Amoreiras, this tiny boutique hotel is like a luxury cottage in the city. **Pros:** delicious breakfast with house-made cakes; quiet surroundings; cozy outdoor patio. **Cons:** rooms not soundproof; far from major attractions; only serves breakfast and snacks. $ *Rooms from: €250* ✉ *Praça das Amoreiras 34, Amoreiras* ☎ *21/163–3710* 🌐 *www.hoteldasamoreiras.com* 🛏 *19 rooms* 🍽 *Free Breakfast* Ⓜ *Yellow Line to Rato, Tram 24 to Jardim das Amoreiras.*

★ Olissippo Lapa Palace

$$$$ | **HOTEL** | Combining the elegance of a 19th-century manor house with the modern amenities of a luxury resort, this hotel is perched at the top of one of Lisbon's seven hills and has spectacular views. **Pros:** beautiful gardens; refined yet relaxed indoor bar; live jazz bands many evenings. **Cons:** location isn't the best for sightseeing; very pricey; far walk to downtown. *Rooms from: €420* ✉ *Rua do Pau de Bandeira 4, Lapa* ☎ *21/394–9494* *www.lapapalace.com* *109 rooms* *Free Breakfast* Ⓜ *Tram 25 to Rua de Saõ Domingos à Lapa.*

Nightlife

BARS

Nexo 1/2

COCKTAIL BARS | Nexo 1/2 is run by a young Portuguese couple whose playfulness comes across in the bar's colorful interior but also in their concoctions, which mix ingredients like blood orange, Japanese spices, and Mezcal. ✉ *Rua Pereira e Sousa 4B, Campo de Ourique* ☎ *21/603–9910* *Closed Sun. and Mon.* Ⓜ *Yellow Line to Rato, Tram 24 to Rua das Amoreiras.*

FADO CLUBS

★ Senhor Vinho

LIVE MUSIC | This Lisbon institution attracts some of Portugal's most accomplished fado singers. It also serves better food than many *casas de fado* and is one of the few touristy spots that still attracts locals. ✉ *Rua do Meio à Lapa 18, Lapa* ☎ *21/397–2681* *www.srvinho.com* *Closed Sun.* Ⓜ *Tram 25 to Rua de São Domingos à Lapa.*

Shopping

Galeria Cristina Guerra

ART GALLERY | Inaugurated in 2001, this gallery regularly presents works by top contemporary Portuguese artists, plus some big international names. ✉ *Rua Santo António à Estrela 33, Estrela* ☎ *21/395–9559* *www.cristinaguerra.com* *Closed Sun. and Mon.* Ⓜ *Tram 25 or 28 to Rua Domingos Sequeira.*

O Melhor Bolo de Chocolate do Mundo

CHOCOLATE | It's right there in the name: "the best chocolate cake in the world." Instead of flour, the bakers use layers of cocoa mousse, so it really is no ordinary chocolate cake. ✉ *Rua Tenente Ferreira Durão 62A, Campo de Ourique* ☎ *21/396–5372* *www.omelhorbolodechocolatedomundobycbl.net* *Closed Sun.* Ⓜ *Tram 25 or 28 to Igreja do Santo Condestável.*

Chapter 10

INTENDENTE, MARTIM MONIZ, AND MOURARIA

Updated by
Ann Abel

Sights	Restaurants	Hotels	Shopping	Nightlife
★★☆☆☆	★★★★☆	★★☆☆☆	★★☆☆☆	★★☆☆☆

NEIGHBORHOOD SNAPSHOT

TOP EXPERIENCES

■ **Atmospheric alleyways.** One of the great joys of Mouraria—one of Lisbon's oldest neighborhoods—is wandering the super-narrow winding streets and seeing where they lead.

■ **Immigrant cuisines.** The blocks around Martim Moniz are home to many of Lisbon's new arrivals, and they're full of restaurants showcasing foods from Southeast Asia and Portuguese-speaking Africa.

■ **Seafood feasts.** Lisbon's most popular seafood hall, Cervejaria Ramiro, is a must-visit for shellfish.

■ **Vintage shopping.** Several of Lisbon's top vintage shops, specializing in fashion and housewares, are among the gentrifying streets of Intendente.

GETTING HERE

Intendente and Martim Moniz have metro stops on the Green Line, but Mouraria is less well served by public transportation. The hyper-popular Tram 28 runs along the edge of Intendente, and Tram 12 runs from Martim Moniz up Rua dos Cavaleiro, which saves you a few minutes' uphill walk into Mouraria, but its hilly location is best reached on foot.

PLANNING YOUR TIME

There's not a bad time to visit this area. The many good restaurants serve lunch and dinner, and the fado houses and craft beer bars come alive at night. Caution is advised late at night when establishments begin to close.

VIEWFINDER

■ **Escadinhas da Saúde.** Two long escalators beside steep stairs connect the main square in Martim Moniz with the windy streets of Mouraria. If they're working, look over your shoulder on the way up to check out the view. If not, pause at the top and congratulate yourself on the workout—the name means "Little Stairs of Health" in English.

PAUSE HERE

■ **Largo de São Cristovão.** One of the smaller and more unassuming squares in Lisbon, São Cristovão is anchored by a historic church and the outdoor seating for one of the coolest restaurants in town. Just a few steps down the hill, the pork sandwiches at As Bifanas do Afonso are beloved by the city's foodies.

Situated on the hillside below Lisbon's iconic Castelo de São Jorge (St. George's Castle), these three neighborhoods are among the oldest in the city. Although parts of them are changing rapidly, a walk around the narrow hilly lanes of the most historic quarters can feel like a step back in time.

Although there are no palaces and little cultural patrimony here, getting lost in the winding lanes is a true Lisbon experience. You don't visit the neighborhood with a checklist of sites to see so much as a spirit of discovery—a willingness to climb one more flight of stairs or to see what's around the next corner.

Following your nose or your eyes is usually a good strategy. The scent of grilled fish mingles with Asian spices and the aromas of African cuisine. Sometimes, from the balconies overhead or from behind the doors of unassuming establishments, the distinctive mournful strains of fado spill out into the streets. Some accounts have it that Portugal's most famous musical style was born in Mouraria, part of the Moorish influence that's still evident in the neighborhood today.

Mouraria and Intendente, along with neighboring Alfama, were among the only areas to survive the devastating earthquake of 1755, and the higgledy-piggledy streets, with laundry lines flapping between buildings, continue to evoke medieval Lisbon. In the past these areas were outside the city walls, so traditionally only the poorest people lived here. Today they are at a crossroads, with some longtime working-class residents living beside recent immigrants from Africa and Asia, as well as wealthy Portuguese hipsters, digital nomads, and other foreigners who are opening specialty coffee shops and craft-beer bars.

Intendente, especially, is gentrifying rapidly—and not always comfortably so. As recently as a decade ago, it was still something of a no-go zone, with many Lisboetas avoiding it because of prostitution and drugs. Thankfully that changed as the city's overall fortunes improved.

But now the artists and other creative pioneers who began living and working here—giving the area its winningly alternative vibe—are getting priced out of their spaces. Although the main square, Largo do Intendente, is much safer than it used to be, it's arguably less interesting. Still, it's a winsome place to admire architecture and vintage ceramic tiles, and to enjoy a (vegan) snack and a glass of (natural) wine.

For now, there's still an interesting mix of vintage stores, designer ateliers, and speakeasy-style bars on the one hand and traditional Portuguese restaurants, holes-in-the-wall specializing in momos or pho, "clandestine" Chinese restaurants inside second-floor apartments, Asian supermarkets, and sari shops on the other. While it's always wise to be respectful of the realities of life for a neighborhood's residents, there are still many simple pleasures to be enjoyed.

At the southern end of Mouraria, you'll find a couple of the country's trendiest tables, as well as a fine-dining restaurant, Prado, that recently picked up one of the country's most coveted culinary awards.

Intendente, Martim Moniz, and Mouraria

Sights

Igreja de São Cristóvão (*St. Christopher's Church*)
CHURCH | Originally dating from the 13th century but reconstructed after a fire in the 16th century, this church was largely untouched by the 1755 earthquake. Its interior, with a painted ceiling and many artworks in gilded frames, illustrates the baroque splendor of Portuguese churches before the earthquake robbed the city of much of its heritage and wealth. ✉ *Largo de São Cristóvão 4, Mouraria* ☎ *92/754–9975* ⏲ *Closed Sun.–Tues.* Ⓜ *Green Line to Martim Moniz.*

Largo do Intendente
PLAZA/SQUARE | This large square at the heart of Intendente is one of the most striking in the city. Neglected for many years, it became a major hipster hub starting in the 2010s. Now gentrification is pushing out some of the trendy cafés and creative spaces, but parts of that edginess remain. It also has some notable architecture, including the beautiful tile-covered facade of the former showroom for the historic ceramics company Viúva Lamego, and Lisbon's answer to New York's Flatiron Building, which is now a fashionable hotel. ✉ *Largo do Intendente, Intendente* Ⓜ *Green Line to Intendente, Tram 28 to Largo do Intendente.*

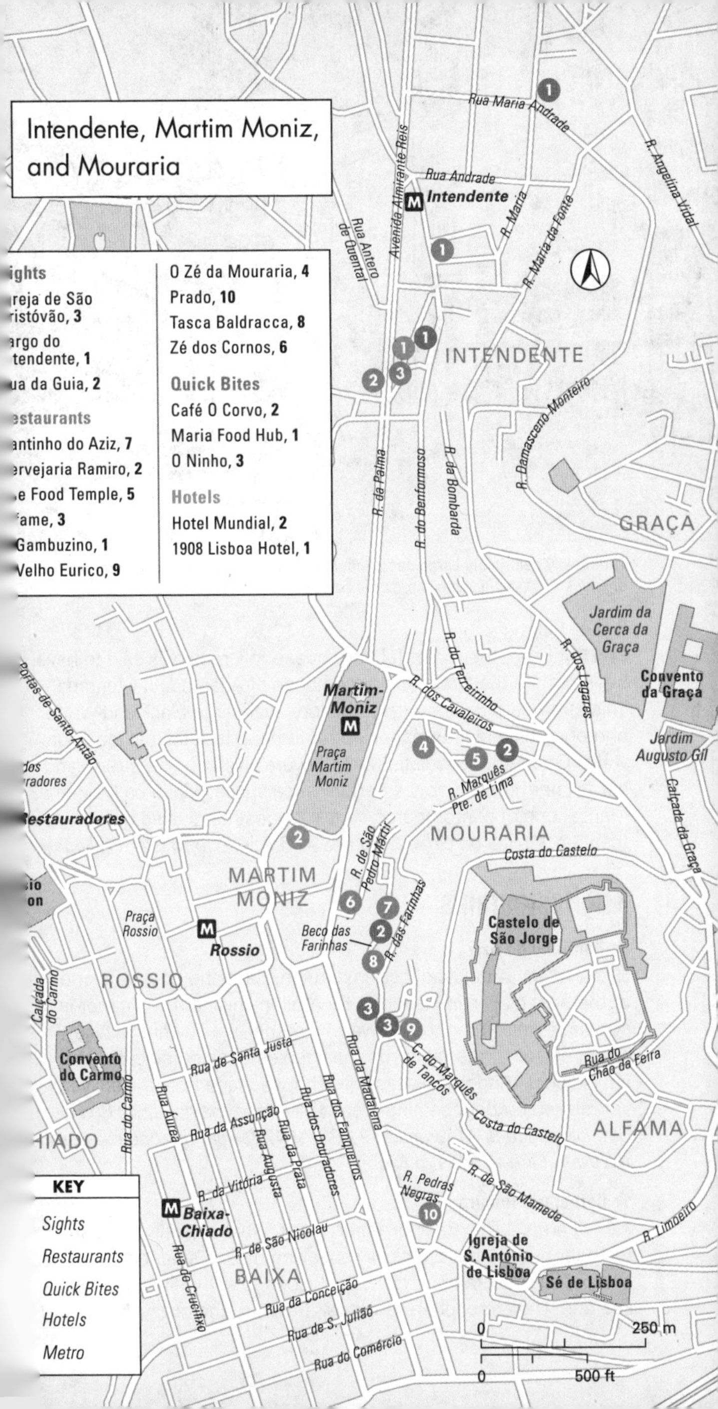

Intendente, Martim Moniz, and Mouraria
ights
reja de São
ristóvão, 3
argo do
tendente, 1
ua da Guia, 2
estaurants
antinho do Aziz, 7
ervejaria Ramiro, 2
e Food Temple, 5
ame, 3
Gambuzino, 1
Velho Eurico, 9
O Zé da Mouraria, 4
Prado, 10
Tasca Baldracca, 8
Zé dos Cornos, 6
Quick Bites
Café O Corvo, 2
Maria Food Hub, 1
O Ninho, 3
Hotels
Hotel Mundial, 2
1908 Lisboa Hotel, 1
KEY
Sights
Restaurants
Quick Bites
Hotels
Metro
Rua Maria Andrade
R. Angelina Vidal
Rua Andrade
Intendente
R. Maria
R. Maria da Fonte
Avenida Almirante Reis
Rua Antero de Quental
INTENDENTE
R. Damasceno Monteiro
R. da Palma
R. do Benformoso
R. da Bombarda
GRAÇA
Jardim da Cerca da Graça
Convento da Graça
Jardim Augusto Gil
R. do Terreirinho
R. dos Lagares
R. dos Cavaleiros
Martim-Moniz
Praça Martim Moniz
Portas de Santo Antão
Restauradores
R. Marquês Pte. de Lima
MOURARIA
Costa do Castelo
Calçada da Graça
R. de São Pedro Mártir
MARTIM MONIZ
R. das Farinhas
Beco das Farinhas
Praça Rossio
Rossio
ROSSIO
Castelo de São Jorge
Calçada do Carmo
Convento do Carmo
Rua de Santa Justa
C. do Marquês de Tancos
Rua do Chão da Feira
Rua da Madalena
Rua dos Fanqueiros
Rua dos Douradores
Rua da Prata
Rua Augusta
Rua da Assunção
Rua Áurea
Rua do Carmo
ALFAMA
HIADO
R. da Vitória
R. Pedras Negras
R. de São Mamede
Baixa-Chiado
R. de São Nicolau
Rua do Crucifixo
BAIXA
Igreja de S. António de Lisboa
Sé de Lisboa
R. Limoeiro
Rua da Conceição
Rua de S. Julião
Rua do Comércio
0
250 m
0
500 ft

The rapidly gentrifying Largo do Intendente is still a great place to stop for a drink or snack and take in some impressive azulejos.

Rua da Guia

STREET | Fado, the mournful Portuguese folk music, is said to have been born in the Lisbon neighborhoods of Alfama and Mouraria. This street is redolent with its history, with large black-and-white photographs and information about famous fadistas pasted on its walls. One famous fadista, Maria Severa, lived on this street, and her former home is now a performance space, Maria da Mouraria. Mariza, one of contemporary fado's biggest stars, also hails from the area. ✉ *Rua da Guia, Mouraria* Ⓜ *Green Line to Martim Moniz.*

Restaurants

★ Cantinho do Aziz

$$ | **AFRICAN** | A beloved local institution, Cantinho do Aziz is one of the best places in Lisbon to try African cuisine. The interior is cozy and welcoming, but in warm weather, you'll want to take a seat at one of the tables on the cobblestones outside. **Known for:** delicious Angolan dishes; killer house-made hot sauce; lively yet relaxed outdoor seating area. Ⓢ *Average main: €18* ✉ *Rua de São Lourenço 5, Mouraria* ☎ *21/887–6472* 🌐 *cantinhodoaziz.com* Ⓜ *Green Line to Martim Moniz.*

★ Cervejaria Ramiro

$$$ | **SEAFOOD** | This traditional *cervejaria* (which literally translates to "beer house" but practically speaking means seafood hall) is one of the most famous places in Lisbon to eat well-priced fresh seafood. The atmosphere is casual, frenetic, and buzzy. **Known for:**

garlic shrimp; fresh lobster; beef sandwiches for "dessert". *Average main: €25* *Av. Almirante Reis 1H, Intendente* *96/983-9472 only for takeaway* *www.cervejariaramiro.com* *Closed Mon.* *Green Line to Intendente.*

The Food Temple

$ | **VEGAN** | This easy-to-miss vegan tapas place is little more than a door in the wall halfway up a public stairway. Despite its location, it was the first fully vegan restaurant in Lisbon, and it's still worth the search for its ever-changing menu of shareable plates and its pretty tables on the outdoor stairway terrace on summer evenings. **Known for:** vegan tapas; outdoor seating; fresh smoothies and juices. *Average main: €12* *Beco do Jasmim 18, Mouraria* *21/839-7874* *www.thefoodtemple.com* *No credit cards* *Closed Mon.* *Green Line to Martim Moniz.*

Infame

$$$ | **CONTEMPORARY** | **FAMILY** | The bar-restaurant at the trendy 1908 Lisboa Hotel is as stylish as the design hotel itself—the space has been tastefully kitted out to make the most of its historical building with a striking tiled floor, high ceilings, an exposed metal staircase, and windows on three sides. A pleasant place for brunch, lunch, or dinner, the eclectic menu features seafood, meat, and vegetarian options, many with Asian influences. **Known for:** modern Asian-influenced menu; contemporary decor and photo-worthy food presentation; extensive Sunday brunch. *Average main: €24* *1908 Lisboa Hotel, Largo do Intendente, Pina Manique 4, Intendente* *21/880-4008* *infame.pt* *Green Line to Intendente.*

O Gambuzino

$ | **VEGETARIAN** | One of the most fun vegetarian restaurants in town, O Gambuzino lists its ever-changing daily specials on a chalkboard menu but always highlights fresh vegetables and other products from a place called the Fruta Feia ("Ugly Fruit") co-op. You get the sustainability angle, but the pleasure is also there, with a menu full of global influences. **Known for:** wildly international menu; zero-waste and other sustainability practices; signature cocktails. *Average main: €13* *Rua do Anjos 5A, Intendente* *21/820-8406* *www.ogambuzino.com* *Green Line to Intendente.*

★ **O Velho Eurico**

$$ | **PORTUGUESE** | A critical darling and a popular favorite, this Portuguese-with-a-twist restaurant had a line out the door almost as soon as it opened; it's the sort of place other chefs go on their days off. A team of young chefs is turning out classic regional dishes to a soundtrack of rock and roll in a resolutely casual dining

room. **Known for:** lamb croquettes; bacalhau à Brás (scrambled eggs with shredded salt cod, onion, and potato topped with black olives); party atmosphere. *Average main: €20 Largo de São Cristovão 3, Mouraria Closed Sun. and Mon. Green Line to Martim Moniz.*

O Zé da Mouraria

$ | PORTUGUESE | One of the city's best *tascas* (traditional no-frills restaurants), O Zé da Mouraria features hearty traditional fare every lunchtime. It's a simple place but the servings are large enough to share, the wine list is decent, and the food is an excellent value. **Known for:** bacalhau (salted cod); grilled meats and stews; traditional Portuguese desserts. *Average main: €12 Rua João do Outeiro 24, Mouraria 21/886–5436 No credit cards Closed Sun. Green Line to Martim Moniz.*

★ Prado

$$$$ | CONTEMPORARY | Seasonal, locally sourced ingredients are the stars of the show at this chic but relaxed fine-dining restaurant, where plants hang from the ceiling and contemporary furnishings keep things feeling serene. The presentation is as sophisticated as the flavors, making this one of the city's most acclaimed and awarded restaurants, with top honors from the influential local publication Mesa Marcada and a recommendation in the Michelin guide. **Known for:** fresh farm-to-table products; good list of natural and organic wines; picture-perfect presentation. *Average main: €32 Travessa das Pedras Negras 2, Mouraria 21/053–4649 www.pradorestaurante.com Closed Sun. and Mon. No lunch Tues. and Wed. Tram 28 or 12E to Sé (Cathedral).*

Tasca Baldracca

$$$ | PORTUGUESE | Located in a former pizzeria of the same name, Tasca Baldracca serves contemporary takes on Portuguese classics with a heavy accent from the chef's native Brazil. The vibe is youthful and playful—the antithesis of fine dining—with chalkboard menus, heavily graffitied bathrooms, and rock music on the sound system. **Known for:** beef tartare; Brazilian dishes like moqueca (fish stew); friendly informal service. *Average main: €25 Rua das Farinhas 1, Mouraria Closed Sun. and Mon. Green Line to Martim Moniz.*

Zé dos Cornos

$ | PORTUGUESE | You'll probably need to wait on the stairs outside for a table and then perch on benches or at tightly packed tables, but it's worth the wait for the excellent Portuguese dishes served at this small neighborhood tasca. The menu changes daily with a selection of fish and meat options. **Known for:** small space that's always busy; pork ribs; roasted codfish. *Average main: €10 Beco dos Surradores 5, Mouraria 21/886–9641 www.facebook.com/ZeCornos No credit cards Closed Sun. and Mon. Green Line to Martim Moniz.*

Coffee and Quick Bites

Café O Corvo

$ | **CAFÉ** | Situated on one of Mouraria's prettiest squares, Café O Corvo is a great place to recharge after a day of wandering the area's hilly streets. There are outdoor tables under shady trees, friendly staff, and a menu that includes brunch, burgers, sandwiches, and snacks. **Known for:** brunch boards; homemade focaccia sandwiches; pretty shaded terrace. *Average main: €10 Largo dos Trigueiros 15A–15B, Mouraria 21/886–0545 www.facebook.com/ocorvocafe Green Line to Martim Moniz.*

Maria Food Hub

$ | **ECLECTIC** | This trendy café and restaurant aims to be exactly what its name implies: a gathering spot for residents and locals in Intendente. The terrace is almost always busy, and laptops are welcome inside, allowing people to work and socialize. **Known for:** very good coffee made from its own house blend; open-faced toasts; good selection of craft beer and low-intervention wines. *Average main: €13 Rua Maria Andrade 38, Intendente 21/812–1281 www.mariafoodhub.com Green Line to Intendente.*

O Ninho

$ | **CAFÉ** | A good selection of pastries, a decent brunch menu, great coffee, and friendly service make this French-style café a good choice at the start of your day, whatever time that may be. Brunch is served until 3 pm, and light lunch options are also available. **Known for:** good coffee; French-style pastries; healthy menu options. *Average main: €13 Rua São Cristóvão 17–19, Mouraria 21/136–1664 Closed Tues. Green Line to Martim Moniz.*

Hotels

Hotel Mundial

$$$ | **HOTEL** | At the bottom of the Martim Moniz square, near major places like Rossio and Restauradores, this large property looks uncompromisingly modern, but inside there's lots of old-fashioned charm combined with modern facilities. **Pros:** stunning views and great lounge bar on the rooftop; central location;

friendly staff. **Cons:** unattractive exterior; no pool; Praça Martim Moniz is still in disrepair. *Rooms from: €220* ✉ *Praça Martim Moniz 2, Martim Moniz* ☎ *21/884–2000* 🌐 *www.hotel-mundial.pt* *349 rooms* *Free Breakfast* Ⓜ *Green Line to Martim Moniz.*

1908 Lisboa Hotel

$$$$ | **HOTEL** | A stunning art nouveau building, interesting modern artwork, and a trendy location combine to make a stay at the 1908 Lisboa Hotel memorable for all the right reasons. **Pros:** balconies that overlook Largo do Intendente; excellent restaurant, Infame; local flavor. **Cons:** area can be noisy; a bit far from the river; bathrooms vary significantly in layout and style. *Rooms from: €300* ✉ *Largo do Intendente, Pina Manique 6, Intendente* ☎ *21/880–4000* 🌐 *www.1908lisboahotel.com* *36 rooms* *Free Breakfast* Ⓜ *Green Line to Intendente.*

Nightlife

BARS

Dois Corvos Intendente Taproom

BREWPUBS | Intendente's cool factor was established with the opening of this taproom, a spin-off of the popular Dois Corvos brewery in hipster Marvila. The train-station-style map here lists an ever-changing array of beers, ranging from oat cream IPAs to dry-hopped sours to breakfast stouts. ✉ *Rua dos Anjos 16B, Intendente* ☎ *21/812–0093* 🌐 *www.doiscorvos.pt* Ⓜ *Green Line to Intendente.*

O Pif

WINE BAR | Both the indoor, heavily pink sitting area and the terrace outside at O Pif offer guests the chance to sip natural wines from small Portuguese producers. It also offers simple Portuguese snacks like black pork chorizo and fresh cheese. ✉ *Rua Maria Andrade 43A, Intendente* Ⓜ *Green Line to Intendente.*

Quatto Teste

COCKTAIL BARS | An Italian and a Basque walk into a bar ... actually, a couple from the two parts of Europe opened one, on what has turned into one of Lisbon's buzziest streets. Quatto Teste emphasizes high-quality cocktails (starting with the obvious ones from their native regions: Negronis, of course, and Kalimotxo, that Basque specialty made with Coca-Cola, Rioja wine, and raspberry). There are also Basque-style *pintxos* (tapas) and ciders on tap. ✉ *Rua de São Cristovão 32, Mouraria* 🌐 *linktr.ee/quattro.teste* Ⓜ *Green Line to Martim Moniz.*

Topo Martim Moniz

BARS | This bustling rooftop bar has great views of the castle and the ancient neighborhoods that sit on the hill beneath it. It can be a little hard to find, but persevere and you'll be rewarded with fine views and a wide selection of drinks along with a lively young crowd. ✉ *Centro Comercial Martim Moniz, Praça Martim Moniz, 6th fl., Intendente* ☎ *21/588–1322* 🌐 *www.topo-lisboa.pt* Ⓜ *Green Line to Martim Moniz.*

 Shopping

Atelier Joana Simão

CERAMICS | Local ceramics artist Joana Simão works and sells from this atelier, which is perfectly located on a pretty square in the heart of Mouraria. Her pieces are simple and contemporary, often in white and gray glazes, with interesting details such as rope handles. She also runs occasional workshops. ✉ *Largo dos Trigueiros 16B, Mouraria* ☎ *91/653–2611* Ⓜ *Green Line to Martim Moniz.*

★ **A Vida Portuguesa**

LOCAL GOODS | It's been described by local and international press as "the prettiest store in the city," and few would argue with that description. The large, beautifully styled emporium stocks finely packaged traditional Portuguese goods at every price point, ranging from soaps and shaving cream to glassware, ceramics, textiles, notebooks, food, and olive oils. Airy and spacious, this contemporary shop is a must-visit for gifts and mementos that truly capture Portuguese life. There's a smaller branch in the Time Out Market, but the Intendente store is the one to see. ✉ *Largo do Intendente, Pina Manique 23, Intendente* ☎ *21/197–4512* 🌐 *www.avidaportuguesa.com* Ⓜ *Green Line to Intendente.*

★ **Cortiço & Netos**

CERAMICS | The Portuguese love affair with *azulejo* tiles is evident on and inside buildings across the country, but buying one as a memento has implications, as many of those for sale have been stolen from historic buildings. For a more ethical option, Cortiço & Netos sells distinctive and beautiful discontinued tiles from the 1950s onward. You can buy just one tile or by the square meter. ✉ *Rua Maria Andrade 37D, Intendente* ☎ *21/136–2376* 🌐 *www.corticoenetos.com* Ⓜ *Green Line to Intendente.*

★ **Prado Mercearia**

FOOD | With tiled floors and vintage fittings, this beautifully designed grocery store and wine bar is run by the team behind the acclaimed Prado restaurant. Its shelves are stocked with seasonal, often organic, locally sourced products including cheeses, tinned fish, bread, fruits and vegetables, and dry goods. The adjoining bistro serves delicious small plates and a range of Portuguese natural and organic wines. ✉ *Rua das Pedras Negras 35, Mouraria* ☎ *21/053–4652* 🌐 *pradomercearia.com* Ⓜ *Tram 28E to Igreja de Santa Maria Madelena.*

Retro City Lisboa

VINTAGE | This store has a wide selection of vintage clothing, mostly dating from the 1980s onward. Its well-curated selection has been chosen to appeal particularly to younger fashion-forward buyers. ✉ *Rua Maria Andrade 43, Intendente* ☎ *21/809–9932* 🌐 *www.facebook.com/Retrocitylisbon* Ⓜ *Green Line to Intendente.*

Retrox Vintage Shop

ANTIQUES & COLLECTIBLES | This little vintage store specializes in furniture, books, and collectibles from the 1950s through 1970s. As with all vintage stores, what you find depends on luck and an eye, but you can often find good Portuguese design and international mid-century-modern pieces. ✉ *Rua dos Anjos 4C, Intendente* ☎ *91/830–3991* 🌐 *www.facebook.com/retroxcoisasvintage* Ⓜ *Green Line to Intendente.*

Tropical Bairro

VINTAGE | This small vintage store is run by an Italian DJ and features a well-curated selection of vintage clothing, including the occasional high-fashion label, along with a broad variety of Latin and "tropical" records from the 1950s to 70s. ✉ *Rua de São Cristóvão 3, Mouraria* Ⓜ *Green Line to Martim Moniz.*

Performing Arts

★ Maria da Mouraria

LIVE MUSIC | This small restaurant is one of the most authentic venues in Lisbon for listening to mournful and soulful fado music. On the site of the former house of famous fadista Maria Severa, the venue hosts regular concerts, sometimes luring big-name singers to perform. You can dine in the restaurant, which serves traditional Portuguese dishes, while you listen, or try your luck arriving just for the concert (but tables may be sold out). ✉ *Largo Severa 2B, Mouraria* ☎ *93/445–0130* 🌐 *mariadamouraria.eatbu.com* Ⓜ *Green Line to Martim Moniz.*

Chapter 11

BELÉM

Updated by
Daniela Sunde-Brown

Sights	Restaurants	Hotels	Shopping	Nightlife
★★★★★	★★★★☆	★★★★☆	★★★☆☆	★★★☆☆

NEIGHBORHOOD SNAPSHOT

TOP EXPERIENCES

- **Mosteiro dos Jerónimos.** This enormous late-Gothic building is one of Portugal's most important.
- **Pastéis de Belém.** The original custard tarts are best enjoyed warm with cinnamon.
- **Walk by the river.** Walk from Belém to the bridge, past monuments and cafés.
- **Torre de Belém.** Built to protect the city from invaders, the striking tower now attracts visitors in droves.
- **Museums district.** Find about a dozen of Lisbon's top galleries and museums.

GETTING HERE

Belém is flat and best explored on foot—a welcome change in hilly Lisbon. From Cais do Sodré, walk about 5 km (3 miles) along the river or catch a train. Alternatively, catch Tram 15 from Baixa.

PLANNING YOUR TIME

Most visitors spend at least half a day exploring Belém's museums and monuments. It's a few miles west of downtown, so plan ahead. Go early to avoid the crowds, buy monastery tickets in advance, and have faith that the Pastéis de Belém lines move fast. The Lisboa Card offers free or discounted entry to many attractions.

PAUSE HERE

- **Jardim Botânico da Ajuda.** Portugal's oldest botanical garden—laid out in 1768 by Italian botanist Domenico Vandelli—is a relaxing place to spend an hour or so. Baroque fountains and stairways, Renaissance-style terraced slopes, and meandering peacocks create a sense of splendor. ✉ *Calçada da Ajuda www.isa.ulisboa.pt/en/visitors/ajuda-botanical-garden.*

OFF THE BEATEN PATH

- **Palácio Nacional da Ajuda.** Built in 1802 as a royal residence, today the ornate neoclassical building functions as a museum; admire 18th- and 19th-century paintings, furniture, and tapestries, then pop into the neighboring Royal Treasure Museum. ✉ *Largo da Ajuda* 🌐 *www.palacioajuda.gov.pt.*

Riverside Belém is a neighborhood steeped in history. Jam-packed with museums and monuments, the suburb is an essential stop on any Lisbon itinerary.

Some make a special pilgrimage to Pastéis de Belém to worship at the home of the original Portuguese custard tart. Others come to explore Portugal's vast seafaring history, modern-day artistic expression, and unique Manueline architecture.

It was from here that explorer Vasco da Gama set sail in 1497. He returned from his pioneering sea voyage to India with riches that kicked off Portugal's 16th- and 17th-century golden age. Taxes from the spice trade built the magnificent Mosteiro dos Jerónimos, set on the site of a chapel where Da Gama prayed the night before his nation-changing voyage, and the fortified Torre de Belém, which guards the mouth of the river. The two UNESCO World Heritage sites are symbolic of Portugal's global expansion.

Arrive early at the monastery to beat the crowds. Then join fast-moving queues at Pastéis de Belém, where the custard tarts remain true to the original 1837 recipe, a well-kept secret known by few. The delightful riverside promenade and parks offer a refreshing break from tightly packed streets downtown. An antique market pops up in Jardim Vasco da Gama on the first and third Sundays of the month.

Down by the river, the Torre de Belém has watched over Lisbon since 1514. Now it supervises joggers, starry-eyed couples, and local families as they cut a well-worn path to the imposing *Padrão dos Descobrimentos* statue, built in 1960 to mark 500 years since the death of Henry the Navigator. He helms the grand caravel ship as it puts to sea, lined on either side with navigators, cartographers, warriors, and symbols of Portugal's exploration and eventual colonization of much of the world. The Discoveries Cultural Centre explores their stories but shies away from Portugal's launch of the transatlantic slave trade.

Art lovers should visit the boundary-pushing Museu de Arte, Arquitetura e Tecnologia (MAAT) and the Museu de Arte Contemporânea (MAC). The Museu Nacional dos Coches is filled with flamboyant royal coaches, the Museu de Marinha dives into the Age of Discovery, and the immersive Quake takes you back to the 1755 earthquake, which shaped the Lisbon you see today.

Jeronimos Monastery

Frightened by the tragedy, Portugal's royals rebuilt their home in nearby Ajuda. The lavish palace is worth a detour, along with the shiny Museu do Tesouro Real (Royal Treasure Museum). Soon after the Portuguese Republic was declared in 1910, ending 800 years of monarchy, the pink Palácio de Belém became the official residence of the President. On the third Sunday of each month, the Guarda Nacional Republicana (Republican National Guard, or GNR) performs a changing of the guard ceremony at 11 am.

Belém

Sights

★ Adega Belém Urban Winery

WINERY | FAMILY | Winemakers Catarina Moreira and David Picard turned an old car repair workshop into Lisbon's only urban winery. Using grapes picked nearby and minimal intervention techniques, the family produces vibrant and lively small-batch wines. The winery tours are an accessible but rigorous journey into wine biochemistry. ✉ *Travessa Paulo Jorge 8–9, Belém* ☎ *96/655–7798* 🌐 *www.adegabelem.com* ⏲ *Closed Sun.–Wed.* Ⓜ *Tram 15E to Altinho.*

Jardim Botânico Tropical

GARDEN | FAMILY | Steps from Belém's Manueline monastery, this tropical botanical garden offers shady respite from the heat and the crowds outside. Towering palm trees provide a grand entrance to a flower-filled space that was created in 1906 as the Colonial Garden, housing some 600 species from Portugal's tropical and subtropical former colonies. There are some grand colonial-style buildings, although most are closed to the public, and resident peacocks stroll amid the flowers and plants. ✉ *Largo dos Jerónimos, Belém* 🌐 *museus.ulisboa.pt* 🎫 *€5* Ⓜ *Train to Belém or Tram 15E to Mosteiro dos Jerónimos.*

★ **Mosteiro dos Jerónimos** (*Jeronimos Monastery*)
RELIGIOUS BUILDING | FAMILY | If you see only one historic landmark in Belém, make it this magnificent monastery. This UNESCO World Heritage site is a supreme example of the Manueline style (named after King Dom Manuel I), which represented a marked departure from earlier Gothic architecture. Much of it is characterized by elaborate sculptural details, often with a maritime motif. João de Castilho was responsible for the southern portal, which forms the main entrance to the church: the figure on the central pillar is Henry the Navigator. Inside, the spacious interior contrasts with the riot of decoration on the six nave columns and complex latticework ceiling. This is the resting place of both explorer Vasco da Gama and national poet Luís de Camões. Don't miss the Gothic- and Renaissance-style double cloister, also designed to stunning effect by Castilho. ■ **TIP→ Lines can be especially long here; buy your timed ticket in advance.** ✉ *Praça do Império, Belém* ☎ *21/362–0034* 🌐 *www.patrimoniocultural.gov.pt* 🎫 *Free for church; €12 for cloister, or free with Lisboa Card* ⏲ *Closed Mon.* Ⓜ *Cascais Line to Belém, Tram 15E to Mosteiro dos Jerónimos.*

★ **Museu de Arte, Arquitetura e Tecnologia (MAAT)** (*Museum of Art, Architecture, and Technology*)
ART MUSEUM | Cementing Belém's reputation as Lisbon's top destination for arts and architecture buffs, the ultramodern Museum of Art, Architecture, and Technology (MAAT) is a striking sight on the banks of the Tagus. Opened in 2016, the curved white building houses immersive exhibitions from the likes of revered Portuguese street artist Vhils. The refurbished 1908 power station next door is part of the same museum complex, and it offers enlightening tours. ✉ *Av. Brasília, Belém* ☎ *21/002–8130* 🌐 *www.maat.pt/en* 🎫 *€11* ⏲ *Closed Tues.* Ⓜ *Cascais Line to Belém.*

★ **Museu de Arte Contemporânea – MAC/CCB** (*Berardo Collection Museum*)
ART MUSEUM | FAMILY | Housed in the minimalist Centro Cultural de Belém, the Museum of Contemporary Art showcases one of Europe's most important private collections of modern art. Works from the Berardo treasure trove—which range from Picasso and

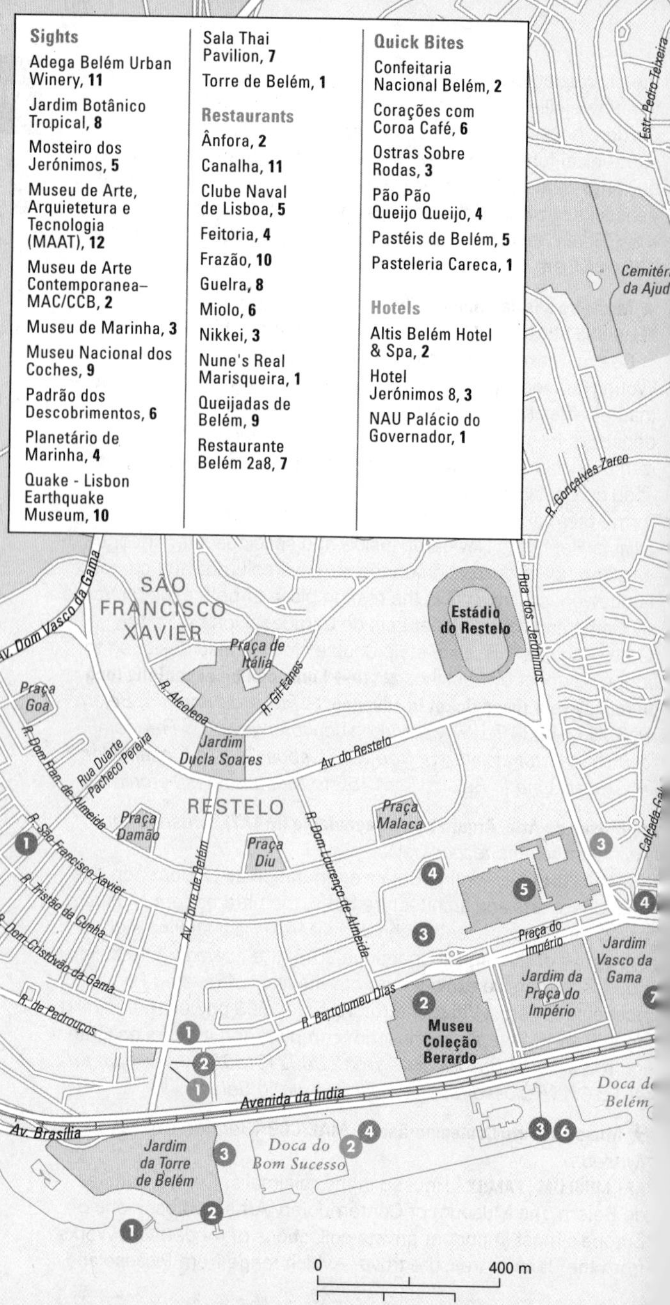
Sights
Adega Belém Urban Winery, 11
Jardim Botânico Tropical, 8
Mosteiro dos Jerónimos, 5
Museu de Arte, Arquietetura e Tecnologia (MAAT), 12
Museu de Arte Contemporanea–MAC/CCB, 2
Museu de Marinha, 3
Museu Nacional dos Coches, 9
Padrão dos Descobrimentos, 6
Planetário de Marinha, 4
Quake - Lisbon Earthquake Museum, 10
Sala Thai Pavilion, 7
Torre de Belém, 1
Restaurants
Ânfora, 2
Canalha, 11
Clube Naval de Lisboa, 5
Feitoria, 4
Frazão, 10
Guelra, 8
Miolo, 6
Nikkei, 3
Nune's Real Marisqueira, 1
Queijadas de Belém, 9
Restaurante Belém 2a8, 7
Quick Bites
Confeitaria Nacional Belém, 2
Corações com Coroa Café, 6
Ostras Sobre Rodas, 3
Pão Pão Queijo Queijo, 4
Pastéis de Belém, 5
Pasteleria Careca, 1
Hotels
Altis Belém Hotel & Spa, 2
Hotel Jerónimos 8, 3
NAU Palácio do Governador, 1
Estr. Pedro Teixeira
Cemitério da Ajuda
R. Gonçalves Zarco
Rua dos Jerónimos
Estádio do Restelo
SÃO FRANCISCO XAVIER
Av. Dom Vasco da Gama
Praça de Itália
R. Gil Eanes
R. Alcoleoa
Praça Goa
R. Dom Fran. de Almeida
Rua Duarte Pacheco Pereira
Jardim Ducla Soares
Av. do Restelo
RESTELO
Praça Damão
Praça Malaca
Praça Diu
R. São Francisco Xavier
R. Tristão da Cunha
R. Dom Cristóvão da Gama
Av. Torre de Belém
R. Dom Lourenço de Almeida
Calçada Gal
Praça do Império
Jardim Vasco da Gama
Jardim da Praça do Império
R. de Pedrouços
R. Bartolomeu Dias
Museu Coleção Berardo
Avenida da Índia
Av. Brasília
Doca de Belém
Jardim da Torre de Belém
Doca do Bom Sucesso
0
400 m
0
1,000 ft

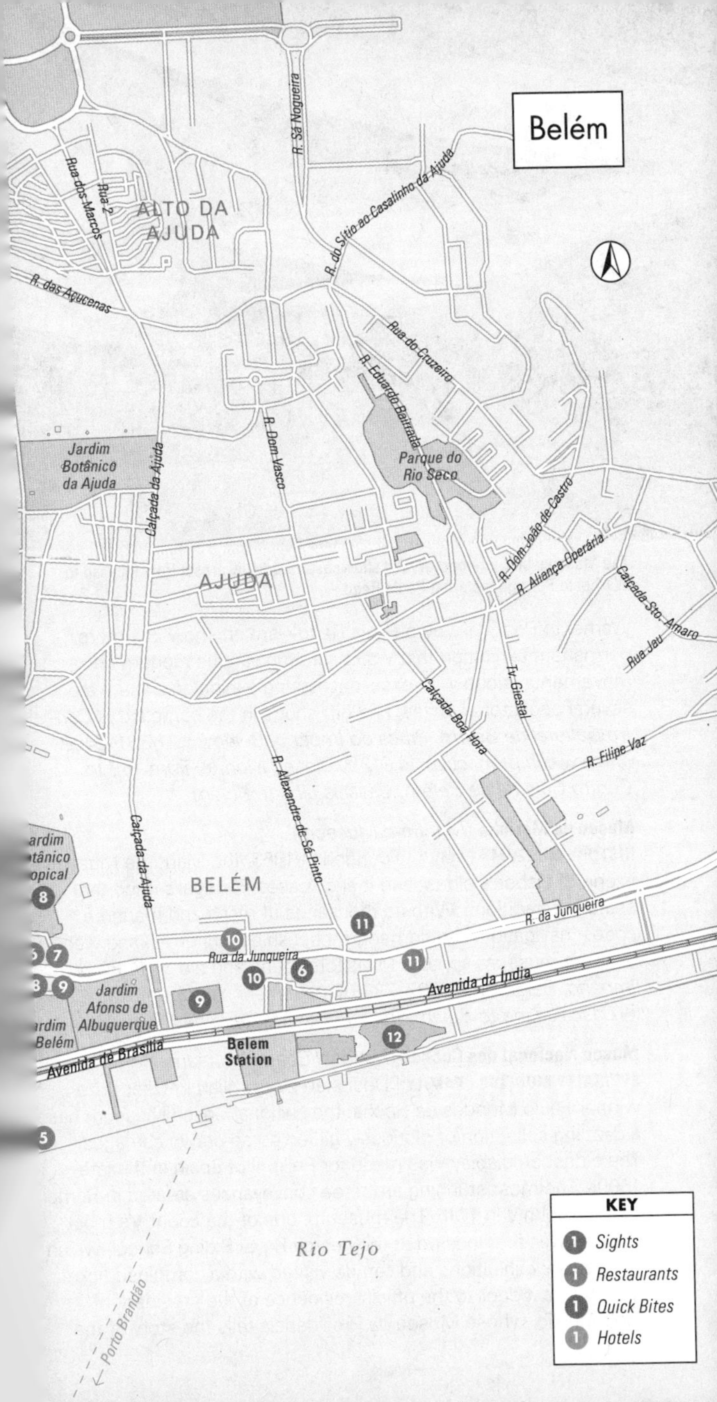
Belém
ALTO DA AJUDA
AJUDA
BELÉM
Rua dos Marcos
Rua 2
R. das Açucenas
R. Sá Nogueira
R. do Sítio ao Casalinho da Ajuda
Rua do Cruzeiro
R. Eduardo Baitrada
Parque do Rio Seco
R. Dom Vasco
Jardim Botânico da Ajuda
Calçada da Ajuda
R. Dom João de Castro
R. Aliança Operária
Calçada Sto. Amaro
Rua Jau
Tv. Giestal
Calçada Boa Hora
R. Filipe Vaz
R. Alexandre de Sá Pinto
R. da Junqueira
Rua da Junqueira
Avenida da Índia
Jardim Afonso de Albuquerque
Avenida de Brasília
Belem Station
Porto Brandão
Rio Tejo
KEY
Sights
Restaurants
Quick Bites
Hotels

The Museum of Contemporary Art showcases works by artists from Picasso to Warhol to Portuguese artist Paula Rego.

Warhol to Portugal's own Paula Rego—are on show in a more permanent exhibition that walks through various modern art movements, along with excellent visiting exhibitions. There are several bookstores, cafés, and gift shops in the complex. ✉ *Centro Cultural de Belém, Praça do Império, Belém* ☎ *21/361–2400* 🌐 *www.ccb.pt/macccb* 🎫 *€12* ⏲ *Closed Mon.* Ⓜ *Tram 15E to Centro Cultural de Belém, Cascais Line to Belém.*

Museu de Marinha (*Maritime Museum*)
HISTORY MUSEUM | FAMILY | Founded in 1853, the Maritime Museum is one of Lisbon's oldest and it showcases Portugal's important seafaring traditions. With its thousands of maps and maritime codes, navigational equipment, model ships, uniforms, and weapons, the museum appeals to visitors young and old. ✉ *Praça do Império, Belém* ☎ *21/097–7388* 🌐 *ccm.marinha.pt/pt/museu* 🎫 *€7* Ⓜ *Cascais Line to Belém, Tram 15E to Mosteiro dos Jerónimos.*

Museu Nacional dos Coches (*National Coach Museum*)
SPECIALTY MUSEUM | FAMILY | Designed by Brazilian Pritzker Prize winner Paulo Mendes da Rocha, the National Coach Museum has a dazzling collection of gloriously gilded horse-drawn carriages. The oldest on display was made for Philip II of Spain in the late 1500s. The most stunning are three conveyances created in Rome for King John V in 1716. The museum, one of the country's most popular, was first located at the nearby Royal Riding School, which still houses exhibitions and can be visited with a combined ticket. It's right next door to the official residence of the president of the republic, whose Museu da Presidência tells the story of the

presidency, profiles the officeholders, and displays gifts they have received on state visits. ✉ *Av. da Índia 136, Belém* ☎ *21/073–2319* 🌐 *museudoscoches.gov.pt/en* 🎫 *€8 or free with Lisboa Card; €10 for combined Royal Riding School ticket* ⏲ *Closed Mon.* Ⓜ *Tram 15E to Altinho.*

★ **Padrão dos Descobrimentos** (*Monument of the Discoveries*)
MONUMENT | FAMILY | The monolithic Monument of the Discoveries was erected in 1960 to commemorate the 500th anniversary of the death of Henry the Navigator. It was built on what was the departure point for many voyages of discovery, including those of Vasco da Gama for India and—during Spain's occupation of Portugal—of the Spanish Armada for England in 1588. Henry is at the prow of the monument, facing the water; lined up behind him are the Portuguese explorers of Brazil and Asia, as well as other national heroes. Walk inside and take the elevator to the top for river views. ✉ *Av. Brasília, Belém* ☎ *21/303–1950* 🌐 *padraodosdescobrimentos.pt/en* 🎫 *€10* Ⓜ *Tram 15 to Mosteiro dos Jerónimos, Cascais Line to Belém.*

Planetário de Marinha
OBSERVATORY | FAMILY | The Navy Planetarium is an immersive space that presents astronomical films with various themes several times per day. Headphones can be used to translate the presentations into English, and there are special sessions designed for kids. ✉ *Praça do Império, Belém* ☎ *21/097–7350* 🌐 *ccm.marinha.pt/pt/planetario* 🎫 *€7* ⏲ *Closed Mon.* Ⓜ *Cascais Line to Belém, Tram 15E to Mosteiro dos Jerónimos.*

Quake - Lisbon Earthquake Museum
HISTORY MUSEUM | FAMILY | In 1755 a catastrophic earthquake changed the face of Lisbon forever. This modern immersive museum aims to take visitors back in time to experience some of the horrors. Wander through a series of themed rooms that explore the quake, fires, and tsunami that rippled across Lisbon, and learn about the history and science of the event. Tickets are timed and the experience takes around 90 minutes. ✉ *Rua Cais da Alfândega Velha 39, Belém* 🌐 *lisbonquake.com* 🎫 *€28* Ⓜ *Cascais Line to Belém, Tram 15E to Museu Nacional dos Coches.*

Sala Thai Pavilion
GARDEN | FAMILY | Your eyes do not deceive you—there really is an ornate gilded Thai pavilion beneath the jacaranda trees in Belém's Jardim Vasco da Gama. Built to celebrate 500 years of diplomatic relations between Thailand and Portugal, the structure was opened by Thai princess Maha Chakri Sirindhorn. ✉ *Jardim Vasco da Gama, Belém* Ⓜ *Tram 15E to Mosteiro dos Jerónimos.*

★ **Torre de Belém** (*Belém Tower*)

NOTABLE BUILDING | FAMILY | The openwork balconies and domed turrets of the fanciful Belém Tower make it perhaps the country's purest Manueline structure. The UNESÇO World Heritage site was built between 1514 and 1520 on what was an island in the middle of the Tagus River to defend the port entrance, and it's dedicated to Saint Vincent, the patron saint of Lisbon. Today the chalk-white tower stands near the north bank—evidence of the river's changing course. Cross the wooden gangway to check out the cannons, then climb the steep, narrow, winding staircase to the top of the tower for a bird's-eye view across the Tagus. Then, descend to the former dungeons. ✉ *Av. Brasília, Belém* ☎ *21/362–0034* 🌐 *torrebelem.pt* 🎫 *€8* 🕒 *Closed Mon.* Ⓜ *Cascais Line to Belém, Tram 15E to Largo da Princesa.*

Restaurants

Ânfora

$$$ | PORTUGUESE | When you eat at this restaurant—situated in the luxurious Palácio do Governador and named for the Roman amphorae uncovered beneath the site—you'll feel as if you're dining in the vaulted halls of a castle. There's nothing old-fashioned about the food though, with a spectacular menu that reinterprets traditional Portuguese dishes with modern techniques. **Known for:** beautifully presented dishes; good advice on wine pairings; incredible desserts. Ⓢ *Average main: €25* ✉ *Nau Palácio do Governador, Rua Bartolomeu Dias 117, Belém* ☎ *21/246–7800* 🌐 *www.nauhotels.com/en/nau-palacio-do-governador/restaurant-bar/anfora* Ⓜ *Tram 15E to Largo da Princesa.*

★ **Canalha**

$$$ | PORTUGUESE | FAMILY | Fresh produce is the hero at this modern neighborhood bistro. Portuguese chef João Rodrigues swapped his Michelin-star kitchen for this modest diner where top-quality seafood and seasonal ingredients shine. **Known for:** top-quality, produce-forward dining; traditional dishes as weekday specials; great wine list and relaxed atmosphere. Ⓢ *Average main: €25* ✉ *Rua da Junqueira 207, Belém* ☎ *96/215–2742* 🌐 *www.instagram.com/restaurantecanalha* 🕒 *Closed Sun. and Mon.* Ⓜ *Tram 15E to Altinho.*

Clube Naval de Lisboa

$$ | PORTUGUESE | Set right on the banks of the Tagus with suitably nautical decor, this restaurant is owned by Lisbon's Naval Club and offers excellent fish and simple traditional dishes. Floor-to-ceiling windows allow diners to enjoy river views when it's too cool for the terrace. **Known for:** fair prices for seafood; traditional

Portuguese dishes; sunny terrace right by the river. *Average main: €19* ✉ *Edifício do Clube Naval de Lisboa, Av. Brasília, Belém* ☎ *21/363–6014* 🌐 *www.restaurantedoclubenavaldelisboa.pt/en* ⏲ *Closed Tues.* Ⓜ *Tram 15E to Mosteiro dos Jerónimos.*

★ Feitoria

$$$$ | FUSION | Expect culinary wizardry at this award-winning restaurant headed by acclaimed chef André Cruz, who honed his talents in Portugal and South America. There's no à la carte menu, but diners can take their pick from traditional or vegetarian tasting menus of seven or nine courses each. **Known for:** inventive set menus; dazzling dining room; expert advice on wine pairings. *Average main: €150* ✉ *Altis Belém Hotel & Spa, Doca do Bom Successo, Belém* ☎ *21/040–0200* 🌐 *restaurantefeitoria.com* ⏲ *Closed Sun. and Mon.* Ⓜ *Tram 15E to Centro Cultural de Belém.*

Frazão

$ | PORTUGUESE | FAMILY | There's no English menu here—just the daily specials scrawled on a piece of paper out front. If you want to eat where the locals do, search these dishes on the Web then step inside Frazão. **Known for:** cheap lunch menu that changes daily; crowd of regulars dining solo; brisk and busy no-fuss service. *Average main: €10* ✉ *Rua da Junqueira 412, Belém* ☎ *21/364–7805* ▭ *No credit cards* ⏲ *Closed Sun.* Ⓜ *Tram 15E to Museu Nacional dos Coches.*

★ Guelra

$$$ | SEAFOOD | FAMILY | Portugal is a nation obsessed with seafood, but more often than not, fish is simply grilled over charcoal with salt. Guelra is changing the game with a fish-focused eatery where you can sit down for creative seafood snacks and wine at the bar, or venture upstairs for a chic meal with Portuguese-influenced dishes. **Known for:** creative approach to seafood; all-day terrace and cocktails; wines aged in terra-cotta amphora vessels. *Average main: €22* ✉ *Rua de Belém 35, Belém* ☎ *93/900–2081* 🌐 *guelraott.com* ⏲ *Closed Mon.* Ⓜ *Tram 15E to Museu Nacional dos Coches.*

Miolo

$ | CAFÉ | FAMILY | This peachy pink all-day café serves breakfast and brunch plates nonstop along with coffee and cocktails. Find plenty of vegetarian and vegan-friendly options in the extensive menu that mixes brunch culture and Portuguese cuisine with a healthy homemade twist. **Known for:** creative and healthy breakfast dishes; dog-friendly space; specialty coffee and homemade treats. *Average main: €12* ✉ *Rua de Belém 36, Belém* 🌐 *www.instagram.com/miololisboa_* Ⓜ *Tram 15E to Museu Nacional dos Coches.*

Built in the 16th century, the Torre de Belém is now a UNESCO World Heritage site and one of Lisbon's most iconic attractions.

Nikkei

$$$ | JAPANESE FUSION | A dressy crowd gathers at this ultramodern dimly lit restaurant specializing in Japanese-Peruvian fusion food. At Nikkei you can sample many varieties of ceviche and sashimi, as well as *tiraditos* (a sashimi-shaped raw fish dish that blends Peruvian and Japanese culinary traditions). **Known for:** excellent sushi, sashimi, and ceviche; close to Torre de Belém; smaller crowds than at nearby restaurants. *Average main: €22* ✉ *Doca de Bom Successo, Belém* ☎ *21/301–7118* 🌐 *www.facebook.com/nikkeilx* Ⓜ *Tram 15E to Largo da Princesa.*

Nune's Real Marisqueira

$$$$ | SEAFOOD | FAMILY | Crustaceans of every shape and size are found at this classic *marisqueira*, the name given to restaurants that specialize in seafood of all kinds. A recent renovation turned this family-run spot into a glitzy, art deco–inspired space where high-quality Portuguese seafood remains the star and loyal locals still attend in droves. **Known for:** huge range of seafood, priced by weight; good wine list; over-the-top art deco–inspired decor. *Average main: €30* ✉ *Rua Bartolomeu Dias 172, Belém* ☎ *21/301–9899* 🌐 *www.nunesmarisqueira.pt/en* ⏲ *Closed Mon.* Ⓜ *Tram 15E to Largo da Princesa.*

Queijadas de Belém

$$ | PORTUGUESE | FAMILY | The namesake tarts, *queijadas*, are super sweet little cheese cakes, but this casual spot can also satisfy a more substantial hunger. For lunch, don't miss the giant grilled tiger prawns, or the grilled sardines when they're in season.

Known for: good coffee and delicious pastries; affordable main meals; friendly service. *Average main: €16* *Rua de Belém 1, Belém* *21/363–02034* *www.facebook.com/QueijadasDeBelem* *Closed Tues.* *Tram 15E to Mosteiro dos Jerónimos.*

Restaurante Belém 2a8
$$ | PORTUGUESE | FAMILY | Even though it's located right at the heart of Belém's sightseeing action, this traditional Portuguese restaurant has avoided becoming a tourist trap. The space is light and airy and the relaxed café downstairs and formal dining room upstairs serve everything from pastries and *petiscos* (small plates) to full meals. **Known for:** well-prepared fish and seafood; welcoming atmosphere; close to major sites. *Average main: €18* *Rua de Belém 2, Belém* *21/363–9055* *Tram 15E to Museu Nacional dos Coches.*

Coffee and Quick Bites

Confeitaria Nacional Belém
$ | CAFÉ | FAMILY | Portugal's oldest bakery has taken over an old pier next to the Torre de Belém. Here dozens of tables are perched over the Tagus River, with one side facing the famous tower and the other toward the city. **Known for:** sweets from Lisbon's oldest bakery; wide range of traditional baked goods; vantage point over the river. *Average main: €5* *Av. Brasília, Belém* *confeitarianacional.com* *Cascais Line to Belém, Tram 15 to Centro Cultural de Belém.*

Corações com Coroa Café
$ | CAFÉ | FAMILY | Sit beneath fragrant orange blossoms enjoying a healthy lunch at this café with a mission. Hidden behind the Belém library, this glass-walled social enterprise café supports a project protecting and empowering vulnerable women and girls. **Known for:** cozy secret terrace away from the crowds; menu designed by famous Portuguese chef Kiko; very good options for vegetarians. *Average main: €8* *Rua da Junqueira 295, Belém* *91/031–2930* *coracoescomcoroa.org* *Closed 2nd and 4th weekend each month* *Tram 15E to Altinho.*

Ostras Sobre Rodas
$ | SEAFOOD | FAMILY | Portugal produces fantastic oysters, and this solar-powered food truck located next to the Discoveries Monument is a top spot to try them. "Oysters on Wheels" brings fresh bivalves from the Sado River, an hour south of Lisbon, to the capital. Pair a couple or a dozen with a glass of Portuguese sparkling wine and enjoy the million-dollar waterfront views. **Known for:** fresh local oysters; sparkling wine; waterfront views. *Average*

main: €14.50 ✉ Av. Brasília, Belém ☎ 92/412–3985 🌐 ostrassobre-rodas.pt/en Ⓜ Tram 15E to Mosteiro dos Jerónimos.

Pão Pão Queijo Queijo

$ | **SANDWICHES** | **FAMILY** | Although the name translates as "Bread Bread Cheese Cheese," this bustling place serves much more than these two staples. Expect lines out the door as hungry sightseers and locals line up to take their pick from a huge variety of sandwiches, salads, falafel, and wraps. **Known for:** Turkish-style meat kebabs; excellent falafel on pita bread; popular with locals. *$ Average main: €9 ✉ Rua de Belém 126, Belém ☎ 21/362–6369 🌐 www.facebook.com/paopaobelem Ⓜ Cascais Line to Belém, Tram 15 to Mosteiro dos Jerónimos.*

★ **Pastéis de Belém**

$ | **CAFÉ** | **FAMILY** | This bakery specializes in *pastéis de nata*: delicious warm custard tarts sprinkled with cinnamon and powdered sugar. Although these sweet treats are ubiquitous in Portugal, the version here is celebrated as the original, made here since 1837 using a secret recipe from the nearby Mosteiro dos Jerónimos. **Known for:** the most famous custard tarts in Portugal; distinctive azulejo tile design; beautifully packaged pastéis to take away. *$ Average main: €8 ✉ Rua de Belém 84–92, Belém ☎ 21/363–7423 🌐 pasteisdebelem.pt/en Ⓜ Tram 15E to Mosteiro dos Jerónimos, Cascais Line to Belém.*

Pastelaria Careca

$ | **CAFÉ** | **FAMILY** | Many a Lisboeta would argue that Careca, which has been cooking up pastries since 1954, serves the best sweet croissants in town. Try them for yourself at this simple-but-smart café—best enjoyed outside on the terrace with a coffee or fresh orange juice. **Known for:** fresh-baked sweet croissants; friendly service; casual local vibe. *$ Average main: €7 ✉ Rua Duarte Pacheco Pereira 11D, Belém ☎ 21/301–0987 🌐 pastelariaocareca.pt 💳 No credit cards ⏲ Closed Tues. Ⓜ Tram 15E to Pedrouços.*

Hotels

★ **Altis Belém Hotel & Spa**

$$$$ | **HOTEL** | The decor at this elegant riverside hotel harks back to Portugal's Age of Discovery, but that's not to say it's stuck in the past—the overall vibe is light and modern, and its relatively small size gives it an intimate feel. **Pros:** chic bar for sunset cocktails; convenient to Belém's attractions; excellent spa area. **Cons:** not that convenient to public transport; restaurant and bar get packed; not much nightlife nearby. *$ Rooms from: €320 ✉ Doca do Bom Sucesso, Belém ☎ 21/040–0200 🌐 www.altishotels.com/EN/*

HotelAltisBelem *50 rooms* *Free Breakfast* *Tram 15E to Centro Cultural de Belém.*

Hotel Jerónimos 8

$ | **HOTEL** | Just around the corner from the monastery of the same name, Hotel Jerónimos 8 is a good base for exploring the many local sights. **Pros:** reasonable rates; views of the nearby monastery; relaxing sundeck. **Cons:** dated design; far from downtown sights; no pool or fitness area. *Rooms from: €125* *Rua dos Jerónimos 8, Belém* *21/360–0900* *www.almeidahotels.pt/pt/hotel-jeronimos-em-lisboa* *65 rooms* *Free Breakfast* *Cascais Line to Belém, Tram 15 to Mosteiro dos Jerónimos.*

★ NAU Palácio do Governador

$$$$ | **HOTEL** | Layers of history are on display at this beautiful retreat that combines fascinating peeks into the past with modern amenities. **Pros:** vast indoor pool and spa; garden terrace great for drinks; peaceful location. **Cons:** a little hard to find; neighborhood is not especially scenic; a bit far from the action. *Rooms from: €280* *Rua Bartolomeu Dias 117, Belém* *21/300–7009* *www.nauhotels.com/nau-palacio-do-governador* *60 rooms* *Free Breakfast* *Free Parking* *Tram 15 to Largo da Princesa.*

Nightlife

Á Margem

BARS | **FAMILY** | The perfect place for a sundowner, Á Margem is a minimalist white cube of a restaurant-bar perched on the banks of the Tagus. *Doca de Bom Successo, Av. Brasília, Belém* *91/862–0032* *www.instagram.com/amargem.belem* *Tram 15E to Centro Cultural de Belém.*

Gastrobar 38° 41'

BARS | Cocktails, DJ sessions, light meals, and glorious sunset views draw a well-heeled crowd to this slick bar on the banks of the Tagus River. *Altis Belém Hotel & Spa, Doca de Bom Successo, Belém* *21/040–0210* *www.altishotels.com/altis-belem-spa/restaurantes-bares* *Cascais Line to Belém.*

Quiosque Belém

BARS | **FAMILY** | Sipping a drink at one of Lisbon's many outdoor kiosks is key to enjoying the city's fine views and fine weather. Belém's own *quiosque* is perfect for a sundown *ginjinha* (sour cherry liqueur) or a chilled white wine overlooking the leafy location. *Rua Vieira Portuense 1, Belém* *21/800–3496* *Cascais Line to Belém, Tram 15E to Museu Nacional dos Coches.*

SUD Lisboa

PIANO BAR | A bar, restaurant, and swimming pool all enjoy gorgeous riverfront views at this super-luxe contemporary space. By day visitors can eat, drink, and swim; at night saxophonists play under the twinkling lights of the poolside bar. ✉ *Pavilhão Poente, Av. Brasília, Belém* ✥ *Next to MAAT* ☎ *21/159–2700* 🌐 *sudlisboa.com* Ⓜ *Tram 15E to Altinho.*

★ Wine with a View

WINE BAR | There's nothing between you and the view where this vintage wine tricycle has a pitch in the gardens of the Torre de Belém. It peddles Portuguese wines of every style and hue, which can be sipped from reusable plastic wine glasses while sightseeing. ✉ *Av. Brasília, Belém* 🌐 *winewithaview.pt* Ⓜ *Cascais Line to Belém, Tram 15E to Centro Cultural de Belém.*

Performing Arts

Centro Cultural de Belém

PERFORMANCE VENUES | **FAMILY** | Known to locals as CCB, this highly regarded cultural center offers a huge range of reasonably priced events, ranging from touring art exhibitions and theatrical or musical performances to outdoor DJ sessions and pilates classes. Within the precinct, you'll also find the contemporary art gallery and a curation of shops and restaurants. ✉ *Praça do Império, Belém* ☎ *21/361–2400* 🌐 *www.ccb.pt/en* 🎫 *From €7* Ⓜ *Cascais Line to Belém, Tram 15E to Centro Cultural de Belém.*

Shopping

Arte Periférica

ART GALLERY | This gallery and arts store at the Centro Cultural de Belém is a good source of contemporary art, particularly by emerging young talent. ✉ *Centro Cultural de Belém, Praça do Imperio, Loja 3, Belém* ☎ *21/361–7100* 🌐 *arteperiferica.pt* ⏲ *Closed Mon.* Ⓜ *Cascais Line to Belém, Tram 15 to Centro Cultural de Belém.*

Next Door Shop

SOUVENIRS | Take home a piece of Portugal from this family-run gift store, which sits next to the world-famous Pastéis de Belém. Inside you'll find an extensive range of Portuguese-made souvenirs, from hand-painted tiles to original artworks, tinned fish to socks. ✉ *Rua de Belém 80, Belém* ☎ *21/363–8024* 🌐 *www.nextdoorshop.pt* Ⓜ *Cascais Line to Belém, Tram 15 to Mosteiro dos Jerónimos.*

Chapter 12

SOUTH OF THE RIVER

Updated by
Daniela Sunde-Brown

Sights	Restaurants	Hotels	Shopping	Nightlife
★★★★★	★★★★☆	★★☆☆☆	★★★☆☆	★★★☆☆

NEIGHBORHOOD SNAPSHOT

TOP EXPERIENCES

- **Costa da Caparica.** Miles of sandy beaches that are perfect for surfing or sunbathing, accompanied by bars and seafood shacks.
- **Parque Natural da Arrábida.** For quiet beach days, nature hikes, and seafood by the water.
- **Views from Cacilhas.** Cross the river for a fresh shellfish lunch and incredible Lisbon views.
- **Azulejos do Azeitão.** Learn about the traditional methods used to make, paint, and glaze Portugal's famous tiles.
- **Trafaria fish lunch.** Locals grill up the day's catch at no-fuss seafood restaurants.

GETTING HERE

A 10-minute passenger ferry bounces between Lisbon and Cacilhas roughly every 20 minutes (5 am–1 am). From here buses connect to Sesimbra (3545) and Caparica (3011). Another ferry runs between Belém and Trafaria, taking 20 minutes and departing less frequently (6 am–9 pm). Trains, buses, and cars cross the red Ponte 25 de Abril or the sweeping Ponte Vasco da Gama. Regular buses leave from Sete Rios for Costa da Caparica (3710), Azeitão (4730), and Sesimbra (3721), calling at Alcântara before crossing the river.

OFF THE BEATEN PATH

- **Setúbal.** About 50 km (30 miles) south of Lisbon lies Setùbal, a historic port city known for its charming historic center, seafood, and Moscatel wine. Drop by the fantastic daily market, then try *choco frito* (fried cuttlefish) for lunch before escaping to Arrábida's beaches or joining a dolphin-watching cruise.

PLANNING YOUR TIME

- This chapter covers a huge region, so stick to one town or consider the time needed to bounce around. Each area offers enough for a relaxed day out, with enough beaches to keep you busy for a month. The furthest areas require a day trip but you can pop to Cacilhas or Costa da Caparica for an easy breezy afternoon.

It's a little more than a mile from Lisbon to the South Bank but with just two bridges and a handful of ferry connections, it feels like another world.

Those willing to make the short hop over the Tagus River to the *Margem Sul* will be rewarded with miles of wild golden beaches, unspoiled nature, lush vineyards, long wine-soaked seafood lunches, and a more relaxed pace.

Colorful Cacilhas has long drawn locals to its many (seafood restaurants), while tourists flock to the Insta-famous Ponto Final, with its enchanting view of Lisbon and months-long reservations list. A free elevator takes those with a creative appetite up to Casa Cerca, a contemporary art center with a café terrace offering the same splendid Lisbon panoramas.

If you want some of Europe's best beaches, head straight for Costa da Caparica, where the sands grow ever more untouched—and unfortunately harder to reach by public transport—the further south you go. But for the romance of being transported from busy downtown Lisbon to a quaint seafood-heavy Portuguese village in under 10 minutes, you can't beat the ferry.

Most of this coast is best reached by car or motorcycle. The same can be said for the truly spectacular secluded beaches of Parque Natural da Arrábida, the wine-growing areas of Azeitão, and the pretty beach town of Sesimbra.

Join a guided day trip, or take yourself to Setúbal for Portugal's best fresh fish market. Venture into Arrábida for a seafood lunch overlooking crystal clear turquoise waters framed by wild green hills. Cross the hills to Azeitão, where you can visit an artisanal *azulejo* workshop, taste the gooey local sheep's cheese or sweet *tortas de azeitão*, and sample wines at historic estates.

Further afield, a 9th-century Moorish castle looms above the palm-fringed Sesimbra, a relaxed seaside town with pretty, historic streets, calm waters perfect for swimming, and a reputation for fresh fish. Admire an outdoor gallery of sea-themed murals while you enjoy a gelato and stroll along the oceanfront.

The glass-fronted Boca do Vento elevator takes you between Almada's riverfront and Old Town, with an amazing view along the trip.

Cacilhas and Almada Velha

A 10-minute ferry ride takes you from Lisbon across to Cacilhas, where seafood restaurants and glorious city views await. Boats run roughly every 20 minutes, 5 am–1 am, between Cacilhas and the terminal at Cais do Sodré, and it's just a few minutes' walk to the main bar and restaurant strip. Almada's old town is also within walking distance—or there's a tram. It's a slightly rough walk along the sea edge to famed waterside restaurants like Ponto Final, where a free elevator connects the riverfront to the clifftop.

Sights

★ Elevador Panorâmico da Boca do Vento

VIEWPOINT | Almada's eye-catching elevator is a fun, free, and extremely photogenic way to travel between Almada's Old Town and the pretty gardens and noteworthy restaurants on the riverfront of Cais do Ginjal. Enjoy the views from the glass-fronted cabin as you ascend or descend. ✉ *Rua do Ginjal 72* 🌐 *www.cm-almada.pt/conhecer/natureza/elevador-panoramico-da-boca-do-vento* 🎫 *Free.*

Olho de Boi

NEIGHBORHOOD | Olho de Boi ("Bull's Eye") is the local name for the riverfront area at the foot of Almada's Panoramic Elevator. From here enjoy incredible views across the shimmering river to Lisbon

Cacilhas and Almada Velha

Sights

Elevador Panorâmico da Boca do Vento, **3**

Olho de Boi, **2**

Santuário Nacional do Cristo Rei, **1**

Restaurants

Atira-te ao Rio, **1**

Cabrinha, **5**

Damasqino, **3**

O Farol, **4**

Olga Gatti, **6**

Tasca D'Avenida, **2**

Quick Bites

Meia Volta de Úrano, **1**

Rio Tejo
Rua do Ginjal
Olho de Boi
R. Carvalho Freirinha
R. Cândido dos Reis
CACILHAS
Cacilhas
Av. Aliança Povo M.F.A
Submarine Barracuda
Frigate Dom Fernando II e Glória
R. Elias Garcia
25 de Abril
Av. 25 de Abril de 1974
R. Dom José de Mascarenhas
R. Dom João de Portugal
R. Francisco de Andrade
R. Serpa Pinto
R. Bernardo Francisco da Costa
Gil Vicente
Cemitério de Almada
R. Leonel Duarte Ferreira
R. Cap. Leitão
Parque Municipal da Juventude
Av. Dom Afonso Henriques
R. M.J de Sousa Coutinho
R. Dom Álvaro Abranches da Câmara
R. Dona Leonor de Mascarenhas
Av. Dom João I
R. Luís de Queiroz
R. Lourenço Pires de Távora
R. Dom Sancho I
R. Irene Lisboa
R. Fernão Lourenço
R. Afonso Galo
S. João Baptista
Av. do Cristo Rei
Av. Dom Nuno Álvares Pereira
R. Dom Francisco Xavier de Noronha
Parque Urbano Comandante Júlio Ferraz
Av. Prof. Egas Moniz
Av. Rainha Dona Leonor
R. Padre Ângelo Firmino da Silva
R. Dom João de Castro
ALMADA
Almada
0 400 m
0 800 ft

KEY

Sights
Restaurants
Quick Bites
Metro

Stroll through the pleasant green space at Jardim do Rio to reach the Naval Museum in one direction and the famous Ponto Final riverfront restaurant in the other. ✉ *Rua do Ginjal.*

★ Santuário Nacional do Cristo Rei

MONUMENT | FAMILY | Lisbon's answer to Rio de Janeiro's Christ the Redeemer was inaugurated in 1959 as a mark of thanks for Portugal's safety during the violence of World War II. Today, it's an important religious site, but most casual visitors come here for the spectacular views from the free lookout or the 262-foot-high viewing platform, reached by elevator. ✉ *Praceta do Cristo Rei 27A* 🌐 *cristorei.pt/en* 🎫 *€8.*

Restaurants

Atira-te ao Rio

$$ | PORTUGUESE | FAMILY | This riverfront restaurant draws crowds for its excellent views and refined cuisine. The mint green chairs of Atira-te ao Rio are easy to spot, and the octopus with roasted potatoes is always a winner. **Known for:** panoramic views; refined Portuguese dishes; busy service. 💲 *Average main: €19* ✉ *Rua do Ginjal 69* ☎ *21/275–1380* 🌐 *atirateaorio.com.*

Cabrinha

$$ | PORTUGUESE | FAMILY | Cabrinha has been doing a roaring business among locals and out-of-towners since 1978. Crustaceans of all kinds are priced by weight, while steaks, grilled fish, and the famous seafood stew will satisfy a hearty appetite without blowing the budget. **Known for:** brisk friendly service; lobster and giant prawns; tasty seafood rice. 💲 *Average main: €20* ✉ *Beco do Bom Sucesso 4* ☎ *21/276–4732* 🌐 *cabrinha.com.pt* ⏲ *Closed Mon.*

Damasqino

$ | MIDDLE EASTERN | FAMILY | When love led Damascus-born Bashar Khabbaz to put down roots in Portugal, he couldn't help but miss the flavors of Syria. So he opened this Syrian bistro in Cacilhas with homestyle dishes from kibbeh to kebabs. **Known for:** homestyle Syrian dishes; lively atmosphere; huge terrace for shisha. 💲 *Average main: €15* ✉ *Rua Commandante António Feio 28A* ☎ *93/058–4246* 🌐 *damasqino.pt* ⏲ *Closed Mon.*

O Farol

$$$ | PORTUGUESE | FAMILY | The oldest *cervejaria* (relaxed dining and drinking spot) in the region, O Farol has been serving cold beer, rich seafood stews, and delicious shellfish since 1890. The local crowd is a testament to the outstanding seafood, and the sunset views over the river to Lisbon are magical. **Known for:** excellent grilled fish and shrimp; efficient friendly service;

waterfront location near the ferry terminal. *Average main: €21* *Largo Alfredo Dinis 1* *21/276–5248* *en.restaurantefarol.com* *Closed Mon.*

Olga Gatti

$ | ITALIAN | FAMILY | The south of the river is more than just seafood. If you're craving Italian, Valdo Gatti serves artisanal wood-fired pizza crafted with Italian and Portuguese ingredients. **Known for:** fresh, organic ingredients; best wood-fired pizza south of the river; modern industrial space. *Average main: €15* *Rua Candido dos Reis 5* *21/276–1721* *www.olgagatti.com.*

★ Tasca D'Avenida

$ | PORTUGUESE | A paper tablecloth stuck to the window detailing the day's dishes is almost always a good sign. At lunch, this chic tavern and marisqueira fills with a crowd of well-dressed regulars who return for the high-quality food and friendly banter. **Known for:** fantastic traditional Portuguese dishes; crowd of regulars; daily lunch specials menu. *Average main: €15* *Av. Dom Afonso Henriques 10C* *96/834–8036* *Closed Sun.*

Coffee and Quick Bites

Meia Volta de Úrano

GATHERING PLACE | FAMILY | This eclectic and bohemian spot is at once a bookshop, gallery, café, and arts space. Align your visit with regular events such as poetry, fado, stand-up comedy, and board game and quiz nights. *Livraria Casa das Artes, Rua Cândido dos Reis 49A e B* *91/850–7478* *meiavoltadeurano.pt.*

Nightlife

Boteco.47

BARS | This bright and breezy spot with nice cocktails and *petiscos* buzzes with Lisboetas after dark. Order a bottle of wine and small plates to share, pull up a seat outside, and watch the party unfold. *Rua Cândido dos Reis 47* *www.facebook.com/boteco.47* *Closed Tues. and Wed.*

Chá de Histórias

BARS | This is a retro-chic spot for drinks and petiscos. The kitsch collectibles and bottle-filled cabinets make the space feel like being at someone's grandparents' house, and the board games and comic books add to the wholesome charm. *Rua Dom Sancho I 7A* *21/809–9712* *www.facebook.com/chadehistoriascacilhas* *Closed Sun.*

★ Ophelia

COCKTAIL BARS | This slick minimalist cocktail bar would easily rank on a list of Lisbon's best bars, but refreshingly put down its roots on the southern bank. The carefully curated cocktail list focuses on the flavors and vibes of each drink, rather than the booze within. ✉ *Largo Gabriel Pedro 7* ☎ *93/460–3940* 🌐 *www.instagram.com/ophelia_cocktailbar* ⏲ *Closed Tues.*

Petisco da Lata

BARS | The Portuguese have turned canned fish into an art form, and at this chic neighborhood bar you can sample a range of tinned tuna and sardines transformed into snacks. There's a good range of wines and Portuguese spirits, as well as live music. ✉ *Rua da Judiaria 22A* ☎ *91/755–9953* 🌐 *www.instagram.com/petiscodalata* ⏲ *Closed Sun. and Mon.*

Performing Arts

★ Casa da Cerca

PERFORMANCE VENUES | This contemporary art museum and live music venue is set in a beautiful 18th-century building. Permanent and visiting exhibitions and installations will appeal to art lovers, and a café-bar with outdoor seating offers incredible panoramic views. ✉ *Rua da Cerca 2* ☎ *21/272–4950* 🌐 *www.instagram.com/casadacerca* ⏲ *Closed Mon.*

★ Cine Incrível

CONCERTS | The colorful art deco building is reason enough to visit this cinema-turned-arts-venue. Today the space hosts a rich roster of live music three days a week, and locals can be found swapping stories at the bar. ✉ *Rua Capitão Leitão 1* ☎ *93/207–2937* 🌐 *www.facebook.com/cineincrivel* ⏲ *Closed Sun.–Wed.*

Shopping

Atelier Arteria

CRAFTS | Atelier Arteria is a free-spirited, inclusive, and ever-changing creative coworking space. Drop by to shop for one-of-a-kind bags and pillows made from textile waste and Portuguese linen, locally made jewelry, original artwork, and more. ✉ *Rua Latino Coelho 27* ☎ *96/263–8024* ⏲ *Closed Sun.*

Retro Queen

VINTAGE | Lisbon's vintage junkies have hopped across the river since 2000 to browse the racks at this small but well-stocked store that specializes in the '80s and '90s. There's a good range of vintage menswear in addition to killer dresses, handbags, and jewelry. ✉ *Rua Cândido dos Reis 60A* ☎ *96/421–8591* 🌐 *www.instagram.com/retroqueen.cacilhas.*

Costa da Caparica, Trafaria, and Cova do Vapor

On summer weekends, Lisboetas flee the heat for the Costa da Caparica, 16 miles of soft yellow sand that feels more like California than the rows of umbrellas and pebbles often associated with European beaches. There are three dozen individual beaches and each has a trendy bar, chic café, or relaxed fish grill, so you're never far from an ice-cold jug of sangria. Consistent swells have made Costa da Caparica a surfer hangout—and if you're brave enough to enter the chilly Atlantic, plenty of surf schools will rent you a board and wetsuit.

Bus 3710 to Caparica departs two or three times an hour from Areeiro, making a few stops in Lisbon before crossing the bridge. A car is needed to reach farther-flung beaches. Trafaria, a riverfront fishing town famed for its seafood restaurants, can be reached by 20-minute ferry ride from Belém, and it's a short cab ride from there to the colorful fishing village of Cova do Vapor, where the beautiful white sands mark the beginning of Costa da Caparica.

Sights

Costa da Caparica Beaches

BEACH | FAMILY | When young Lisboetas want to go to the beach, they'll often cross the bridge for the Costa da Caparica, which packs out in summer with bronzed locals. As a former fishing village, the town itself lacks charm but the beachfront is lively with dozens of cafés and bars catering to a relaxed surf-loving clientele. The further south you go, the quieter it gets. Each beach is different: the areas nearest Caparica are family-oriented, while more southerly ones attract a younger crowd with beach parties (there are some nudist beaches, too). **Amenities:** food and drink; lifeguards; parking (fee); showers; toilets; water sports. **Best for:** partiers; sunset; swimming; walking.

Praia da Cova do Vapor

BEACH | FAMILY | Still under the radar even among Lisboetas, Cova do Vapor is a fishing hamlet perched at the point where the Tagus meets the Atlantic. The soft-sand beach is Caparica's closest point to Lisbon, and while there are glorious views over the city, the rustic beach shacks make it feel like another world. While crowds

Costa da Caparica's many beaches offer something for everyone under the sun, from families to surfers to the beach party crowd.

of surfers pack most of the Costa da Caparica, there are still vast swaths of space on the sands and gentle dunes here. **Amenities:** food and drink; parking (no fee). **Best for:** solitude; swimming; walking.

Restaurants

Borda d'Água

$$ | ECLECTIC | This restaurant—a glassed-in wooden cabana built in the sand dunes—has a laid-back beach vibe with white-washed interiors, colorful deck chairs, and swinging hammocks. The menu is strong on daily fish specials, with sandwiches and salads on offer, too. **Known for:** caipirinhas and other beachy beverages; sand-in-your-shoes atmosphere; vegetarian and vegan dishes. *Average main: €19 Praia da Morena 21/297–5213 bordadagua.com.pt Closed Dec. 1–Jan. 15.*

★ Casa Ideal

$ | PORTUGUESE | FAMILY | Trafaria is a tiny fishing village with a charming view of small boats and Lisbon in one direction and a huge grain silo in the other. Hidden down a back street, cozy Casa Ideal has been welcoming diners for more than 40 years with a humble menu of grilled fish and delicious seafood rice dishes. **Known for:** homely 40-year-old restaurant; seafood rice cooked to order; fresh fish grilled over charcoal. *Average main: €13 Rua Tenente Maia 22 21/295–0898 www.facebook.com/casaidea restaurante Closed Wed.*

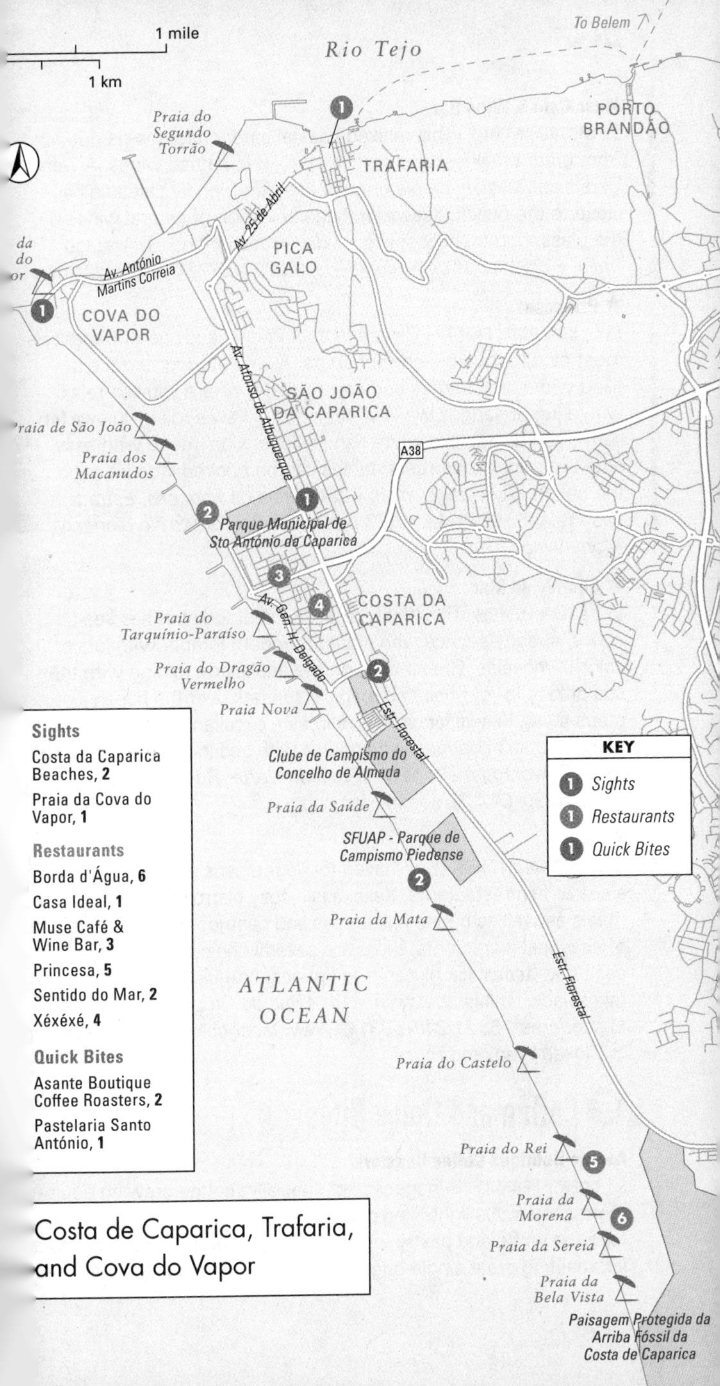

Costa de Caparica, Trafaria, and Cova do Vapor

Muse Café & Wine Bar

$ | **BISTRO** | **FAMILY** | This relaxed coastal eatery runs the gamut from great breakfast and brunch options to natural wines. A warm Ukrainian-Russian couple opened this dog-friendly café and bar close to the beach. **Known for:** huge selection of natural wines by the glass; dog-friendly space; all-day brunch menu. *Average main: €12 Av. 1º de Maio 36G 93/723–6772 musecafe.pt.*

★ **Princesa**

$$$ | **SEAFOOD** | **FAMILY** | Calm and cool Princesa is one of Caparica's most picturesque beachfront spots. A vast outdoor terrace is filled with sun loungers and comfy chairs where you can relax with a jug of sangria while watching the waves roll in. **Known for:** light fresh dishes like white fish ceviche; kids' menu with easy eats like mini hamburgers; tables can be booked indoors or on the beach. *Average main: €22 Praia da Princesa, Estrada das Praias 93/464–7138 praiaprincesa.com No dinner Mon.–Wed.*

★ **Sentido do Mar**

$$ | **ASIAN FUSION** | This highly regarded seafood spot has sea views, speedy service, and a bright modern interior with lots of colorful mosaics. Grab a table on the esplanade to dine with the sea breeze in your hair and magical sunsets over the ocean just steps away. **Known for:** super fresh fish; excellent sushi and ceviche; vegetarian options like noodles with seasonal vegetables and tofu. *Average main: €20 Praia do Norte, Rua Muralha da Praia 7 21/290–0473 sentidodomar.pt.*

Xéxéxé

$ | **VEGETARIAN** | **FAMILY** | A haven for vegetarians and vegans amid a sea of fish restaurants, Xéxéxé is a cozy bistro serving delicious meals as well as house-baked pies and pastries. With creative use of seasonal ingredients, there are several choices of set meals each day. **Known for:** gluten-free options; enthusiastic staff; creative salads. *Average main: €14 Rua do Grupo Desportivo dos Pescadores 1 21/243–5031 www.facebook.com/xexexevegan Closed Wed. and Thurs.*

Coffee and Quick Bites

Asante Boutique Coffee Roasters

$ | **COFFEE** | **FAMILY** | A huge wall of specialist coffee brewing equipment shows this light-filled café means business. Join the locals for a flat white and pastry while catching up on the news. **Known for:** roasting great single-origin coffee; tasty pastries and flat whites; space to meet Caparica's expat crowd. *Average main: €4 Av. Dom Sebastião 69E 21/291–4259 asante.coffee Closed Mon.*

★ **Pastelaria Santo António**

$ | BAKERY | FAMILY | Since 1942 this bakery has been a cornerstone of the Costa da Caparica community. Sit out on the terrace beneath the pine trees, where you can taste its famous (custard tarts with coconut), along with coffee roasted on-site. **Known for:** pastéis de Santo António; delicious chorizo bread; coffee roasted on-site. *Average main: €3 Av. Afonso de Albuquerque 227 21/290–0065 pastelariasantoantonio.pt No credit cards.*

Nightlife

★ **Leblon**

BARS | Named for Rio de Janeiro's most upmarket beach neighborhood, Leblon attracts the same type of well-groomed beachgoer as its Brazilian namesake. Locals come here for tasty post-swim petiscos and strong caipirinhas. *Praia das Palmeiras 96/423–0203 www.instagram.com/leblonrestaurante Closed Mon.*

Waikiki

BARS | Steps from the water at the popular Praia da Sereia, Waikiki is a place for late-night summer beach parties or for daytime drinking and sunbathing during the warm spring months. *Praia da Sereia 21/296–2129 waikiki.com.pt Closed Oct.–Mar.*

Sesimbra and Arrábida

These relatively secluded towns are home to pretty beaches, excellent seafood, and worthwhile local sights.

Bus 3721 runs roughly once an hour from the Carris bus terminal at Praça da Espanha and Sesimbra, also calling at Alcântara-Terra, and takes about 75 minutes. Buses are slightly more frequent in the summer. Another option is to take the ferry from Cais do Sodré to Cacilhas, where Bus 3536 runs out to Sesimbra. Exploring Parque Natural da Arrábida is better with a car or an organized day trip, though some roads close during the summer months. To reach Arrábida with public transport, take a train to Setúbal then ride Bus 4472 or 4474 to various beaches along the coast.

Sights

Praia da California

BEACH | FAMILY | Sesimbra's beachfront stretches the entire length of the historic downtown area, divided in the middle by a whitewashed fort jutting out to sea. The eastern side, known as Praia da California, is rocky at the far end, with some currents and small waves. During the summer it's packed with sun loungers, pedal boats, and splashing families, but it's blissfully quiet from mid-October through June. **Amenities:** food and drink; lifeguards (summer); showers (summer); toilets (summer). **Best for:** snorkeling; swimming; walking. ✉ *Rua Heliodoro Salgado 2C.*

★ Praia de Galapinhos

BEACH | FAMILY | Frequently cited as one of the most beautiful beaches in Portugal, Galapinhos has such white sand and crystalline water that it appears almost Caribbean. Surrounded by the wild nature of Arrábida's hills (wild boar have been spotted taking a dip here), it's best visited outside the July–September season, when things get busy and access to vehicles is restricted. **Amenities:** food and drink (summer). **Best for:** snorkeling; solitude; swimming; walking. ✉ *Praia dos Galapinhos.*

★ Praia do Ouro

BEACH | FAMILY | Calm and clear water, a workout station, and a diving platform make the western stretch of Sesimbra Beach a favorite with families and athletic young folk. Boats docking here in the summer whisk beach-hoppers off to hard-to-reach strands, but with the pine-covered hills stretching right down to the sand and a café-bar doing a brisk trade in wine, ice cream, and seafood, there's plenty of reason to stay put. The beach has wheelchairs and an access point during the July–September high season and has won national awards for accessibility. **Amenities:** food and drink; lifeguards (summer); parking (fee); showers; toilets (summer). **Best for:** snorkeling; swimming. ✉ *Av. dos Náufragos 20.*

Praia do Portinho da Arrábida

BEACH | FAMILY | One of the most celebrated of the famous Arrábida beaches, Portinho is a photogenic crescent of golden sand and turquoise waters, flanked on all sides by pine-covered hills. A high-season car ban makes access tough in the summer months, but it's a joy to visit at any other time of year. **Amenities:** food and drink. **Best for:** snorkeling; swimming; walking.

Restaurants

★ Casa Mateus

$$ | **PORTUGUESE** | **FAMILY** | In this relaxed fishing village with charcoal grills on every corner, Casa Mateus offers a refreshing reinterpretation of seafood. The Sesimbra favorite is well-known for plating local flavors and traditional dishes with a more refined chef flair. **Known for:** traditional Portuguese dishes with modern twists; daily specials; outdoor terrace. *Average main: €17 Largo Anselmo Braancamp 4 96/365–0939 casamateus.pt Closed Mon.*

★ Tasca do Isaias

$ | **SEAFOOD** | **FAMILY** | The huge queues that form outside this tiny family-run tavern are a testament to the fact that the fish served here is the best in town. **Known for:** lively atmosphere; outdoor tables on the cobblestones; charcoal-grilled fish. *Average main: €13 Rua Coronel Barreto 2 91/457–4373 No credit cards Closed Sun.*

Coffee and Quick Bites

★ ECHO Gelato Lab

$ | **ICE CREAM** | **FAMILY** | Creativity and chemistry combine at this Italian-style gelato shop on Sesimbra's waterfront. Choose from 18 traditional and fun flavors, including many that make use of fresh fruits. **Known for:** super creamy gelato with just enough sugar; seasonal flavors that highlight fresh fruits; terrace with sea views. *Average main: €4 Av. 25 de Abril 6C 21/584–7756 www.instagram.com/echogelatolab Closed Mon.*

Fini

$ | **ICE CREAM** | **FAMILY** | There's no shortage of places to eat ice cream in Sesimbra, but Fini serves superior Italian scoops and has a sunny patio overlooking the sea. Flavors vary daily (the banana and peanut butter is particularly delicious), plus there's a wide range of toppings and good coffee. **Known for:** fresh contemporary decor; huge range of fresh fruit and nut toppings; jars of ice cream to go. *Average main: €5 Av. dos Náufragos 15 21/193–1795 fini.pt Closed weekdays Oct.–Apr.*

Galé

$ | **SEAFOOD** | **FAMILY** | This friendly café-bar has a wonderful vantage over the sea. The seafood, toasted sandwiches, and house white wine are all good, but the main attraction is the sheltered terrace. **Known for:** friendly family owners; good shellfish and seafood snacks; popular with locals. *Average main: €13 Rua Capitão Leitão 7 21/223–3170 No credit cards Closed Tues.*

Azeitão, Meco, and Lagoa de Albufeira

From rolling hills to vineyards to an artisanal azulejo workshop, you'll find plenty to do and see here.

Sporadic Carris Metropolitana buses (Bus 4730) run weekdays between Lisbon's Sete Rios and Setúbal, stopping in Azeitão. The ride takes about an hour. Even more limited bus services (3201, 3208, 3210) run between Sesimbra, Meco, and Lagoa de Albufeira. If time is of the essence, it's easier to hire a car, catch a cab, or take a trip with a guide. Driving in the region is lovely, with lots of scenic small villages, rolling hills, and dramatic ocean views.

Sights

★ José Maria da Fonseca Casa-Museu

WINERY | Intriguing tours cover this winery's long history and allow you to see all stages of production, including a peek into its dark and mysterious prized Moscatel cellars, where 100-plus-year-old bottles are still aging gracefully. ✉ *Rua José Augusto Coelho 11–13* ☎ *21/219–8940* 🌐 *jmf.pt* 🎫 *From €7.50 for tours* ✍ *Reservations recommended for tours.*

Palácio da Bacalhôa

WINERY | The jewel in the crown of this winery set in a late-16th-century mansion is its box-hedged garden and striking azulejos. Visitors can tour the building, gardens, and wine cellars (advance bookings are advised). Among the highlights is the so-called Casa do Fresco, which houses the country's oldest azulejo panel. ✉ *N10* ✥ *4 km (2½ miles) east of Vila Nogueira de Azeitão* ☎ *21/219–8067* 🌐 *bacalhoa.pt/en/palacio-da-bacalhoa* 🎫 *€12* ⏲ *Closed Sun.*

Praia da Lagoa de Albufeira

BEACH | **FAMILY** | Mammoth white sand dunes separate the calm lake at Lagoa de Albufeira from the crashing Atlantic waves on the other side. Kite surfers whiz by, families splash in the waters, and locals wade through the shallows, harvesting shellfish. **Amenities:** food and drink; parking (fee); water sports. **Best for:** walking.

Praia do Meco

BEACH | Crashing waves, jagged cliffs, and tall dunes make for a dramatic view at Praia do Meco, which found fame in the 1970s as one of the first nudist beaches in Portugal. Today, this 5-km (3-mile) sweep of beach is a popular spot with surfers and day-tripping families, but those keen to get an all-over tan can

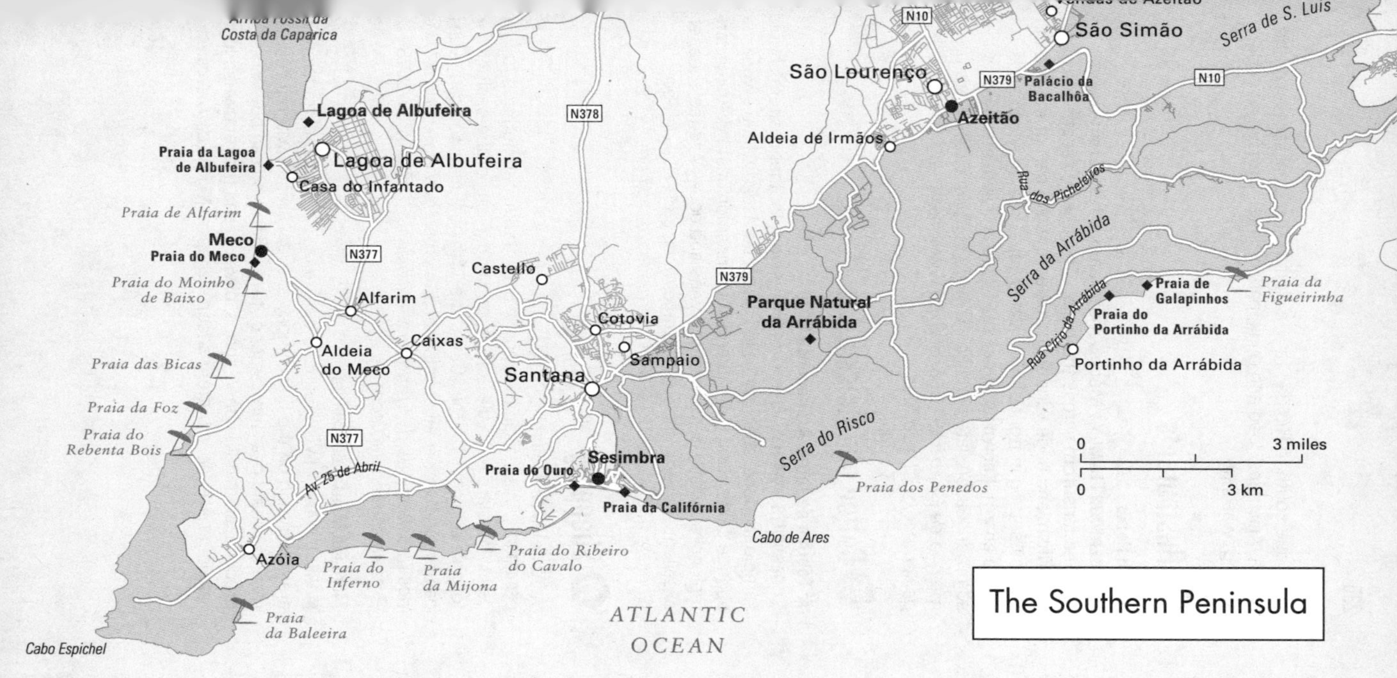
The Southern Peninsula
Costa da Caparica
Lagoa de Albufeira
Praia da Lagoa de Albufeira
Lagoa de Albufeira
Casa do Infantado
Praia de Alfarim
Meco
Praia do Meco
Praia do Moinho de Baixo
Alfarim
Aldeia do Meco
Caixas
Praia das Bicas
Praia da Foz
Praia do Rebenta Bois
Av. 25 de Abril
Azóia
Praia da Baleeira
Cabo Espichel
Praia do Inferno
Praia da Mijona
Praia do Ribeiro do Cavalo
Castello
Cotovia
Sampaio
Santana
Sesimbra
Praia do Ouro
Praia da Califórnia
Cabo de Ares
Serra do Risco
Praia dos Penedos
ATLANTIC OCEAN
N378
N377
N379
N10
São Lourenço
São Simão
Serra de S. Luis
Palácio da Bacalhôa
Azeitão
Aldeia de Irmãos
Rua dos Picheleiros
Parque Natural da Arrábida
Serra da Arrábida
Rua Círio da Arrábida
Praia do Portinho da Arrábida
Praia de Galapinhos
Praia da Figueirinha
Portinho da Arrábida
0
3 miles
0
3 km

head due south to Rio da Prata, a clothing-optional section of the beach. **Amenities:** food and drink; parking (fee). **Best for:** solitude; surfing; walking.

Restaurants

Bar do Peixe

$$$ | SEAFOOD | FAMILY | Meco's most famous restaurant draws seafood fans from across the region. The freshly caught sea bass, swordfish, and huge variety of crustaceans are part of the appeal, but the setting in front of wild windswept Praia do Meco adds to the charm. **Known for:** great sea views and sunsets; oysters in summer season; late opening. *$ Average main: €25 ✉ Praia do Moinho de Baixo ☎ 91/308–8097 🌐 www.instagram.com/bardopeixemeco ⏲ Closed Tues.*

Coffee and Quick Bites

★ Fábrica de Tortas Azeitonense

$ | DESSERTS | FAMILY | When in town, sweet-toothed visitors should sample the local specialty called *tortas de Azeitão,* little sweet sponge cakes filled with an egg-and-cinnamon custard. **Known for:** regional specialty desserts; local wine and gooey Azeitão cheese; excellent souvenir shop. *$ Average main: €8 ✉ Rua de São Gonçalo 438 ☎ 21/210–2189 🌐 tortasdeazeitao.com.*

Shopping

★ Azulejos de Azeitão

CERAMICS | This artisanal company uses traditional methods to paint and glaze each tile sold in the shop. Many of the designs for sale originated in the 16th to the 19th centuries. You can even paint your own tile—just call ahead to organize a workshop. *✉ Rua dos Trabalhadores da Empresa Setubalense 15 ☎ 21/218–0013 🌐 azulejosdeazeitao.com.*

Mercado Mensal do Azeitão

MARKET | FAMILY | Vila Nogueira de Azeitão's agricultural traditions are trumpeted on the first Sunday of every month, when a country market is held near the center of town. Here you can buy wine, produce, clothing, kitchen goods, olive oil, and the renowned local *queijo de Azeitão,* a buttery sheep's cheese. *✉ Rua do Mercado.*

Chapter 13

13

AVENIDAS NOVAS

Updated by Joana Taborda

Sights	Restaurants	Hotels	Shopping	Nightlife
★★★☆☆	★★★☆☆	★★★☆☆	★★☆☆☆	★★☆☆☆

NEIGHBORHOOD SNAPSHOT

TOP EXPERIENCES

■ **Museu Calouste Gulbenkian.** Spend a day browsing through this art museum, where you'll find masterpieces by the likes of Renoir alongside contemporary Portuguese artists like Almada Negreiros.

■ **Get your pastry fill.** Take your pick from the dozens of pastries filling the counter of the art noveau–style café Pastelaria Versailles.

■ **Museu Bordalo Pinheiro.** Learn about Portugal's most famous ceramicist, known for his iconic fruit-and-vegetable-shaped bowls, at this local museum.

■ **Travel back in time.** Uncover layers of the city's history at the Museu de Lisboa, which houses a miniature replica of pre-earthquake Lisbon.

■ **Palácio dos Marqueses da Fronteira.** Book a guided tour of this 17th-century palace to admire one of the largest tile collections of its time.

GETTING HERE

The Metro is the best way to reach Avenidas Novas. All four lines go through the district, but the Yellow Line stops at the main avenues and squares. Unlike the other parts of the city, it does not have tram service, but Buses 736, 738, and 744 connect it to downtown and beyond.

PLANNING YOUR TIME

There's hardly a bad time to visit this neighborhood, as most sites are open every day, though restaurants may be packed with local workers at lunchtime during the week.

PAUSE HERE

■ **Museu Calouste Gulbenkian gardens.** Before or after touring the exhibits at the Museu Calouste Gulbenkian, take some time to wander through the surrounding gardens, where you'll find ducks and turtles basking in the sun. In the summertime, the garden welcomes a lively jazz festival. ✉ *Av. de Berna 45* 🚇 *Blue Line to São Sebastião or Praça de Espanha.*

OFF THE BEATEN PATH

■ **Mercado de Arroios.** About a five-minute walk from the Fonte Luminosa is the Mercado de Arroios, a food market that houses one of Lisbon's first Syrian restaurants, Mezze, alongside other international treats. ✉ *Rua Ângela Pinto* 🚇 *Green Line to Arroios or Alameda.*

Avenidas Novas witnessed Lisbon's blossoming into a modern city. You'll see it in its boulevards dotted with art nouveau buildings, metro stations adorned with contemporary tiles, and the iconic Museu Calouste Gulbenkian.

Soon after the Avenida da Liberdade was inaugurated in the 19th century, long broad avenues started radiating from Praça do Marquês de Pombal to the northern and eastern parts of the city. Portuguese engineer Frederico Ressano Garcia and his team were responsible for mapping this new area, largely inspired by Parisian boulevards. People referred to them as the *avenidas novas* (new avenues), and that's what this district is officially called today.

Art nouveau buildings filled the neighborhood in its early days. Many have since been replaced by dull office and apartment blocks, but there are still a few glimpses of the past, like the Casa-Museu Dr. Anastácio Gonçalves or the Pastelaria Versailles, an iconic pastry shop.

Lisboetas have fond memories of Avenidas Novas, mainly because of the Feira Popular, a large amusement park that took over the city for over half a century. These days, the biggest attraction here is the Museu Calouste Gulbenkian, an art museum whose gardens have become the meeting spot of the neighborhood.

When the metro opened in 1959, it cut through Avenidas Novas, signaling the beginning of a new era. Even the stations were works of art, featuring tile panels designed by prominent artists of the time like Maria Keil and Júlio Resende, an underground gallery that continues to this day in the new lines that have emerged since.

This sprawling district was also the stage for Paulo Rocha's *Os Verdes Anos*, a film that spurred the birth of the Portuguese New Cinema. The 1963 drama depicts the reality of the time, when countryfolk were making their way to the big city. Since then, Avenidas Novas has become the city's business hub, with many offices establishing their headquarters here.

While it may lack the soul of old Lisbon and doesn't have many major attractions, it's home to several large hotels, making it a great place to base yourself.

Avenidas Novas

Sights

Casa-Museu Dr. Anastácio Gonçalves

HISTORIC HOME | The former home of renowned 20th-century doctor and art collector Anastácio Gonçalves houses around 3,000 of his most prized pieces. Those include paintings by major Portuguese artists like Columbano Bordalo Pinheiro and José Malhoa, ancient Chinese porcelain, and 19th-century furniture from around Europe. The building is an art nouveau mansion from 1904. ⊠ *Av. 5 de Outubro 6–8, Avenidas Novas* ☎ *21/354–0823* ⊕ *culturaportugal.gov.pt/pt/conhecer/local/mmp-locais/casa-museu-dr-anastacio-goncalves* 🎫 *€5* ⊙ *Closed Mon.* Ⓜ *Yellow Line to Picoas.*

Fonte Luminosa

FOUNTAIN | This monumental fountain was built from 1938 to 1948, when World War II raged across Europe but Portugal remained a neutral war-free country. It's called "Luminous Fountain" because of a light show that takes place daily after the sun sets. The water falls from an upper platform to a large basin, but also only at set times—during the light show in the evening, and at lunchtime, between noon and 3. In the water are four sculptures of mermaids and another showing Triton on horseback. ⊠ *Alameda Dom Afonso Henriques, Areeiro* Ⓜ *Green or Red Line to Alameda.*

Galeria 111

ART GALLERY | This gallery is one of the few dating back to before the 1974 revolution, presenting some of the best contemporary Portuguese artists from the 20th and 21st centuries. You may find works by big names like Paula Rego and Maria Helena Vieira da Silva together with pieces by emerging artists. ⊠ *Rua Dr. João Soares 5B, Campo Grande* ☎ *21/797–7418* ⊕ *111.pt* ⊙ *Closed Sun. and Mon.* Ⓜ *Green or Yellow Line to Campo Grande.*

Igreja de São Sebastião

CHURCH | This church was built in 1652 and is one of the few survivors of the Great Earthquake of 1755. Behind a plain exterior is typical Portuguese baroque decoration, with walls lined with 18th-century paintings and tile panels illustrating the life of Saint Sebastian. The 17th-century goldwork of the main altar has been carefully restored and shines as you enter. ⊠ *Rua Tomás Ribeiro 64, São Sebastião* ☎ *21/354–5470* ⊕ *www.paroquia-s-sebastiao-pedreira.pt* Ⓜ *Blue or Red Line to São Sebastião.*

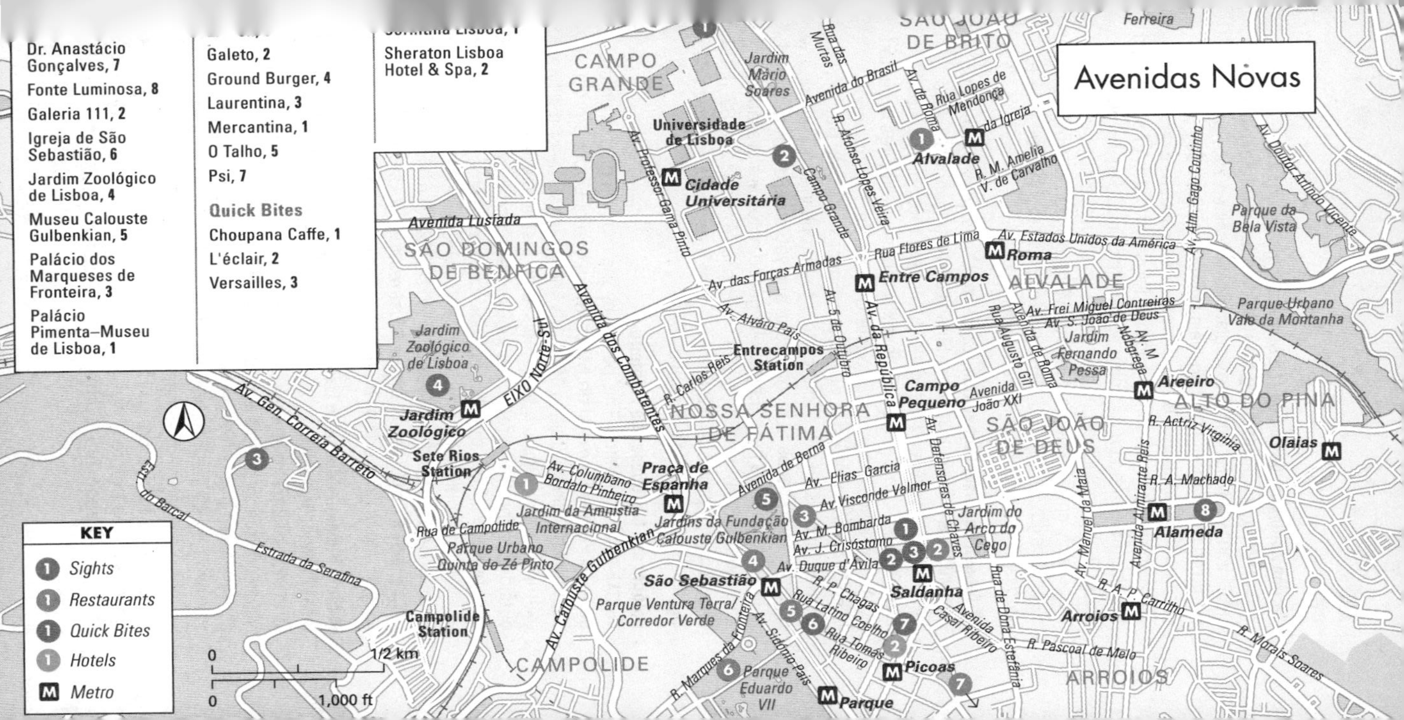

Avenidas Novas
Dr. Anastácio Gonçalves, 7
Fonte Luminosa, 8
Galeria 111, 2
Igreja de São Sebastião, 6
Jardim Zoológico de Lisboa, 4
Museu Calouste Gulbenkian, 5
Palácio dos Marqueses de Fronteira, 3
Palácio Pimenta–Museu de Lisboa, 1
Galeto, 2
Ground Burger, 4
Laurentina, 3
Mercantina, 1
O Talho, 5
Psi, 7
Quick Bites
Choupana Caffe, 1
L'éclair, 2
Versailles, 3
Sheraton Lisboa Hotel & Spa, 2
KEY
Sights
Restaurants
Quick Bites
Hotels
Metro
0
1/2 km
0
1,000 ft
CAMPO GRANDE
SÃO JOÃO DE BRITO
SÃO DOMINGOS DE BENFICA
ALVALADE
NOSSA SENHORA DE FÁTIMA
SÃO JOÃO DE DEUS
ALTO DO PINA
CAMPOLIDE
ARROIOS
Universidade de Lisboa
Cidade Universitária
Alvalade
Roma
Entre Campos
Entrecampos Station
Campo Pequeno
Areeiro
Olaias
Alameda
Arroios
Saldanha
Picoas
Parque
São Sebastião
Praça de Espanha
Jardim Zoológico
Sete Rios Station
Campolide Station
Jardim Zoológico de Lisboa
Jardim Mário Soares
Parque da Bela Vista
Parque Urbano Vale da Montanha
Jardim Fernando Pessa
Jardim do Arco do Cego
Jardins da Fundação Calouste Gulbenkian
Jardim da Amnistia Internacional
Parque Urbano Quinta do Zé Pinto
Parque Ventura Terra/ Corredor Verde
Parque Eduardo VII
Ferreira
Rua das Murtas
Avenida do Brasil
Av. de Roma
Rua Lopes de Mendonça
da Igreja
R. M. Amelia V. de Carvalho
R. Afonso Lopes Vieira
Campo Grande
Av. Professor Gama Pinto
Avenida Lusíada
Av. Alm. Gago Coutinho
Av. Doutor Arlindo Vicente
Av. Estados Unidos da América
Rua Flores de Lima
Av. das Forças Armadas
Av. Frei Miguel Contreiras
Av. S. João de Deus
Av. M Nóbrega
Avenida de Roma
Rua Augusto Gil
Av. Álvaro Pais
Av. 5 de Outubro
Av. da República
R. Carlos Reis
Avenida dos Combatentes
EIXO Norte-Sul
Av. Gen. Correia Barreto
Estr. do Barcal
Estrada da Serafina
Avenida João XXI
R. Actriz Virgínia
R. A. Machado
Avenida Almirante Reis
Av. Manuel da Maia
Av. Defensores de Chaves
Avenida de Berna
Av. Elias Garcia
Av. Visconde Valmor
Av. M. Bombarda
Av. J. Crisóstomo
Av. Duque d'Ávila
R. P. Chagas
Rua Latino Coelho
Rua Tomás Ribeiro
Avenida Casal Ribeiro
Rua de Dona Estefânia
R. Pascoal de Melo
R. A. P. Carrilho
R. Morais Soares
Av. Columbano Bordalo Pinheiro
Rua de Campolide
Av. Calouste Gulbenkian
Av. Sidónio Pais
R. Marquês da Fronteira

Jardim Zoológico de Lisboa (*Lisbon Zoological Gardens*)
ZOO | FAMILY | Families should set aside a full day to explore this deservedly popular and immaculately maintained zoo, which is home to more than 3,000 animals from more than 330 species. The grounds are huge, but visitors can leap aboard a cable car to whiz from one attraction to another. Those who don't have a head for heights can board a miniature train (not included in entrance price) that trundles around the gardens. There's a petting zoo and twice-daily animal shows. ✉ *Praça Marechal Humberto Delgado, Sete Rios* ☎ *21/723–2900* 🌐 *www.zoo.pt* 🎫 *€29* Ⓜ *Blue Line to Jardim Zoológico, Train to Sete Rios.*

★ **Museu Calouste Gulbenkian** (*Calouste Gulbenkian Museum*)
ART MUSEUM | Set in lovely gardens filled with leafy walkways, blooming flowers, and waddling ducks, the museum of the celebrated Fundação Calouste Gulbenkian houses treasures collected by Armenian oil magnate Calouste Gulbenkian. The collection is split in two; one part is devoted to Egyptian, Greek, Roman, Islamic, and Asian art, and the other to European acquisitions. The quality of the pieces is magnificent, and you should aim to spend at least two hours here. English-language notes are available throughout. ✉ *Av. de Berna 45A, Avenidas Novas* ☎ *21/782–3000* 🌐 *gulbenkian.pt/museu* 🎫 *€13* 🕒 *Closed Tues.* Ⓜ *Blue Line to São Sebastião or Praça de Espanha.*

Palácio dos Marqueses de Fronteira
CASTLE/PALACE | FAMILY | This palace by the modern district on the edge of Parque Florestal de Monsanto is one of Lisbon's most beautiful buildings. Built in 1670, it's known for some of the finest examples of Portuguese tile panels, both inside the palace and outside around the garden. It's tricky to reach by public transportation, but a taxi from the Jardim Zoológico metro stop, about a mile away, will be quick and inexpensive. ✉ *Largo de São Domingos de Benfica 1, Avenidas Novas* ☎ *21/778–2023* 🌐 *fronteira-alorna.pt* 🎫 *From €7* 🕒 *Closed Sun.* ✍ *Must reserve guided tours* Ⓜ *Blue Line to Jardim Zoológico (then 20-min walk, taxi, or Bus 770).*

Palácio Pimenta–Museu de Lisboa
HISTORY MUSEUM | FAMILY | A palace built in the 1700s for a nun (one of the king's mistresses) is now the main branch of the Museu de Lisbon. There are peacocks roaming around the formal garden, as well as a few ceramic animals created by the great 19th-century sculptor Rafael Bordalo Pinheiro. The museum houses a collection of archaeological finds, historic tile panels, paintings, and sculptures. A highlight is a model of the city, showing it as it was before it was laid to ruins in the 1755 earthquake. ✉ *Campo Grande 245, Campo Grande* ☎ *21/751–3200* 🌐 *www.*

The serene Museu Calouste Gulbenkian is home to a magnificent collection of artworks from Europe, Asia, North Africa, and the Middle East.

museudelisboa.pt/pt/nucleos/palacio-pimenta €3 Closed Mon. Green or Yellow Line to Campo Grande.

Restaurants

★ Eleven

$$$$ | ECLECTIC | Sitting at the top of Parque Eduardo VII, this was the first modern restaurant to bring a new wave of Michelin stars to Lisbon. Its à la carte and tasting menus change every season and attract businesspeople for lunch and couples at dinnertime. **Known for:** view over Avenida da Liberdade; matured rack of lamb; fish from the Portuguese coast. *Average main: €55* *Rua Marquês de Fronteira, Jardim Amália Rodrigues, Avenidas Novas* *21/386–2211* *www.restauranteleven.com* *Closed Sun.* *Blue Line to São Sebastião.*

Galeto

$ | PORTUGUESE | The large counter facing the bar makes this 1960s establishment a prime spot for solo diners. It's also one of the few places in the neighborhood open from breakfast to dinner. **Known for:** late-night meals; prego (traditional steak sandwich); breakfast menu. *Average main: €12* *Av. da República 14, Avenidas Novas* *21/354–4444* *Yellow or Red Line to Saldanha.*

Ground Burger

$$ | AMERICAN | Located next to the Museu Calouste Gulbenkian, this may be Lisbon's best burger joint. It serves American-style burgers, and there's a new one on the menu every month, plus a vegetarian option. **Known for:** 100% Black Angus burgers; American-style milkshakes; craft beers. $ *Average main: €16* ✉ *Av. António Augusto de Aguiar 148A, Avenidas Novas* ☎ *21/371–7171* 🌐 *www.groundburger.com* Ⓜ *Blue or Red Line to São Sebastião.*

Laurentina

$$ | PORTUGUESE | FAMILY | For cod dishes prepared with great pride, come to this restaurant that's been specializing in all things *bacalhau* (salted codfish) since 1976. Expect a few Mozambican dishes alongside excellent renderings of Portuguese favorites. **Known for:** bacalhau à Brás; grilled meat and fish; codfish moqueca. $ *Average main: €20* ✉ *Av. Conde Valbom 71A, Avenidas Novas* ☎ *21/796–0260* 🌐 *www.restaurantelaurentina.com* ⊗ *Closed Sun.* Ⓜ *Blue or Red Line to São Sebastião.*

Mercantina

$ | ITALIAN | FAMILY | Shortly after opening, this restaurant was distinguished with the Associazione Verace Pizza Napoletana certificate of authenticity. The ingredients are imported directly from Naples and used not just in the pizzas but in all the Italian specialties. **Known for:** good-value lunch menus; fresh pasta; Italian desserts. $ *Average main: €14* ✉ *Praça de Alvalade 6B, Lojas 9 e 10, Alvalade* ☎ *21/796–0313* 🌐 *mercantina.pt/restaurantes/mercantina-alvalade* Ⓜ *Green Line to Alvalade.*

O Talho

$$$$ | INTERNATIONAL | Chef Kiko has several restaurants in Lisbon, each with its own specialty, but this was his first. O Talho means "The Butcher Shop," and this elegant meat-centric restaurant does double-duty as a working butcher shop. **Known for:** signature drinks; dry-aged meat; inventive international dishes. $ *Average main: €35* ✉ *Rua Carlos Testa 1B, Avenidas Novas* ☎ *21/315–4105* 🌐 *www.otalho.pt* Ⓜ *Blue or Red Line to São Sebastião.*

Psi

$ | VEGETARIAN | Blessed by the Dalai Lama on one of his visits to Lisbon, this is one of the city's oldest vegetarian restaurants. It's now mostly vegan but has maintained its Asian-inspired menus. **Known for:** seating in a covered Zen garden; sugar-free desserts; good selection of teas. $ *Average main: €14* ✉ *Alameda Santo António dos Capuchos, Avenidas Novas* ☎ *21/359–0573* 🌐 *www.restaurante-psi.com* ⊗ *Closed Sun.* Ⓜ *Blue Line to Avenida.*

Coffee and Quick Bites

Choupana Caffe

$ | INTERNATIONAL | It's always difficult to get a table at this café, as it's a favorite of young crowds who crave its pancakes and pastries all day. By the entrance is a display of Portuguese and international gourmet products to take home. **Known for:** weekend brunch; organic yogurt; house-made croissants. *Average main: €12 ✉ Av. da República 25A, Avenidas Novas ☎ 21/357–0140 🌐 www.choupanacaffe.pt Ⓜ Yellow or Red Line to Saldanha.*

L'éclair

$ | FRENCH FUSION | In a city with so many traditional pastries, a menu dedicated exclusively to French éclairs and macarons certainly didn't seem to have great appeal. But turns out Lisboetas were looking for just that, and L'éclair is now one of the city's most popular sweets spots. **Known for:** special salted éclairs (only at lunchtime); organic juices; international teas. *Average main: €7 ✉ Av. Duque de Ávila 44, Avenidas Novas ☎ 21/136–3877 🌐 www.l-eclair.pt Ⓜ Yellow or Red Line to Saldanha.*

★ Versailles

$ | PORTUGUESE | Open since 1922, this is one of Lisbon's surviving grand cafés and arguably its most beautiful. It's still mostly a place for locals, who often meet here and stay chatting for hours over coffee. **Known for:** palatial mirrored interior; variety of Portuguese pastries; traditional Portuguese lunch. *Average main: €8 ✉ Av. da República 15A, Avenidas Novas ☎ 21/354–6340 🌐 grupoversailles.pt Ⓜ Yellow or Red Line to Saldanha.*

Hotels

Corinthia Lisboa

$$$ | HOTEL | An excellent option for business travelers, the luxe Corinthia Lisboa offers comfortable accommodations and impeccable service. **Pros:** three restaurants and two bars; walking distance to the Museu Calouste Gulbenkian; excellent swimming pool and spa. **Cons:** extra charge for breakfast; not Lisbon's most beautiful neighborhood; uninspiring exterior. *Rooms from: €254 ✉ Av. Columbano Bordalo Pinheiro 105, Sete Rios ☎ 21/723–6300 🌐 www.corinthia.com/Lisbon 518 rooms No Meals Ⓜ Blue Line to Jardim Zoológico, Train to Sete Rios.*

Sheraton Lisboa Hotel & Spa

$$$ | HOTEL | Traveling executives flock to this business hotel overlooking modern Lisbon for its many pluses including nicely appointed guest rooms. **Pros:** staff goes above and beyond; comfortable bar; excellent fitness center. **Cons:** not the best location for sightseeing; unattractive building; expensive. *Rooms from: €240 ✉ Rua Latino Coelho 1, Saldanha ☎ 21/312–0000 🌐 www.marriott.com/en-us/hotels/lissi-sheraton-lisboa-hotel-and-spa/overview/ 369 rooms No Meals Ⓜ Yellow Line to Picoas.*

Inspired by Madrid's bullfighting arena, the massive Campo Pequeno stadium also hosts events from rock concerts to exhibitions.

Nightlife

Jupiter Lisboa Rooftop Bar & Piscina

BARS | One of Lisbon's least-known rooftop bars, this one is located at the top of the Jupiter Lisboa Hotel. Open for drinks and light meals throughout the day, it attracts workers from the neighboring offices. ✉ *Jupiter Lisboa Hotel, Av. da República 46, Avenidas Novas* ☎ *21/073–0104* 🌐 *www.jupiterlisboahotel.com/pt/page/rooftop-hotel-lisboa.5823.html* Ⓜ *Yellow or Red Line to Saldanha.*

Old Vic

COCKTAIL BARS | Old Vic is one of Lisbon's oldest and most beautiful bars, but it's hidden between apartment buildings and you have to ring a bell to get in. Red velvet booths and the low-lit, Victorian-inspired interior are conducive to sipping cocktails late into the night. ✉ *Travessa Henrique Cardoso 41, Avenidas Novas* ☎ *91/407–6170* 🕓 *Closed Sun.* Ⓜ *Green Line to Roma.*

Performing Arts

Praça de Touros do Campo Pequeno (*Campo Pequeno Bullring*)

PERFORMANCE VENUES | **FAMILY** | These days this monumental structure hosts more rock concerts than bullfights. Holding up to 9,000 people, the Moorish-style auditorium hosts big names like Pixies and Arcade Fire. There's a multiscreen cinema here, too. ✉ *Av. da República, Campo Pequeno* ☎ *21/799–8450 for tickets* 🌐 *www.sagrescampopequeno.pt* Ⓜ *Yellow Line to Campo Pequeno.*

Chapter 14

SIDE TRIPS FROM LISBON

Updated by
Joana Taborda

Sights	Restaurants	Hotels	Shopping	Nightlife
★★★★★	★★★★☆	★★★★☆	★★★☆☆	★★★☆☆

WELCOME TO SIDE TRIPS FROM LISBON

TOP REASONS TO GO

★ **Fairy-tale getaway.** Sintra—a UNESCO World Heritage site—has gorgeous palaces and gardens, and a landscape that inspires poetry. The combination makes it ripe for romantics.

★ **Endless beaches.** All along the Cascais and Sintra coast, beautiful beaches await. Take your pick from remote coves like Praia da Ursa or Praia da Adraga in Sintra, test your surf skills at Praia do Guincho, or head anywhere between Cascais and Estoril for a livelier atmosphere and access to bars and restaurants.

★ **Fabulous seafood.** *Marisqueiras* (seafood restaurants) are an essential component of Portuguese culture, and this region has some of the best in Portugal.

1 Sintra. The undeniable romance of Sintra makes it a UNESCO World Heritage site. Here you'll find breathtaking castles and mist-shrouded palaces at every turn, and the steep streets are lined with cafés, restaurants, and wine-tasting rooms.

2 Estoril. Famous for its swanky casino (said to have inspired James Bond creator Ian Fleming), Estoril has long

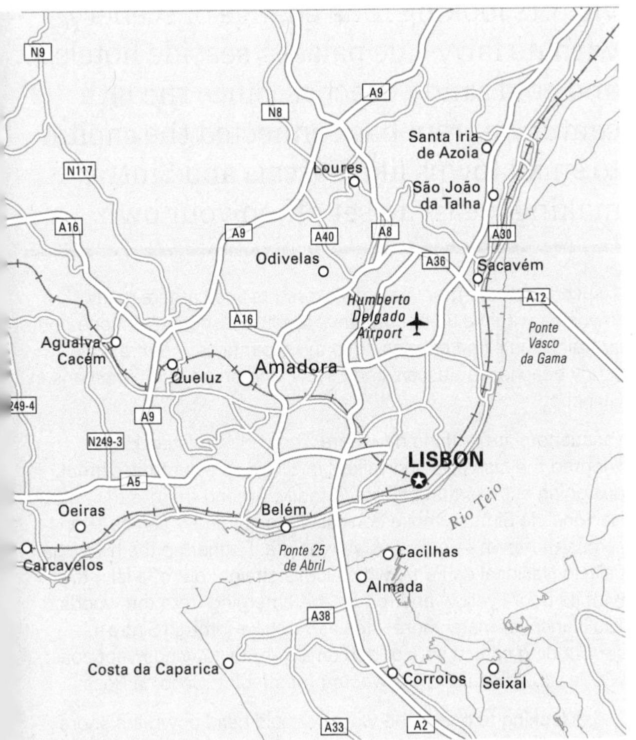

attracted high-living types. But you don't need to be a millionaire to appreciate the string of family-friendly beaches.

3 Cascais. Like neighboring Estoril, the resort town of Cascais has a succession of beaches that appeal to everyone from parents looking for gentle waves to surfers in search of a challenge. It also has some notable museums and galleries.

4 Guincho. One of the most famous beaches in the area, Praia do Guincho is a wild windswept stretch of sand that's hugely popular with surfers. Located within the Parque Natural de Sintra-Cascais, it has some excellent seafood restaurants.

Long coveted by royalty, spies, and surfers, Lisbon's west coast continues to draw visitors looking for a change of scenery, with its fairy-tale palaces, seaside hotels, and gold sandy beaches. Since the 19th century, a train has connected the capital to small towns like Cascais and Sintra, making it easy to set off on your own.

A succession of attractive coastal resorts and camera-ready towns lie within a 30-minute drive west of Lisbon (about one hour by train). You'll find palaces amid the mountains in Sintra, long sandy beaches in Cascais and Estoril, and prime surf conditions in Guincho.

Vacationers are nothing new here. The early Christian kings adopted the lush hills and valleys of Sintra as a summer retreat, designing estates that still stand today. Among them is the Palácio Nacional de Sintra, whose conical white chimneys can be seen across the town's numerous viewpoints. Further up the hill is the Palácio Nacional da Pena, which looks straight out of a fairy tale, with its bright yellow and red facade emerging from the woods. You'll uncover many more sites as you hike through Sintra's surrounding natural park or hop on a tram to its windswept coast, where you'll find Europe's westernmost point, Cabo da Roca.

Those looking to chase the waves should head down the shore to Praia do Guincho. This exposed beach break is famous among windsurfers and kitesurfers, but when the wind dies out, it is a prime spot for surfing, too. Guincho is one of the many towns that make up the sea-facing Cascais district, which stretches all to way to Carcavelos, where Portuguese surf was born.

In between, you'll find a string of more urbanized family-friendly beaches and mansions that belonged to the country's nobility. Many of these have since been converted into hotels. Indeed, this has always been a bit of an upmarket district, especially around Estoril, where you'll find Portugal's first casino. During World War II, spies of every nationality and beleaguered refugee gentry occupied the Estoril's villas and hotels. British writer Ian Fleming was here around that time, and some say this is where he got the inspiration to create his James Bond character.

Wealthy families still make up most of the residents, as this is one of the most expensive districts for housing around Lisbon. Still, many come here to walk or cycle along its coastal trails, take a refreshing dip (the Atlantic is mighty cold), or sample delicious seafood from one of the local marisqueiras, some of which have been running for more than 50 years.

Planning

Getting Here and Around

All the main towns and most of the sights are accessible by train or bus from Lisbon, so you can see the entire region on day trips from the capital.

BUS

Although the best way to travel from Lisbon to Sintra and most of the towns on the Costa do Estoril is by train, there are some useful bus connections between these towns. From the bus terminal in Cascais, MobiCascais buses travel to Guincho (30 minutes) and Carris Metropolitana connects you to Sintra (45 minutes). Bus 1623 is faster, but Bus 1624 travels along a more scenic route. Meanwhile, Scotturb runs two sightseeing buses for Sintra's monuments.

Tickets are cheap (less than €5 for most single journeys), and departures are generally every hour (less frequently on weekends). Always arrive at least 15 minutes before your bus is scheduled to depart.

CONTACTS Carris Metropolitana. ☎ *21/041–0400* 🌐 *www.carrismetropolitana.pt.* **MobiCascais.** 🌐 *mobi.cascais.pt.* **Scotturb.** ☎ *21/469–9100* 🌐 *scotturb.com.*

CAR

Highways connect Lisbon with Sintra (A37/IC19) and with Estoril and Cascais (A5/IC15). Try to avoid departing from Lisbon at the start of a weekend or public holiday. Parking can be problematic, too, particularly in summer along the Costa do Estoril and around Sintra on weekends.

TAXI

Lisboetas use ride-hailing apps like Bolt (a local favorite) and Uber to visit the towns around Lisbon. If you take a traditional taxi, agree on a fixed price for the round-trip journey. Estoril should be about €40 each way, while Sintra should cost roughly €45 each way. Prices will be higher on weekends and public holidays.

TRAIN

Comboios de Portugal (CP) commuter trains travel the entire Costa do Estoril, with departures every 15 to 30 minutes from the waterfront Cais do Sodré station in Lisbon, west of the Praça do Comércio. The scenic trip to Estoril takes about 40 minutes, and there are four more stops along the seashore to the end of the line at Cascais. A one-way ticket to either costs €2.40. Trains from Lisbon's beautiful Rossio station depart roughly every 30 minutes to Sintra (40 minutes) via Queluz (20 minutes). One-way tickets cost €1.75 to Queluz and €2.40 to Sintra. **■TIP→ Save money by getting a rechargeable Navegante ticket and selecting the Zapping option from the ticket machines.**

CONTACTS Comboios de Portugal (CP). ☎ *21/090–0032* 🌐 *www.cp.pt/passageiros.*

Hotels

Accommodations are more limited once the bright lights of Lisbon have been left behind, but the options—both old and new—are truly diverse. Historic lodgings are understandably popular, and *pousadas* (inns, often in converted buildings, that generally have superior facilities) are the top pick for many travelers. Modern alternatives may not have the same cultural cred, but they compensate by having up-to-date amenities and, in some cases, an eco-friendly outlook. No matter what you choose, advance booking is essential in summer. Out of season, many places offer substantial discounts.

Sintra

30 km (18 miles) northwest of Lisbon

History buffs, architecture enthusiasts, literature lovers, and hopeless romantics all fall under Sintra's seductive spell. The lush northern slopes of the Serra de Sintra have been inhabited since prehistoric times, although the Moors were the first to build a castle on their peaks. Later Sintra became the summer residence of Portuguese kings and aristocrats, and its late-medieval palace is the greatest expression of royal wealth and power from the time. In the 18th and 19th centuries, English travelers, poets, and writers—including an enthusiastic Lord Byron—were drawn by the region's beauty. Poet Robert Southey described Sintra as "the most blessed spot on the whole inhabitable globe." Its historic importance has been recognized by UNESCO, which designated it a World Heritage site in 1995.

GETTING HERE AND AROUND

By far the easiest way to get to Sintra is by train. Trains from Lisbon's Rossio station run every 30 minutes to Sintra (40 minutes). One-way tickets cost €2.40. Sintra's small train station gets packed during the peak summer season (July–early September), and queues at the information desk are huge. Driving to Sintra takes around 30 minutes, but once you get there parking is a hassle.

Once you're in town, the nearest attractions are within walking distance. If you'd rather not tackle steep hills on foot, you can opt for a tuk tuk ride; a guided tour (easily arranged through the tourist office); a hop-on, hop-off bus; or a tour by taxi. The most useful bus service for getting around Sintra is Scotturb Bus 434, which connects Sintra Station, the town center (there's a stop outside the tourist office), Castelo dos Mouros, and Palácio da Pena. The fare is €13.50 and is valid all day. Bus 1253 covered by Carris Metropolitana also passes through some sites, including Cabo da Roca on the coast.

The Sintra Elétrico tram runs from the town center to the pleasant beach village of Praia das Maçãs, a scenic 45-minute ride costing €5 each way. The service is less frequent in winter.

TOURS

Eléctrico de Sintra

OTHER TOURS | FAMILY | Antique red streetcars make the 45-minute scenic journey from the center of Sintra through the countryside and down the mountain to the ocean at Praia das Maçãs. Seafood restaurants line the beach at the last stop. During the summer season, there are three trams a day in each direction. ✉ *Rua General Alves Roçadas, Sintra* ☎ *21/923–8766* 🌐 *visitsintra.travel/pt/descobrir/electrico-de-sintra* 🎫 *€5.*

VISITOR INFORMATION

CONTACT Ask Me Sintra. ✉ *Praça da República 23, Sintra* ☎ *21/923–1157* 🌐 *visitsintra.travel.*

Sights

Castelo dos Mouros (*Moorish Castle*)

CASTLE/PALACE | FAMILY | The battlemented ruins of this 10th-century castle still give a fine impression of the fortress that finally fell to Christian forces led by Dom Afonso Henriques in 1147.

You'll need to wear sturdy shoes when walking along the sometimes steep stone walls of Castelo dos Mouros, but the views are well worth it.

Panoramic views from the serrated walls explain why the Moors chose the site. It's visible from various points in Sintra itself, but for a closer look follow the steps that lead up to the ruins from the back of the town center (40 minutes going up, about half that coming down). No cars are allowed, but you can save your legs by catching Scotturb Bus 434 or taking a tuk tuk ride from town. ■ **TIP→ The castle is walkable from the Palácio da Pena, since it's accessed from the same road and its entrance is somewhat below that of the Palace park.** ✉ *Estrada da Pena, Sintra* ☎ *21/923–7300* 🌐 *www.parquesdesintra.pt/pt/parques-monumentos/castelo-dos-mouros* 🎫 *€12* Ⓜ *Bus 434.*

Convento dos Capuchos (*Convent of the Capuchos*)
RELIGIOUS BUILDING | The entrance to this extraordinarily austere convent, 13 km (8 miles) southwest of Sintra, sets the tone for the severity of the ascetic living conditions within. From 1560 until 1834, when it was abandoned, eight friars—never any more, never any less—prayed in the tiny chapel hewn out of the rock and inhabited the bare cells, which were lined with cork in attempt to maintain a modicum of warmth. Impure thoughts meant a spell in the Penitents' Cell, an excruciatingly dark space. ✉ *Convento dos Capuchos, Colares* ☎ *21/923–7300* 🌐 *www.parquesdesintra.pt/pt/parques-monumentos/convento-dos-capuchos/* 🎫 *€11.*

Palácio e Parque Biester
CASTLE/PALACE | This 19th-century palace was featured in Roman Polanski's *The Ninth Gate*. Much of the decor has been kept in its original form, from the ornate wooden staircases to the painted

ceilings with floral motifs. The highlight, however, is the large windows that look out into Sintra's hills. Take a stroll around the surrounding gardens, and you'll spot the town's major sites rising in the distance. ✉ *Av. Almeida Garrett 1A, Sintra* ☎ *21/870–8800* 🌐 *www.biester.pt* 🎟 *€12* Ⓜ *Bus 435 or 1253.*

★ **Palácio Nacional de Sintra** (*Sintra Palace*)
CASTLE/PALACE | FAMILY | The enormous twin chimneys rising out of Sintra Palace are among the town's most iconic landmarks. There has probably been a palace here since Moorish times, although the current structure dates from the late 14th century. It is the only surviving royal palace in Portugal from the Middle Ages and displays a combination of Moorish, Gothic, and Manueline architecture. The chapel has Mudéjar (Moorish-influenced) *azulejo* tiles from the 15th and 16th centuries. The ceiling of the Sala dos Brasões is painted with the coats of arms of 72 noble families, and the grand Sala dos Cisnes has a remarkable ceiling of painted swans. ✉ *Largo Rainha Dona Amélia, Sintra* ☎ *21/923–7300* 🌐 *www.parquesdesintra.pt/pt/parques-monumentos/palacio-nacional-sintra/* 🎟 *€13* Ⓜ *Sintra Line from Rossio to Sintra.*

★ **Parque e Palácio de Monserrate** (*Monserrate Park and Palace*)
CASTLE/PALACE | FAMILY | This estate was laid out by English gardeners in the mid-19th century at the behest of a wealthy Englishman, Sir Francis Cook. The centerpiece is the Romantic-style, three-dome Palácio de Monserrate, which combines Gothic and Indian architectural influences with Moorish touches. The gardens, with their trickling streams and waterfalls, are famed for an array of tree and plant species. ✉ *Estrada de Monserrate, Sintra* ☎ *21/923–7300* 🌐 *www.parquesdesintra.pt/pt/parques-monumentos/parque-e-palacio-de-monserrate/* 🎟 *€12* Ⓜ *Bus 435.*

★ **Parque e Palácio Nacional da Pena** (*Park and National Palace of Pena*)
CASTLE/PALACE | FAMILY | The biggest draw in Sintra, this colorful palace is a glorious conglomeration of turrets and domes awash in bright pastels. In 1836, the ruins of a 16th-century monastery were purchased by Maria II's consort, Ferdinand of Saxe-Coburg and Gotha. Inspired by the Bavarian castles of his homeland, Ferdinand commissioned Baron Eschwege to build the palace of his fantasies, in styles that range from Arabian to Portuguese Gothic. The surrounding park is filled with trees and flowers, as well as hidden temples, grottoes, and the Valley of the Lakes, where swans glide the mystical surrounds. Inside the palace is an ostentatious and often bizarre collection of European furniture, ornaments, and paintings. Visitors can walk along high palace walls, peek into turrets, and refresh at one of two cafés. A path

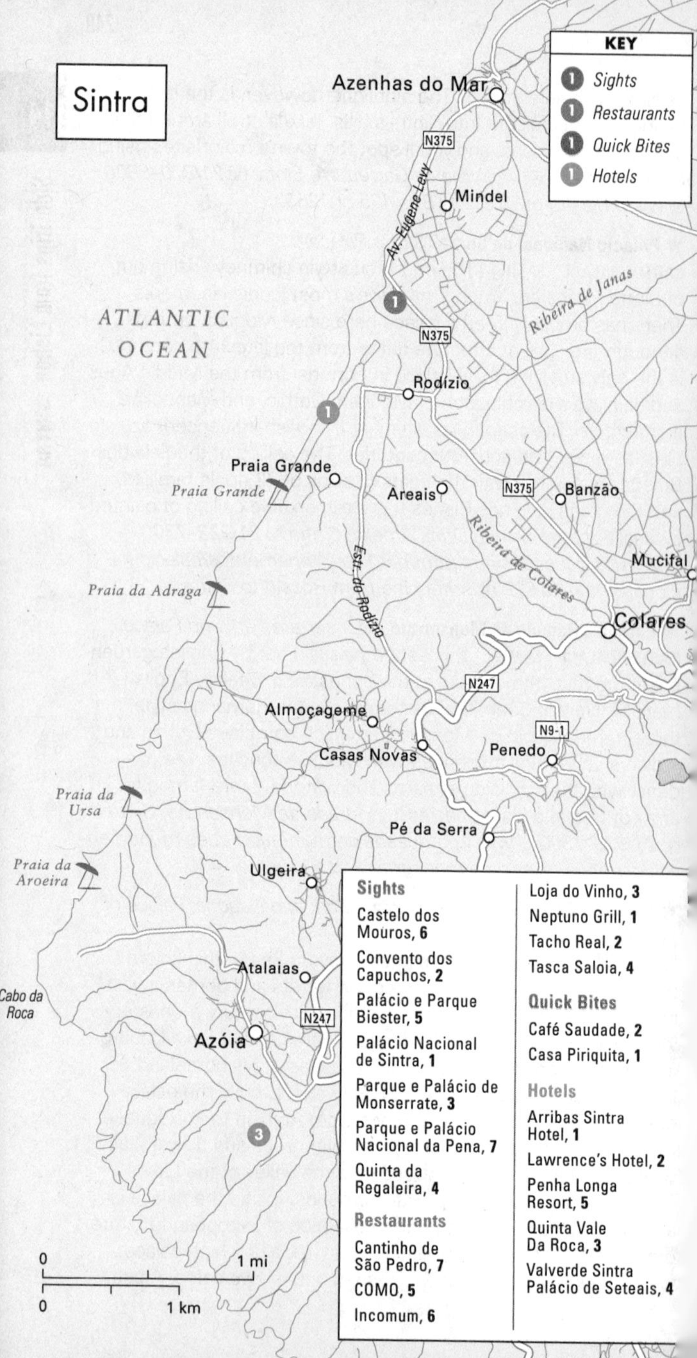
Sintra
KEY
Sights
Restaurants
Quick Bites
Hotels
Azenhas do Mar
N375
Av. Eugene Levy
Mindel
Ribeira de Janas
ATLANTIC
OCEAN
Rodízio
Praia Grande
Praia Grande
Areais
Banzão
Ribeira de Colares
Estr. do Rodízio
Praia da Adraga
Mucifal
Colares
N247
Almoçageme
N9-1
Casas Novas
Penedo
Praia da
Ursa
Pé da Serra
Praia da
Aroeira
Ulgeira
Atalaias
Cabo da
Roca
N247
Azóia
0
1 mi
0
1 km
Sights
Castelo dos Mouros, 6
Convento dos Capuchos, 2
Palácio e Parque Biester, 5
Palácio Nacional de Sintra, 1
Parque e Palácio de Monserrate, 3
Parque e Palácio Nacional da Pena, 7
Quinta da Regaleira, 4
Restaurants
Cantinho de São Pedro, 7
COMO, 5
Incomum, 6
Loja do Vinho, 3
Neptuno Grill, 1
Tacho Real, 2
Tasca Saloia, 4
Quick Bites
Café Saudade, 2
Casa Piriquita, 1
Hotels
Arribas Sintra Hotel, 1
Lawrence's Hotel, 2
Penha Longa Resort, 5
Quinta Vale Da Roca, 3
Valverde Sintra Palácio de Seteais, 4

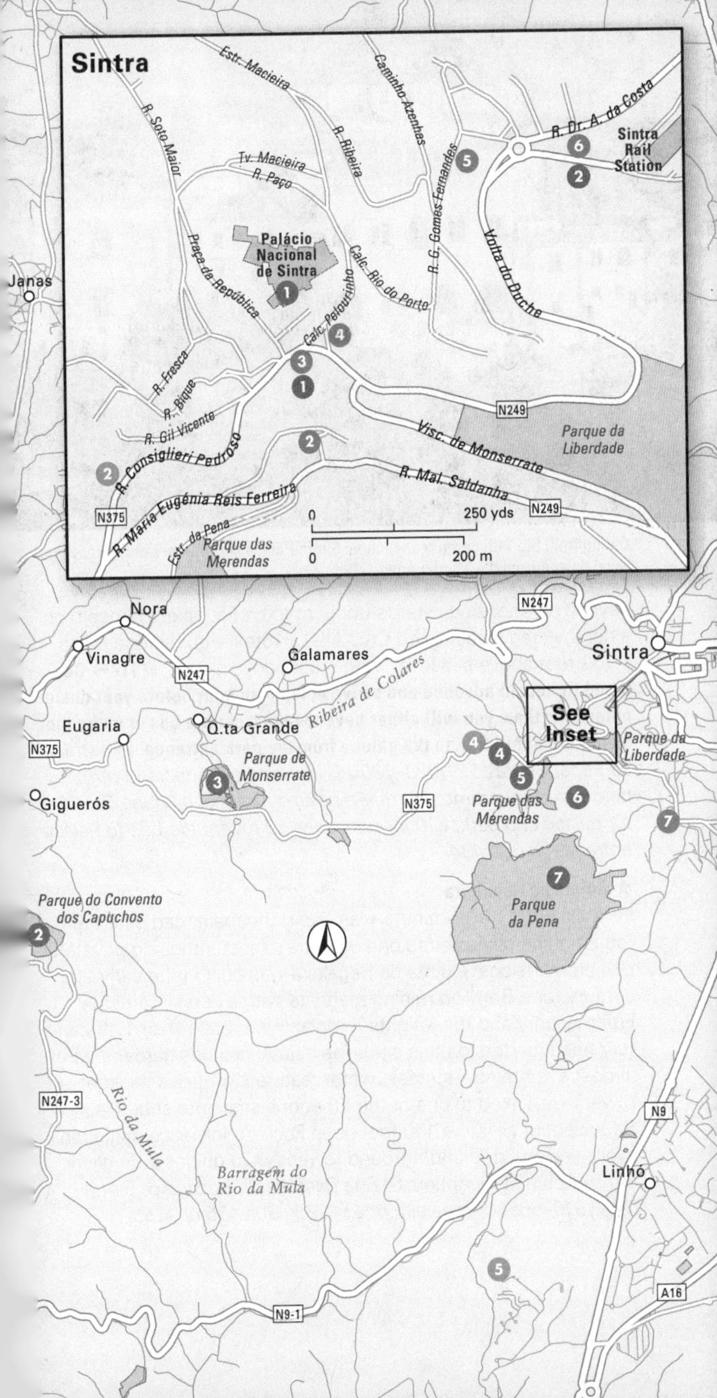

Sintra
Estr. Macieira
Caminho Azenhas
R. Soto Maior
R. Ribeira
Tv. Macieira
R. Paço
R. Dr. A. da Costa
Sintra Rail Station
R. G. Gomes Fernandes
Palácio Nacional de Sintra
Praça da República
Calc. Rio do Porto
Calc. Pelourinho
Volta do Duche
R. Fresca
R. Bique
R. Gil Vicente
R. Consiglieri Pedroso
N249
Parque da Liberdade
Visc. de Monserrate
R. Mal. Saldanha
R. Maria Eugénia Reis Ferreira
N375
Estr. da Pena
Parque das Merendas
0
250 yds
200 m
Janas
Nora
Vinagre
N247
Galamares
Sintra
Eugaria
Q.ta Grande
Ribeira de Colares
See Inset
N375
Parque de Monserrate
Giguerós
Parque das Merendas
Parque do Convento dos Capuchos
Parque da Pena
N247-3
Rio da Mula
Barragem do Rio da Mula
N9
Linhó
A16
N9-1

Dating from the 14th century, the iconic Sintra Palace is Portugal's only surviving royal palace from the Middle Ages.

beyond an enormous statue (thought to be Ferdinand himself) on a nearby crag leads to the Cruz Alta, a 16th-century stone cross 1,732 feet above sea level, with stupendous views. **■ TIP→ Buy timed tickets in advance and arrive at least an hour before your designated tour time; you will either have to take a shuttle bus or make the 30-minute uphill trek to the palace from the park entrance.** ✉ *Estrada da Pena, Sintra* ☎ *21/923–7300* 🌐 *www.parquesdesintra.pt/pt/parques-monumentos/parque-e-palacio-nacional-da-pena* 🎫 *€20 for palace and park; €10 for park only; €3 for shuttle bus to palace entrance* Ⓜ *Bus 434.*

★ Quinta da Regaleira

HISTORIC HOME | A 10-minute walk along the main road past the tourist office takes you to one of Sintra's most intriguing privately owned mansions. Quinta da Regaleira was built in the early 20th century for a Brazilian mining magnate with a keen interest in Freemasonry and the Knights Templar (who made their 11th-century headquarters on this site). The estate includes gardens where almost everything—statues, water features, grottoes, lookout towers—is linked to one or the other of his favorite subjects. Spookiest of all is the 100-foot-deep Poço do Iniciático (Initiation Well)—an inverted underground tower. Audio guides in English are available at reception. ✉ *Rua Barbosa do Bocage 5, Sintra* ☎ *21/910–6650* 🌐 *regaleira.pt* 🎫 *€12* Ⓜ *Bus 435 or 1253.*

Restaurants

Cantinho de São Pedro

$ | **PORTUGUESE** | **FAMILY** | Inside white stucco walls beneath a barrel-tile roof, this tavern is said to be one of the oldest in Portugal. The interior has exposed brick walls, expansive windows, and a huge fireplace that keeps the place cozy in cooler weather. **Known for:** anything from the grill is excellent; long and interesting history; variety of meat cuts served with house-made sauces. *Average main: €14 Praça Dom Fernando II 18, Sintra 96/703–3520 cantinhosaopedro.com Closed Wed. Bus 1252 or 1253.*

COMO

$$$ | **INTERNATIONAL** | Dine with a view of the Palácio Nacional de Sintra at this contemporary restaurant inside the Moon Hill Hostel. The menu combines traditional Portuguese flavors with touches of Italian and French cuisine. **Known for:** regional wines from Colares; generous portions; palace views from the window-facing tables. *Average main: €22 Moon Hill Hostel, Rua Guilherme Gomes Fernandes 19, Sintra 96/015–4129 comoorigins.com Closed Mon. No dinner Sun. Sintra Line from Rossio to Sintra.*

★ **Incomum**

$$ | **ECLECTIC** | Not far from the town's main train station, this restaurant's location on one of Sintra's major thoroughfares means that it is always busy. The dining room is elegantly lighted with crisp linens on the tables, but the favorite seats are on the street. **Known for:** dishes are prepared and presented with great care; elegant dining room; tasting menu showcasing talents of chef Luís Santos. *Average main: €20 Rua Dr. Alfredo da Costa 22, Sintra 21/924–3719 incomumbyluissantos.pt Closed Wed. Sintra Line from Rossio to Sintra.*

Loja do Vinho

$$ | **TAPAS** | One of the city's first wineshops, Loja do Vinho has a cozy cellar lined with hundreds of bottles from all over the world. Plates of cured meats, boards of local cheeses, and bowls overflowing with olives make good companions to the many varieties of wine on offer here or on the tiny outdoor terrace. **Known for:** tapas-style plates; huge range of wines from the region; extremely cozy setting. *Average main: €16 Praça da República 3, Sintra 21/924–4410 www.screstauracao.com/en/venues/Loja-do-vinho/148 No dinner Sintra Line from Rossio to Sintra.*

Neptuno Grill

$$$ | **SEAFOOD** | **FAMILY** | One of the best oceanside restaurants in nearby Praia das Maçãs, glass-fronted Neptuno is where sandy-footed diners can feast on freshly grilled fish caught just

hours before. Try the octopus ceviche and the seafood rice with shrimp. **Known for:** huge variety of shellfish dishes; diners can take their pick from daily catch; lovely beachfront location. *$ Average main: €22 ✉ Rua Pedro Álvares Cabral, Praia das Maçãs ☎ 21/929–1222 🌐 www.facebook.com/rest.neptuno.praiamacas ⏲ Closed Tues. No dinner Mon. M Bus 1242, 1248, or 1254.*

Tacho Real

$$ | PORTUGUESE | Locals make their way up a steep hill to this restaurant for traditional dishes like roasted cod that are cooked with panache and served by a friendly staff. Steaks are a specialty, as are the mouthwatering desserts that include house-made cakes and tarts. **Known for:** elegant dining room bordered with azulejo tiles; good advice on Portuguese wines; terrace is an escape from the crowds. *$ Average main: €20 ✉ Rua do Ferraria 4, Sintra ☎ 21/923–5277 🌐 www.facebook.com/RestauranteTachoReal ⏲ Closed Wed. No dinner Tues. M Sintra Line from Rossio to Sintra.*

Tasca Saloia

$$ | PORTUGUESE | FAMILY | At this restaurant in the center of town, the handful of tables in the convivial dining room spill out onto the sidewalk in warmer weather. Seafood *petiscos* (the Portuguese version of tapas) and a good wine selection are the main attractions. **Known for:** excellent shrimp and other seafood dishes; relaxed atmosphere on outdoor terrace; friendly service. *$ Average main: €16 ✉ Largo Dr. Gregório de Almeida 2, Sintra ☎ 21/910–5863 🌐 www.screstauracao.com/espacos/Tasca-Saloia/188 M Sintra Line from Rossio to Sintra.*

Coffee and Quick Bites

Café Saudade

$ | CAFÉ | FAMILY | A short stroll downhill from the train station, this cozy spot has marble-topped tables and an elaborately decorated ceiling. It serves delicious scones, cakes, and pastries in a setting that evokes the grandeur of another era. **Known for:** wine available by the glass or the bottle; strong coffee and hearty breakfasts; retro-chic interior and outdoor seating on the terrace. *$ Average main: €12 ✉ Av. Dr. Miguel Bombarda 6, Sintra ☎ 21/015–0055 🌐 www.saudade.pt/cafesaudade.html ⏲ Closed Mon. and Tues. No dinner M Sintra Line from Rossio to Sintra.*

★ Casa Piriquita

$ | PORTUGUESE | This bakery in Sintra's old town has been dishing out regional pastries to visitors since 1862. It is known for its *travesseiros*, a pillow-shaped puff pastry filled with almond and egg custard and dusted with sugar. **Known for:** affordable breakfast; historic interior with tiles and marble. *Average main: €5* *Rua Padarias 1, Sintra* *21/923–0626* *piriquita.pt* *Sintra Line from Rossio to Sintra.*

Arribas Sintra Hotel

$$ | HOTEL | FAMILY | Keen swimmers will be in their element at this family-focused hotel: not only does it sit right on the beachfront at Praia Grande, Colares, but it also boasts one of Europe's largest saltwater swimming pools. **Pros:** right on the ocean; great for familes; good dining options on-site. **Cons:** exterior of the building not very attractive; it's a drive from Sintra sights; pool is busy with nonguests. *Rooms from: €200* *Av. Alfredo Coelho 28, Colares* *21/928–9050* *www.arribashotel.com* *60 rooms* *Free Breakfast* *Bus 1250 or 1254 to Praia Grande.*

★ Lawrence's Hotel

$$$ | B&B/INN | The oldest lodging on the Iberian peninsula, this 18th-century grande dame has hosted such illustrious guests as Lord Byron and, more recently, Queen Beatrix of the Netherlands. **Pros:** terrace restaurant has spectacular views; light meals served in the cozy bar; lovely gardens. **Cons:** no gym or swimming pool; some rooms are small; decor can feel twee. *Rooms from: €210* *Rua Consigliéri Pedroso 38–40, Sintra* *21/910–5500* *www.lawrenceshotel.com* *16 rooms* *Free Breakfast* *Sintra Line from Rossio to Sintra.*

★ Penha Longa Resort

$$$$ | RESORT | FAMILY | Hidden among the rolling green hills of the Parque Natural de Sintra-Cascais, this dreamy resort has breathtaking views of the surrounding forest and the gorgeous grounds. **Pros:** 14th-century monastery in the gardens; on-site boutiques offer designer clothing; some of the region's best dining. **Cons:** the huge scale can feel impersonal; you need to drive to town; lots of added costs. *Rooms from: €415* *Estrada da Lagoa Azul, Sintra* *21/924–9011* *penhalonga.com* *204 rooms* *Free Breakfast.*

★ Quinta Vale Da Roca

$$ | B&B/INN | With its own winery on-site, chic boutique hotel Quinta Vale Da Roca will delight fans of Portugal's excellent *vinhos.* It's tucked away in the hills between Sintra and Cascais, and makes a relaxing retreat for hikers and outdoor enthusiasts as well as city-weary Lisboetas arriving by car. **Pros:** only lodging in the area with its own winery; welcoming owners; stunning setting. **Cons:** far from major sights; need a car to get around; can be windy. *Rooms from: €230* *Rua Casal Farripas 8, Colares* *96/607–6761* *www.valedaroca.com* *8 rooms* *Free Breakfast.*

★ Valverde Sintra Palácio de Seteais

$$$$ | **HOTEL** | Built in the 18th century as a home for the Dutch consul, this suitably grand hotel is surrounded by pristine grounds. **Pros:** peaceful location 1 km (½ mile) from the center of Sintra; romantic dining experience in the gardens; excellent facilities for kids. **Cons:** very expensive; not many dining options; formal feel. *Rooms from: €520* *Rua Barbosa du Bocage 8, Sintra* *21/923–3200* *www.valverdepalacioseteais.com* *30 rooms* *Free Breakfast.*

FESTIVALS

Festival de Sintra

FESTIVALS | First held in 1957, Sintra's annual music and dance festival takes place during early fall (usually September or October) at the Centro Cultural Olga Cadaval, as well as in the many palaces and gardens around Sintra and Queluz. The Gulbenkian Symphony Orchestra, Gulbenkian Ballet Company, and other international groups perform. **TIP→ Buy tickets at the Ask Me Sintra tourist information offices.** *Praça Dr. Francisco Sá Carneiro, Sintra* *festivaldesintra.pt.*

Sintra is a noted center for antiques, curios, and ceramics. Keep an eye out for displays of hand-painted ceramics, many of them reproductions of 15th- to 18th-century designs, signed by the artists. As you walk into town from the train station, you'll see people selling all manner of handicrafts and jewelry.

GOLF

★ Penha Longa Golf Courses

GOLF | With magnificent ocean views, the Sintra Hills, and Estoril and Cascais in the foreground, architect Robert Trent Jones Jr. had a wonderful setting in which to create one of Portugal's most memorable courses. The Atlantic Championship Course has great sweeping changes in elevation and often tight fairways that put a premium on driving accuracy. With the elevation often come strong breezes that add another dimension to what is in any case a demanding layout. ✉ *Estrada da Lagoa Azul, Sintra* ☎ *21/924–9031* 🌐 *penhalonga.com* 🎫 *From €105* ⛳ *27 holes; 6904 yard; par 72.*

Estoril

26 km (16 miles) west of Lisbon, 13 km (8 miles) south of Sintra

Having long ago established its reputation as an affluent enclave, Estoril is still the place to go for glitz and glamour. In the 19th century, it was favored by the European aristocracy, who wintered here in the comfort and seclusion of mansions and gardens. In the 20th century, it became popular among international stars and was a top playground for Europe's rich and famous. Although the town has elegant hotels, restaurants, and sports facilities, reminders of its genteel history are now few. It presents its best face right in the center, where today's jet set descends on the casino at the top of the formal gardens of the Parque do Estoril.

Across the busy main road, on the beachfront Tamariz esplanade, are alfresco restaurants and an open-air seawater swimming pool. The best and longest local beach is at Monte Estoril, which adjoins Estoril's beach; here you'll find restrooms and beach chairs for rent, as well as plenty of shops and snack bars.

Estoril is also very sports oriented. As well as being a magnet for golfers, it hosts major sailing, windsurfing, tennis, and equestrian events, as well as motor races at the old Formula 1 track.

GETTING HERE AND AROUND

The best way to arrive is via the Comboios de Portugal urban train (Cascais Line) departing from Lisbon's Cais do Sodré station in Lisbon. The drive by car will take around 25 minutes from Lisbon, either by the A5 highway or the scenic Avenida Marginal running along the coast. Avoid driving during the afternoon on summer weekends, as the traffic is horrendous.

VISITOR INFORMATION

CONTACT Cascais and Estoril Tourism. 🌐 *visitcascais.com.*

Sights

★ Casino Estoril

CASINO | Thought to have inspired the James Bond novel (and subsequent movie) *Casino Royale,* the glitzy Casino Estoril retains a glamorous allure. It's one of the largest casinos in Europe, with a nightclub, art gallery, bars, and restaurants alongside the gambling salons. You can make an evening of it here, with dinner and dancing to live music or DJs, but it's a pricey night out. *Av. Dr. Stanley Ho, Estoril* *21/466–7700* *casino-estoril.pt* *Cascais Line from Cais do Sodré to Estoril.*

Restaurants

Cimas

$$$$ | ECLECTIC | In a half-timbered building, this family-run restaurant features baronial surroundings of burnished wood, heavy drapes, and oak beams that have played host to royalty, high-ranking politicians, and celebrated authors. The menu spans continents, with everything from French to Indian and Portuguese selections. **Known for:** wine cellar with more than 22,000 bottles; excellent fish and seafood dishes; roasted partridge and other game dishes. *Average main: €34* *Av. Marginal, Estoril* *21/468–1254* *Closed Sun.* *Cascais Line from Cais do Sodré to Monte Estoril.*

Villa Saboia

$$ | FUSION | Owned by Portuguese actor Lourenço Ortigão and his brother Tomás, Villa Saboia is a stylish space for sushi and light Mediterranean meals. Fish and seafood takes the starring role, cropping up on the "Mediterranean Menu" in dishes like octopus carpaccio and truffle risotto, as well as in the beautifully presented sashimi and sushi. **Known for:** sushi menu with à la carte and combo options; trendy crowd; good cocktails and lengthy wine list. *Average main: €20* *Av. de Sabóia 515A, Estoril* *93/939–3966* *villasaboia.com* *Cascais Line from Cais do Sodré to Monte Estoril.*

Coffee and Quick Bites

Azimut

$ | INTERNATIONAL | There are plenty of beach bars and restaurants on the esplanade between Cascais and Estoril, but this one at Monte Estoril, a 10-minute walk from either town, is the pick of the bunch. Right by a small sandy beach called Praia das Moitas, the vibe is peaceful and there's a broad menu ranging from snacks, hamburgers, toasted sandwiches, and salads to seafood and fish. **Known for:** beachside dining; hamburgers, salads, and sandwiches; kids' menu. *Average main: €12* *Praia das Moitas, Estoril* *21/482–0433* *Cascais Line from Cais do Sodré to Monte Estoril.*

Garrett do Estoril

$$ | CAFÉ | FAMILY | This *pastelaria* has been serving delicious cakes, pastries, and other goodies since 1934, and is more popular now than ever. It serves full meals at lunch, but the real pleasure comes in taking your pick from the glass display cases of custard tarts and other confections before sitting down to devour them alongside an espresso, fresh juice, or a glass of Portuguese wine. **Known for:** elaborate fruit tarts and iced macarons; good breakfasts, brunches, and set-lunch plates; handsome design and period furniture. *Average main: €18 Av. de Nice 54, Estoril 21/468–0365 garrettestoril.pt Cascais Line from Cais do Sodré to Estoril.*

Hotels

Amazónia Estoril-Cascais Hotel

$$ | HOTEL | This four-star boutique hotel sits on a hill just far enough off the main drag that it's hidden from the noise and crowds but still convenient walking distance to all the star attractions, including Casino Estoril and Praia do Tamariz. **Pros:** tucked-away location gives it a tranquil feel; ocean views from top-floor rooms; children's play area. **Cons:** steep walk uphill to the property; restaurant only serves breakfast; some areas in need a refresh. *Rooms from: €180 Rua Engenheiro Álvaro Pedro de Sousa 175, Estoril 21/468–0424 www.amazoniahoteis.com 28 rooms Free Breakfast Cascais Line from Cais do Sodré to Estoril.*

Hotel Inglaterra

$$ | HOTEL | FAMILY | The name of this sparkling boutique hotel reflects the long-standing English love affair with Costa do Estoril, but it remains at heart a grand mansion that is unmistakably Portuguese. **Pros:** lovely garden with small playground; discounts to a local spa; rooftop pool with sea views. **Cons:** contemporary decor not to everyone's taste; some small rooms; extra charge for breakfast. *Rooms from: €195 Rua do Porto 1, Estoril 21/468–4461 www.hotelinglaterra.com.pt 69 rooms No Meals Cascais Line from Cais do Sodré to Estoril.*

★ **InterContinental Cascais-Estoril**

$$$$ | HOTEL | Just steps from the seafront, InterContinental Cascais-Estoril is a plush base for exploring both Estoril and neighboring Cascais. **Pros:** large outdoor pool and L'Occitane spa; beautiful pool and bar overlooking the ocean; sea views from rooms and dining areas. **Cons:** can be busy with business travelers; some areas used for private events; chain-hotel feel. *Rooms from: €380 Av. Marginal 8023, Estoril 21/829–1100 for reservations* *www.estorilintercontinental.com/en* *59 rooms* *No Meals* *Cascais Line from Cais do Sodré to Monte Estoril.*

★ **Palácio Estoril**

$$$$ | HOTEL | This luxurious 1930s hotel hosted exiled European aristocrats as they waited out World War II; today it draws golfers who play on the nearby course and weary travelers in need of pampering at the spa. **Pros:** impeccable old-world service; excellent dining options; golf packages. **Cons:** the old-fashioned style will not appeal to everybody; pool area can be very crowded in summer; stuffy formal atmosphere. *Rooms from: €320* *Parque do Estoril, Rua Particular, Estoril* *21/468–0000* *www.palacioestorilhotel.com* *161 rooms* *Free Breakfast* *Cascais Line from Cais do Sodré to Estoril.*

Nightlife

Estoril's nightlife scene is quieter than one might imagine, and bars and clubs tend to open and close within a short space of time. At night the casino is a big draw, while other barhopping typically takes place within the hotels and, during the summer, at a handful of open-late spots along the beachfront.

Tamariz Summer Club

DANCE CLUB | The biggest and busiest nightspot in the area, at least during high season, Tamariz Summer Club attracts a young dressed-up crowd keen to dance until dawn. This place is strictly for night owls: it only opens at midnight. *Praia do Tamariz, Rua Olivença, Estoril* *www.facebook.com/TamarizSummerClub* *Cascais Line from Cais do Sodré to Estoril.*

Shopping

Feira Internacional de Artesanato do Estoril

CRAFTS | FAMILY | From late June to early September, Estoril hosts a huge open-air arts-and-crafts fair near the casino. Vendors sell local art, crafts, and food and drink every evening until midnight. With live music, dancing, and kid-friendly shows, FIARTIL is a major event on Estoril's cultural calendar. The same location is used for Chefs on Fire (*www.chefsonfire.pt*) in mid-September, which invites several chefs to cook over a large outdoor barbecue. *Av. Amaral, Estoril* *21/468–0185* *fiartil.pt* *Cascais Line from Cais do Sodré to Estoril.*

Activities

GOLF

The superb golf courses near Lisbon attract players from far and wide. Most are the creations of renowned designers, and the climate means golfers can play year-round. Many hotels offer golf privileges to guests; some even have their own courses. Package deals abound.

★ **Clube de Golfe do Estoril** (*Estoril Golf Club*)

GOLF | Founded in 1929, Club de Golfe do Estoril has an immaculately maintained 18-hole championship course with some very challenging holes. Guests at Palácio Estoril receive special rates and privileges. The welcoming clubhouse serves Portuguese dishes and a good range of drinks, all of which can be enjoyed overlooking the 18th hole and out to sea. ✉ *Av. da República, Estoril* ☎ *21/468–0176* 🌐 *www.clubegolfestoril.com* 🎫 *€85 (€95 on weekends) for 18 holes; €45 for 9 holes* ⛳ *18 holes; 5810 yards; par 69* Ⓜ *Bus M06, M11, or M38 to Golf do Estoril.*

SCUBA DIVING

Cascais Dive Center

DIVING & SNORKELING | Scuba courses are available through the PADI-accredited Cascais Dive Center. Other services include specialized dive trips. ✉ *Impact Beach House, Av. Marginal 6538, Estoril* ☎ *91/991–3021* 🌐 *cascaisdive.com* 🎫 *From €35 for dives* Ⓜ *Cascais Line from Cais do Sodré to São João do Estoril.*

Cascais

32 km (20 miles) west of Lisbon

Once a simple fishing village, the town of Cascais—with three small sandy bays—is now a heavily developed resort town packed with shops, restaurants, and hotels. Despite the masses of people, though, Cascais has retained some of its small-town character. This is most visible around the harbor, with its fishing boats and yachts, and in the old streets and squares off Largo 5 de Outubro, where you'll find lace shops, cafés, and restaurants. Although the water is cold year-round, the beaches are very attractive, from the packed sands in the center of town to wild and windy remote surf beaches and dramatic grottoes like Boca do Inferno. There's been a lively dining scene around what has been dubbed Rua Amarela ("Yellow Street")—a pedestrianized section of downtown where restaurants and taverns set out tables and chairs on the yellow-painted flagstones. Cascais is also something

Cascais, with its pedestrian-only streets lined with colorful buildings, is ideal for strolling.

of a cultural hub, with the best of its galleries and arts centers clustered in the town's Museum Quarter.

GETTING HERE AND AROUND

From Lisbon's Cais do Sodré (Cascais Line), Comboios de Portugal urban trains arrive close to downtown Cascais. To visit the surrounding area, MobiCascais and Carris Metropolitana provide connections to Sintra, Estoril, and Oeiras. Motorists can make the 25-minute drive from Lisbon, either on the A5 highway or the more scenic Avenida Marginal along the coast. Traffic congestion is common around rush hour and summer weekends.

VISITOR INFORMATION

CONTACTS Cascais Visitor Center. ✉ *Praça 5 de Outubro, Cascais* ☎ *21/587–0256* 🌐 *visitcascais.com.*

Sights

★ **Boca do Inferno** (*Mouth of Hell*)

NATURE SIGHT | The most visited attraction in the area around Cascais is the forbiddingly named "Mouth of Hell," one of several natural grottoes in the rugged coastline. Located just 2 km (1 mile) west of town, it is best appreciated at high tide or in stormy weather, when the waves crash high onto the surrounding cliffs. You can walk along the fenced paths to the viewing platforms above the grotto and peer into the abyss. A path leads down to secluded spots on the rocks below. The bleakly beautiful spot is where English occultist Aleister Crowley faked his own suicide in

1930, shocking onlookers when he appeared at a Berlin art gallery three weeks later. ✉ *Av. Rei Humberto II de Itália, Cascais* Ⓜ *Bus M27 to Boca do Inferno.*

Museu dos Condes Castro Guimarães

HISTORIC HOME | FAMILY | Visitors to this grand mansion can get a peek into how local aristocracy once lived while admiring an impressive display of 18th- and 19th-century paintings, ceramics, and furnishings. The canary-yellow building makes a dramatic backdrop to the small beach next door, which is open to the public. ✉ *Av. Rei Humberto II de Itália, Cascais* ☎ *21/481–5303* 🌐 *bairrodosmuseus.cascais.pt/list/museu/museu-condes-de-castro-guimaraes* 🎫 *€5* ⏲ *Closed Mon.* Ⓜ *Cascais Line from Cais do Sodré to Cascais.*

Parque Marechal Carmona

CITY PARK | FAMILY | Take respite from the crowds at this relaxing park next to the palacial Museu dos Condes Castro Guimarães. There are tree-shaded spots for picnickers, plus a large lawn for sunbathers (expect strolling ducks and peacocks for company). There's also a playground and a pleasant café. ✉ *Praceta Domingos D'Avillez, Av. da República, Cascais* Ⓜ *Cascais Line from Cais do Sodré to Cascais.*

Restaurants

Beira Mar

$$$ | SEAFOOD | One of several well-established seafood restaurants in town, Beira Mar has won a string of awards for its fish and seafood. An impressive glass display shows off the best of the day's catch. **Known for:** platters of lobster; simple vegetarian options; fresh fish grilled to perfection. 💲 *Average main: €25* ✉ *Rua das Flores 6, Cascais* ☎ *21/482–7380* 🌐 *restaurantebeiramar.pt* ⏲ *Closed Mon. No dinner Sun.* Ⓜ *Cascais Line from Cais do Sodré to Cascais.*

★ Cantina Clandestina

$$ | ECLECTIC | A standout on the pedestrianized Rua Amarela strip, Cantina Clandestina serves delicious tapas, light meals, and cocktails (try the Clandestina, which combines gin with lemon, basil, and ginger beer) to a relaxed crowd. You can take a seat in the cozy confines of Cantina Clandestina itself, at sister restaurant-bar Taberna Clandestina across the road, or arrive early to grab one of the much-coveted tables on the famous yellow-painted street itself. **Known for:** delicious swordfish carpaccio; inventive focaccia sandwiches; friendly service. 💲 *Average main: €17* ✉ *Rua Afonso Sanches 47, Cascais* ☎ *91/622–9630* 🌐 *www.facebook.com/*

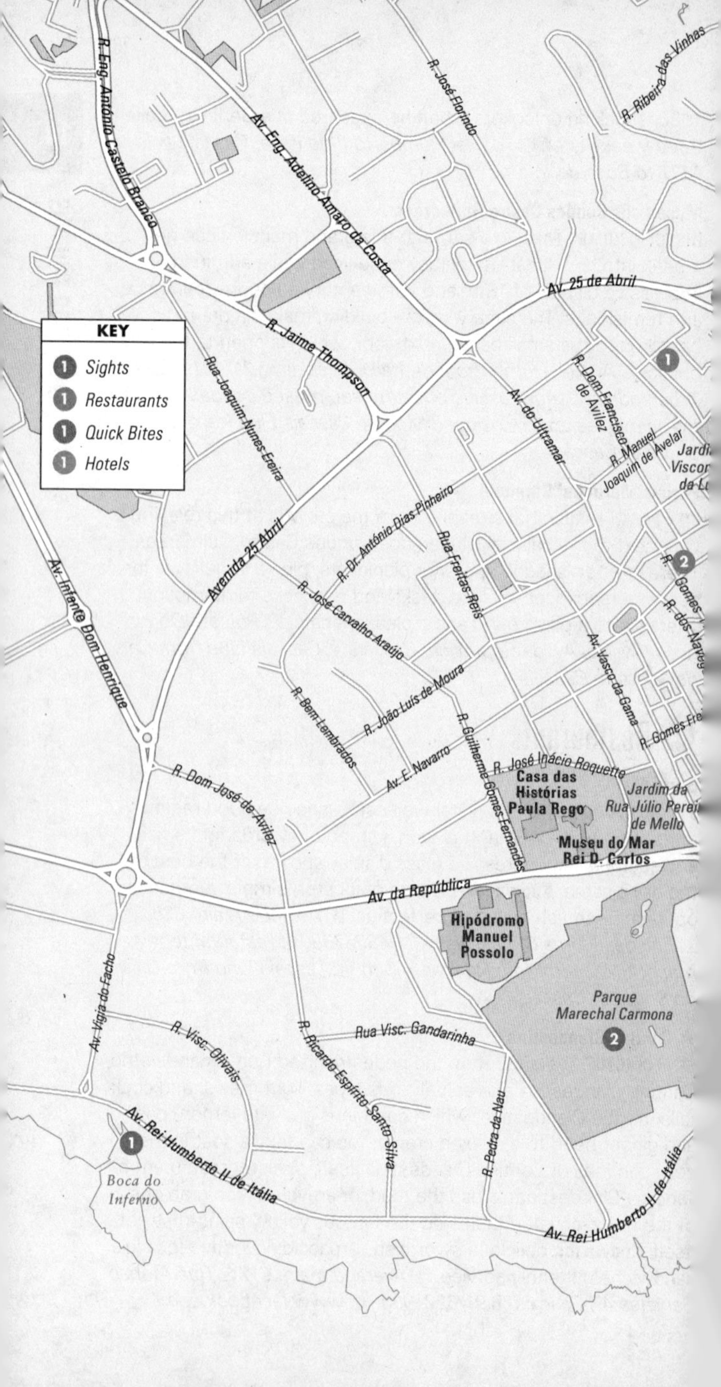
KEY
Sights
Restaurants
Quick Bites
Hotels
R. Eng. António Castelo Branco
Av. Eng. Adelino Amaro da Costa
R. José Florindo
R. Ribeira das Vinhas
Av. 25 de Abril
R. Jaime Thompson
Rua Joaquim Nunes Ereira
R. Dom Francisco de Avilez
Av. do Ultramar
R. Manuel Joaquim de Avelar
Avenida 25 Abril
R. Dr. António Dias Pinheiro
Rua Freitas Reis
R. José Carvalho Araújo
Av. Vasco da Gama
R. dos Navegantes
Av. Infante Dom Henrique
R. Bem Lembrados
R. João Luís de Moura
R. Guilherme Gomes Fernandes
Av. E. Navarro
R. José Inácio Roquette
Casa das Histórias Paula Rego
Jardim da Rua Júlio Pereira de Mello
R. Dom José de Avilez
Museu do Mar Rei D. Carlos
Av. da República
Hipódromo Manuel Possolo
Parque Marechal Carmona
Av. Vigia do Facho
R. Visc. Olivais
Rua Visc. Gandarinha
R. Ricardo Espírito Santo Silva
R. Pedra da Nau
Av. Rei Humberto II de Itália
Boca do Inferno

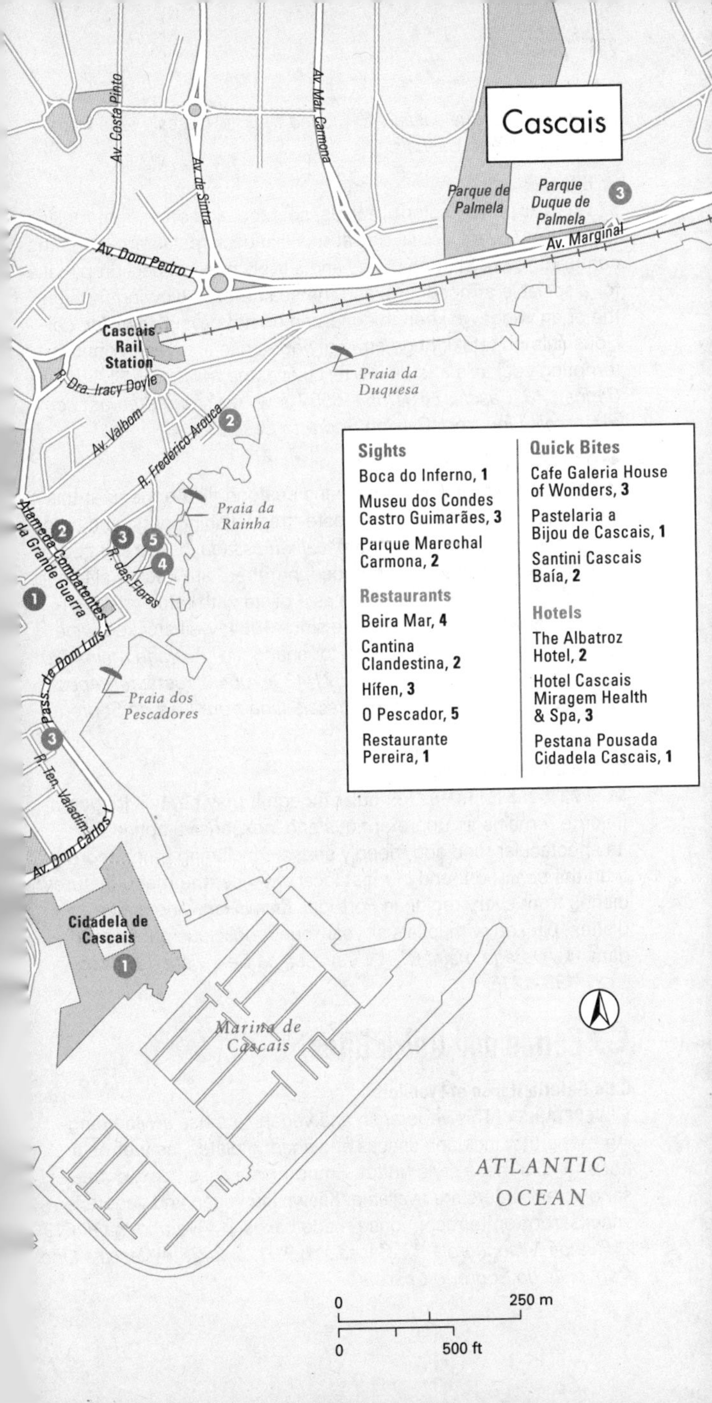
Cascais
Av. Costa Pinto
Av. de Sintra
Av. Mal. Carmona
Parque de Palmela
Parque Duque de Palmela
Av. Marginal
Av. Dom Pedro I
Cascais Rail Station
R. Dra. Iracy Doyle
Praia da Duquesa
Av. Valbom
R. Frederico Arouca
Praia da Rainha
Alameda Combatentes da Grande Guerra
R. das Flores
Pass. de Dom Luís I
Praia dos Pescadores
R. Ten. Valadim
Av. Dom Carlos I
Cidadela de Cascais
Marina de Cascais
ATLANTIC OCEAN
0
250 m
0
500 ft
Sights
Boca do Inferno, 1
Museu dos Condes Castro Guimarães, 3
Parque Marechal Carmona, 2
Restaurants
Beira Mar, 4
Cantina Clandestina, 2
Hífen, 3
O Pescador, 5
Restaurante Pereira, 1
Quick Bites
Cafe Galeria House of Wonders, 3
Pastelaria a Bijou de Cascais, 1
Santini Cascais Baía, 2
Hotels
The Albatroz Hotel, 2
Hotel Cascais Miragem Health & Spa, 3
Pestana Pousada Cidadela Cascais, 1

cantinaclandestina.cascais ⏲ *Closed Tues.* Ⓜ *Cascais Line from Cais do Sodré to Cascais.*

★ Hífen

$ | **ECLECTIC** | Enjoy colorful salads, seafood, and other light meals with a view over Cascais Bay at this laid-back restaurant-bar in the center of town. Sharing plates and a lively musical backdrop make for a sociable atmosphere, and the sea breezes blowing through the open windows keep things fresh on hot days. **Known for:** delicious salmon tataki; huge array of vegetarian and vegan options; tempting cocktails and desserts. 💲 *Average main: €15* ✉ *Av. Dom Carlos I 48, Cascais* ☎ *91/554–6537* 🌐 *www.hifenrestaurant.com* Ⓜ *Cascais Line from Cais do Sodré to Cascais.*

★ O Pescador

$$ | **SEAFOOD** | **FAMILY** | Fresh fish and seafood fill the menu at this relaxed restaurant filled with lobster traps, fishing nets, and other maritime-related artifacts. The *bacalhau assado* (baked salt cod) is one of the specialties of the house, but there are usually also one or two vegetarian options, such as a pasta with tofu and mushrooms. **Known for:** a local favorite since 1964; well-stocked wine cellar; fish and seafood platters for sharing. 💲 *Average main: €20* ✉ *Rua das Flores 10, Cascais* ☎ *21/483–2054* 🌐 *restaurantepescador.com* ⏲ *Closed Wed.* Ⓜ *Cascais Line from Cais do Sodré to Cascais.*

★ Restaurante Pereira

$$ | **PORTUGUESE** | **FAMILY** | Popular though it may be, this longtime favorite remains an unpretentious and inexpensive option for its spectacular food and friendly service. Including much more than the seafood found in most local eateries, the menu features dishes from every region in Portugal. **Known for:** various rice dishes; packed with locals all year round; delicious pumpkin fondant. 💲 *Average main: €18* ✉ *Travessa da Bela Vista 42, Cascais* ☎ *21/483–1215.*

Coffee and Quick Bites

Cafe Galeria House of Wonders

$ | **VEGETARIAN** | This vegetarian and vegan café has a wide-ranging menu that includes snacks and sharing plates, as well as a hot and cold meze-style buffet. Smoothies, juices, teas, coffee, sangria, and beers are available. **Known for:** vegan and vegetarian snacks; rooftop terrace; house-made cakes. 💲 *Average main: €13* ✉ *Rua da Misericórdia 53, Cascais* ☎ *91/170–2428* Ⓜ *Cascais Line from Cais do Sodré to Cascais.*

Pastelaria a Bijou de Cascais

$ | **PORTUGUESE** | The Portuguese have a sweet tooth—not a morning, or afternoon, goes by without a stop for a coffee and pastry—and this traditional little shop, with its wide selection of tarts, cakes, biscuits, and croissants, is a great introduction to typical Portuguese sweets. It's also a good spot for a light breakfast. **Known for:** Portuguese pastries; coffee; local favorite. *Average main: €4 Rua Regimento 19 de Infantaria 55, Cascais 93/231–2526 www.bijoudecascais.pt Cascais Line from Cais do Sodré to Cascais.*

★ Santini Cascais Baía

$ | **ICE CREAM** | **FAMILY** | In the heart of old-town Cascais, Santini Cascais has what many people consider to be the country's best Italian-style gelato. **Known for:** more than 20 flavors of handcrafted gelato; satisfying cup of coffee; popular with families. *Average main: €5 Alameda dos Combatentes da Grande Guerra 100, Cascais 21/096–6779 www.santini.pt Cascais Line from Cais do Sodré to Cascais.*

Hotels

★ The Albatroz Hotel

$$$$ | **HOTEL** | On a rocky outcrop above the crashing waves, this gorgeous hotel was once the summer residence of the dukes of Loulé. **Pros:** worth paying extra for rooms with a sea view; spectacular beach-adjacent location; beautiful historic building. **Cons:** one of the most expensive options in the area; nearby beach can get crowded; small swimming pool. *Rooms from: €395 Rua Frederico Arouca 100, Cascais 21/484–7380 www.thealbatrozcollection.com 51 rooms Free Breakfast Cascais Line from Cais do Sodré to Cascais.*

Hotel Cascais Miragem Health & Spa

$$$$ | **HOTEL** | **FAMILY** | Perfectly integrated into the landscape, this luxurious hotel is built in steps up the side of the hill above the sea. **Pros:** great drinking and dining options on the premises; beautiful views of the marina; plenty of amenities for kids. **Cons:** some rooms look dated; fitness facilities open to public; parking is pricey. *Rooms from: €285 Av. Marginal 8554, Cascais 21/006–0600 www.cascaismirage.com 192 rooms Free Breakfast Cascais Line from Cais do Sodré to Monte Estoril.*

★ Pestana Pousada Cidadela Cascais

$$$$ | **HOTEL** | Housed in a beautifully restored 17th-century fort, the Pousada Cidadela Cascais is a real treat for lovers of art, architecture, literature, and history. **Pros:** unique setting; luxurious

indoor and outdoor pools, spa, and fitness center; characterful rooms with sea or citadel views. **Cons:** it's not cheap; lots of visitors on the site; some areas can be a bit dark. $ *Rooms from: €340* ✉ *Av. Dom Carlos I, Cascais* ☎ *21/481–4300* 🌐 *www.pestanacollection.com/en/hotel/fortress-cascais* 🛏 *126 rooms* 🍽 *Free Breakfast* Ⓜ *Cascais Line from Cais do Sodré to Cascais.*

Nightlife

Cascais has plenty of bars on and around the central pedestrian street (Rua Frederico Arouca) and in Largo Luís de Camões. The marina is also a lively place to barhop, with a wide choice of places that stay open until around 2 am. Three streets in the historic center are closed to traffic to allow for outdoor drinking and dining. Painted bright yellow and dubbed Rua Amarela or "Yellow Street," this restaurant district is a good place to come for cocktails and tapas-style sharing plates.

Cascais Jazz Club

LIVE MUSIC | This soulful little bar presents live jazz, blues, and bossa nova jams and performances. Its diminutive size belies the quality of the musicians that it features. ✉ *Largo Cidade de Vitória 36, Cascais* ☎ *96/277–3470* ⏲ *Closed Mon.–Wed.* Ⓜ *Cascais Line from Cais do Sodré to Cascais.*

Holy Wine Cascais

WINE BAR | At this spacious yet cozy bar dedicated to natural wines, you can hunker down for a drink and nibble on anything from pulled-pork sandwiches to creamy Basque cheesecake (classic and chocolate-based). ✉ *Rua Afonso Sanches 21A, Cascais* ☎ *91/212–2038* Ⓜ *Cascais Line from Cais do Sodré to Cascais.*

John Bull

PUB | On hot summer nights, patrons of this English-style restaurant-pub spill out into the square. A log fire in the lounge keeps things cozy when the weather turns chilly. ✉ *Largo Luís de Camões 4, Cascais* ☎ *21/483–3319* 🌐 *johnbull.eatbu.com* ⏲ *Closed Mon.* Ⓜ *Cascais Line from Cais do Sodré to Cascais.*

Shopping

Cascais is arguably the best shopping area on the Costa do Estoril, with pedestrian streets lined with small market stalls. For clothing and handmade jewelry, browse around Rua Frederico Arouca. To stock up on local fruit, vegetables, and cheeses, head to the food market on Rua Padre Moisés da Silva held every Wednesday and Saturday morning.

★ Casa da Guia

MALL | Housed in a beautiful 19th-century palace, Casa da Guia combines shopping, art, and gastronomy in grand style. It's poised on a cliff edge west of Cascais, beyond Boca do Inferno, and it's worth the trip. ✉ *Av. Nossa Senhora do Cabo 101, Cascais* ☎ *21/484–3215* 🌐 *casadaguiacascais.pt* Ⓜ *Bus M15 to Casa da Guia.*

Ceramicarte

CERAMICS | Luís Soares presents his own carefully executed, modern ceramic designs alongside more traditional jugs and plates at Ceramicarte. There's also a small selection of tapestries and an art gallery. ✉ *Largo da Assunção 3–4, Cascais* ✣ *Near the main Catholic church in the Old Town* ☎ *21/484–0170* 🌐 *ceramicarte.pt* ⏲ *Closed Sun.* Ⓜ *Cascais Line from Cais do Sodré to Cascais.*

Activities

GOLF

★ Oitavos Dunes

GOLF | Portugal's best golf course is consistently rated as one of the top 100 in the world. It lies within the Parque Natural de Sintra-Cascais, and makes the most of three distinct landscape forms: umbrella pine forest, dunes, and the open coastal area. Every hole has a view of the Atlantic Ocean. This was the first course in Europe to be recognized as a Gold Certified Signature Sanctuary by American Audubon International. ✉ *25 Quinta da Marinha, Cascais* ☎ *21/486–0600* 🌐 *oitavosdunes.com* 🎫 *From €161 for greens fees* ⛳ *18 holes; 6526 yards; par 71* Ⓜ *Bus M05 to Rua das Pereiras.*

Guincho

8 km (5 miles) northwest of Cascais

The wide beach at Guincho is one of the most famous in the country. Atlantic waves pound the sand even on the calmest of days, providing perfect conditions for windsurfing (the annual world championships are often held here). Be sure to savor some fresh fish at one of the restaurant terraces overlooking the beach.

GETTING HERE AND AROUND

You can get to Guincho by bus from Cascais (Buses M05 and M15). MobiCascais buses leave Cascais's bus terminal roughly every hour (30 minutes). Driving will take 15 minutes from Cascais, 20 minutes from Sintra, and 35 minutes from Lisbon.

The distinctive building of the Casa das Histórias Paula Rego houses the works of Portugal's best-known contemporary artist.

Sights

★ Casa das Histórias Paula Rego

ART MUSEUM | Designed by Eduardo Souto de Moura, one of Portugal's preeminent architects, the striking terra-cotta-colored buildings of this museum are as intriguing as the works of Portugal's best-known contemporary artist, Paula Rego, shown inside. ✉ *Av. da República 300, Cascais* ☎ *21/482–6970* 🌐 *bairrodosmuseus.cascais.pt/list/museu/casa-das-historias-paula-rego* 🎫 *€5* 🕓 *Closed Mon.* Ⓜ *Cascais Line from Cais do Sodré to Cascais.*

★ Praia do Guincho (*Guincho Beach*)

BEACH | Surfers can always be seen braving the waves here regardless of the season. The undertow can be dangerous, and even accomplished swimmers have had to summon lifeguards. If you prefer something more sedate, this beach—with the Serra da Sintra serving as a backdrop—is an ideal spot to watch the sunset. **Amenities:** food and drink; parking (no fee); showers; toilets. **Best for:** sunset; surfing; windsurfing. ✉ *N247, Cascais* Ⓜ *Bus M05 or M15 to Praia do Guincho.*

Restaurants

★ Bar do Guincho

$$ | **PORTUGUESE** | **FAMILY** | Raise a glass to life's simple pleasures as you nibble on freshly caught shellfish at this feet-in-the-sand bar and restaurant. There are grilled slabs of meat and fish on the menu, alongside a lengthy cocktail list. **Known for:** small plates for sharing; surfer hangout; beautiful spot on the beach. *Average main: €18 Estrada do Abono 547, Cascais 21/487–1683 www.bardoguincho.pt Bus M05 or M15 to Praia do Guincho.*

★ Monte Mar
$$$$ | SEAFOOD | Superior seafood and steaks come with equally impressive sea views at this highly regarded restaurant that attracts everyone from rock stars to heads of state. **Known for:** grilled fish and fresh shellfish; large wine selection; wonderful service. *Average main: €38 Av. Nossa Senhora do Cabo 2845, Cascais 91/602–5305 www.montemar.pt Closed Mon. Bus M15 to Monte Mar.*

Hotels

Dream Guincho
$$$ | B&B/INN | Loved equally by outdoor enthusiasts and the fashion press, Dream Guincho offers boutique hillside lodgings away from the tourist trail. **Pros:** beautiful views over the hills and out to sea; peaceful retreat; stylish rooms and living areas. **Cons:** hard to find; far from most attractions; can be very windy. *Rooms from: €260 Rua do Moleiro, Alcabideche 21/804–2230 dreamguincho.pt 8 rooms Free Breakfast Bus 1624 to EN 247 572 (Almoinhas Velhas).*

★ Fortaleza do Guincho
$$$ | HOTEL | Standing on the cliffs facing the ocean, this historic fort may look austere from the outside, but walk through the entrance and you'll find all the luxury of an old-world palace. **Pros:** award-winning restaurant; gorgeous location on the ocean; eye-popping architecture. **Cons:** standard rooms are quite small; small bathtubs; pricey. *Rooms from: €230 Estrada do Guincho, Cascais 21/487–0491 www.fortalezadoguincho.com 27 rooms Free Breakfast Bus M05 to Guincho.*

Activities

Guincho Wind Factory
WINDSURFING | Call ahead for lessons in kitesurfing, windsurfing, and stand-up paddleboarding; you can also buy or rent boards and all the equipment you need. *Rua da Torre 1476A, Cascais 21/486–8332 www.guinchowindfactory.com From €45 for surf lessons Bus M04, M15, or M34 to Rua Jayme Thompson.*

Index

D

E

I

J

K

L

M

Q

R

U

V

W

Z

Photo Credits

Front Cover: John Peter Photography/Alamy Stock Photo[Descr: The Discoveries Monument on the north bank of The Tagus River in Lisbon Portugal.] **Back cover, from left to right:** Sean Pavone/iStockphoto. LucVi/iStockphoto. Armando Oliveira/iStockphoto. **Spine:** Trabantos/iStockphoto. **Interior, from left to right:** Alexandr Spatari/GettyImages (1). Sean Pavone/iStockphoto (2-3). **Chapter 1: Experience Lisbon:**Georgios Tsichlis/iStockphoto (6-7). Acnaleksy/Dreamstime (8-9). Hemis/Alamy Stock Photo (9). Tatiana Bralnina/Shutterstock (9). Interpixels/Shutterstock (10). Tastytravels/Shutterstock (10). Hemis/Alamy Stock Photo (10). Malajscy/Dreamstime (10). Tamas Gabor/Shutterstock (11). Sean Hsu/Shutterstock (11). Dmitry Rukhlenko/iStockphoto (12). Saiko3p/Shutterstock (12). Alexandr Spatari/GettyImages (13). Viach Abein/Shutterstock (18). Malajscy/Dreamstime (18). Joao Manita/Shutterstock (18). Bruno Ismael Silva Alves/Shutterstock (18). BooFamily/Shutterstock (19). Rosa Irene Betancourt/Alamy Stock Photo (20). George Stamatis/Shutterstock (20). Lerner Vadim/Shutterstock (20). BooFamily/Shutterstock (20). BooFamily/Shutterstock (21). **Chapter 3: Baixa:** TTstudio/Shutterstock (55). Eskystudio/Shutterstock (62). Henglein & steets/GettyImages (68). ESB Professional/Shutterstock (71). **Chapter 4: Chiado and Bairro Alto:** Zts/Dreamstime (73). Expose/Shutterstock (80). Milosk50/Shutterstock (93). Agenzia Sintesi/Alamy Stock Photo (100). **Chapter 5: Avenida da Liberdade, Príncipe Real, and Restauradores:** David soulsby/Alamy Stock Photo (103). Dudlajzov/Dreamstime (106). Bill Perry/Shutterstock (110). **Chapter 6: Alfama, Graça, and São Vicente:** Martin Thomas Photography/Alamy Stock Photo (125). Anatolii Lyzun/Shutterstock (131). Tomas1111/Dreamstime (133). Zts/Dreamstime (140). Gerasimovvv/Dreamstime (144). **Chapter 7: Beato and Marvila:** Zuma Press, Inc./Alamy Stock Photo (147). Marcin Jamkowski/Adventure Pictures/Alamy Stock Photo (153). Martin Thomas Photography/Alamy Stock Photo (154). **Chapter 8: Alcântara, Cais do Sodré, and Santos:** Alexandre Rotenberg/Shutterstock (157). Konrad Zelazowski/Alamy Stock Photo (160). Curioso.Photography/Shutterstock (166). **Chapter 9: Estrela, Campo de Ourique, and Lapa:** Bennymarty/Dreamstime (175). Ian Pilbeam/Alamy Stock Photo (181). **Chapter 10: Intendente, Martim Moniz, and Mouraria:** Sónia Pereira (185). Dudlajzov/Dreamstime (190). **Chapter 11:Belém:** Photosbypatrik/Shutterstock (197). Altezza/Dreamstime (200). MPauline/Shutterstock (204). Milosk50/Shutterstock (208). **Chapter 12: South of the River:** Mairu10/Shutterstock (213). Rik Hamilton/Alamy Stock Photo (216). Mauricio Abreu/Alamy Stock Photo (222). **Chapter 13: Avenidas Novas:** Tamas Gabor/Alamy Stock Photo (231). Gustavo JF Ramos/Shutterstock (237). Policas/Shutterstock (240). **Chapter 14:Side Trips from Lisbon:** Taiga/Shutterstock (241). Andrei Nekrassov/Shutterstock (248). Sean Pavone/Shutterstock (252). Trabantos/Shutterstock (262). Radub85/Dreamstime (270). **About Our Writers:** All photos are courtesy of the writers.

*Every effort has been made to trace the copyright holders, and we apologize in advance for any accidental errors. We would be happy to apply the corrections in the following edition of this publication.

Notes

Notes

Notes

Notes

Notes

Fodor's InFocus LISBON

Publisher: Stephen Horowitz, *General Manager*

Editorial: Douglas Stallings, *Editorial Director;* Jill Fergus, Amanda Sadlowski, *Senior Editors;* Brian Eschrich, Alexis Kelly, *Editors;* Angelique Kennedy-Chavannes, Yoojin Shin, *Associate Editors*

Design: Tina Malaney, *Director of Design and Production;* Jessica Gonzalez, *Senior Designer;* Jaimee Shaye, *Graphic Design Associate*

Production: Jennifer DePrima, *Editorial Production Manager;* Elyse Rozelle, *Senior Production Editor;* Monica White, *Production Editor*

Maps: Rebecca Baer, *Map Director;* Andrew Murphy and Mark Stroud (Moon Street Cartography), *Cartographers*

Photography: Viviane Teles, *Director of Photography;* Namrata Aggarwal, Neha Gupta, Payal Gupta, Ashok Kumar, *Photo Editors;* Jade Rodgers, Shanelle Jacobs, *Photo Production Intern*

Business and Operations: Chuck Hoover, *Chief Marketing Officer;* Robert Ames, *Group General Manager*

Public Relations and Marketing: Joe Ewaskiw, *Senior Director of Communications and Public Relations*

Fodors.com: Jeremy Tarr, *Editorial Director;* Rachael Levitt, *Managing Editor*

Technology: Jon Atkinson, *Executive Director of Technology;* Rudresh Teotia, *Associate Director of Technology;* Alison Lieu, *Project Manager*

Writers: Ann Abel, Alison Roberts, Daniela Sunde-Brown, Joana Taborda

Editor: Brian Eschrich

Production Editor: Jennifer DePrima

1st Edition

ISBN 978-1-64097-736-5

ISSN 2998-1905

All details in this book are based on information supplied to us at press time. Always confirm information when it matters, especially if you're making a detour to visit a specific place. Fodor's expressly disclaims any liability, loss, or risk, personal or otherwise, that is incurred as a consequence of the use of any of the contents of this book.

SPECIAL SALES

This book is available at special discounts for bulk purchases for sales promotions or premiums. For more information, e-mail SpecialMarkets@fodors.com.

PRINTED IN CANADA

10 9 8 7 6 5 4 3 2 1

About Our Writers

Ann Abel is an American travel writer living in Lisbon and frequently traveling around her adopted country. When she is not soaking up the sun on an Algarvian beach or eating garlicky Portuguese seafood, she writes about travel in Portugal and beyond for publications including *Condé Nast Traveler, Forbes, Departures, Afar, Robb Report,* and *Well + Good.*

Alison Roberts is a freelance journalist, writer, and translator based in Lisbon who has worked for international broadcasters as well as newspapers and magazines. Born in London, she has also lived in Canada, India, and Germany but now spends as much time as possible exploring Portugal. Her interests include travel, languages, and culture.

Daniela Sunde-Brown is an Australian travel writer who landed in Lisbon for a "gap year" in 2018 and never left. Since then she's been on a mission to discover all things made, grown, and created in Portugal, which she shares on her website (🌐 *oladaniela.com*) and in articles and guides for Fodor's, *Telegraph Travel,* and in-flight magazines. Her perfect day might include getting lost in Lisbon's colorful tiled streets with a camera, attending strange cultural festivals, and meeting traditional artisans. She hopes that by traveling deeper she can inspire others to explore Portugal's rich history, culture and cuisine beyond the surface. You can connect with her via @daniela.sundebrown.

Joana Taborda is a Portuguese travel writer and editor. Over the years, she has written articles and guidebooks on Portugal for Fodor's Travel, DK Eyewitness, Lonely Planet, and many others. She loves sharing her favorite spots around her home country, from craft beer bars to local artist workshops. Splitting her time between Lisbon and the semitropical island of Madeira, she is always on the lookout for new stories (and the sunniest spot). You can follow her latest adventures @cityodes.